DAIMLER STUDIOS

THE FINAL
POLISH

MATCHING AN OWNER'S
COMPLEXION

TRIMMING A
NEW BONNET

PUTTING ON
THE FINISHING
TOUCH

RED

BLUE

BUFF PINK RED

GREY

W
HEATH
ROBINSON

Daimler

DAIMLER'S

PAINT
SHOP

As part of our ongoing market research, we are always pleased to receive comments about our books, suggestions for new titles, or requests for catalogues. Please write to: The Editorial Director, Patrick Stephens Limited, Sparkford, Near Yeovil, Somerset, BA22 7JJ.

Daimler
CENTURY

The full history of Britain's oldest car maker

LORD MONTAGU & DAVID BURGESS-WISE
Foreword by HRH The Duke of Edinburgh

Patrick Stephens Limited

First published in 1995

British Library Cataloguing-in-Publication Data:
A catalogue record for this book is
available from the British Library

ISBN: 1 85260 494 8

Library of Congress catalog card no. 95 78123

Patrick Stephens Limited is an imprint of Haynes Publishing,
Sparkford, Nr Yeovil, Somerset BA22 7JJ.

Designed and typeset by G&M, Raunds, Northamptonshire
Printed in Britain by Butler & Tanner Ltd, London and Frome

CONTENTS

The first motor-cars must have been most intriguing gadgets, and I can well understand King Edward VII's fascinated interest in these 'horseless carriages' when they were introduced to him by Lord Montagu's father. His acquisition of one of the very earliest products of the Daimler Company set a trend for the next four monarchs. I can still remember watching King George V and Queen Mary driving past my Prep School in a Daimler on their way to Ascot in the early 1930s. By contemporary standards, theirs was an immense car with wheels big enough for a London bus.

The present Queen owned a small Daimler saloon in the 1950s and now uses a Jaguar-built Daimler 'Double Six'. Two of the last Daimler DS 420 Limousines to be built are also presently in the Mews. They all retain the vestiges of the famous Daimler fluted radiator.

Daimler will always be associated with the beginning of motoring in this country and I am sure that all enthusiasts will welcome this official history of that famous company, written by such a great authority on the motor industry.

INTRODUCTION
by Lord Montagu of Beaulieu

Since the first car my father bought was an 1898 6 hp Daimler, it is not surprising that I grew up fascinated with the history of Daimler and the various models that it produced. Now, nearly 100 years after my father's purchase, I am driving the latest Daimler and it has long been my ambition to record the history of this remarkable company, Britain's oldest motor manufacturer, which is not – nor ever was – a subsidiary of Daimler in Germany.

It therefore seemed very appropriate to publish an authoritative history of the

My passenger on the 1899 Daimler is Denise Critchley Salmonson, grand-daughter of the Hon Evelyn Ellis, Daimler's pioneering customer.

Company to coincide with its 100th birthday, which is celebrated on 14 January 1996. I am most grateful for the support and encouragement of Jaguar, who have been responsible for keeping the Daimler flag flying since 1960 when the two companies were merged.

There was, of course, an enormous amount of research to be undertaken, not only from the original Minute Books of the Daimler Company but also from former employees and dealers. This history could never have been written without the hard work, knowledge and investigative persistence of motoring historian David Burgess-Wise, who assembled the material which was essential to ensure that an objective story emerged. I would like especially to thank him, as without him the book would have been deficient both in content and in style.

So many people helped us that it is invidious to mention them all. However, very special thanks go to Nick Scheele, Chairman and Chief Executive of Jaguar Cars; Bruce Blythe, who played a pivotal role in Ford's take-over of Jaguar-Daimler and Walter Hayes, former Vice-Chairman of Ford of Europe (and now Life President of Aston Martin Lagonda). Special help was given by David Boole, Director of Communications & Public Affairs at Jaguar, Steve Bagley of the Museum of British Road Transport, Coventry, and Ann Harris of the

Jaguar Daimler Heritage Trust.

Much so far unpublished material was provided by Jack Fairman (who trained at the Daimler in the 1930s before making his name as a racing driver), and Gordon Asbury and James Smillie, former senior executives of Stratstone. Particular thanks go to my neighbour Desmond Stratton, son of the co-founder of Stratstone, a company whose history is intimately bound up with that of Daimler, especially with supplying Daimler cars to the Royal Family.

Needless to say, the Library and Photo Library of the National Motor Museum at Beaulieu have contributed much and I would like to thank Annice Collett, Marie Tieche and Lynda Springate for all their hard work.

Finally, I would like to express my appreciation to His Royal Highness Prince Philip, Duke of Edinburgh, for contributing the Foreword.

Everybody in Britain should be proud of the achievements of the Daimler Company over the past 100 years and will wish it every success as it enters its second century.

St George's Day, 1995

Chapter 1

UNDERNEATH THE ARCHES

Young Frederick Simms was enchanted: the little knifeboard-seated railcars with the jolly canopy tops, tirelessly ferrying passengers around the Bremen showground as if by magic, seemed to hold the answer to his quest for a compact, independent power source for his 'Aerial Flights'.

It was the year 1888; Simms, then aged 25, was an Englishman who had been born in the German port of Hamburg where his grandfather, a native of Birmingham, had established a trading company to equip the Newfoundland fishing fleet. Young Frederick had inherited that entrepreneurial spirit and, in company with a friend from Blackpool named Stansfield, was attempting to market an overhead passenger cableway that would give visitors to showgrounds and exhibitions the sensation of flying. He sought out the builder of the railcars, a short, bearded 54-year-old Swabian named Gottlieb Daimler, 'an inoffensive person, rather benign and weak-eyed in appearance'. Despite the great difference in their ages, the two men became firm friends.

Technical director of the Deutz gas engine factory from 1872–82, Daimler had then set up in business with his protégé Wilhelm Maybach (formerly chief designer at Deutz) to develop the world's first high-speed

The sight of these motor railcars at the 1888 Bremen Exhibition inspired Frederick Simms to establish a British agency for the Daimler engine. [DBW]

FAR LEFT *Frederick R. Simms. [DBW]*

LEFT *Gottlieb Daimler. [M-BA]*

BELOW *Daimler ran this railcar at an exhibition in his home town of Cannstatt in 1887. [M-BA]*

lightweight internal combustion engine, able – thanks to Daimler's invention of 'hot tube' ignition – to run at speeds up to a dizzy 900 rpm, rather than the 180 rpm which was the top speed of the clumsy Deutz units. He gave it independence and the ability to power

vehicles (he had built his first 'horseless carriage' in 1886) by running it on liquid petroleum – *Benzin* in German – instead of connecting it to a fixed gas main.

Though progress with the 'Aerial Flights' seems to have been intermittent – Stansfield did instal one at London's Crystal Palace in 1891 – Simms could see beyond his immediate needs to envision the wider potential of Daimler's 'universal power source'.

The press, too, was fascinated by the Daimler engine. That year the popular German family paper *Die Gartenlaube* reported of 'the modern goblin' in 1888 that 'this type of railway uses neither horses nor any visible engine – not even the well-known electric power. One can only see one man operating the vehicle, and next to him is a box which makes a rattling "tick-tick" noise.'

Daimler's big breakthrough had been the invention of a new ignition system to replace the crude Deutz method which fired the explosive mixture by mechanically opening a little sliding trap-door in the cylinder at the crucial moment to expose the flammable gas to a naked flame. Given the feeble nature of electric ignition systems at the time, Daimler's solution to the problem was brilliant. He retained the idea of a burner outside the cylinder, but used it to raise a

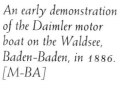

An early demonstration of the Daimler motor boat on the Waldsee, Baden-Baden, in 1886. [M-BA]

hollow platinum tube projecting into the combustion chamber to near-incandescence. As the piston rose in the cylinder, the gas/air mixture was forced into the hot tube and detonated.

Though Daimler did achieve some early success supplying his power units to tramway companies, the advent of cheap electrical power soon closed that particular avenue. Motor boats proved a more fruitful source of sales, and as early as 13 October 1886 he had given a public demonstration of his marine engine at the fashionable spa town of Baden-Baden. Reported the newspaper *Schwäbischen Chronik*: 'Yesterday afternoon at 3 o'clock, a motor-boat driven by a petroleum engine constructed by mechanical engineer Daimler, who has a small business in Cannstatt, was to be seen in full flight on the Waldsee near the town. All the civic dignitaries were present.

'We understand that the inventor has made three boats built to this system, of which the biggest holds ten people and the second two. Meanwhile Daimler, who has named his boat *Rems*, demonstrated it, serviced the motor and took the helm himself. The first is positioned in the middle of the boat and takes up little space; equally, the mechanism is also positioned in a practical, simply constructed space and sets the craft in swift and steady

motion. The motor functions smoothly and with negligible noise so that the consumption of petroleum is minimal. The speed is considerable and the manoeuvrability is light and sure. Despite the lake's being only 3,600 square metres, the boat shot through the water as swift as an arrow. Mr Daimler was awarded full recognition of his handsome invention.'

Daimler was convinced that the motor launch was largely responsible for removing the prejudice that existed against the use of inflammable *Benzin* as a fuel; in one notable confrontation, the Frankfurt police had banned Wilhelm Maybach from entering his racing boat in a regatta on the River Main, 'because it was reckoned that a boat filled with *Benzin* would fly up into the air'. Undeterred, Maybach ran his little boat on the regatta course anyway, beat all the other craft – and was arrested by the police! When Daimler first took his own motor-boat on to the River Neckar, he had to take refuge behind an awful pun – *Es lauft Öl-lecktrisch* ('It runs by licking oil') – to give the impression that it was powered by electricity. Acceptance by high society came in 1888, when an elaborately-finished Daimler motor launch named *Marie* was presented to the Iron Chancellor, Prince Otto von Bismarck.

One of Daimler's most impudent publicity stunts took place on the River Elbe in Hamburg on 15 October 1888, when the new Kaiser, Wilhelm II, was inspecting the recently-completed Hamburg harbour by tug – and a 2 hp Daimler motor boat named *The Seven Swabians* unofficially slipped into line behind. A watching stoker reckoned that it was something to do with the American inventor Thomas Edison, for the electrical experiments of the 'Wizard of Menlo Park' were attracting much attention at the time; many of the onlookers were surprised that the mystery boat had no smoke stack.

Cheaper and less complex than steam, and capable of running at a heady 750 rpm, the new power unit attracted a good deal of interest. One likes to think that Daimler's newfound friend Simms was at least partly responsible for that cheeky display in Hamburg . . .

Certainly in 1890 Simms was Daimler's principal accomplice in a daring demonstration of the capabilities of the motor boat at Potsdam, in the heartland of German military imperialism. Daimler had just built a 32-foot launch capable of an impressive 12 knots and, though it was already sold, hit upon the idea of publicizing his engine by using the launch to gatecrash a demonstration being given by the Marine Salvage Corps to Kaiser Wilhelm II and his admirals on the Wannensee, near the imperial palace of Sans Souci.

When the owner of the boat got wind of the scheme, he refused permission for his property to be used in so disrespectful a manner, and issued a writ against Daimler. But too late: the boat was already on the water when the official attempting to serve the writ arrived at the Wannensee, and he was forced to give chase in a slower launch. With Simms at the helm, engineer Wilhelm Bauer – who would die in a high-speed crash in his 24 hp Phönix-Daimler at La Turbie in March 1900 – controlling the power unit and Daimler's eldest son Paul in the bows, the launch successfully outran the law. Later in the day Simms was invited to explain the Daimler engine to the Kaiser, who had watched the chase from a torpedo boat.

Simms – also involved in promoting other money-making schemes like an automatic ticket machine which worked rather like the old penny-in-the-slot chocolate dispensers – decided that there were distinct possibilities for the Daimler engine on the British market, and asked Gottlieb Daimler if he could be granted the agency.

An early problem was finding a suitable source of fuel, for refined petroleum spirit of a sufficiently volatile nature was hard to come by in Britain. Eventually, the London company of Carless, Capel & Leonard said that they could supply Simms with the right kind of 'double-distilled petroleum spirit', but that it would be liable to the provisions of the Explosives Act and would have to be labelled 'highly inflammable'. Both Simms and Carless, Capel & Leonard subsequently claimed to have decided that this fuel should be sold under the anodyne trade name 'Petrol' to reassure the public that it was not dangerous. German sources are equally definite that Gottlieb Daimler had recalled the term being used when he was a student in England in the 1860s, and had adopted it when he began demonstrating his motor boats in the late 1880s to allay the popular fear of the word *Benzin*, which conjured up visions of an explosive liquid. Whoever invented the name, it soon became the generic word for motor fuel.

Once Simms had decided to take up the Daimler agency, things began to move quickly. On 8 February 1891 he wrote from Berlin to his solicitor Alfred Hendriks in London: 'I have started a department for petrol motor boats and cars, and I have concluded an agreement with the Daimler Motor Company of Cannstatt which has just been turned into a limited company. I am going to exhibit a motor car at the German Exhibition at Earl's Court, London, and I want to run a beautiful motor boat on the Serpentine to show the grand thing in England which I have secured. The motor is

unequalled; no smell, quite dangerless, fifty per cent cheaper than all other motors and with a very small consumption, viz. 2 lbs. per horse-power hour. One horse-power weighs 60 lbs. and takes very little room; 6 horse-power weighs about 140 lbs. and is very little bigger. The motor may be set off within two minutes and has many advantages.'

One interesting sidelight on this letter is that it was the first recorded use of the term 'motor car', though this name – a straight translation by Simms of the German phrase *Motor-Wagen* – was not generally accepted by the British for a number of years, hence the birth in 1895 of a new magazine called *The Autocar*, which was to play a crucial role in the early history of Daimler in Britain.

On 15 February 1891 Simms wrote again to Hendriks: 'Kindly let me know to 6 Moorgate Street when you are in for certain as my time is only limited and I must settle my motor-affairs either in one way or another. Naturally we have all the English patents for our petrol motors, boats, cars, etc, which are very good ones, too – the motor is very light, small, powerful and cheap, the best qualities that can be expected.'

Three days later, Gottlieb Daimler appointed Simms as the sole English agent for his patents 'for use as you think fit . . . we

In 1891, Simms was loaned this 2 hp Daimler launch by the Cannstatt factory. [JDHT]

have complete confidence in you.' And as evidence of the Daimler company's support for Simms's efforts, it loaned him 'a Daimler motor boat constructed of oak and fitted with a 2 hp engine and also an engine in addition'.

On 24 February Hendriks was asked to draft out a contract to form a syndicate to administer the British patent rights and Simms – planning his display at the Earls Court German Exhibition – confidently predicted: 'I believe we shall have the motor-boat over here in latest six weeks – the motor car in three weeks, or do you prefer having for this car a motor to drive anything as perhaps you may not be able to find a place for the car. It is no use to simply show same, we must run it somewhere.' Simms obviously had great confidence in Hendriks, for the agreement between the two men was purely verbal – a bad mistake, as it turned out.

Nor did he bring a motor car to England, where it would surely have caused a sensation, for the idiotic Locomotives on Highways act was in full flower and private 'self-propelled' carriages, being equal in the eyes of the law with full-blown traction engines, were supposed to carry both a driver and an engineer and be preceded by a man on foot (who usually carried a red flag, even though it had not strictly been necessary since the law was amended in 1878).

Unsurprisingly, most of the builders of light steam carriages had given up in frustration and not a single internal-combustion engined car was then running on British roads; the number of Britons who had even seen a motor vehicle (which were only to be found in private hands in France at that time) was almost certainly still in single figures.

So the 1 hp engine No 164, consigned to Simms by Daimler on 6 March 1891, was to be used to drive a Chocolate and Cocoa Making Machine on the stand of a Dresden company at the show. The late St John Nixon claimed that the exhibition organizers got cold feet and would not allow the engine to be shown, let alone run, though there doesn't seem to be any evidence of this in Simms's surviving (and voluminous) correspondence. Indeed, after the show closed, Simms proudly boasted: 'We have more orders than we can execute for five months!'

He was still operating the British Daimler agency out of the Berlin office of his patent ticket dispensing company, and obviously bursting with optimism. The motor boat had turned out to be 'perfection in every way, running about 7 to 8 knots an hour.' Nevertheless, Simms asked Hendriks to 'secure a good lake for our boat, for I am afraid the Thames will be too rapid for this 2 hp motor. For the Thames there ought to be

The 'wonderfully fast' launch built by Simms in 1892. [DBW]

An ideal customer

The Hon Evelyn Ellis was the ideal client for the Daimler Motor Syndicate, wealthy and well-connected, with inherited landholdings in Jamaica and relatives at Court. Modest but adventurous, Ellis had sailed before the mast aged 13 and recalled, from bitter experience, that 'a good flogging is the best cure for sea-sickness that I know'. Maybe it was his early nautical experience that inspired him to become such a good customer for Daimler motor launches. A pioneer motorist, he had bought and used his Daimler-engined Panhard in France before he imported it into England, and thus knew the capabilities of the new mode of transport. And when his car became outmoded, he simply removed its body, fitted it with a pump, and used it as a fire engine at his house in Datchet.

about a 4 hp motor.' Then he added: 'We have just finished a boat (fast) for the boat races, running 11 knots an hour, taking 6 people, length only 7 yards, and wonderfully lively in turning . . . We have so many orders for boats and motors and cars that we are full up to October and think of erecting another factory in Berlin.'

In mid-May Simms sent his mechanic Johann van Toll ('one of the earliest pioneers of the internal combustion engine, not only in this country, but in the world') over to England to look after the boat and on 10 June he triumphantly wrote: 'I have the boat at Putney.' He had also secured a London base for the Daimler agency, a two-room office in the 'new and magnificent' Billiter Buildings at 49 Leadenhall Street – which boasted both a built-in lift and electric light – at an annual rent of £50, and formalized the business in June 1891 under the name Simms & Company, Consulting Engineers, with Hendriks as partner.

Simms was attempting to sell the British Empire rights to the Daimler engine, but when he offered a Mr Stecken the Australian and New Zealand rights at the end of June 1891, he was told: 'During my stay in the City I have seen two other motors using mineral oil instead of Benzine or so-called purified Petrol, so that I do not see my way to taking up the Daimler Motor, which I consider rather dangerous for a warm climate.' Never one to miss the chance of making money, Hendriks introduced Stecken to another of Simms's many ventures, the 'Refuse Disposal Business'.

Simms had been seeking a permanent base on the Thames for his motor launch, appropriately named *Cannstatt*, and in late May 1892 he took on a mooring at Putney Pier, owned by the Metropolitan District Railway. However, the bill for the first two months' rent (£2) describes *Cannstatt* as a 'steam launch': Simms was perhaps being 'economical with the truth', for exactly a year later the Metropolitan District Railway Company told Simms to remove his launches

from their Putney mooring **immediately** as they had discovered that they were 'driven by some kind of petroleum'!

A significant demonstration took place early in August 1892 when Johann Van Toll informed Simms: 'Have had a most successful trip with boat to Maidenhead. Mr E seems fairly keen on it now.' ('Mr E' was the Hon Evelyn Ellis, 50-year-old son of the late Lord Howard de Walden and a Member of Parliament; he ordered his first Daimler-engined launch soon after and would be perhaps the most influential of Simms's early customers.) Simms's launch business quickly gathered momentum. On 29 October he received Daimler marine engine No 471: this represented a major step forward in terms of power, for it was a 10 hp four-cylinder unit, a type of engine first built by Maybach in 1890.

In mid-December Simms took delivery of the mahogany hull and fittings for a 38-foot pinnace – to be powered by a 10 hp four-cylinder Daimler motor – for the London County Council, from yacht-builders Watkins & Company of Blackwall, along with an invoice for £307 16s. When Simms came to pay this bill, he was surprised to find that there was less money in the company's account than he had anticipated: it soon became apparent that the apparently trustworthy Hendriks had been cooking the books . . .

On drawing up the year-end accounts, Simms discovered that Hendriks had been abstracting large sums of money from the business, including £214 3s 8d 'petty cash applied to own purposes'. The auditor commented that 'the books show many irregularities . . . the banking account has been used to a large extent for the private purposes of Mr Hendriks.' Further examination showed that Hendriks had also misappropriated one of two payments of £210 made to cover the purchase of Evelyn Ellis's launch and attempted to cover the fraud by depositing a cheque for £249 10s 0d received from the LCC. On 1 February 1893 Hendriks announced that he was severing his

connection with Simms & Company and moving to 3 Circus Place, Finsbury Circus. He offered to pay off the missing money – which eventually turned out to total over £514 – in instalments, but by June had repaid just £100.

Further investigation proved that Hendriks had not even been professionally qualified to handle Simms's affairs, for he had been struck off the rolls of the Law Society on 7 April 1884 and had County Court Judgements made against him in 1881, 1883, 1884 and 1890. Furthermore, a bankruptcy injunction had been filed against him as recently as 4 April 1892.

It was definitely time to make a fresh start . . .

* * *

In the wake of the Hendriks debacle, Simms asked lawyer Henry C. Warry to examine his existing contract with Daimler, for he had plans to expand the business. He had already sent a telegram to Stuttgart on 11 April, asking for a binding five year sole agency for 'England and the Colonies', followed by a further two years' patents option: his original agreement, it seems was for just three years. This was followed by a circular letter announcing that Simms was converting 'Simms & Co, Engineers' into a limited company under the name of 'The Daimler Motor Syndicate, Ltd', with a capital of £6,000, with its principal activity listed as 'selling . . . the Daimler Motor, with its many applications'. Simms was to be Managing

Director and 'entitled to hold the office for life'. The first directors were both, as it happens, 'something in the City': one was Simms's cousin, a vintner named Robert Gray, and the other was Theo Vasmer, described as 'a merchant'.

The Daimler Motor Syndicate was duly incorporated on 26 May 1893, and the early entries in its minute book reveal that despite its lofty ambitions, its staff was modest (as were their salaries): apart from Simms, it only had a secretary, Edward Canning Glass (a former merchant), on £150 a year, two engineers – Ebenezer W. Tonkin and Joh van Toll – on £2 5s and £2 10s a week respectively (and van Toll – described by a colleague as 'a man of enormous strength' – also got up to £2 10s 'for every motor fixed by him'); an assistant engineer, J.T. Pearse, on £1 a week; and a clerk from Stoke Newington named Henry M. Scott, who made just 9 shillings a week (but must have proved a good worker, for his salary was increased to 12s a week in August 1893). The Syndicate's engineering workshop was at 'Arch No 71 by Putney Bridge Railway Station' and was once again the property of the Metropolitan District Railway who were, presumably, at that point still in blissful ignorance of the motive power of the Daimler engines.

Trade was steady, and orders for motor boats included a powered lifeboat for Pembrokeshire, which must have been the first example of its kind, at a time when many lifeboats still depended on oars: the accounts

The Daimler launch supplied to the London County Council in 1893.

for the period 27 May 1893 to 31 October 1894 reveal that sales of engines totalled £6,623 10s 11d, against which Simms's other agencies seemed very poor performers: the 'Rapid Pump' had sold to the tune of £116 15s 7d, the 'Patent Automatic Railway Ticket Selling Box' had brought in just £72 19s 9d, and the net result was a loss on trading of £577 3s 2½d. Nevertheless, the increased business of the Daimler agency justified a move into larger offices within Billiter Buildings, and No 95 was rented for £140 annually from the end of September.

Frederick Simms's relationship with Cannstatt was often more that of friend and advisor than a client; on one of his visits to the German works in 1893, Gottlieb Daimler's gifted amanuensis Wilhelm Maybach complained to Simms that the crude surface carburettors then fitted were proving troublesome. 'Why not have an automatic feed?' Simms suggested.

The advice seems to have been taken seriously, for six months later Maybach brought out his famous float-feed carburettor which, though it was subsequently found to have been anticipated by the carburettor fitted to the English pioneer Edward Butler's 1887 'Petrol-cycle' – a name which certainly indicates that the word 'petrol' was in use before Simms claimed to have invented it – was eventually adopted throughout the motor industry.

But in those days, the only real motor industry was on the Continent, where the Daimler engine was dominant. It had been adopted by both leading French companies, Panhard & Levassor (which held the French Daimler engine agency) and Peugeot, while, apart from Daimler, the only German company selling motor cars was Benz of Mannheim, whose engines were a development of the old-fashioned horizontal gas-engine.

While there may not yet have been a market for motor cars in Britain, demand for the motor launches was steady, and some of those early boat engines proved wonderfully reliable; one was in use in the yard launch at Marvin's of Cowes for over 30 years, while another powered William Summer's launch *Phoebe* on Southampton Water for more than 20 years. By October 1894 Evelyn Ellis had three Daimler launches ('very fast craft') named *Albicore, Geyser* and *Mercury* moored on the Thames near his home at Datchet, while another titled client was Baron de Barreto of Brandon Park, Suffolk, who took delivery of a 3 hp sea-going launch engine, despite a serious disagreement earlier in the year.

In January de Barreto had ordered two 20 hp engines for his yacht *Asteroid*; by August 'difficulties' had arisen between the Daimler Motor Syndicate and de Barreto, and between the Daimler Motor Syndicate and the Daimler Motoren Gesellschaft. Precisely what the 'difficulties' had been is not revealed in the company minutes, but eventually de Barreto dropped a threatened court action after the Daimler Motor Syndicate had paid him a total of £1,050. Possibly the answer lay in another minute book entry made in August 1894, revealing that history had shown an unfortunate tendency to repeat itself: 'In view of the irregularities in the secretary's accounts and of his gross neglect of his duties, it was decided to request his immediate resignation.' One of the company's engineers, Ebenezer Tonkin, temporarily stepped into the breach left by the unlamented Edward Canning Glass.

In December 1894, an acquaintance of Simms named Thomas Instone (a former ship's engineer from Burntisland in Scotland who had moved south to Birmingham and then been appointed the London manager of the West Bromwich scale makers George Salter) recommended Edward Atkinson as General Manager. Instone, a member of the Institution of Mechanical Engineers since 1883, subsequently stepped in to fill the vacancy on the board, when Simms, who was still trying to develop sales of his ticket machine in Germany, resigned as Managing Director of the Syndicate with effect from 31 December (though he continued to act as an honorary director) and returned to Hamburg.

When the continuingly poor sales of the ticket machine at last convinced even Simms that it was a lost cause, he attempted to unload the patent on to the Daimler Motor Syndicate in February 1895, but was firmly told that the offer 'could not be entertained'. With the ticket machine venture now a secondary issue, Simms returned to London on a permanent basis by April and was duly re-elected managing director, Instone standing down to make room for him. The recently-appointed general manager, Atkinson, was summarily given a month's notice, while Ebenezer Tonkin was put on three months' notice, though he was subsequently allowed to continue as acting secretary, subject to a month's notice.

With Simms back at the helm, business was flourishing: at the board meeting on 7 June he announced that he was negotiating to buy part of Eel Pie Island, Twickenham, in order to provide servicing facilities for the Daimler-engined launches that were now running on the Thames, and then unveiled his major plan: to form the Daimler Motor Company Limited, with a capital of £50–100,000, 'for the purpose of acquiring the British Daimler Patents and the manufacturing of the said motors in this country'. The meeting gave him full authority to proceed.

At the same meeting, Simms proudly produced 'the first licence, for the carriage of the Hon Mr Ellis'. This was a 3½ hp Daimler-engined Panhard & Levassor, which Ellis had bought and run in France: now it was officially licensed by the Syndicate, he shipped the Panhard from Le Havre to Southampton on 3 July and then drove north to Micheldever, one station from Winchester on the London & South-Western Railway, where he was met by Simms, who accompanied him on the last leg of the journey to Datchet. He later went on to Malvern; it was the first long journey made by a motor car in England, and passed without any interference from the law. Seventy years later, his daughter – then Mrs Mary Critchley Salmonson – still recalled the excitement this caused: 'My father brought the first car to England and he drove it all the way from Marseille . . . and then brought it down to our country home at Rosenau, Datchet. I remember him arriving there and I often drove in that first car with him – the average speed was 8 miles per hour. He took King Edward VII [then Prince of Wales] for his first drive in that car and old King Edward said to my Father: "Evelyn, don't drive so fast – I am frightened!"'

Simms subsequently described his historic ride in a long letter to the *Saturday Review*: 'During the previous night a long and much-wanted steady rainfall had laid the dust on the roads, and thus we had every prospect of an enjoyable journey. We set forth at exactly 9.26 a.m. and made good progress on the well-made old London coaching road. The sky appeared somewhat over-clouded, but the easterly winds keeping off the rain and the roads being in good condition, it was delightful travelling on this fine summer morning.

'We were not quite without anxiety as to how the horses we might meet would behave towards their new rivals, but they took it very well. Out of 133 horses we passed on the road only two little ponies did not seem to appreciate the innovation . . . Meanwhile the sun brightened up the scenery all around us, and it was a very pleasing sensation to go along the delightful roads towards Virginia Water at speeds varying from three to twenty miles per hour. Our iron horse behaved splendidly . . . The average speed we attained was 9.84 miles per hour, the usual travelling speed being from eight to twelve miles per hour.

'In every place we passed through, we were not unnaturally the object of a great deal of curiosity. Whole villages turned out to behold, open-mouthed, the new marvel of locomotion. The departure of coaches was delayed to enable their passengers to have a look at our horseless vehicle, while cyclists

Inveterate inventor

Throughout his life, Frederick Simms kept on inventing things. He designed the first petrol motor mower – made by Ransome, Simms & Jeffries – and designed and built Britain's first aero-engine, which powered the Spencer airship that flew from the Crystal Palace round St Paul's Cathedral in 1903. He designed a magneto and devised the first – pneumatic – car bumpers. Even during the Second World War, the septuagenarian Simms studied metallurgy in order to perfect an invention.

Cannstatt celebrates the building of its 1,000th engine in 1895. [JDHT]

would stop to gaze enviously at us as we surmounted with ease some long and (to them) tiring hill.

'Mr Ellis' Panhard-Daimler motor-carriage – one of which, as will be remembered, gained the first prize in the recent carriage race, is a neat and compact four-wheeled dog-cart with accommodation for four persons and two portmanteaux. The consumption of petrol is a little over a halfpenny a mile and there is no smoke, heat or smell, the carriage running smoothly and without vibration. The simple and ingenious gear puts the carriage under complete control. The steering is likewise extremely simple, and either of the two powerful brakes can bring the carriage to a complete standstill within a little over a yard.'

Ellis subsequently 'ran the car in many parts of England, doing what he could to induce the authorities to take proceedings against him . . . in order to test the question of the legality of using such motors, intending

to take the case to the House of Lords, but the authorities did not accept his challenge'. One interesting sidelight on history is that when Ellis adapted part of his stables to house the Panhard, he called it a 'garage' – derived from the French verb *garer*, to store – and the word has been in use ever since.

In July Simms announced that since he and Ellis had made that pioneering journey in the Panhard (referred to coyly as a 'Daimler Motor Carriage'), 'over 80 enquiries had been received as well as many orders for carriages and also offers to make the motors and have licences granted'. A deal with Panhard & Levassor was concluded the following month in which the Daimler Company would receive a 10 per cent commission on British sales, 'plus 2 per cent on all orders sent'.

Frederick Simms, one of those archetypal Englishmen who feel compelled to found clubs to perpetuate their interests, drew up the constitution of an organization which he called the Self-Propelled Traffic Association, calling a meeting in late 1895 at which the S-PTA was successfully formed. Simms quickly felt that he was being pushed into the background by other members, and resigned; the S-PTA proved short-lived but did some useful work in organizing trials of commercial vehicles and in lobbying for the drafting of a new 'Locomotives on Highways' Bill which took account of private motor cars. Simms, undeterred, next formed a new organization called the Motor Car Club and this time ensured that he was declared vice-president . . . Sadly, he was to be railroaded out of that position, too.

As the scheme for the conversion of the Syndicate into a full company progressed, Simms announced that the purchase price for the Syndicate would be £40,000 – half in cash, the rest in cash or shares at the option of the directors. He also invited his old friend Gottlieb Daimler to join the new company as consulting engineer.

His plans were certainly ambitious: he wanted to build a brand-new factory with a staff of 400 workmen and modelled on the Deutz engine works at Cologne, with incoming raw materials distributed in sequence by light railway lines passing through the works 'to avoid all possibility of a repetition of transport to and fro, [through] which now-a-days in many Works hundreds of pounds are being lost without being noticed'.

By now the works on Eel Pie Island, formerly an electric motor works owned by soap king Alfred Pears, had been bought for £4,000–£1,000 cash, £3,000 on mortgage – and requests for licences to build the Daimler engine had been received from some well-known engineering companies, including Hornby, Ackroyd & Co, Easton, Anderson & Goolden Ltd, Singer of Coventry, T.B. Barker of Birmingham, John Fowler of Leeds, Crossley Brothers of Manchester, the Bristol Waggon Company and Marsden & Company of Birmingham.

On 15 October the Mayor of Tunbridge Wells, Sir David Salomons, organized Britain's first automobile exhibition on the showground of the local agricultural society: Ellis's Panhard & Levassor was prominent among the handful of vehicles present and, according to *The Autocar*, 'excited much interest, as it is practically a duplicate of the vehicle that arrived first in the Paris–Bordeaux race'. Peugeot and de Dion-Bouton vehicles were demonstrated, and the local fire brigade, led by Captain Tinne, demonstrated a fire engine 'designed for a country house and worked, so far as the water jets were concerned, by a Daimler petroleum engine'. A 19-year-old eyewitness recalled many years later: 'The Show Field was a soft grassy meadow on a considerable incline, hopeless conditions for these newly-born infants to show what they could do – or couldn't do – and they just sulked!'

So, armed with the full dignity of his mayoral office, Salomons cocked a snook at the requirements of the Locomotives on Highways law by leading the motor vehicles out on to the road linking the Show Field with the town. 'The motor vehicles were shown to be under perfect control and not one of the horses so much as lifted an eye as the horseless carriages sped somewhat noisily by,' wrote *The Autocar*, adding: 'At the close of the proceedings, it was felt by all that the occasion undoubtedly heralded the dawn of a new era in vehicular propulsion on the high roads of this country, and that for manifold purposes the horse would shortly be reckoned to be *de trop*.'

Just over a month later, on 22–30 November 1895, the first indoor British exhibition of internal combustion motor vehicles took place at the Stanley Cycle Show in the Agricultural Hall, London. The five cars displayed again included Ellis's Daimler-engined Panhard, along with a l'Hollier-Benz, Gladiator 'mineral naphtha' tricycle, and a Facile 'heavy oil' carriage.

But by now Simms's ambitious plans had all changed, for on the very day of the Tunbridge Wells Show, the Daimler Motor Syndicate had been approached by a firm of

This Daimler fire-engine was demonstrated at the 1895 Tunbridge Wells exhibition.

lawyers – Steadman, Van Praagh, Campion & Simmons – representing a cocky little company promotor named Harry J. Lawson. Short and pop-eyed, Lawson had been involved in a number of spectacular flotations along with his mentor, Terah Hooley, and was now setting up the British Motor Syndicate with a view to obtaining a stranglehold on the manufacture and sales of motor vehicles before an industry had a chance to get established in Britain.

Then aged 43, Lawson claimed to have invented 'the first British motor-car' – he had patented a curious gas-driven tricycle in 1880 – and had been a prime mover in the bicycle boom on the early 1890s along with Harvey Du Cros Sr, Martin Rucker and Terah Hooley; all of them had made considerable fortunes out of floating bicycle and tyre businesses and converting them into heavily over-capitalized limited companies. The latter pair were Lawson's partners in the British Motor Syndicate, founded in July 1895 with a capital of £150,000. Its 1895 promotional brochure was short on size and long on hyperbole: the tiny booklet

described Lawson as the 'Pioneer of Fin-de-siècle Locomotion' (as well as patenting his gas-propelled tricycle he claimed to have invented the safety cycle), adding, in an obvious dig at Ellis and Simms: 'Men were wily enough to earn cheap popularity by bringing a French car over and running it about parks, but until Mr Lawson's advent on the motor-car stage, no-one had sufficient courage or foresight to risk any hard cash.'

Lawson's offer was straightforward: £35,000 in cash for the Daimler patent rights, and Simms instantly decided to sell the Daimler Motor Syndicate as a going concern. It came as no surprise that he failed to persuade Lawson to take on the rights to the ticket machines or another of his sidelines, weighing machines, and these were pointedly omitted from the deal. But before the deal could be concluded and the rights to the Daimler patents transferred to a new company, there was a major problem to overcome in Cannstatt, where Gottlieb Daimler, having fallen out with the directors of the Daimler-Motoren-Gesellschaft (formed in 1890 with capital provided by two armament manufacturers named Lorenz and Duttenhofer), had, along with Maybach, withdrawn from the company – which was concentrating on its low-speed stationary engine business – at the end of 1892 to develop horseless carriages, working in a converted summerhouse behind an abandoned hotel.

Without Daimler and Maybach, the Daimler-Motoren-Gesellschaft was drifting towards bankruptcy and Simms left post-haste for Cannstatt after the meeting with Lawson's representatives to try and reunite the former partners, for the takeover depended on both parties accepting Lawson's offer. Simms's tactics were simple: he offered Lorenz and Duttenhofer 350,000 Marks (£17,100) for the Daimler licence on condition that Gottlieb Daimler rejoined the company, and though they were reluctant, they were over-ruled by their fellow directors and a 'contract of reassociation' was signed on 1 November.

Four days later, the DMG's business manager Gustav Vischer wrote to Wilhelm Deurer, the company's Hamburg representative since the days of that famous incident with the Kaiser and the motor-launch: 'Do not disturb yourself any more; today I am in the happy position of letting you know that everything is in order. The merger has been effected and the contract signed by Herr Lorenz. The whole of Daimler-Maybach's assets are joined with ours. Daimler will be General Inspector, Maybach the chief Technical Director, Moeves at the head office of the Technical Bureaux, Linck wishes to enter the Commercial Directorate (which is not quite certain) and I will be journeying to London in the next few days to carry out the formalities of the transfer of patents and to take receipt of the money. In England, no business will be built but a consortium will take over patents and issue licences, for which they will pay in cash, which would be more than the business and shares together.

'That, in short is the outcome. Can you imagine how pleased I am about the way things have turned out? The struggle and strife is ended and we stand financially A-1. Hopefully in other respects, we shall shortly be on the top rung technically. With such an outlook, not only we, but all our friends who have supported us with their cooperation – with you and your friends in the forefront – can face the future with new confidence.

'In all, these discussions have benefited greatly from Herr *Geheimrat* [privy councillor] Duttenhofer's wide outlook and business acumen, without which a merger on such a sound basis would not have been possible. Nevertheless, I do not wish to diminish the efforts of Herr Simms, who has gone to so much trouble, especially in

Company promotor Harry J. Lawson. [DBW]

THE DAIMLER MOTOR CARRIAGE.

Highest Awards.

The Daimler
Motor Syndicate,
Limited.

Telegraphic Address—
" DAIMLER, LONDON."

Inspection Invited.

The Daimler Patent Gas and Oil Motors.

For driving all kinds of Machinery, Electric Lighting and other purposes.
For Carriages, Bi-and Quadri-cycles, Tramways, Locomotives, Railway Inspection Cars, Delivery Vans,
and Vehicles of all kinds; for Launches and all Marine Purposes.

95, Billiter Buildings.
49, Leadenhall Street.

Frederick R. Simms, Esq.,   London, 26th November, 189 5.
                                              E.C.

    95, Billiter Buildings,

        49, Leadenhall Street, E.C.

Dear Sir,

    I have much pleasure in handing you on behalf of the
Trustees of the Daimler Motor Syndicate, Limited, elected at an
extraordinary general meeting held on the 18th inst., the enclosed
cheque for £5,900 (Five thousand nine hundred pounds) being dividend
of 200% per Share. Further payments in accordance with the resolution of the Shareholders at the above-mentioned general meeting, will
be forwarded in due course, as well as statement of account.

                Yours truly,

                Frederick R. Simms

(Encl.)

securing the signature of Herr Daimler, which was no mean feat.' In effect, the persuasive Simms – and Lawson's money –

had assured the futures of both the English and German companies in one move.

Back in London, on Wednesday 20 November Simms and his fellow directors of the Daimler Motor Syndicate met Lawson and his solicitor, Bertram Van Praagh, to finalize the details of the sale and it was proposed that a company should be formed with a capital of £100,000.

The new company would acquire the right to use the name Daimler and operate all the Daimler patents, taking over 'the offices, works, assets, debts, furniture and effects of [the] late Syndicate . . . thus enabling it to continue the business as heretofore with increased capital and the greatly increased demand which we expect to create'. Simms was to act as managing director ('or otherwise as may be agreed').

The shareholders in the Daimler Motor Syndicate were delighted: when the sale was completed at the end of November, Simms was able to return them their original capital plus dividends totalling £19,147 – a profit of 200 per cent – and they presented him with a massive silver loving cup mounted on a silver pedestal to show their gratitude.

He had, deservedly, done rather well out of the sale: on 26 November he solemnly sat down and wrote himself a formal letter – addressing himself as 'Dear Mr Simms' and signing his name in full – which contained a cheque for £5,900, representing his share of the 200 per cent dividend, and equivalent to well over £300,000 in today's terms.

Chapter 2

THE MOTOR MILLS

Harry J. Lawson, whose British Motor Syndicate now controlled the Daimler patents, was by any standards, a remarkable man. By today's squeaky-clean standards, it's easy to brand him an opportunist rogue, but he was a highly-successful businessman in a far more robust era, when insider trading was the quick way to a fortune and the guiding principle of many a large company was to gain absolute control of an industry by the establishment of a water-tight monopoly.

He certainly made vast sums of money out of his business dealings but then so, too, did many of his investors until boom turned to bust, and, recalled his former associate Herbert Osbaldeston Duncan in his monumental book *The World on Wheels:* 'He was neither a greedy man nor an egoist. On the contrary, he was always fair and extremely generous. He paid largely and was most liberal in the golden days of his success. A cheque was always ready to be handed over with a kindly smile to friends who assisted him either with his dealings or company-promoting schemes. Lawson was a clever man. Perhaps his greatest misfortune was in not being supported properly in his business by others equally intelligent.'

Born in the City of London in 1852, Lawson came from an unlikely background, for his father was a renowned Puritan preacher and technical model maker. In the 1870s Lawson went into the nascent cycle industry, setting up in business in Brighton where in 1876, at the height of the craze for high-wheeled 'penny-farthing' bicycles, he and James Likeman patented a curious lever-driven bicycle with a low-set saddle which made falling off less hazardous. Lawson recalled helping his father make a replica of George Stephenson's famous 'Geordy' safety lamp while still a student at a Mechanics' Institute, and registered the name 'safety' for the new bicycle.

He subsequently sold his Brighton business to W.H. Halliwell and moved to Coventry – already established as the centre of the cycle industry – where he joined the Tangent & Coventry Tricycle Company. In 1879 Lawson patented a new safety cycle, this time with chain drive, which he called the 'bicyclette' in order to attract French customers, who did not appear to recognize the concept of 'safety' when applied to cycling. The design of the 'bicyclette' was widely copied – the word even managed the near-impossible feat for an English coinage of being accepted into French dictionaries – and in 1880 Lawson became sales superintendent of the newly-formed Rudge Cycle Company, the fruit of a merger between Tangent & Coventry and the cycle company founded by Dan Rudge, the recently-deceased landlord of the 'Tiger's Head' public house, engineered by an astute Coventry lawyer named George Woodcock, who became chairman of the concern.

Lawson's career as a company promotor began in 1887, when he assisted Woodcock convert Rudge into a joint stock company, a flotation which proved so successful – 'the shares went to £15 each and one year a profit of £36,000 was earned' – that, as the financial weekly *The Rialto* commented: 'Coventry afterwards was too circumscribed for his expanded views, and the metropolis became his arena'.

His first independent venture was the Cattle Foods Company, 'to which the public liberally subscribed, but only to find what in the prospectus appeared an attractive speculation, develop into a miserable fiasco, and result in liquidation'. Undeterred, in 1889 Lawson floated the London & Scottish Trustee & Investment Company, with a capital of £100,000, which soon became the London & Scottish Issue Company, with a capital increased to £350,000 ('of which fully-paid shares representing £250,000 were allotted to Mr H.J. Lawson for past and future services') and ended in liquidation after giving birth to the Financial Trust & Agency, one of four companies launched by Lawson in 1890.

The pattern was remarkably similar: Lawson's companies paid spectacular – and unsustainable – dividends for a couple of years before collapsing 'in the throes of insolvency'. Nevertheless, in the get-rich-quick climate of the early 1890s there followed a string of Lawson-promoted flotations: the Brewery Assets Company; the Discount Banking Company of England & Wales; the Hounslow Brewery Company; the Humber Bicycle Company and the Humber Extension Limited; the Mortgage Loan & Discount Company; the Stockbrokers' Banking Corporation; the Spring Water Company; the Hop Ale Company; Prestons of Liverpool; the Licences Insurance Company; Moore & Burgess and the Beeston Tyre Company, 'launched in 1893, with a capital fully subscribed of £60,000, but after undergoing

reconstruction – a favourite process with Mr Lawson – it failed to yield any dividend for the shareholders'.

Somewhere along the way – probably when he and Martin Rucker, then general manager of Humber, sought City finance for the conversion of that firm into a limited company – Lawson had become involved with the astounding Ernest Terah Hooley, five years his junior in age, but the undisputed master of over-capitalized company flotations, starting respectably enough with companies like Schweppes and Bovril but moving into increasingly dubious territory with the promotion of concerns like the Simpson Lever Chain ('an invention that would enable a novice to attain speeds of from forty to sixty miles an hour!') and culminating with the acquisition in 1896 – along with the Du Cros brothers and, among others, Adolphe Clément and Martin Rucker – of the Dunlop Pneumatic Tyre Company for £3 million and its flotation as a new concern for £5 million. Lawson, it was said, had personally made £500,000 from dealing in Dunlop shares.

The well-connected Hooley, who had a 'league table' of fees for noble names to dress up his boards of directors (£10,000 for a duke, £5,000 for an Earl, and so on) was to help Lawson find backing for his various ventures. However, after one flotation – Venice Limited, with a capital of £150,000 – had flopped, *The Rialto* commented: 'Mr H.J. Lawson, a City celebrity, has been so much in the background of late that we were afraid he had retired altogether from the promoting world, satisfied to rest on the laurels earned in by-gone days; but if rumour be correct, he is maturing several schemes in connection with horseless carriages.'

But though Lawson was controversial, he was also a visionary, and well ahead of most people he foresaw the potential of the horseless carriage and realized that if he could corner the industry that would inevitably follow the easing of the legislative restrictions on motor cars, the potential fortune that could be made would overshadow anything that he had previously accumulated. Taking Hooley's Dunlop Tyre Syndicate as a pattern, Lawson had formed his British Motor Syndicate in an attempt to buy up every key patent relating to the motor car so that he could levy a royalty on every motor vehicle built or used in the United Kingdom.

The acquisition of the Daimler Syndicate had been the first step in that master plan.

* * *

On 14 January 1896 Lawson incorporated Britain's first motor manufacturing company, the Daimler Motor Company Limited, which – even if it didn't actually possess a factory or its own product – had impressive headed notepaper bearing the address of Lawson's premises at 40 Holborn Viaduct. It carried an engraving of a Peugeot car ('The Daimler Motor Carriage – Highest Awards') and promoted 'The Daimler Patent Gas and Oil Motors for driving all kinds of Machinery, Electric Lighting and other purposes. For Carriages, Bi- and Quadri-cycles, Tramways, Locomotives, Railway Inspection Cars, Delivery Vans and Vehicles of all kinds; for Launches and all Marine Purposes.'

One of the first uses for the new notepaper came when Lawson sent a hastily-typed note to Simms on 5 February: 'Since leaving you just now, I notice these expensive premises on the Viaduct, with a glorious front and shop window being wasted. Why not placard it from top to bottom with "Daimler Motor Co Ltd" and have a table with a clerk in the show-room and let the issue take place here? It is just the sort of thing we go and pay a big sum for in the city, ie a shop window from which we can advise the floating of a public company. My Daimler Motor Carriage will stand in the window and I will create such a sensation as has never been created in London before. I am quite certain that is the right thing to do, much better than climbing a second floor in Leadenhall Street. Here we have these very expensive premises in the

City. Let the issue take place here.' A hand-written afterthought added: '& we shall have a grand advertisement.'

Lawson's enthusiasm, it must be admitted, was hardly shared by the financial press: 'No doubt [the Daimler Motor Company] will be the pioneer of other like companies,' wrote *The Rialto*, 'and thus the record of Mr Lawson's enterprise in the promotion of companies may again, like history, repeat itself. We cannot protect people from the consequences of their own imprudence and recklessness, but we can place on record the wonderful enterprise of Mr Lawson as a promotor, developed, too, within the short period of a few years, and leave the public to draw its own conclusions as to the relative positions, financially, of a promotor and a shareholder. The maxim of Caveat Emptor appears to have been ignored by the clients of Mr Lawson, and no legislation can protect fools.'

The *Stock Exchange Gazette* was broadly in agreement: 'The Daimler Motor Company Ltd, which appeals for support today, is no doubt a good thing. But the fact that Mr H.J. Lawson is the controlling spirit is a very bad omen for the company and augurs a speedy acquaintance with the bankruptcy court rather than the success the patent deserves.'

But when the prospectus for the Daimler Motor Company ('Capital £100,000, divided into 10,000 shares of £10 each') was issued on 15 February, announcing 'the Lists will open for Subscription on Monday February 17th at 10 am and close the following day for town and country', Lawson's name was not on the list of directors, who seemed to have been carefully chosen to allay any fears that this was a typical Lawsonian flotation: Gottlieb Daimler ('Inventor of the Daimler Motor'); Hon Evelyn Ellis; William Wright ('Director of Moor & Robinson's Nottinghamshire Banking Co Ltd'); J.J. Mace ('Director of London Road Car Co Ltd'); J.J. Henry Sturmey ('Iliffe & Sturmey, Coventry'); and H.E. Sherwin Holt MA MIEE ('Chairman of

J.J. Henry Sturmey as a young journalist. [DBW]

opening of the lists meant that they were ignorant of a clause which allowed the British Motor Syndicate to place two nominees on the board of Daimler (though it should have come as no surprise to anyone familiar with his methods that Lawson would be one of them, or that he would be appointed the company's first chairman).

And while the prospectus made it clear that the British Motor Syndicate was to receive 4,000 shares or their equivalent in cash (naturally, Lawson chose the cash option) in payment for a non-exclusive United Kingdom licence to the Daimler patents, it did not mention 'an obligation on the part of the Daimler Motor Company Limited to assign to the British Motor Syndicate Limited all improvements the said Daimler Company might effect or become the owners of in respect of the invention or the mode of applying it.' In effect, this meant that the new Daimler Company was compelled to hand over the results of any product development to the British Motor Syndicate, who were free to either produce the improved design themselves or issue licences to any number of third parties.

Amazingly, however, the issue proved to be ten per cent over-subscribed when the lists closed on 18 February, which meant that the new company had the £60,000 working capital it needed (in addition to the £40,000 'licence money'); now it had to find a factory. It also needed friends in high places to speed the promised revision of the Locomotives on Highways Act through Parliament, for until motor cars could move freely on the roads of Britain, sales would inevitably be restricted.

To mark the flotation of the Daimler Motor Company, Lawson organized a reception at the Imperial Institute on Saturday 15 February under the umbrella of the Motor Car Club, which, complained Simms, had become 'the direct instrument of Mr Harry J. Lawson and others, in the promotion of their motor car schemes'. Now based on the second floor of Lawson's headquarters at 40 Holborn Viaduct, the

Swinburne & Company Ltd, Electrical Engineers'). Simms – far from being managing director – was not even on the board, but was appointed consulting engineer.

The secretary of the company, Charles Osborn, was also the secretary of the British Motor Syndicate – and that was not the only conflict of interest on the list of company officials. Henry Sturmey was certainly a director of the publishing company Iliffe & Sturmey, but he also edited *The Autocar*, the only British publication dealing with the new locomotion, and his seat on the Daimler board might, one would have thought, have unduly influenced his views on the new company (and, indeed, the entire Lawson empire).

In addition, the fact that there was no time allowed for would-be investors to inspect the company's articles of association before the

Motor Car Club described itself as 'a society for the protection, encouragement and development of the motor-car industry'. It had Lawson as its chairman and C. Harrington Moore as secretary.

Among the nearly 1,700 people who crowded the galleries of the Imperial Institute to see a demonstration of four of the handful of motor cars in Britain demonstrate their capabilities were members of both Houses of Parliament – and the Prince of Wales, who had asked for a private view the previous day and been driven around the Institute by his equerry's cousin, Evelyn Ellis on the Daimler-engined Panhard, the only car which had actually turned up on the Friday.

'I cannot forget,' Simms later recalled, 'with what concern I watched my friend running His Majesty up a narrow wood ramp of a grade of one in ten and safely back again to the level. This may seem strange to the motorman of to-day, but I believe that my feelings were quite justified, knowing the responsibility which my expert friend was taking, for the combined weight of the two occupants was no small matter!' Asked his opinion after his first motor-ride on British

soil, the Prince is reported to have remarked that he was delighted, but thought it would be a pity if the motor car ousted the horse entirely.

On the Saturday, three other cars were present: a Benz-Acme, a Pennington and a Garrard & Blomfield electric car, which 'arrived late, and burst a tyre after a few circuits'. The event opened with a solemn procession of the cars down the Institute's North Gallery preceded by a small child carrying a red flag, after which the machines demonstrated their speed and manoeuvrability as best they could within the confines of the building.

As soon as the Daimler issue was successfully concluded, it was time for a junket, concluded Lawson: 'We decided that the directors themselves should be able to thoroughly grasp the fact of what these motors were, and for that purpose we personally visited each of the Continental works, which took some time. The works we visited in a body were, first of all, those in Paris, and the sight we saw there was such as I should very much like the people of Great Britain to be able to see. There were hundreds

Harry Lawson, in the extravagant costume of his Motor Car Club, is seated in the middle of the front row of this photo taken after the 1896 Emancipation Day Brighton Run. Other Daimler pioneers present are Otto Mayer (back row, left), J.S. Critchley (back row, second from left), A.J. Drake (back row, right), Charles Osborn (seated, left) and J.J. Mace (seated, second from right). [JDHT]

Fanciful advertising like this engraving of a flying motor-cycle enabled E.J. Pennington to sell his patent rights to Lawson for £100,000. [DBW]

of these cars in large works such as Panhard-Levassor and Peugeot . . . I suppose there are now some 20 or 30 big factories turning out these motors as hard as ever they can. The cars we saw were of every description. We went for rides in omnibuses, which were entirely self-acting, through streets, up and down hills and over mountains without the slightest difficulty or danger. If anything were in the way we were pulled up with a jerk. Our only objection was in being pulled up so suddenly – in half the space that it takes for an average horse to pull up in. After that we went to Germany and saw Mr Daimler, the inventor of our motor . . . We saw everything that would convince the most sceptical man that this is going to be one of the biggest industries in this country.'

Through his British Motor Syndicate, Lawson was spending huge sums of money buying up 'master' patents, though the value placed on each was not always a measure of its practicability. One of his earliest and most spectacular acquisitions had been the purchase of the British rights to the inventions of Edward Joel Pennington, subsequently described by patent agent Eric Walford (who was employed by the London firm of Boult & Wade, which handled Lawson's patents work) as 'that mechanical charlatan'.

'Airship' Pennington was, if you like, America's answer to Lawson, and had first attained notoriety in 1890 by his plans to build a flying machine; he then became obsessed with the internal combustion engine and attempted to build a motor bicycle. With backing from Thomas Kane of Racine, Wisconsin, he put a curious engine into production which had tubular steel cylinders devoid of cooling and with no carburettor – just a primitive needle valve which dribbled raw fuel into the air intake. Ignition was taken care of by another Pennington speciality – the 'long-mingling spark'. For reasons which defy rational explanation, the two-, three- and four-wheeled vehicles built by Pennington actually ran – 'as far, perhaps,' recalled Walford, 'as ten miles without a breakdown, though on most occasions the ignition failed very quickly.'

A published description of the Kane-Pennington engine poetically described it as 'a heat engine of such exquisite simplicity that a child might remember all of its few parts and their uses' and inspired a young Detroit mechanic named Henry Ford to build his first 'quadricycle'. At the end of 1895 Pennington, inspired by reports from a Londoner named Baines (who had an option on his designs) that there were rich pickings to be had, sailed to England to negotiate with prospective licensees.

Martin Rucker of Humber introduced him to Lawson, who was doubtless much impressed by a spectacular engraving of a Pennington motorcycle leaping a river 'to illustrate its suitability for cross-country work'. The upshot of the meeting was an agreement to purchase the largely spurious Pennington rights for £100,000 'in hard cash'. 'As an engineer and inventor,' remarked Lawson, 'I think a great deal of the Pennington motor, so much so that I am doing my hardest at present to get a contract for manufacturing the Pennington motors, which would require similar machinery to what we require to make our Daimler motors. By that means we would get into the first position for making motors in this country.'

Further acquisitions by Lawson included the British rights to the 'past, present and future patents of De Dion-Bouton', bought for £20,000 – half in cash, half in British Motor Syndicate shares – and £20,000 in cash for similar rights to the designs of Léon Bollée, a mechanical genius from Le Mans, who had designed a three-wheeled 'voiturette'. By mid-1896, the Syndicate had acquired over 70 such patents – and, incidentally, the cash payments proved the salvation of several companies which were to become household names in the Continental motor industry – and Lawson now revealed the next stage of his complex scheme, the formation of a company intended 'to carry on and establish the Great Horseless Carriage Industry in this country'.

Since the Daimler company had been formed to exploit the Daimler patents, this new company – appropriately named 'the Great Horseless Carriage Company' – would 'purchase a license to use all or any of the applications for patents, patent rights or letters patent of or belonging at the present time to the British Motor Syndicate' (for which the purchase price would be '50,000 shares or cash in lieu thereof' – neatly accounting for £500,000 of the issued capital of £750,000).

With a list of aims and objects that seemingly left no self-propelled stone unturned, the new promotion would be 'a new parent company to immediately take up, work and develop this immense industry; to acquire licences for working the patents mentioned herein; to purchase master patents and receive royalties therefrom; to license and form subsidiary companies thereunder; to sell foreign rights and concessions; and to generally establish and work the trade in this country.' Consequently, added the new company's prospectus, it would be 'the first great joint stock enterprise in this country to attempt to take in hand and immediately launch upon the streets in sufficient quantity these vehicles for immediate sale'. And this at a time when the use of motor vehicles on British roads was so hedged about with restrictions as to make it almost impracticable.

Lawson, whose basic plan, according to Duncan, was 'to form a string of subsidiary companies and ensure a ceaseless flow of royalties into his coffers', knew just how to appeal to his avaricious audience, hopefully anticipating that the flotation of a British motor industry would rival the Railway Mania of the early nineteenth century: 'The magnitude of this enormous industry takes us back to the days of George Stephenson and the birth of Railway Motors, the first departure from animal traction. The feverish rush and excitement attending upon the great

A rose by any other name

One charge made against early motor cars was that they smelt of oil, but, as Harry Lawson commented in 1896, 'some oils smell a great deal less than others and it all depends on getting oils of the right gravity . . . and you must remember that the horse has a smell! . . . When you see the car standing still, you form an absolutely wrong conclusion as to both the smell and the vibration. When you go along, the little smell that there is is left behind you, and even those who are near you as you pass do not smell it. [Your servant] must be educated to keep the machine clean, and then there will be no smell at all.'

Railway Boom fifty years ago, when some of the greatest fortunes of the present day were founded, are about to be repeated.'

Obviously none of these ambitions could be achieved if his new empire had nowhere to build 'the New Motor Broughams, Landaus, Phaetons of the future! Motor Pullman Cars, Omnibuses, Tramcars, Wagonettes! Motor Express Vans, Parcels Delivery, Trucks and Waggons!' foreshadowed by the prospectus for the Great Horseless Carriage Company, and Frederick Simms was sent to look for suitable buildings.

He discovered what seemed like the perfect solution in the shape of the purpose-built Trusty Oil Engine Works, a freehold property 'in splendid condition and repair' on a six-acre site at Cheltenham with its own foundry, machine shop and testing facilities, fully equipped with machines and tools 'of the latest type and pattern throughout . . . they seem to be very fine tools indeed, especially for heavy work'. The Trusty Company was in receivership and for sale as a going concern with a staff of 80 workmen and, remarked Simms, 'with regard to skilled labour, I have been informed that plenty is to be got at Cheltenham, Gloucester and Stroud at a fair price, in fact I feel sure that I could reduce the average of 22s [£1.10], which is very moderate, to about 20s [£1.00]'.

Concluded Simms: 'My opinion with regard to the Cheltenham Works is that the Company should buy them immediately, as I feel sure that we shall not be able to do better. We should have in these works no, or little, loss of time, which in the face of the many competitors which are starting up seems to be of the utmost importance. We should also get a certain number of tried men, as well as a works manager, whom I am informed is a very smart man, and last, but not least, we could save a great deal in cash, for we certainly could not buy freehold ground, build buildings on same, and equip the works with such machines as the price that is being asked for the Cheltenham Works.'

Unfortunately for Simms, he was abroad

when the Daimler Motor Company held its first statutory meeting, on Friday 27 March at 40 Holborn Viaduct under the chairmanship of Harry Lawson. Only J.A. Bradshaw, Henry Sturmey and J.H. Mace were present, along with the new company secretary A.H. Deaville Altree and a solicitor named Piercy. After a couple of salary cheques – £18 15s representing six weeks' pay for an employee named Osborn and Altree's £20 8s 4d monthly stipend – had been made out, the British Motor Syndicate licence for making Daimler engines was sealed and signed. Piercy confirmed that it was now in order to hand over the balance of the purchase money and Altree was instructed to send the Syndicate a cheque for £10,000.

The board members then discussed the purchase of a factory highly recommended by Harry Lawson. Just placed on the market 'by a lucky fluke . . . these magnificent works . . . offered to us on what we consider reasonable terms', consisted of an empty cotton mill built in the 1860s by the recently-defunct Coventry Cotton Spinning & Weaving Company on a large leasehold site by the Coventry Canal. Badly damaged by fire in 1891, the mill had largely been rebuilt by its insurers, so the upper three floors of the four-storey structure were practically new. It was too large for Daimler as it then existed – and, logically, a multi-storey factory was hardly ideal for the production of wheeled vehicles – but it was exactly what Lawson wanted, for it fitted neatly into his larger plan. And the old mill had another – hidden – advantage: it belonged to Ernest Terah Hooley . . .

Lawson was obviously his old persuasive self, for the directors quickly authorized him to send Hooley a telegram stating: 'Company agrees to purchase Cotton Mills £17,500 will send deposit £1,000 on your confirming this.' And then they went to lunch. When the directors came back, bathed in a post-prandial glow, there was Hooley waiting to conclude the deal as soon as possible!

It was quickly agreed that Daimler should

'purchase all that estate known as the Coventry Cotton Mills for the sum of £18,000 comprising 4 storey factory, outbuildings, manager's residence, fixed plant and machinery and the surrounding land including in the lease about 11½ acres', and a cheque for £4,000 was handed to Hooley on account, in exchange for a receipt assigning his contract for the mills to the Daimler Company.

Simms was not at all pleased about this when he returned from the Continent, and urged the Daimler directors 'to sell the Cotton Mill at Coventry with a profit if possible', and buy the Trusty Oil Engine Factory, but he was ignored, for all too obvious reasons. And that flagrant piece of insider trading between Hooley and Lawson was the sole reason why Coventry – which, despite its recent history of making sewing machines and cycles, had not the slightest experience of heavy industry or engine manufacture – became the centre of the British motor industry rather than Cheltenham.

Lawson informed shareholders at the company's statutory general meeting on 19 May that the Coventry building was 'an almost perfect place for manufacturing these machines. We made an advantageous arrangement which, however, I am not at liberty to give you in detail.' This 'advantageous arrangement' was brilliant in its simplicity: Daimler sub-let the main building (grandly rechristened 'the Motor Mills') to the Great Horseless Carriage Company for considerably more than it had paid for the entire site, showing a profit of nearly £12,000 on the transaction. The Great Horseless Carriage Company, in turn, let off the upper floors to other companies within the combine: the Beeston Tyre Syndicate took the top storey, the British Motor Syndicate the first floor and – purely as a temporary measure while their fire-damaged factory was rebuilt – Humber had the ground floor, and fitted-up the shafts and machinery so that the area was ready for the Great Horseless Carriage Company to move straight into.

Since the British Motor Syndicate had recently declared a 30 per cent interim dividend on its first year's trading even though none of Lawson's companies had even started building a motor car, the 'little man' obviously still possessed his Midas

This engraving of the Motor Mills accompanied Lawson's publicity for the British Motor Syndicate: one suspects that the serried ranks of the work force are largely artist's licence . . .

touch. He even managed to persuade Simms of the advantages of the Motor Mills and, in a handwritten report dated 16 June, Simms boasted of the 'splendidly arranged works with some of the finest & modern machinery at Coventry, for abt. 250 men capable of an annual output of abt. 1,000 motors . . . The fact of ready motor works, well-organized & capable of coping with the rush of business in a very short space of time is of greatest importance in view of the early passing of the amended Locomotion Act'.

The factory was not, however, as 'ready' as it might have been for, admitted Lawson the following year, 'when we took the building, the shops were fitted with cotton-spinning machinery, and that was broken up and cleared out. Then we had simply the four walls and the shafting in position. The fitting up of the shops took some time . . . a large proportion of the machines ordered in May were not received until December and some ordered in June are not in yet.'

Much of the credit for the Coventry factory's transformation lay with its works manager, James Sidney Critchley, who had been an early recruit to the Daimler Company. Critchley was a qualified patent agent by training, but had made his career in the design and construction of factory plant and machinery. He was also, it seems, related to the Instones by marriage. He was thrown in at the deep end, acquiring a gas engine to power the machinery, drawing up plans for a blacksmith's shop, buying machine tools, recommending that the tenants in the houses on the mill property be given notice to quit as soon as possible, 'as it would be better for those employed here to live as close to the works as possible and houses are not easily to be found'.

In addition, at the end of May 1896 Critchley travelled to Cannstatt to meet Otto Mayer who, though he had been working with Daimler and Maybach since 1887, was originally from Lincolnshire, where he had been born in 1866 and served his apprenticeship with the great steam engine manufacturers Robey & Co before moving to Germany. Critchley's task was to collect drawings and blueprints selected by Simms during his visit to the German factory in March and redrawn by a small team of draughtsmen under Mayer's supervision so that production of Cannstatt-Daimlers could begin at Coventry as soon as possible; Mayer, who between 1889–92 had worked in New York to enable the American Daimler Company to get into production, would initially carry out liaison between Simms (appointed a director of the Daimler Motoren Gesellschaft early in 1896) and the Cannstatt firm but then joined the Coventry Daimler company and spent the remainder of his long career in England.

During Simms's visit to Cannstatt he had, aided by Herr Engineer Director Wilhelm Maybach himself, assembled 'a complete Daimler Motor Carriage frame on the Cannstatt System, as distinct from the Paris system'. With the assistance of Mayer and Van Toll, Simms had also chosen the new Phönix vertical-twin engine – 'at present constructed in four sizes, viz: 2, 4. 5 and 10 hp, and which type we have christened "Type N", comprises nearly all the advantages of all the previous Daimler motors' – as the most suitable type for production at Coventry. Not only, wrote Simms, was the engine easily adaptable for marine use but 'the other reason why I selected this Mobile type of Motor is that the Company will be able to get a better price for products of locomotion be it on land or water, than by producing stationary Motors, where a very powerful and well-installed competition already exists.'

One of Simms's plans which came to nothing was his scheme for setting up a small experimental shop where he and Van Toll could work on two of his pet projects, 'a 4 hp horizontal carriage motor on the newest lines . . . and as a second experiment, a horizontal 8 hp crude oil motor, there being a great demand for horizontal motors from 8 to 28 horse power'.

Simms's new position on the Cannstatt

board enabled him to buy the German products at a 25 per cent discount and he had also taken over the stock on consignment at a 34 per cent reduction. He had ordered various vehicles and components for urgent delivery, including a narrow-gauge tram, two 3 hp launch engines and 'some complete sets, so as to enable us to start manufacturing quickly on good lines'. These 'sets' – bodiless belt-drive chassis – consisted of four 3 hp, three 4 hp and one 10 hp, while Simms had also ordered three complete motor cars, a 3 hp two-seater with child's seat at 4,560 Marks (£223), a 4 hp *vis-à-vis* Victoria at 5,360 Marks (£262) and a 4 hp 'Freight Car' at 4,650 Marks (£227).

But the Coventry Company already had other strings to its bow, for during that board trip to Paris, arrangements had been made with the two French companies using Daimler engines in their products (Panhard & Levassor and Peugeot Frères) for the supply of cars and components. Noted Simms: 'The order given to Messrs P & L is well in hand, and they have already sent over the omnibus bought when in Paris and it is now at the Imperial Institute for exhibitional purposes. I expect by the 1st of May, two complete carriage frames from Messrs P & L, one of which is for our own study and the other for Messrs. Mulliner, Ltd., of Birmingham, to be fitted with a carriage body; and then sent to the exhibition

'A 10 hp carriage motor has also since been ordered from Messrs P & L as a pattern, and I am now laying down the lines of a powerful carriage with Sir Somers Vine, who has been authorized by the well-known mining engineer, Mr George Gray, to buy such a carriage for Western Australia, which, if it turns out a success, will be followed by a large order. We shall have to send out an engineer specially, of course at the expense of the purchaser. The three carriages ordered from Messrs Peugeot Frères have also been despatched, after several little improvements have been made on them, according to my instructions.'

Read the Imperial Institute poster carefully: it was the Institute of which Queen Victoria was Patron, not Lawson's Horseless Carriage Exhibition! [DBW]

The need for all these vehicles was reasonably urgent, for Lawson had organized an exhibition of motor vehicles at the Imperial Institute, to be held between 9 May and 8 August, and, since Queen Victoria was Patron and the Prince of Wales President of the Imperial Institute, the use of their names and the Prince of Wales's insignia on the poster advertising the exhibition gave the impression that the event itself was under Royal patronage. 'The exhibition', commented H.O. Duncan, 'was made up of all the motor vehicles that could be brought together from the inventors and firms from whom Lawson had purchased the patents. Hence, the chief exhibitors were Daimler, De Dion-Bouton, Pennington and Bersey (electric carriages).'

Around this time, Ernest Martyn Critchley Instone, the 23-year-old son of Thomas Instone, joined the Daimler Company, and reported to the Imperial Institute, where he saw 'with feelings of awe and curiosity' his first motor car – a 3½ hp Cannstatt-Daimler

Petrol pioneer

One of the first cars imported into England was this belt-driven Cannstatt-Daimler, seen here at the Crystal Palace in 1895 with its owner Frederick R. Simms at the tiller. Simms was perhaps the most remarkable figure of the early history of motoring, for he was the father of the British motor industry and personally instigated its governing body, the Society of Motor Manufacturers & Traders, as well as its policy of official motor shows: five years earlier, in 1897, he had also founded the country's leading motoring organization, which became the Royal Automobile Club. He was, remembers his daughter, Mrs Rosie Ramsay, a good organizer and a man who trusted people (a trust which, sadly, was often betrayed). 'My father was always working,' Mrs Ramsay recalls. 'Nowadays you would call him a workaholic. He was full of ideas, always inventing things. He helped develop Bakelite and even devised a sticking plaster; I remember him working on a diesel engine in the 1930s. But the other directors of his company – Simms Motor Units – didn't like him developing this new power unit. He was taken ill while shooting in Austria and was 13 weeks in hospital in Innsbruck; when he came home he found he had been ousted. He was 71 and he had to start all over again. He became a consultant, studied metallurgy and formed the Elmet Metal Company, with laboratories provided by GEC (whose managing director was a good friend). He was a very strict Victorian disciplinarian, but a conscientious father to my sister and me, with great foresight to determine our futures (which, alas, did not materialize owing to the war).' [JDHT]

phaeton, a real horseless carriage imported by Simms, with belt drive and the even then out-dated feature of centre-pivot steering.

A few days later, instructed by Johann van Toll, young Instone was driving the Cannstatt-Daimler round the grounds of the Imperial Institute 'at a speed approximating 10 miles an hour'. It was the beginning of an association with Daimler which was to last – with the exception of a two-year period in 1899–1901 when he lived in Paris (as the representative of the Automobile Club of Great Britain & Ireland in connection with the organization of the Gordon Bennett race) – until his death in June 1932.

Once again, the Prince of Wales came to see the horseless carriages at the Imperial Institute, this time – on the opening day – accompanied by a party including HRH the Grand Duchess of Mecklenburg-Strelitz and Prince Edward of Saxe-Weimar, and accompanied by his equerry Sir Arthur Ellis (cousin of Evelyn). These Imperial Institute demonstrations were the beginning of the long association between the Royal Family

and the Daimler Motor Company. Lawson also held further receptions for Members of Parliament and the press: the exhibition was said to have cost £10,000 to stage.

The motor launch business was still doing well and the company boasted that over 600 (doubtless including Cannstatt sales) were running worldwide: in April a Daimler employee with the splendidly Dickensian name of Megginson piloted the Daimler-engined launch *Twaddler* from Putney to Margate – where the company's directors were spending Easter at the Queen's Hotel and wanted to combine publicity for their products with some seaside fun – in 11 hours, and a local newspaper remarked that motor launches would become popular 'when they have been got into thorough working order and sufficiently powerful engines have been placed in them'. There were plans, too, to build launch engines, propellers and stern tubes at Eel Pie Island from drawings sent from Cannstatt.

At the company's first statutory meeting on 19 May, shareholders were told that 'it is the intention of the directors as soon as possible to make their own motors in Coventry.' Furthermore, it was added that 'satisfactory working arrangements have been entered into between Daimler Motor Company and the Great Horseless Carriage Company', which basically provided for Daimler supplying the chassis and the Great Horseless Carriage Company building the bodies. The same month Deaville Altree, recently appointed general manager of Daimler, was interviewed by the *Daily Courier* and claimed that he had received 5,000 enquiries from all round the world, 30 from Bombay alone. He added that Daimler would start building motor cycles 'as soon as the weight of the engine has been reduced a little'.

The Daimler Works held its first press reception during the first week of June; there may not have been any cars for the journalists to see, but Humber-Pennington and Hildebrand & Wolfmüller motor cycles and a De Dion tricycle were demonstrated until a shower of rain stopped play. In mid-June, Simms returned to Cannstatt to complain about the slow delivery of drawings and components and was assured that everything – working drawings, casting patterns and sample iron and brass castings – would be shipped by the end of the month.

Critchley's own frenzy of activity ended in his being taken ill, but his assistant Arthur Drake carried on commissioning the factory and, as Critchley neared recovery early in July, Drake told Simms: 'We have the tool room now running, the pattern shop will start on Monday next, also the smithy. Many machines are also running in the machine room. We hope during the next week to get the whole of the works in running order.'

Though Simms, with his vested interest in the German Daimler company, built a replica of the new Coventry smithy at Cannstatt, there was a notable lack of traffic the other way. Small engine parts began arriving from Germany but there was still a distinct shortage of blueprints, and as late as September Mayer was complaining that most of the drawings ordered by Simms had not arrived. And when they did, said Lawson, 'as far as the drawings from Germany were concerned, they were useless, because they were drawn to a scale and system we could not adopt*. As far as the motors and parts in the rough which we got from Germany, all I can say is they were "Made in Germany" – and most of you know what that means in England!'

However, the delay seems to have started the Coventry staff thinking along independent lines, and, rather than wait for fresh drawings from Germany, they built 'four carriages upon experimental lines for the purpose of understanding something about the machines ourselves' and dismantled a Panhard parcels van that was

*The plans had been drawn in the metric system; Lawson was a Euro-sceptic ahead of his time! However, when Automotor & Horseless Vehicle Journal visited the Motor Mills in August 1897, it noted with approval that 'in the Daimler factory the metric system prevails' . . .

standing in the works so that they could make drawings and patterns of the working parts.

It was a crucial decision: while the Panhard still used the tube-ignition Daimler vertical-twin engine, it was the first proper motor car, with an engine in the front under a bonnet, driving the rear wheels through variable-ratio gearing, a layout devised by Simms's friend Emile Levassor that would still be recognizable a century later. It was a much better starting point for the new British industry than the antediluvian Cannstatt design, which was a crude horseless carriage with a multiple belt drive little advanced on the Daimler-Maybach prototype motor-wagon of 1886.

As soon as he was back at work, Critchley ordered twenty 3 hp cylinders from Cannstatt and subsequently began planning for a rear-engined 2 hp engine/chassis unit, though the directors halted work on that project on 21 September. The following month, axle ends and steering arms were ordered from the well-known French company Lemoine.

Drawings surviving among Simms's papers include a plan of the Motor Mills revealing that the original plan was to divide the main building equally between the Great Horseless Carriage Company and Daimler; however, it didn't work out in practice. The late H.P. Small – later mechanic to Charles Jarrott, one of the many motoring notables whose careers began within the Lawson empire – started work at the Motor Mills in 1897 and recalled 70 years late: 'The Great Horseless Carriage Company occupied the main building and Daimlers were in the shed round the back . . .'

Orders were apparently flowing in, even though production of actual vehicles seemed as far away as ever: on 6 August Altree reported: 'This week I have succeeded in booking the following orders: R.H. McDowell, Southport, 25 vehicles, various; Brighton Cycle & Motor Co, 1 vehicle, 4-seated; The Great Horseless Carriage Co, 20 motors & frames.'

At the end of October Otto Mayer visited the Motor Mills: not everything proved to his satisfaction, as he informed Simms in a heavily underlined letter: 'The general arrangements and equipment of the shops are excellent and everything that can be desired. The machine work that is being done is very good but:- the vice *work* and *erecting* which is of very great importance is *not up to the mark* and leaves *much* to be desired.'

There may not have been production, but a few cars were being brought in from the foreign companies whose licences Lawson had bought, and on 14 November *The Autocar* published an artist's impression of 'the first British-built Daimler Autocar', a strange-looking machine with an unsprung rear axle (the springs were attached to the bodywork instead) and what appeared to be a bevel-driven rear axle, which would have been the first of its type. This car certainly existed, for it was photographed outside the Motor Mills with Critchley at the tiller, accompanied by A.J. Drake, Otto Mayer and 'head tester' Bush. However, the gear lever doesn't appear to be connected to anything, the nearside front spring is apparently missing, and altogether it seems to have been a mock-up to keep the investors happy rather than a genuine functioning vehicle.

Certainly the excitement was building and the Daimler/British Motor Syndicate London office at 40 Holborn Viaduct was becoming a magnet for young men who were fascinated by motor cars. Among those who 'spent many hours damaging our shins with confounded starting handles or pushing obstinate starters along the gutters of Holborn Viaduct in a vain endeavour to experience a ride of three or four hundred yards in a motor car' were Billy Letts (the future Sir William Malesbury Letts KBE, President of the Society of Motor Manufacturers and Traders), Percival Perry (later Lord Perry, chairman of Ford) and Charles Jarrott (founder of the Automobile Association and vice president of the SMMT), who was secretary of the British Motor Syndicate.

'The first British-built Daimler Autocar' photographed outside the Motor Mills with Critchley at the tiller, accompanied by A.J. Drake, Otto Mayer and 'head tester' Bush appears to have been a mock-up. However, its specification included a constant-mesh transmission (apparently missing here!) and the motor industry's first-ever use of a shaft-driven rear axle incorporating differential gearing. [DBW]

Over the years, Daimler would continue to attract the brightest talents in the motor industry.

* * *

'Every sign betokens that the firms engaged in the manufacture of horseless carriages and motor cycles in Coventry do not intend to take any but the premier position, and the fact that these vehicles are Coventry made will be as good a guarantee for first-class workmanship as in the case of cycles,' wrote the *Coventry Times* in September 1896.

Lawson had every reason to be pleased that the industry – and with it his patent monopoly – was beginning to take off so well. Though the Cannstatt designs were late, the Panhard and Peugeot cars were dominating the new and thrilling sport of automobile racing and of the 54 entrants in the Paris–Marseille–Paris race, which started on 24 September, 'in 32 cases the patents are the property of the British Motor Company,' commented the *Sheffield Telegraph*. And, boasted Lawson, 'winners first, second, third, fourth and fifth were British Motor Syndicate patents, thus finally proving the enormous

value and superiority of our patents!'. He had indeed, just paid 30,000 Francs (£1,200) each for the first three cars – all Panhards – and had them shipped to England.

Small wonder that the French were calling him *Le Roi Anglais de l'Automobile*, and he had responded to this praise by donating a 'magnificent objet d'art . . . which represents the "Triumph Universelle" of the motor car movement in the shape of a goddess in a motor chariot' as a prize for the Paris–Marseille race. This curious image – which also appeared on the metal plate fitted to all motor vehicles licensed by the British Motor Syndicate – is still used on the medals issued to competitors in the London–Brighton Veteran Car Run, the annual event which celebrates the passing of the revised Locomotives on Highways Bill on 14 November 1896 (which Lawson and his companies had played a considerable part in bringing about) and the 'procession to Brighton' organized by the Motor Car Club to mark 'Emancipation Day'.

'Automobilists' had not got everything they had hoped for: while MPs had said privately that there was unlikely to be a speed

Lawson's Cannstatt-Daimler landau photographed outside the Metropole Hotel, Brighton, two days after the 1896 Emancipation Day Run, with the benign countenance of Gottlieb Daimler beaming from the rear seat, though Frederick Simms, who drove the car in the event, has already left for London. [NMM]

McRobie Turrell and Jack Dring in 'No 5' Panhard after the Emancipation Day Run: Lawson's Syndicate licence plate can be seen on the dashboard. [JDHT]

limit for motor cars, popular opinion had dictated a 14 mph limit, and the Local Government Board had shaved a further 2 mph off this: but nevertheless it was better than being preceded by a pedestrian (though the police admittedly did pay much more attention to motor vehicles and their speed from then on).

As a curtain-raiser, Lawson ran his stately Cannstatt-Daimler landau *Present Times* in the Lord Mayor's Show, the first motor vehicle to take part in this historic parade. He and his colleague C. McRobie Turrell rode on the box seat, wearing the elaborate uniform of the Motor Car Club, which it was unkindly said made them look like admirals in the Swiss Navy. Riding inside the car was a correspondent from the *Daily Telegraph*, who wrote of experiencing 'the sensation of making a tour through the City of London and a part of the West End in a steam launch . . . its smart appearance, admirable qualities of steering and capability of varying its speed at the shortest notice were all critically appreciated, and again and again cheers came from working men in hearty approval of the invention'. Of course, some pettifogging official attempted to bring a summons against Lawson for not having a flag man in front: but he was rightly treated with contempt (though the following week the police successfully prosecuted a driver who went out at 10.00 p.m. the night before the Act came into force).

Present Times was a prominent entrant in the London–Brighton Run exactly a week after the Lord Mayor's Show, driven by Frederick Simms, with Gottlieb Daimler – who told Lawson 'You did excellent business the day you bought the British Daimler Patents and I wish the English Daimler company every success!' – as passenger.

Another driver was a Daimler employee named A.O. Bradley, in a twin-cylinder 5 hp Panhard which the British Motor Syndicate had recently sold to a London company: 'This car had iron tyres, no gear box – because all the gears were wholly exposed – chain drive from a countershaft to the rear wheels, tiller steering and tube ignition . . . The day in question was a horrible one; it was pouring with rain and a most unpleasant fog had settled over London. The cars were lined up near the Hotel Metropole, London, where engines had to be stopped. Each person taking part was presented with a map, specially printed by Iliffe and Son, showing the route to be taken. Then we were told to start our engines, and the real fun began, because many engines flatly refused to fire at the critical moment. The vibration and the noise made by those which responded to their driver's efforts frightened several onlookers.

'The president of the Motor Car Club, H. J. Lawson, mounted the pilot car, carrying a flag bearing the letters "MCC" and off the whole procession went on the long journey to Brighton, via Westminster Bridge, Lambeth Palace Road, Brixton and on through Croydon to Reigate, where lunch was to be served.

'As the run progressed the weather became worse and worse; we were all soaked to the skin and every time I stood up the water ran down my legs into my boots . . . My poor old Panhard kept steadily mud-plugging through the rain for hour after hour until darkness set in, when I was obliged to stop to buy some candles for the lamps. Within ten miles of Brighton I was unfortunate enough to break a link in one side chain . . . Unfortunately I had no spare links, and was benighted by the roadside, unable to move another yard.'

It may have been an awful day, but the huge crowds – over half a million are said to have watched the start – which lined the road all the way to Brighton showed the tremendous public interest in motoring. The run was a severe test for the primitive autocars, and things were not helped when the official breakdown van lived up to its name, and broke down. Though most of the vehicles made the journey under their own power, some of the 22 or so participants – particularly the electric cars – were rumoured to have come by train!

In 1935 the then Mayor of Brighton, who had been a journalist covering the original Brighton Run, recalled that Lawson had handed out the report of the Run to the press a day or two before the event actually happened, 'not the least of the joke being Lawson's description of how well his own car performed in this preamble, as against its actual performance in the run'.

But if there had been an element of farce, the event had proved conclusively that the motor car was a practical means of transport, and the illustrated paper *The Graphic* was scarcely exaggerating when it trumpeted: 'We are on the eve of one of our greatest epochs! The world's traffic is to be revolutionised, but naturally not without cost. Millions of money are to change hands! Huge fortunes are to be amassed by the poorest, and that perhaps quickly! From the baker's cart to the loveliest of equipages, all are interested.

Fire down below

Tube ignition – in which the compressed petrol/air mixture was ignited by a platinum tube kept red hot by an external Bunsen burner – was more reliable than electricity in the pre-1900 era but, recalled G.H. Allsworth, who drove a 4 hp Daimler wagonette, 'it soon became apparent that performance was noticeably affected by ignition timing and . . . the distance of the ignition tube from the inside wall of the cylinder was varied . . . in the hope of obtaining greater speed. Generally speaking, however, little advantage resulted, mainly for the reason that in those pioneer days the carburettor was not automatic . . . at 750 rpm the mixture was cut off completely by a centrifugal governor.'

'Saturday's great London–Brighton test has proved that we may travel much faster, much easier and at less cost. A four-in-hand makes five changes and employs twenty horses to do what one little Motor can easily accomplish. Those who have this great industry in hand may make fortune after fortune out of a great patent monopoly for an entirely new traffic. The Railway excitement and wild mania of our forefathers will soon be entirely eclipsed by a greater public Motor boom than has ever been witnessed.'

* * *

'What will happen?' asked an amazingly prescient article in a broadsheet issued by the British Motor Syndicate shortly after Emancipation Day, quickly answering its own question with the phrase: 'Prosperity is now dawning for many trades. Engineers will be wanted everywhere. Dwelling houses are necessary no longer in towns. Houses need no longer be let as in Brighton, with annual season ticket included, but everywhere builders now building, who include a strong Motor Car in the stable, join it to town . . . The price of land twenty miles outside towns may yet become as valuable as in the town itself. All landowners need only to provide good roads, hotel, restaurant and motor accommodation to welcome the arrival of crowds of pleasure seekers . . . Wherever the horse and inferior animal power is at present, there immense saving and increased efficiency is to be effected.

'The bus companies and tram companies are already beginning to move in the matter. The Army no longer needs to waste money on horse-flesh where roads are available. The Police on machines will be swifter and more economical. The Parcels delivery will only be served properly by motor. The Post Office and Parcels Post must become immense users. The railway mania will be superseded by the steadily growing, saving and money making advantages daily being discovered in the new motor.

'The wildest excitement will be that of competition. The Motor Derby is to present a far more wonderful scene than the Derby of quadrupeds ever has. The owners can themselves race: the weakest and the fairest may urge their own steed in front of the strongest. Fancy prices may be offered for the fastest possible cars, and the greatest excitement will be produced by higher speeds than the world has ever yet witnessed . . .

'The British Motor Syndicate is the sole owner of the Master Patents and its shares will see very extraordinary and sensational prices.'

* * *

The first opportunity the Syndicate had to exercise its monopoly came when Lord Llangattock's son, the Hon Charles S. Rolls, imported a Peugeot car from France and was promptly taken to court for infringement. In January 1897 Mr Justice North found him guilty and granted an injunction and £15 damages: Rolls was allowed to pay a royalty and continue using his car (and cannot have been too upset, because in August Daimler resolved to sell him the 'No 6 carriage', the Paris–Marseille winning Panhard, 'for not less than £300'). However, other 'infringers' were threatened with confiscation of their vehicles and one even committed suicide (so his royalty payment was reduced!).

Having shown its strength, Daimler now felt confident to show its factory in action, even though it had not actually built a single vehicle. The visitors to the Motor Mills that January were greeted by the impressive figure of Pennington and then went on to see the Humber factory across town, recently rebuilt after a fire which had gutted the original building the previous July, and the New Beeston Cycle Works.

After lunch in the Queen's Hotel, Lawson told shareholders of the wonderful prospects of the British Motor Syndicate, though even by his grandiose standards, his claim that his knowledge of motor vehicles was based on the fact that 'I own more motor cars than any man in the world . . . I own about forty different kinds, and I suppose the next biggest owner owns three or four' sounded improbable. Nevertheless, his shareholders were in the mood for impressive statistics. Boasted Lawson: 'Nothing you have read in the prospectus conveys an idea of the huge proportions of our works, and the immense amount of labour it must have entailed to fit them with machinery. No one could have any idea of the work that has been involved unless they were engaged in it.'

He was still obsessed by Pennington's 'wonderful little engine which . . . is practically silent, and which does not vibrate before the rider or riders get into the car', and promised 'a perfectly saleable machine . . . without disagreeable smell or vibration . . . This little engine you can hold up with one finger, and there is 2 hp in it, and you have seen it propel a car along the road with nine people sitting on the car.' Over the subsequent century, how many other motor magnates have boasted of having discovered the perfect alternative power unit, only for it all to end in tears?

But Lawson brought the message his investors wanted to hear; during his long peroration to the gathered throng, he boasted: 'Before the end of the year you will see millions of capital in motor companies all over the country. In different towns you will see little companies with hundreds of thousands of capital. These will not be formed by me or by the British Motor Syndicate; but I hope they will find it worth their while – to put it mildly – to come to us for licences and for the benefit of the experience which we have gained at such an enormous cost.

'I should point out . . . that we have only issued capital which ranks for dividend to the amount of between £200,000 and £250,000, and the Directors have come to an arrangement with the patentees and inventors and myself that no shares further beyond the said £250,000 shall be issued in this Company, neither to me nor to anyone else, as fully paid until the shares stand at over

£3 in the market and until a handsome dividend is paid to the shareholders on the present issued capital, sufficient to justify the price of £3 on the market. To this I most cordially and willingly agree, knowing very well, as you will know after what you have seen to-day, that "that will not be long."

'Last year we paid dividends, in hard cash, 40 per cent, apart from a bonus in shares. That 40 per cent was principally on £150,000; that is to say, it was paid in instalments, and while those payments were being made the capital went on increasing. Now if we do only as well as we did last year, you can see your way to 20 per cent on £200,000. But after what you have seen you can judge whether we shall not do many times better, please God we have life and health and strength, with a common amount of luck.' Lawson had obviously learned a lot from his father, the hellfire and brimstone preacher!

Housing the workers, the investors were told, was a real problem: 'Dwelling accommodation cannot be found for the workpeople engaged, and many families are camping out in gipsy vans in the fields. Every night, also, a number of workmen have to be allowed to sleep in the casual wards of the workhouse because they are unable, though possessed of sufficient money, to find beds elsewhere.'

There was, perhaps more than an element of exaggeration in this, as pioneer motoring journalist H. Massac Buist, who was one of the visitors to the Motor Mills, revealed nearly 30 years later in the foreword to the souvenir booklet for the motor section of the 1924 Empire Exhibition at Wembley: 'A party had been brought down from London by special train to verify the mere existence of this alleged new industry. On the ground floor of the factory they saw men busily at work. After due inspection they proceeded up curtained stairs to the first floor, where a halt was called in a partitioned space and light refreshments were proffered. Then the work doing on the first floor was inspected. The same process was repeated on proceeding to the second floor, some visitors, more curious than the rest, who ascended the curtained stairway, being now conscious of a seeming echo of footsteps at the opposite end of the building. After yet another pause for refreshments, on emerging from the partitioned space the visitors were conducted round the second floor, whereupon one of the Paul Prys was prompted to enquire whether it was the policy of this pioneer company of a new industry to make a point of recruiting members of the same families, placing brothers to work on different floors? The answer is not recorded. But there was yet one more storey to which to ascend. The sequence of events was repeated, including the echoing of footfalls from opposite, and the subsequent recognition, this time in a still greater number of cases, of increasingly familiar faces among the operatives . . .'

However, Lawson had laid on an impressive display of motor vehicles for his visitors in the Kenilworth Road: 'Some were very silent, some extremely fast, some really handsome. Such for instance as the coach of the Lord Mayor's Show. Noticeable a Lady's Motor Safety, designed by Mr Lawson, which many said would make most money.'

Next, it was Daimler shareholders' turn to view progress at the Motor Mills. Deaville Altree advised them of a meeting at Coventry at 3.30 p.m. on Thursday 4 March: 'Saloon coaches will be provided for shareholders on the train leaving Euston at 10.10 a.m. and also on the train leaving Coventry at 6.13 p.m. and return railway tickets at the ordinary third class fare of 15/8 may be obtained from the secretary of this company not later than Tuesday 2 March. A cold luncheon (price 2/6) will be served at the Queens Hotel, Coventry at 1 p.m. and the Company will endeavour to arrange for a sufficient number of autocars to be at the hotel at 2 p.m. for the purpose of conveying shareholders to the Motor Mills, where the staff will be prepared to conduct them over the works previous to the meeting'.

Some 45 shareholders took up the invitation to visit the Motor Mills 'and the works of kindred enterprises', where Lawson informed them that the Daimler Works were 'the most perfect manufactory of 4 hp and 6 hp motors in the world – in some respects superior to the Continental works'. He added that the company's first vehicle had made its maiden run two days earlier, on 2 March: 'We have completed the first of our commercial carriages which, although the painting is not quite finished, was run to the station today, and some of you had the pleasure of riding upon it. It was the smaller carriage of the two, and made the less noise and vibration. We had it out for the first time on Tuesday and were very well satisfied with our efforts.'

H.M. Carter, who had joined Daimler in November 1896, vividly recalled that maiden run (which he placed in February) in an article he wrote for the house magazine *The Pre-Selector* in 1939: 'What pride and joy was experienced by those 60-odd employees of the Daimler Company who had helped to build it. I recall the intensely amusing spectacle of our dapper little Manager, Mr Drake, starting off on this very first car drive, looking anything but happy. You see, no one had up to then driven a British-built Daimler motor-car, so I can assure you we all felt the thrill, glamour, and glory of this, the beginning of the motor age. The car, which weighed about 1 ton, and had only a 4 hp engine, could not be expected to go more than 12 miles per hour, but even this speed was considered very wonderful.'

Interestingly enough, the Coventry Daimler engines – the first of which was, apparently, built in 1896 by William Alfred Perkins, who was still working for Daimler 50 years later – were not blind copies of the Continental design, as Veteran Car Club member Tim Moore, who has restored 1897 examples of both Panhard and Daimler, notes: 'While the overall design is very similar, Panhard's metallurgy is not over-special; many of the castings are full of blow-holes . . . the Daimler is better in that respect. Another difference is that the valves are on opposite sides on the Coventry Daimler and Panhard engines.'

These detail differences were due to Critchley, as a surviving (and somewhat acrimonious) letter written to Simms in March 1897 reveals: 'I must take strong exception to your remarks in connection with the cam shafts as we have after much consideration discarded the very method now employed by Messrs Panhard & Levassor. Our cams are certainly formed separately from the shaft and are made at *one* operation on a profile milling machine. Our method is no more expensive than the one you mention as no marking out is required & by hardening the cams before they are fitted to the shaft we get them absolutely true with each other . . . I certainly think that our methods of manufacture will compare very favourably with Messrs P & L and every day we are bringing into use more jigs and other labour-saving appliances.'

While working on its own first car, Daimler had begun shipping chassis to meet an order worth £13,000 for 50 'machines with motor covers' placed shortly after the company's formation by John Stirling's Hamilton Carriage, Motor Car & Cycle Works, an old-established Scottish coachbuilder. Stirling had actually completed its first body – a double phaeton with a varnished walnut body and vermilion chassis and wheels – on a chassis shipped from Coventry in January 1897, but this was only partly a Daimler, for it was powered by a Paris-built Panhard twin-cylinder engine. Stirling claimed they could deliver a car a fortnight.

The first 'all-Coventry' Daimler chassis reached Hamilton at the beginning of March; a few days later, on 10 March, Stirling wrote the British motor industry's very first unsolicited testimonial to Sturmey: 'We have made a very careful study of the Daimler Motor since we got the first one down, and we think we thoroughly understand both the new one and the old one. The alterations in the former, we think, are improvements, but we shall be able to speak more definitely after a few days' trial.

'PS – We have just returned from a twelve miles' run and we are highly pleased with the behaviour of the car. We got a much higher

Engine assembly at the Motor Mills in 1897. [NMM]

speed than ever we obtained on the first car and we anticipate still better results over dry roads.'

Ten days later, he wrote again: 'We have now had further trials of the second motor and frame sent down, and we are pleased to inform you that its running qualities are giving us very great satisfaction. The — company have delivered a motor van to a Glasgow warehouseman this week and as this is the very first motor carriage that has been sold in Glasgow, it is creating a very bad impression. It was partly on account of this that we spent several days in the city this week with the Daimler car and we think that the behaviour of our car on these occasions has counteracted the bad effect and opened the eyes of thousands to the capabilities of your motor. We find the car is astonishingly easy to manipulate in the traffic. It is quite a revelation to the public to see it picking its way through the densest traffic. It gives us very great pleasure to write thus and we are pleased to learn that each subsequent motor sent down will be to some extent an improvement on the previous ones.'

At that time, Daimler claimed that it was building about two cars a week, 'which rate of output would very speedily be increased'. Sturmey had taken another large order, from the London Motor Van and Waggon Company for a hundred chassis 'without motor covers'. the first of which was completed at the end of March. This, however, proved to be a difficult job, and the rest of the year was occupied with the clients complaining that their vans needed constant repair and threatening to curtail the order, which was being met at the rate of two chassis a week, rising to three after works extensions were completed in mid-1897. It ended with George Foster Pedley being seconded to the London Motor Van & Waggon Company in November on a weekly salary of £3 10s to sort out the problems, and Daimler lost money on the deal.

During March, the company also loaned a motor wagonette to the Brighton Cycle & Motor Company Ltd of 9 Marine Parade, Brighton, which gave sixpenny rides from the Brighton Aquarium to the Devil's Dyke and back, taking 45 minutes out and 25 minutes for the downhill return journey. By January 1898 the car had covered 'about 5,000 miles in Sussex and adjoining counties and it has climbed the hills in a satisfactory manner. In our opinion, it is superior to every other form of motor carriage that has at present come under our notice'.

The first complete Daimler car delivered to a private owner was apparently the one collected in mid-April by Ernest Estcourt of Canfield Gardens, South Hampstead, who had a two hour lesson 'in the arts and mysteries of motor driving and autocar control' on arrival at Coventry and the next day drove the car the 90 miles home to London in 10½ hours, 'inclusive of two and a half hours for meals, watering and getting past restive horses'.

Estcourt's description of the trip reveals something of the blind hope with which the first motorists ventured on to roads which had been largely neglected since the coming of the railways 70 years earlier: 'It was nearly seven o'clock when we started. For the first ten miles one of the Daimler motor men was with us, and we lost some time by taking the wrong turning and by his giving my two friends a lesson in driving, as we thought it best for more than one to know something about it.

'After leaving him to return on another car, we got on faster, and, considering the state of the road, which was very rough and heavy, as it had been raining in the night, we made good time, arriving in Daventry at 8.20, at Towcester (thirty-three miles) at ten, where we had breakfast, filled up with oil and water, got away at 11.05, passed through Stony Stratford at 11.50, Fenny Stratford at 12.45 (roads much worse).

'As we were afterwards informed, a gentleman with a dogcart and a fast trotter told his friends he would be into Dunstable before us, and passed us at the start. We soon got by him, when we were stopped by a horse in a cart left without attendance. By the time we got someone to look to the horse he had again passed us, but not for long, as we soon passed him again, and arrived in Dunstable at two o'clock. He arrived at 2.15, and we then heard about his intention of being first. We had lunch, again filled up with water and oil, and got away at three o'clock. The roads were now in fine condition, and we had a delightful run, arriving at St. Albans at four, Barnet five, Canfield Gardens 5.30.

'I may mention that we all thoroughly enjoyed the trip; had no trouble with the motor, and think, considering the state of the roads, and the fact that it was our first experience of a motor car [neither one of the three had ever been on a motor car of any description before], that it proves the Daimler motor to be thoroughly reliable, and much more perfect than is generally believed.'

Demand was obviously increasing: on 2 April, Daimler sought the Great Horseless Carriage Company's permission to make 25 more carriage bodies and also ordered three 'Siamese' bodies from A.J. Mulliner, but still had sufficient spare capacity to supply a chassis to a steam car manufacturer in the Midlands. In mid-May, Daimler claimed to have built five cars in a single week ('two small brakes, two dogcarts and one parcel car') and its leading position was confirmed in June when *The Autocar* surveyed the British motor industry and stated that 'six motor companies were actually delivering autocars – Daimler, Thornycroft, the Beeston Cycle Co, Stirling, the Coventry Motor Co and the Anglo-French Co . . . Twenty-five British-built cars in all had been delivered.'

Another early Daimler owner was T.R.B. Elliot, of Kelso, Scotland, whose earlier purchase of a Panhard & Levassor had earned him the title of 'the first independent autocar user in Scotland'. Elliot took delivery of his Stirling-Daimler on 17 June and had covered about 1,200 miles by 12 October: 'One day I ran it 110 miles in 10 hours 20 minutes, which included all stoppages, and it went well in heavy mud and rain from start to finish. On another occasion I ran it 58½ miles at an average of 13 miles an hour, carrying three

A fanciful engraving of a meet of Lawson's Motor Car Club in 1897 shows the variety of cars licensed by his Syndicate.

In May 1897, Daimler claimed to have built these five cars – 'two small brakes, two dogcarts and one parcel car' – in a single week. [JDHT]

persons. With two persons I have, with perfect weather conditions, averaged as much as 15 miles an hour for 20$\frac{1}{2}$ miles of anything but flat country. I find the consumption of petrol varies from 12 to 14 miles per gallon. Since I had rubber tyres fitted, I have run 900 miles and I find they wear very well; in fact they don't seem to have worn at all. My running has been entirely done between the Tyne and the Forth and chiefly in hilly districts.'

In mid-June Sturmey declared that the number of paid hands in the Daimler Works was 223: 'I may add, however, that the space at our command is all too small and that we have just finished the erection of an additional factory, measuring 120 ft x 130 ft, which, as soon as the necessary machinery has been installed, will give employment to additional hands . . .

'The Daimler Co. are manufacturing motors for launch and stationary purposes, as well as for motor vehicles . . . Three months ago we produced our first finished vehicle, and our output of the finished article was one per week. Our output has now risen to three per week, and as soon as our new factory is completed, and our additional staff of erectors trained and organized, we are

expecting to treble it, this in addition to launch and stationary motor work . . . We have, as a matter of fact, orders for carriage motors, frames, gearing, and complete carriages in hand to the tune of close upon £40,000 in addition to a large amount of work in launch motors. In short, we have over 350 motors of different classes in hand, and to the orders of customers at the present time.'

Daimler became Britain's first car manufacturer to organize a press road test, in July 1897, when two lady journalists from *The Gentlewoman* rode from Northampton to their offices in Arundel Street, just off the Strand in London, driven by coachbuilder Arthur Mulliner. One of them, Mrs Sutherland Morris, was reportedly 'so nervous that she made her will before setting out from home', and they found motoring like 'tobogganing or riding on a switchback railway'. But when the ladies asked Mulliner why he called the car 'she', he tactlessly replied that 'it took a man to manage her'.

To prove him wrong, the ladies both took the controls on the drive south and wrote ingenuously of 'the colossal appetites which motoring gave them'.

* * *

Henry Sturmey had placed an order for his own car with the aim of making Britain's very first long-distance motor tour, but the company was 'two or three months behind the time guaranteed', so, as a good company executive, he stood aside in favour of a paying customer, Major-General Montgomery of Winchester, who collected a 4 hp Cranford wagonette from the works on 20 August and rode home in it, driven by a Daimler employee named Slater, 'one of the company's highly-skilled and most-trusted workmen, who has come to Winchester at General Montgomery's request to instruct his groom in the management of the motor carriage'.

They accomplished the 102 mile journey at an average running speed of just over 10 mph, staying overnight at the Mitre Hotel in Oxford and arriving in Winchester around 6 p.m. When Montgomery died, as 1901 passed into 1902, *The Autocar* claimed that he 'was the first gentleman unconnected with the industry in this country to purchase an English-built motor carriage . . . the general was an enthusiast on the subject of automobilism and did much to remove prejudice and educate the people in his neighbourhood . . . we heard some personal friends of his resident a few miles distant say: "We never go to see the general now because he always wants us to go for a ride in his horrid motor car." It is further interesting to record that those same people are now autocarists themselves, and as keen on the subject as was their old friend.'

Daimler was already establishing a strong technical lead: in mid-1897 Critchley was investigating the use of X-rays, discovered only a year earlier by Professor Röntgen of Würzburg, for the detection of flaws in axles and castings.

A long-running saga had come to an end in July when the launch works on Eel Pie Island were sold – at a loss – to a Mr Kerbey Brown, though shortly before they closed Deaville Altree took a 31 ft launch from Twickenham to the Spithead Diamond Jubilee Naval Review on 26 June. Johann Van Toll had already been transferred to Coventry, and in October took part in the acceptance trials of Evelyn Ellis's new *dos-à-dos* bodied Daimler, 'specially built for touring both at home and abroad' (and grandly referred to as the 'Alpine' model).

'It was his desire to have a gear sufficiently low for him to be able to climb anything,' and on 12 October James Critchley – accompanied by Ellis, his daughter Mary, Otto Mayer and Van Toll – drove it to the top of Worcestershire Beacon, the highest of the Malvern Hills. 'This is 1,395 feet above the sea,' reported *The Autocar*, 'and is approached by long rises (many of them very steep) from Malvern Link Station, which only stands a few feet above the level of the Severn Valley. The last part is over a rough track, not a proper carriage road, and varies in steepness from one in six to one in four . . . This machine, with its specially low gear and three separate brakes, is the outcome of two years of practical experience in autocaring, and in it its owner has a carriage in which he can face any mountain pass . . . either up or down.'

Sturmey had taken delivery of what he claimed was the ninth Daimler car completed – perhaps he meant the ninth car to be built *and* bodied in the Motor Mills – on 9 September, and began planning for the first-ever car journey from John o' Groats to Land's End, or what he quaintly termed 'from end to end on an autocar'. Having arranged for Carless, Capel & Leonard to provide petrol supplies along his route, Sturmey had his car transported northwards by train to Wick station, the nearest railhead to John o' Groats, and drove the 60-odd miles from Wick to John o' Groats and back on 2 October, accompanied by Daimler mechanic Richard Ashley as a prelude to an epic drive of some 1600 miles, reaching Land's End on 19 October before returning to Coventry by road.

Mechanical troubles were remarkably few – the clutch slipped on occasion and had to be dosed with resin to restore its grip, while

Evelyn Ellis and his daughter Mary in his new Daimler dos-à-dos 'Alpine' model reach the top of Worcestershire Beacon on 12 October 1897. Also present were James Critchley, Otto Mayer and Johann Van Toll. [JDHT]

liquid mud clogged the driving chains and caused a distressing sound which Sturmey called 'machinery grinding'. The brakes failed in the Lake District and the Daimler ran away downhill, though the resourceful Sturmey was equal to the crisis: 'I took the situation in at a glance and seeing that the foot of the hill was followed by a stiff ascent, I felt that all I had to do was to keep a straight course, so jambing both brakes on with all my force (although this appeared to have as much effect as water on a duck's back) I set my teeth and gripping the steering handle, steered a dead straight course in as near a bee line as possible with the result anticipated, and the car pulled up on the opposite slope.' As Sturmey had claimed on the little printed information cards which he carried aboard the Daimler to hand out to interested bystanders that 'there are eight ways of stopping it so it can't run away', it's as well that there were no spectators watching this desperate feat to demand technical details of the car!

By now Daimler was asserting its independence from the other members of the Lawson empire; it had given notice to the Great Horseless Carriage Company to quit the painting shed and informed the British Motor Syndicate that there would be no further deliveries until they had paid their account, though Harry Lawson, in his capacity as chairman of the Syndicate met Altree and went through the accounts 'with a view to early settlement'. Nevertheless, Daimler decided not to pay the British Motor Syndicate's account for licence plates supplied: the patents monopoly was starting to crumble.

In July Daimler agreed to supply the Great Horseless Carriage Company with 'one new set of Panhard frame and gearing without charge', but in the same breath asked for settlement of its account, pointing out that 'unless this was received at an early date, all further supplies would be stopped.' There was a falling out with the Daimler Motoren Gesellschaft, too, and Daimler refused to hand Cannstatt working drawings of its 4 hp 'motor frame'. A couple of weeks later, in mid-

July, Frederick Simms – whose sympathies lay more with Cannstatt than Coventry – resigned as consulting engineer.

Daimler was experiencing the onset of the financial troubles that were to plague it during its early years: Critchley was instructed by the board to 'exercise the utmost economy in conducting the works . . . to complete the manufacture of all motors now in hand and not to make any further parts except such as are required for the completion of these motors . . . not to engage any more workmen.' The board followed the economy theme by deciding to accept half fees 'in view of the present reduced funds of the Company' and cut back its travelling expenses to second class railway fares. Sturmey and Mace were appointed to examine the company's accounts.

'In view of the present restricted funds of the company,' Evelyn Ellis told the board, 'I will offer to advance £10,000, provided thoroughly satisfactory work is turned out.' It obviously was, for the company soon drew £3,000 against Ellis's loan, even though an order placed with Arthur Mulliner for a body for a new car being built for Evelyn Ellis along the lines of Sturmey's 'end to end' car was cancelled at the beginning of October. There

had been complaints of 'very unsatisfactory finish' on Mulliner bodies and Daimler was talking to alternative coachbuilders like Thrupp & Maberley.

Orders were obviously being taken to keep the works running rather than to make money: having been quoted a minimum price of £225 each for an extra 50 4 hp chassis, to be delivered at the rate of six to eight a month 'before long', Stirling was then offered a hundred 'motors & gearing' for just £180 each with a further 2.5 per cent discount if they ordered 150 chassis 'promptly'. It must have worked, for by the end of the year Stirling, with sales of 'over a score [Daimlers] within the past six months', had become Daimler's exclusive Scottish agents and placed an order for a hundred chassis (though the price had risen in the interim). There was also the chance to make a quick profit when a quantity of 4 hp engines, which had cost £59 8s each, were sold to the Great Horseless Carriage Company for £80, 'guaranteed to run a hundred miles'.

One of the first agents to be appointed was Albert Farnell of Bradford, who recalled in 1932: 'My first agency was for the Daimler . . . At that time it was a closed territory and my area was Yorkshire. I am unable to give the date when the first car was delivered to me. It

'Progressive prelate' Dr Kennion, Bishop of Bath and Wells, frequently hired this early twin-cylinder Daimler to visit the various churches in his see. [DBW]

Percy Richardson demonstrating the hill-climbing abilities of the 6 hp Daimler to an Irish coachbuilder. [NMM]

The search for more power was on: Professor B. Boverton Redwood, one of the company's earliest customers, ordered a new and more powerful car, and Critchley created Britain's first 'home-grown' four-cylinder engine for Redwood's Daimler by simply mounting two 4 hp motors in tandem and marketing the result, upholstered in morocco, for £350. In December, a further six sets of castings for 'coupled 4 hp engines' were ordered, but there was clearly a market for a purpose-built four-cylinder model.

On 7 October, Harry Lawson resigned from the Daimler board, saying that the Great Horseless Carriage Company and the British Motor Syndicate were taking up too much of his time. That was an understatement: the Coventry cycle industry was trembling on the brink of depression and eventually collapsed in 1898, resulting in Hooley's bankruptcy (though he managed to hold on to some £200,000 which he had put in his wife's name).

In January 1898 the Great Horseless Carriage Company went into liquidation, and Daimler wanted to know if its agreement with that firm was still legally binding with its successor, the Motor Manufacturing Company. However, Nemesis did not finally catch up with Lawson until he floated the 'Electric Tramways Construction & Maintenance Company' in 1904, and he and Hooley stood trial for fraud. 'After a three weeks' hearing,' wrote cycle historian Geoffrey Williamson, 'Hooley – brilliantly defended by Rufus Isaacs – was found not guilty; but Lawson was found guilty of false statements and was sentenced to twelve months' hard labour.'

But that was in the future: in the meantime Daimler could celebrate a lucky escape by considering an increase in output from five 4 hp chassis per week to eight.

* * *

During the nine months to 28 February 1898, Daimler had sold and delivered 89 complete vehicles or motors and frames, plus '24 single

was, however, a 6hp twin cylinder, governed, detachable head, tube ignition – making a cylinder head joint was a work of art, grinding with putty powder and sealing with boiled oil – tiller steering, dial control, 4 speeds (5,10,15 and 20 mph), solid tyres. How many men could be found today able to time a tube ignition engine?'

This period also saw Daimler's first venture into car hire, when half-a-dozen of the Coventry workforce were 'put through a thorough course of tuition on the motor and driving' so that carriages could be 'let out on hire with a competent driver for a period not exceeding three months at a charge of £5 per week – this amount, less driver's wages to be refunded in the event of purchase'. The company also supplied the well-known carriers Carter Paterson with their first motor vehicle, a 5½ hp twin-cylinder van, in 1897.

engines for carriage, launch or other purposes'. Reported the new chairman, Henry Sturmey: 'These sales represent an aggregate value of over £23,000 and at the present time sufficient orders are in hand to keep the factory fully employed for many months to come . . . With the view of keeping the present foremost position of the Daimler Carriage amongst motor vehicles, experimental work is being carried forward and has already resulted in important improvements. A school of instruction for drivers is in course of organization and development and a number of army reserve men are now undergoing a period of training so that customers can be supplied with thoroughly reliable and competent drivers.'

The year 1898 saw the newly independent Daimler company shift into a position of ascendency, which was subtly underlined by the decision made that June to rename the Motor Mills 'Daimler Works'. When the MMC was granted permission to erect its own foundry on land leased from Daimler, it had to undertake 'not to manufacture Daimler motors (except those Daimler

Motor Company are unable to supply)' for a period of three years, and when Daimler sold MMC a hundred 4 hp engines marked

The hirsute W.H. Roberts of the West of England Carriage Works used this early twin-cylinder Coventry Daimler to promote the motor car as 'the horses' friend'. [NMM]

Charles Crowden, general manager of the Great Horseless Carriage Company, driving an early Daimler. When the GHCC went into liquidation in 1898, Crowden set up on his own account in Leamington Spa and built one of the first motor fire engines. [JDHT]

A party of motorists visits the Motor Mills in a fleet of Daimlers (plus a lone Benz Velo) circa 1897. [JDHT]

'Daimler', it was able to insist that the name should not be defaced or removed. Subsequently Henry Sturmey, having succeeded Lawson as chairman, spoke to his predecessor regarding the prolongation of Daimler patents, lodging a strong protest with the British Motor Company (which had succeeded the British Motor Syndicate) over the way it had handled this business and demanding compensation 'in view of their abandonment of their application for prolongation of one of the said patents.'

Another link with the origins of the company was broken in July when Gottlieb Daimler resigned from the board, never actually having attended a board meeting (he died two years later), but when one Richard Bannister, of 59 Tregunter Road, London SW, was proposed as his successor, Sturmey protested 'strongly and emphatically', sensing a plot to diminish his power, since Bannister was 'not even a shareholder of the company, and [his] knowledge of our business is nil'.

The upshot of these protests was the appointment of a committee of investigation, which, while vindicating Sturmey's opposition to Bannister, condemned the past management of the company, from the nomination of the original board, apparently by the British Motor Syndicate 'or its principal proprietors' to the misleading nature of the prospectus. It felt that the £40,000 paid for the Daimler licence was excessive, as 'the licence . . . was not a sole licence, but the British Motor Syndicate Limited retained the power to subsequently licence any number of competitors, the only restriction being that no other licences were to be granted on as favourable terms'.

The lack of manufacturing experience of the board was also criticized, as was the fact that the contracts with Stirling and the London Motor Van Company had proved unprofitable and the first balance sheet, which represented business expenses as stock in hand, was 'not such as to accurately convey to the shareholders the position of the company'. In short, said the committee's report, 'the business of the company has not been conducted in the efficient and energetic manner which is indispensable for the success of any commercial enterprise'. In recommending the reorganization of the company, and the appointment of a paid managing director to run it, the committee commented: 'Only energetic and efficient management, with the command of a fair working capital, are required to make this company a success.'

Faced with this criticism of their integrity and competence, the board closed ranks and issued a joint statement which urged the shareholders 'to strenuously resist such a suicidal step as winding up' – a course now advocated by the committee – and while they won the day, the company continued under a reformed board. Evelyn Ellis was one of the two directors who had not sought re-election, though he continued to fund the company with debenture loans until October 1900. The vacancies on the board were filled by E.H. Bayley JP (who became the new chairman) and Sir Edward Jenkinson KCB, a director of the Manchester Ship Canal and a man of high moral principles. Together they set about a thorough reorganization of the company which left Sturmey more isolated than ever, and in May 1899 he resigned in a fit of pique and bad grammar 'as I object to be a "director" of a business I have practically no voice in the direction of'.

* * *

Fortunately, these boardroom squabbles had no effect on the cars, which already had acquired a fine reputation and were much liked by their owners, among whom was the Hon John Scott Montagu, Conservative MP for the New Forest and heir to the first Lord Montagu of Beaulieu. Fired with enthusiasm for the new sport of motoring after a ride in his friend Hugh Wegulin's Panhard in the autumn of 1897, John Montagu decided to buy his own car, and his recollections – broadcast in a radio talk in 1928 – give a vivid picture of the early days: 'First of all, I attempted to get a Panhard like some of my

friends, including Charlie Rolls, but after various letters and negotiations I found that to get a foreign car over here presented considerable difficulty. So I eventually got into touch with the Daimler company, and in the spring of 1898 ordered my first motor-car.

'I cannot describe the joy which this first Daimler car gave me when it was delivered at my country house at the end of the summer of 1898. I began to realize at once that the mechanical vehicle was going in time to produce a wonderful revolution in our transport methods. Often I waxed eloquent before older men about its possibilities, but of course was generally laughed at and severely snubbed. Later on, when some of my prophecies became true, I became much disliked especially by my "horsy" friends. Such is the fate of most prophets.

'The 6 hp engine was two-cylindered with tube ignition; that is, there were two platinum tubes heated by a forced draught petrol flame, and by this means the mixture of air and petrol vapour in the cylinder was exploded. The body consisted of a six-seater yellow wooden wagonette, the hind seat being sideways as in a horse-drawn vehicle.

'The car had tiller steering, was chain driven, and the gear change was by the front

The Motor Mills in 1898, the year that it became the Daimler Works (even though the MMC sign is more prominent). [DBW]

seat on a metal pillar, on which there were two levers on dials. One of these moved the bevel wheel in or out of its connection with the drive, while the other lever operated four speeds in the gearbox. The gear rings were made of ordinary steel, which, as they were not case-hardened, after a few hundred miles began to show many signs of wear.

'There was no radiator, but a tank containing about twelve gallons of water was carried at the back, the water being pumped through the cylinder block by a semi-rotary pump; and as soon as it had boiled away the tank had to be refilled. One tankful generally lasted for about 20 or 30 miles. The brake consisted of a foot brake operating a wood-lined metal band on the countershaft

By 1898, wheel steering had begun to replace tillers, which could be jerked out of the driver's hand with disastrous effect if the front wheels hit a stone or pot-hole. [JDHT]

while the hand-brake was merely a metal shoe which could be applied to the tread on the hind wheels.

'One of the anxieties of those early cars was that if there was a strong wind, the ignition lamps generally blew out. When they had to be relit, it was a risky job sometimes, for the petrol which had not been consumed after the lamp had been blown out occasionally exploded. As to steering, if one struck even a small obstacle on the road the tiller was nearly wrenched out of one's hand. The springing was primitive and the bumping severe on any except a really good road.

'And the press of those days was by no means kind.. All kinds of abusive terms were used: "rattling, stinking vehicles", "juggernauts", "dread engines of death", "destroyers of the peace of the countryside" . . . Parliament was urged, by horse interests and others . . . to re-enact the Red Flag Act, and some opponents went so far as to declare that there would be a revolution among the people of England if the "rich" – a term of abuse then as now – were seen going at any speed which was not possible for the poor.

'The result of this abuse was seen in various directions. Stones were often thrown at passing motorists, and many persons would hardly speak to a well-known motorist like myself. Indeed, I was considered by some of my relations to be a dangerous revolutionary. Hotel-keepers generally regarded us as people not to be admitted, and I remember being rudely treated in two hotels one day, and told we were not wanted. One irate proprietor said he was not going to have any of these contraptions near his place, for they might blow up at any time. It was no use arguing; one had to submit, and cherish the thought that pioneers have a hard life.'

Sadly, John Montagu's first Daimler came to a spectacular end one winter's day when his original chauffeur, young Jack Stephens, overturned the car 'at the top of Dark Lane, just before the fork three-quarters of a mile or so short of Buckler's Hard', and it was completely burnt out – a lurking hazard with hot tube ignition.

Another keen Daimler owner was Dr W.W. Barrett of Park Crescent, Hesketh Park, Southport, Lancashire, one of the first doctors to use a car on his rounds instead of a horse and trap. Dr Barrett took delivery of a Knightley Victoria in May 1898, and acquired a second Daimler – a 'specially covered-in car' which was probably the world's first fully-enclosed saloon car – the following December. Not only that, but Dr Barrett had the world's first purpose-built private garage constructed to house his two Daimler cars and equipped it with hot-water heating and an inspection pit. The inventive doctor also devised the first quick-lift jack and electric wander-light to make servicing his cars – which were kept in constant readiness in case their owner was called out to an urgent case – easier for his two chauffeurs, who worked an alternating 'one hard day, one soft day' rota 13 days a fortnight.

* * *

In June 1898 the Prince of Wales – who had first ridden in a Coventry Daimler in the grounds of Buckingham Palace on 27 November 1897 – was staying with his old friend Daisy, Countess of Warwick, and her husband at Warwick Castle, just 10 miles from Coventry, and commanded that some motor cars should be sent over by Daimler for him to sample. Despite the short notice, the company arranged for five cars to be available, including Boverton Redwood's new four-cylinder (though this only made a brief appearance, as it was actually on its delivery run).

Critchley drove the Prince and his party – Daisy Warwick, the Duke of Marlborough and Lady Randolph Churchill – in a twin-cylinder wagonette, while Altree, Drake and Meyer followed in the other cars (which included Sturmey's 'John o' Groater') with other members of the Royal entourage. They drove over to Compton Verney House and when they left after a brief rest, were directed to leave the grounds by the lower drive, which had a steep incline. Critchley's car began to falter on the hill, at which members of the Compton Verney staff crept quietly

By the turn of the century, the Daimler motor car had established itself as part of the social scene in Britain and had been used, as here, for weddings – and a funeral . . . [JDHT]

Photographed in 1899, this 6 hp Daimler is similar to the car involved in the Grove Hill accident, with large-diameter rear wheels lacking in lateral strength. [JDHT]

out of the ditch and pushed the car from behind.

The Prince – maybe tongue-in-cheek – 'expressed his surprise at the absence of vibration and the hill-climbing capability of the car . . .'

* * *

By now, Daimler had a London depot in Shaftesbury Avenue, and on 25 February 1899 Samuel Greenhill, manager of the carriage department of the Army & Navy Stores, who wanted to display a Daimler in the stores, arranged for a trial trip with the London depot's engineer, E.R. Sewell, 'a clever, if somewhat daring driver'. With five senior employees of the stores as passengers, Sewell drove out to Harrow-on-the-Hill and, after a leisurely tea at the King's Head Hotel, volunteered to demonstrate 'that he could pull it up quickly, and that the machine was under perfect control.'

Greenhill said that he was 'rather alarmed' at the speed of the car going down Grove Hill from the hotel – 'I should think we were going quite twenty miles an hour; at any rate I was uncomfortable' – when Sewell 'made a beautiful curve to turn round the bend, the tyre flew off, the wheel collapsed and the car came down.' Everyone flew out of the car; Sewell was killed instantly and one of the passengers, Major James Richer, died later. On the pavement was the 14-year-old J.T.C. Moore-Brabazon (later Lord Brabazon of Tara), walking back to Harrow School after seeing his parents off at the station: 'People were afraid to come near as they thought the car would blow up – a characteristic that motors were supposed to possess in those days. You can guess with what pride it was that I turned off the burners of the ignition and stopped the engine. This accident impressed all the boys very much, myself included, and most of them took the view that motors were very dangerous and that it was silly to drive them. I very bravely stuck up for them, but was frowned on for being rather a half-wit for not seeing the light in the obvious way.'

The accident appeared to have been

caused by over-enthusiastic braking causing the wood-spoked carriage wheels (which Daimler bought in from a specialist wheel-making company named Smith & Parfrey) to collapse, rather than excessive speed, but Henry Sturmey compounded the situation by writing an article in *The Autocar* entitled 'A Terrible Object Lesson'. As he was still a Daimler director, this was a trifle unwise, and the company had to pay £655 in damages for this, the first car accident in Britain involving the death of the driver.

One of the expert witnesses at the inquest was Sidney Straker, the newly-appointed 'advisor on matters of design'. One of the best of the first generation of British motor vehicle designers, Straker would later be responsible for the Straker-Squire luxury car (and some fine commercial vehicles) and was, ironically, to die by falling from a horse near his Surrey home in the 1920s. His first task was to create a new and more powerful Daimler that would match the products of the leading Continental factories, as he later recalled: 'On the instructions of the directors of the Daimler Company, I studied the four-cylinder Maybach engine and eventually designed the four-cylinder touring car, of which the Daimler Company built six [presumably this was the initial trial batch], one of which was purchased by the Hon Scott Montagu.'

The time between design and production was not hedged about with the myriad legal and technical impediments that make it impossible nowadays to bring a new car to market in less than three years, and John Montagu's new four-cylinder car was ready for him in May. That summer he became perhaps Britain's (and the world's?) first long-distance commuter, using his new Daimler to travel between Beaulieu and the Palace of Westminster, where he sat as Conservative Member for the New Forest.

On 3 July, the car made parliamentary history, for it became the first car to enter the precincts of the House of Commons, as Montagu told listeners to a 1928 wireless broadcast: 'I well remember driving from the New Forest to London in those days on several occasions and not meeting one motor car the whole way in the 90 miles. When driving into the House of Commons one day in my 12 hp Daimler, I was stopped by the policeman on duty and refused entrance on the grounds that "them things is excluded by the order of the Speaker". On my appeal to Mr Speaker Peel, then in the Chair, and reminding him of the Sessional Order which guaranteed "free ingress and egress" to Members of the House of Commons, he at once gave orders that my car was to be admitted, and I drove proudly into the inner recesses of Palace Yard. The drivers of hansoms and four-wheelers who were there on the cabstand gazed wonderingly, for I expect in the back of their minds they knew that their doom was coming.'

He was soon claiming a speed record 'from his seat in the New Forest to Clapham Common', and in June 1900 it was noted that Arthur J. Balfour, Leader of the House of Commons, had been a passenger in Montagu's Daimler. Balfour, already a motor tricyclist, was about to buy a 3½ hp De Dion: in July 1902, he would become Prime Minister, the first motorist to hold this great office of state.

In August 1899, John Montagu was invited to lunch with the Prince of Wales, who was staying at Highcliffe Castle, half an hour's drive from Beaulieu, and took the Prince for a ride in the Daimler. The Prince, recalled Montagu, 'displayed immense interest in the details of the car, asking the most intelligent and penetrating questions as to the machinery.'

In September 1899, Montagu took his car to France and competed in the Paris–Ostend Race: it was the first entry by a British-built car in an international motor race – and Montagu's third place in the Tourist Class won Britain's first motor racing prize, too. Montagu's Daimler was also the first car ever fitted with a mascot, a small bronze St Christopher sculpted by Charles Sykes (who

Royal beginning

'The real start of Royal motoring came in August 1899 when my father was invited to lunch with Edward, Prince of Wales, at Highcliffe Castle, the home of his friends the Cavendish Bentincks, and drove over in his new four-cylinder Daimler. During the afternoon he took the Prince for a drive through the New Forest, as a consequence of which he was invited to take the Daimler to Marlborough House for examination by the Prince's staff (not one of whom knew the slightest thing about motor cars). Shortly afterwards, the Prince ordered his first Daimler.'
M

in later years created the well-known 'Spirit of Ecstasy' mascot, apparently modelled on Eleanor Thornton, John Montagu's secretary and secret lover, for Rolls-Royce).

* * *

In 1899 Daimler first made its mark on military history when Frederick Simms commissioned it to build the chassis for his 'War Car', a massive military vehicle with Vickers armour plating, to be powered by a four-cylinder 3.3-litre German Daimler engine which Simms had ordered specially from his associates in Cannstatt. It all started amicably enough, for in April the Daimler Company informed Simms: 'We are putting on a larger staff of men to enable us to push on with the completion of the War Car quickly.' But the atmosphere quickly turned sour. In mid-May Critchley wrote to Simms: 'We are surprised at the tone of your letter. In the first place the motor was promised to us in December. It is not yet delivered . . . Your threat to advertise at the Automobile Show that the Motor War Car is not completed . . .

is, we think, not justifiable, and we certainly resent such threats . . . We, ourselves, intended to show . . . a heavy oil motor van and ordered from your firm in December last a cylinder head. This is not delivered although we have been promised delivery long ago. We can in equal fairness advertise . . . that owing to the non-delivery of this head by your firm we have not been able to enter for the competition.'

By September, when the War Car was completed and undergoing its road tests, there was increasingly acrimonious correspondence over payment for the machine. This grew even more bitter after Simms's engineer Rowbotham drove the cumbersome device into a ditch while descending Stoneleigh Hill and it had to be dug out, its gear casing broken by the impact. 'The war-car was quite finished on the date of our invoice, Sept. 30th,' wrote Daimler company secretary John Ware, 'and . . . we have frequently pressed you to let us have your cheque and remove the car. It is very much in our way . . .'

Racing record

'My father entered his 12 hp Daimler in the 1899 Paris–Ostend Race: it finished in third place in the Tourist Class, winning the first motor racing prize awarded to a British car and driver, while its "on the road" average running speed of 23.9 mph matched that of the winning Peugeot, even though the 130 minutes spent repairing its cooling pipe brought his overall average down to 18.7 mph.' **M**

Finally, in November Ware accused Simms – who had asked Daimler for a commission on the £509 18s cost of the German engine – of 'not seeming to understand commercial terms, since you fail to comprehend what we mean by debit and credit. It is quite true that your commission, or your right to a commission, has nothing to do with us, and this is the very point of our argument. Since it has nothing to do with us, it is not we who are going to pay it you.'

Simms must eventually have paid up, for in July he drove his War Car from Coventry to London to be fitted with its armour plating and machine guns. Fully equipped, it measured '28 ft overall, with a beam of 8 ft . . . and is further equipped with two rams – one fore and aft – two turrets and two guns, and is capable of running on very rough surfaces.' Commented *The Autocar*: 'It is a most warlike monster, and if we mistake not its military value will be great.'

But the War Car took too long to complete: by the time it was ready for demonstration at the Crystal Palace in April 1902, the Boer War was virtually over. Its projected use for coastal defence failed to materialize, the War Office failed to attend the trials and the project died. However, Daimler's role in the development of armoured military vehicles was far from over.

* * *

The year 1899 saw Daimler's first venture into mail delivery by motor vehicle. Critchley developed a forward-control 12 hp mail van which took part in a 'long distance' trial in June, driven by its designer. The Daimler took exactly 4 hr 59 min to cover a distance of 20 miles and was later exhibited in the Old Deer Park in Richmond in the first-ever motor show organized by the Automobile Club of Great Britain & Ireland – but no orders were forthcoming.

The first delivery of mail by motor took place that Christmas, when the Lincoln carrier C.H. Gilbert used a Daimler motor lorry to take the post to the romantically-named (and remote) village of New York. The experiment was 'most successful' and the

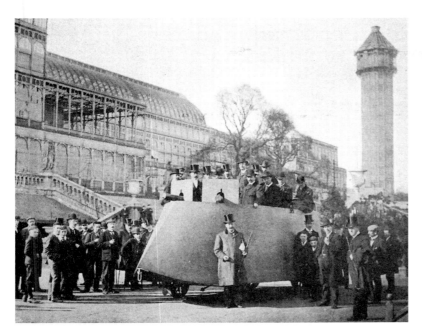

Frederick Simms's War Car of 1899 had Daimler running gear and armour plating by the Vickers, Sons & Maxim armaments giant; it never saw active service. [DBW]

unwanted 4 hp engines which were left over from the company's initial association with Cannstatt. Designed with cheapness in mind – the maximum price was guaranteed at £200 – the 'Critchley' Daimler had a curious belt drive from the engine flywheel to the rear axle which could only be tensioned by moving the engine backwards and forwards, and a vertical steering column on the side of the bodywork so that the wheel could only be operated by the driver's right hand. It was not a good car but it did at least get rid of those old engines, and it seems that the hired Daimler which gave author Rudyard Kipling his first taste of motoring at a cost of three guineas a week 'in the days when motoring was looked upon as a cross between pitch-and-toss and manslaughter' was a Critchley. What other Daimler could have been described as a 'belt-driven, fixed-ignition Embryo which, at times, could cover eight miles an hour'?

* * *

There were few women motorists on the

Daimler did a round trip of 68 miles that Christmas morning 'over a route which could not possibly be reached by means of the railway service.'

Another of Critchley's designs had been completed in January 1899 to use up 50

Designed with cheapness in mind – the maximum price was set at £200 – the 'Critchley' Daimler had a curious belt drive from the engine flywheel to the rear axle. [JDHT]

The lovely Thea Weblyn at the wheel of Evelyn Ellis's 12 hp Siamese Phaeton with Montie Grahame-White beside her in the front seat. [NMM]

roads of Victorian Britain, but Montague Grahame-White – who as an 18-year-old city clerk had cycled down to Datchet in 1895 to look at Evelyn Ellis's Panhard – taught several of them to drive when he was working at Daimler's London depot: 'With one or two exceptions I found that the fair sex became more proficient more rapidly than men,' he commented. 'One of the most beautiful and at the same time most intelligent of my pupils was Miss Thea Weblyn, of Molesey, the youngest of three daughters all noted for their good looks and charming personality. In 1899, after a course of six lessons of an hour's duration, Miss Weblyn drove the Hon Evelyn Ellis's four-cylinder 12 hp Daimler from Hampton Court to Datchet and back, without any outside assistance or control, handling the big car in traffic encountered through Staines in a manner that certainly merited the admiration bestowed on her.'

Grahame-White often borrowed Ellis's 12 hp Daimler – a massive yellow 'Siamese Phaeton' with an identical chassis to John Montagu's car and fitted with an out-rigged 'spider seat' – to give demonstration runs to guests at house parties in the Midlands, and in August 1900 the ever-generous Ellis made him a gift of the car. It subsequently ran away down the hill from Dover to Folkestone with Lord Wolverton and his family aboard when the wooden brake linings caught fire and was only stopped by Grahame-White swinging the car violently round in the station yard at the foot of the hill and running back up the gradient. After new brakes had been fitted, the intrepid nobleman invited 'the iron-nerved' Grahame-White to bring the car to a house party he was holding at Newmarket, adding, pointedly, 'where the country is flat'.

Chapter 3

FIT FOR A KING

When Frederick Simms selected Claude Johnson as the first Secretary of the Automobile Club in 1897, he could not have chosen better. The enterprising Johnson was just the man the Club needed to steer it through the first difficult years of its existence. And the finest demonstration of Johnson's 'great organizing talents, combining the very rare qualifications of quality and quantity of work', came early in 1900, when the Club decided to organize the first long-distance trial of motor vehicles in order to demonstrate their capabilities to the public, an event in which Daimler was to play a dominant role.

While the real dawn of motoring in England was marked by that 1,000 Miles' Trial, held in April–May 1900, the planning of the route – largely carried out in atrocious weather, and mostly using Daimler cars –

Speed trial

'Driving his 1899 12 hp Daimler, my father won a bronze medal in the 1900 1,000-Miles' Trial. Here, he prepares for the speed trials on the Duke of Portland's Estate at Welbeck Park, in which he took fifth place at just over 26 mph.'
M

actually represented a more severe test of the primitive motor vehicles of the day, since it took place without the elaborate back-ups arranged for the Trial itself by the energetic Johnson.

Naturally, when Johnson wanted the loan of 'a car and a capable assistant' to help him in the survey, he turned to Daimler, as the country's leading motor manufacturer. Critchley had no hesitation in offering both the car and the services of the promising 22-year-old Montague Grahame-White, whom he had taken on a couple of years earlier as a personal assistant and subsequently promoted to demonstration driver, thanks to his 'practical knowledge and exceptional skill'. Grahame-White drove works cars in the tours, trials and hillclimbs organized by the Automobile Club.

Johnson and Grahame-White carried out a detailed survey of the route between 19 December 1898 and 5 January 1900, starting by covering the initial westward leg of the 1,000 miles route on Alfred Harmsworth's 8 hp Panhard. Then the pair picked up a modified 'Critchley' Daimler at the Coventry works for the northern section of the run. In an effort to improve its miserable performance, the 'Critchley' had been fitted with a 5½ hp twin-cylinder engine instead of the original 3½ hp unit, but the layout of its troublesome belt drive was unchanged. This proved to be an oversight which, as the little Daimler headed north, Johnson and Grahame-White would regret as they repeatedly rejoined breaks and laboriously adjusted the tension of the belt with worm-threaded trunnions which moved the engine back and forth in the frame.

This engrossing activity was interspersed by further pauses to relight the ignition burners as they blew out in the high winds which accompanied the rain, sleet and snow falling throughout the 74-mile run from Manchester to Kendal (a dismal journey which took from 5.30 a.m. to 5 p.m. on December 20, an average of less than 6.5 miles an hour).

Grahame-White's recollections of the ten-mile ascent of Shap Fell ('during which the road rises from 1,300 to 1,400 feet above sea level') were vivid: 'The ascent . . . was begun with three inches of snow on the road. The driving snow and sleet made it extremely difficult to see, the car having neither hood nor windscreen, and the higher we climbed the more wind we encountered. I suggested to Johnson that we should stop at a local haberdashery and provide ourselves with some black veiling to place under our caps and over our faces to obtain protection and better visibility. In the higher stretches of the pass, however, we found it necessary to remove these, the snow clogging the net and rendering sight impossible . . .

'Between the start of the ascent and reaching the summit of Shap, Johnson and I must have got out on more than a score of occasions, either to fit new belt fasteners, new sections of belting or to light the extinguished burners. To endeavour to reduce the belt slip, powdered resin was dropped on the inside of the belts whilst the car was running, by means of a small funnel penetrating a hole drilled in the flooring of the car. It took us 6¼ hours to cover the ten miles to reach the summit, where we encountered half a gale which drove the loose snow into snowdrifts in the most exposed places.'

Continued Johnson: 'Then followed a weird drive in the dark along the Thirlmere road, the car gradually losing speed and the belts either slipping or breaking continuously. Stopping the car, we discovered that although the engine, when running free, was quite in order, it required considerable effort to even move the car on the level by hand. Getting underneath it and feeling the back axle and brake drum, Grahame-White discovered considerable overheating of the former which he cooled down with the snow from the road, and subsequently oiled by the aid of two carriage lamps.'

But when Grahame-White jacked up the

back axle, he found that the wheels were virtually locked solid: 'The strain to which it had been subjected in crossing and recrossing Shap, with an almost continuous jerk in bringing up side slips on the borders of the ice-covered roads, had twisted the interior shaft, causing its misalignment.' The axles were one of the many weak features of the little belt driven Daimler – one private owner (who actually preferred the belt drive) had two front axles break under him. Johnson had the miserable 'Critchley' Daimler and Grahame-White sent back to Coventry by train and telegraphed to the Edinburgh Autocar Company for another car.

On 27 December a 5½ hp gear-driven Daimler arrived in Keswick, driven by the owner of the Edinburgh Autocar Company, T. Rowland Outhwaite, who was probably the first Briton to operate a sizeable fleet of motor cars. In October 1899 he had placed an order for 20 Daimler cars 'including one 12 bhp car seated for 16 passengers' and declared in 1900 that he was the operator of a fleet of 40 Daimlers, 'and among these are cars which will run over one hundred miles on four gallons of oil'. The remarkable Mr Outhwaite drove Johnson on to Newcastle, where Grahame-White took over once more,

this time with a more reliable 5½ hp gear-driven Daimler, to take Johnson all the way back to London.

Three months of intensive organization followed, and when the Trial actually began, from Hyde Park Corner at 7 a.m. on St George's Day, 1900, the entry included 20 Daimlers and MMC-Daimlers out of a total of 83 entries ('65 started,' noted the Judges' Committee afterwards, 'and with the exception of a few vehicles, most of which ought never to have started, all covered the whole or greater part of the course.' Just two MMC-Daimlers and two Daimlers failed to make the start, so that it was still true that 25 per cent of the competing cars had been built in the Motor Mills).

'It was a notable gathering that started from Grosvenor Place to drive to Bristol the first day, and afterwards, by various stages, to Edinburgh and back again to London,' recalled John Montagu, who had entered his faithful 1899 12 hp Daimler, adding: 'A curious feature was the number of motorists who knew each other, for those who actually owned their own car in this country were very few, and in fact, so small was the number that one knew almost everyone who owned a car of any importance at all.'

Also among the competing Daimlers were several 6 hp twins, including one newly-acquired by newspaper magnate Alfred Harmsworth (who hosted the contestants to breakfast on the opening day of the run) and another driven by a pseudonymous 'Mr William Exe', whose cover was neatly blown by *The Autocar*, which published a photo of that car, No A31, with the caption 'Mr C. Johnson's arrival at Marlborough on his Daimler'. Driving a twin-cylinder Daimler wagonette was Percy Richardson, whose engine began losing water on the first day when the water pump rotor cut through its bronze casing. He repaired the leak with a cigarette tin, using hemp and fish glue as packing.

In addition to the official entries, several Daimlers ran as baggage vehicles (one was

W.B. Jeavons with his frail 1900 belt-driven 6 hp 'Light Daimler', which had already broken two front axles by the time this photo was taken in June that year. [DBW]

driven by Johann van Toll, who was now in business on his own account, building Belgian Vivinus cars under licence in Twickenham under the name 'New Orleans' in partnership with H.G. Burford, formerly with the Motor Manufacturing Company – but the car he had entered for the trial had been put out of action in a crash).

These 'camp-followers' performed unsung, but valiant duties as breakdown vehicles *en route*.

Harry Swindley, who rode on Oswald Lord's 7 hp Peugeot which followed the trial as a non-competitor, recalled: 'The Daimler waggonette used [as a baggage waggon] by the company was one of the best cars on the run. In connection with Mr Straker's breakdown with the char-à-banc she did good service . . . practically towing the char-à-banc through the night. The larger car required constant fresh supplies of water, and the drivers tell weird tales of tramping over the moors with lamps and canvas buckets in search of the necessary fluid, the while they floundered deep in bog holes and otherwise enjoyed themselves at two o'clock in the morning.'

Critchley, who drove one of the works-entered Daimlers, recalled another of the unforeseen problems of the Trial: 'Newspapers naturally had their representatives and in some instances these gentlemen were not enthusiastic. I well remember my scribe, who joined me at Newcastle. The morning was as bad as could be, rain and wind, and he was ill-prepared to face the driving blast and also I felt sure he had not fortified the inner man. His bowler had refused to remain where he put it, and between keeping his hat on and his knee-apron in position, he was having a hard struggle. I warned him to be careful, and to keep the rug away from the exposed driving chain. At this request, he flew into a violent rage and consigned the car and the driver to Hades. I thereupon said that if he so desired, he could get out and walk, but he failed to see the point as to walking!'

The Daimler cars did remarkably well: of the dozen vehicles which completed the Trial at the required average speed – equal to the legal limit (12 mph in England, 10 mph in Scotland) – three (including John Montagu's car) were Daimlers and all five prizes in Class C (works entries costing £300–500) were either Daimlers or MMC-Daimlers. Though the outright gold medal winner was C.S. Rolls's 12 hp Panhard, five out of 10 silver medals and three out of four bronze medals awarded went to Daimler cars, a most remarkable achievement in an event which had really succeeded in its aim of putting motoring on the map as far as the general public was concerned.

Perhaps the most curious award was made to Montague Grahame-White: it was the personal medal awarded by Sir David Salomons 'for conspicuous merit', displayed when the 'Parisian' Daimler of which Grahame-White was in charge was ditched near Alnwick by Basil Johnson (brother of Claude) and its steering gear broken beyond the scope of roadside repair. But the ingenious 'Montie' came up with a solution which at first sight appeared, in the words of one of his passengers, 'sheer lunacy'. By standing on the off-side step of the car with his left foot and keeping his right instep on the long hub casing of the front wheel, he found he could steer the car by pushing the wheel in the required direction, 'with the assistance of Mr Basil Johnson using the foot brake when required'.

Amazingly, the crippled Daimler covered the remaining 52 miles to the over-night stop at Newcastle at an average of nearly 10 mph, though the sole of Montie's boot was nearly worn through by the time the car limped into the Drill Hall where the entrants were garaged. 'The true automobilist is a resourceful man,' remarked an eye-witness. 'After Mr Grahame-White's exhibition of steering a heavy Daimler car with his foot some fifty miles on the public roads, who can contend that the motor car is a dangerous and unmanageable vehicle?'

Out to grass

What to do with old cars when they became outmoded (which, in the early days of motoring, they did all too rapidly) was a problem for keen motorists. After less than four years of use, Lord Montagu's 24 hp Daimler was relegated to estate duties in 1906 and, with a 26-inch channel steel insert let into its chassis, was fitted with a 12-seat shooting brake body. Less dignified was the fate of three old tiller-steered Daimlers which in 1903, fitted with tall superstructures proclaiming them to be 'Oxo Motor Cars', distributed beef extract to competitors in the marathon walking races which had become popular.

Certainly not the redoubtable Montie, who – dismissed from Daimler in May 1900 'for absenting himself from the works without permission' and working as a freelance automobile expert – repeated the feat later that year on a French nobleman's Panhard which broke its steering gear near Amiens.

* * *

Though the Prince of Wales had first ridden in a motor car on the Continent in 1893, it was not until his trips in Daimler cars in the late 1890s that he decided the time was ripe to buy his own automobile. It seems to have been his ride in John Montagu's new 12 hp that tipped the balance, for a few weeks later Montagu had been requested to take his car to Marlborough House, where it was closely examined by members of the Prince's staff (even though their knowledge of cars was nil). The upshot of this inspection was that when Montie Grahame-White returned from that eventful reconnaissance trip for the Thousand Miles' Trial, works manager Critchley ordered him to drive one of the new 6 hp 'Parisian' Daimler twin-cylinders down to the company's London showrooms at 221–229 Shaftesbury Avenue for inspection by Lord Knollys.

The intimation had been given that the Prince would like to see a car bodied as a 'Mail Phaeton' – a handsome leather-hooded two-seater with an occasional bench seat behind, which had been displayed amid the potted palms at the National Show at the Crystal Palace in November 1899 – but for some reason, the Daimler which Grahame-White drove to town had no hood, its wings were mundanely made of wood rather than the more elegant patent leather, and the seat cushion was too shallow.

Knollys also thought the wheels – which had spokes retained by steel sockets on the rim rather than being jointed into wooden felloes – too flimsy, and rejected the car out of hand. Daimler, suitably chastened, arranged to send down a Mail Phaeton that was nearing completion at the works so that the

Prince could approve the bodywork, even though the car was on the old-type chassis with wheel-operated handbrake and gear quadrants on a vertical column ahead of the driver. 'As is well known,' recalled Grahame-White in 1943, 'the Prince was of portly build. Comfortable seating was of first importance, whilst the general details of coachwork had to pass his critical eye and conform to the standard of finish of all carriages built by Hoopers for the Royal Family.'

The replacement car was shown to the Prince in January 1900 in the grounds of Buckingham Palace and Daimler soon received its first Royal order, for a Mail Phaeton on the Parisian chassis – which had side gear and brake levers, a new design of bonnet and a more steeply-raked steering column – through the agency of Oliver Stanton, 'automobile expert'. The Prince's car was also one of the first Daimlers to be fitted with 'double ignition' – hot tube and battery-and-coil electric, with the hot tube being kept as a reserve – and pioneered the use of an accelerator pedal instead of a hand lever. A non-standard feature seemingly adopted in tribute to the impressive embonpoint which had earned Edward his irreverent nickname 'Tum-Tum' was a steering column 'pivoted at the bottom so that it may instantly be placed in a vertical position to facilitate mounting and dismounting'.

Oliver Stanton was, by all accounts, a very smooth man. An American citizen, he gave the impression of being wealthy: but he had first come to public notice when he gave cycling lessons to society folk in Battersea Park, hardly the expected occupation for a gentleman of leisure. However, it did bring him to the attention of the Royal family, some of whose members – including the Prince of Wales – he taught to ride cycles, acquiring a sort of semi-official status.

When in 1897 Lord Iveagh was entertaining the Duke of York (the future George V) at his shoot at Thetford, he hired a car from the Great Horseless Carriage Company. It was, said works manager Francis E. Baron, 'one of the first dozen built by me . . . Lord Iveagh allowed a similar type of car to be advertised by my firm as the "Iveagh Phaeton".' The hired car – a Daimler in all but name – intrigued the Duke so much that Stanton was sent to Coventry to investigate 'as a preliminary to the use of cars by other members of the Royal Family'.

The elegant Stanton – he affected lavender kid gloves and a long cigarette holder – soon became known as 'the automobile instructor to the Prince of Wales and friend of many notabilities on all matters connected with the autocar, its use and management'. Daimler was obviously impressed by his society connections, for as early as July 1898 the company was offering him 5 per cent commission 'on orders emanating from his introductions', and in November 1899 he was allowed to buy a car on the new hire purchase system. In April 1900, Daimler decided to lend a car 'as similar as possible to the one sold to the Prince of Wales' to Stanton free of charge while he was giving tuition to the Prince, and soon afterwards awarded him a bonus of £25 on the Prince of Wales's car 'in addition to the commission of 10 per cent which will be due to him when the car is paid for'. Stanton presumably spent his bonus fairly rapidly, for soon afterwards Daimler offered him an advance of £10 to attend upon the Prince of Wales.

The Prince's car was bodied by Hooper of St James's (who had held the Royal Warrant since 1830) and painted in the royal colours of chocolate and black, picked out in red, to create a 'quiet and stylish appearance'. It was delivered to Sandringham on 28 March 1900 by Sydney Letzer, who had been working for Daimler for some two-and-a-half years and ran a dancing school in the Priory Rooms at Coventry in his spare time; he was shortly afterwards appointed 'mechanician to the Prince of Wales' – the first Royal chauffeur – and was to remain in the Royal Service for many years.

The Prince requested some modifications to be made to the coachwork, and the car was subsequently brought back to him at the Royal Stables at Ascot, where he was holding a large house party, on Monday 11 June, with his friend Lord Suffield and Henry Chaplin, President of the Local Government Board, as passengers.

In the interim, the Prince had been 'fully instructed in the art of motor management' on Oliver Stanton's new Mail Phaeton, and two days after the Daimler had been delivered, rode the 10 miles over to Cumberland Lodge in it accompanied by the Duke of York and a mechanic named Coke, and preceded by a groom on horseback to act as pilot until the Prince got tired of having to 'rein in' the car to match the horse's pace – it took less than a mile – and sent horse and groom back to Ascot.

It seems as though the Prince ('a fearless automobilist . . . although he does not drive himself') soon tired of his 6 hp Daimler and wanted something larger, for in June 1900 it was announced that not only had Stanton sold 12 hp Daimlers to the great divorce judge Sir Francis Jeune and the MP C.H. Wilson but that 'largely through the instrumentality of Mr Oliver Stanton, HRH the Prince of Wales has just ordered two more cars from the Daimler Motor Co'.

On 3 July the Daimler board was told that 'Lord Suffield was desirous of acquiring the car which had been submitted to the Prince of Wales' and offered to sell him the car on 'easy terms of payment' of four six-monthly instalments of £103, 'the price to include motor and frame only and Lord Suffield to make his own arrangements with the builders of the body'. Suffield only kept the car until November; it was then sold to Lord Hastings for £700. Hastings had the Mail Phaeton bodywork converted into a four-seat tonneau by Mr Prentice of the Eagle Carriage Works, Lambeth. Subsequently owned by Daimler for many years, this first Royal Daimler was offered to Queen Elizabeth II in the late 1960s and is now, after restoration to its 1902

Photographed after it had been found in a junk yard in 1924 and bought by Ernest Instone for £10, the first Royal Daimler became a valued museum piece. [NMM]

condition in the workshops of the National Motor Museum at Beaulieu (to celebrate the Queen's Silver Jubilee in 1977), the star exhibit in the Royal Motor Museum at Sandringham.

The cars which the Prince had ordered to replace the 6 hp Mail Phaeton – which he nevertheless drove during the summer of 1900 after Suffield had taken it over – were more powerful but utilitarian vehicles, a 12 hp wagonette for the Prince's personal use (which Stanton test-drove before it was delivered), fitted with a Lonsdale hood which folded to either side of the body or could be closed up to create an almost windowless oubliette, and 'a Titanic machine known as the Beaters' Car'. This massive 14-seater was bodied by Hooper and had the unusual feature of forward control, with the engine concealed beneath the driver's seat. The company charged the Prince £870 for his 'hooded wagonette' and £975 for the 'large wagonette brake'.

The two cars were driven through King's Lynn in mid-November, piloted by the enterprising local Daimler agent, Frank

Morriss, who 'had the honour of supplying petrol and spare parts and executing minor repairs for HRH', and 'caused more than a mild sensation among the market folk'. Morriss was definitely a marque expert, manufacturing replacement parts for Daimler cars and specializing in 'the replacing of old rudder-steering apparatus by the approved wheel-steering gear'.

Stanton's automotive advice could hardly be called disinterested, for he took commission on car insurance and acted as Daimler's agent among the great and the good of society. His market value had increased since the sale of the first Royal car, and he was now paid 10 per cent commission on sales 'on satisfactory proof to the board within a week of signature of the contract that the order has been obtained through his influence'.

When in September 1900 *The Autocar* announced that Stanton had acquired a new 12 hp four-cylinder Daimler, it also reported that the car had originally been built for press magnate Alfred Harmsworth and that its body remained Harmsworth's property: 'He

The first car actually purchased by the Prince of Wales was this 12 hp Daimler Lonsdale wagonette; spare-time dancing master Sydney Letzer, the first royal chauffeur, is at the wheel. [JDHT]

has lent it to Mr Stanton for the time being, but will not part with it, as he has driven thousands of miles in it and is naturally somewhat attached to what has proved such a very comfortable method of seating.'

The truth was a little different: Harmsworth was trying to drum up custom for Daimler with his new car, which was delivered to Stanton on 13 September, and soon after, car and driver were sent off to the Riviera 'with a view to procuring orders'. By November the car had covered nearly 2,000 miles, including a busy mid-October spell of canvassing for the successful candidate in Caithness during the general election campaign ('and on the night before the election had come to be recognized as such a power that it had to be carefully guarded to protect it from the evil designs of irresponsible members of the opposite party').

With the death of Queen Victoria on 22 January 1901, the Prince of Wales succeeded to the throne as King Edward VII and for the first time Britain had a motoring monarch. By mid-year the Royal Daimlers had become a regular means of transport and at King Edward's suggestion the 'beaters' car' had been turned into a practical everyday vehicle by the fitting of a canopy with side-curtains and a glazed back. The King used it for the first time at the beginning of July to travel from Marlborough House to inspect alterations that were being made at Windsor Castle and declared himself very pleased with the car's new configuration. The 12 hp wagonette, meanwhile, was in continuous use, and by the time the King took it on a Continental trip in September it had covered several thousand miles.

Shortly before Christmas, the King placed an order with Stanton for his 1902 car, a 22 hp four-cylinder which was to be 'delivered in good time for Ascot Week'; the company took the King's old car plus £200 cash in exchange. In January came an order for a 14-

seat omnibus, 'a larger edition of the King's 12 hp beaters' car'; this coincided with the announcement that Daimler had been honoured with the Royal Warrant of Appointment as 'motor manufacturers to the King'. Daimler expressed its gratitude by giving Oliver Stanton, 'through whose exertions the royal warrant was obtained', a bonus of £404, '£200 to be paid by cheque, and £204 to be credited to Mr Stanton's repair account'.

'It is a happy coincidence,' wrote Walter Staner, who had just taken over as editor of The Autocar from Henry Sturmey (retired prematurely from injuries received while road-testing a car) 'that the first firm to commence to manufacture motor cars in Great Britain should also have been successful in satisfying the King'.

* * *

Early in 1900, Lawson paid a visit to America, where he met Colonel Albert Pope, whose newly-formed American Bicycle Company was a trust after Lawson's own heart, combining some 45 cycle companies, while the Columbia & Electric Vehicle Trust – another Pope combine – had recently started operating the so-called 'master patent' of George B. Selden, which proved to be a far more effective stranglehold over the American industry than Lawson's combine ever had been. The far-sighted Pope, whose first Columbia car had appeared in 1897, predicted that there would be 100,000 motor vehicles in New York within 10 years and that they would drive every other form of traffic off the streets.

Maybe Lawson (who passed himself off as 'Sir Harry' while he was in the USA) was hoping to form a transatlantic trust by joining with the Colonel's combine, but his power over the British industry was visibly ebbing away. The sole tangible result of the meeting between the two was that Pope's Western Wheel Works began producing the Lawson Sociable – a spidery two-seater tricycle whose single front wheel was driven by a 2¼ hp single-cylinder engine – under the name 'Trimoto' in their Chicago factory. There was, it is believed, 'significant production' of the Trimoto in the period 1900–1. Priced at $425, the Trimoto was capable of 12 mph, and had its brief moment of fame when Trimoto owner Mrs John Howell Phillips claimed to be the first American woman motorist to be issued with a driving licence (State of Illinois No 24).

Lawson also planned production of the Sociable in England, when he attempted a reconstruction of the ailing British Motor Company in July 1900: the idea was that the cash raised by the refinancing of the company would be used to complete the purchase by Lawson of the old Starley-Westwood works in Coventry for the production of the Sociable in England. While the British Motor Company was certainly reborn under the name 'British Motor Traction Company', with Lawson still owning a large tranche of shares, manufacture of the Sociable seems to have been restricted to a few prototypes.

The reconstituted firm attempted to set up a company under the name 'Daimler Waggon Company' in 1901, but though Daimler of Coventry took them to court on the grounds that there was an intention to deceive, the British Motor Traction Company perversely won the case: but there seems to have been no consequent manufacture. Once again, the main aim of this new Lawson company was to claim royalties against 'master patents', but this time it was one master patent too far. In July 1901 the company proceeded against Peugeot agent Charles Friswell for allegedly infringing the Maybach spray carburettor patent – and lost ignominiously when Friswell successfully pleaded that Maybach's patent had been anticipated by two British inventors, Butler and Wilkinson.

Daimler board minutes reveal that the Lawson combine which had been started with such an impressive roster of master patents had failed to keep pace with the development of the industry, for when

Daimler – which was still paying royalty money to Lawson's new company – enquired which of the 'master patents' were still valid, and which had been allowed to lapse, it eventually transpired that only three were left, and the most important of these was the soon-to-be-discredited patent on the carburettor, which was where Daimler put its licence plate, virtually out of sight.

After its factory had shut down, the British Motor Traction Company was finally put into receivership in February 1903 at the petition of Harry Lawson himself, as holder of £7,750 out of the issued capital of £50,000. But the 'house of cards' empire established by Lawson had already begun its inevitable collapse as the old century gave way to the new. In November 1900 Pennington & Baines, whose idiosyncratic vehicles had been such a high-profile product of the Motor Mills, were taken to court by John Harvey of Manchester, who had signed up as their sole agent for Manchester two years earlier, paying £500 for the privilege. He was expecting delivery of at least 30 cars a year and was 'anxious to do business, but no motor cars were sent by the defendants. They kept writing to say that things were going on swimmingly and that they were going to do an enormous business, but the plaintiff had only received one motor car, and that would not work.'

A letter from Harvey's solicitor had got his £500 back, and he was awarded £75 in damages by the court. 'I think these motor cars are horrible things,' pronounced the judge. 'I think so too, my Lord,' sagely agreed the plaintiff's solicitor.

Pennington returned to the United States where, at the time of his death in 1911, he was trying to sue Indian Motocycles for infringing his invention of the motorbike . . .

* * *

Daimler was already establishing a reputation for innovation. In April 1900 the company had exhibited cars fitted with sheet aluminium bodies at the Agricultural Hall Show (it was not until November that the leading coachbuilder Rothschild of Paris would ship the aluminium body for the revolutionary new Mercedes which was nearing completion at Cannstatt). Nor was the company averse to learning from its rivals: in July 1900 Lord Carnarvon brought his racing Panhard to Coventry so that it could be inspected by the works manager, for which he was formally thanked by the directors.

For its normal touring car, Daimler regarded the new 8 hp Napier as its closest competitor and Critchley was asked to design a car to counter its rival from Lambeth. Oddly enough, S.F. Edge, whose Motor Power Company marketed the Napier, was not only a shareholder in Daimler and a director of the British Motor Traction Company, but in May 1900 ordered 50 'motors and frames' from Daimler through his company, though whether these were ever delivered seems unlikely.

Daimler was making progress in engine design, with the pair-cast cylinders now having enveloping water jackets which 'did not leave them uncooled at the point where the two cylinders hitherto joined', as well as wider seating for the detachable cylinder heads, while a double water pump (complete with indicator) also aided the cooling. Critchley was experimenting with electric ignition and trying to get extra power out of the ageing 6 hp engine by 'alterations to the clearance of the induction valve and by increasing the compression, and estimate approximate cost of carrying out the alterations on customers' cars.' Moreover, the internal layout of the gearbox had been redesigned so that it was more compact.

Engine size was on the increase. A visitor to the factory in November 1900 was shown a 'gigantic twenty horsepower machine built for the conveyance of milk and fruit produce . . . of immense length and has specially-designed framework in which long radius rods and compensating levers play a prominent part'.

THE DAIMLER CO. have pleasure in announcing that they have been honoured with the Royal Appointment to HIS MAJESTY THE KING OF SPAIN.

THE DAIMLER MOTOR CO. (1904), Ltd.

COVENTRY—Daimler Works. LONDON—219-229, Shaftesbury Avenue, W.C. MANCHESTER—60, Deansgate. NOTTINGHAM—96-98, Derby Road. BRISTOL—18, Victoria Street. BRIGHTON—Palmeira Works, Hove.

DAIMLER CARS may be obtained through Messrs. Wm. Whiteley, Ltd., Westbourne Grove.

King Edward VII was the first of many monarchs to own Daimlers: by 1907 the worldwide list of Royal customers even included the memorably-named Scorkarta Pakoe Boewono X, Emperor of Java, with a Milverton landaulette supplied by the company's agent in Soerabaya. [DBW]

And the dismal little Critchley voiturette had been transformed into the Kimberley, described at the 1900 board meeting as 'a practical and saleable machine'. But by then Critchley was no longer there to protest at the scarcely-veiled criticism. He had for some time felt that his position was being undermined by the management, and resigned from Daimler in May to become 'motor expert' with the British Electric Traction Company in London. Between 200 and 300 men were present when he was presented with a silver tea service and an illuminated address hand-lettered by Montague Grahame-White. In one of the speeches, it was remarked that 'Mr Critchley was not afraid of work himself, but had the faculty of making others work.' George Foster Pedley, who had been in charge of Daimler's London depot since 1899, took over Critchley's duties as general manager, travelling representative Percy Richardson became London manager, and Critchley's assistant Arthur J. Drake was appointed works manager.

Drake didn't stay in charge long; he handed in his notice in October 1900 and in mid-January 1901 left 'to undertake the management of a very large and important autocar manufacturing enterprise in Edinburgh, which bids fair to become one of the leading firms in the automobile business in Great Britain'. The firm in question – the Kingsbury Motor Construction Company – planned to build a Panhard-type car in its purpose-built 3.5 acre works, complete with quarter-mile test track, at Granton Harbour, near Edinburgh.

Though a prototype of Drake's new Daimler-engined twin-cylinder 2,265 cc car – a heavy six-seater running on solid tyres – successfully ran 10,000 miles as a public service vehicle in Edinburgh during 1901–2, the Kingsbury company was taken over in the spring of 1902 by Stirling, largely, it seems, for the extra production facilities offered by its four-year old factory. Drake stayed on as chief designer, but Stirling ceased production a year or so later, despite a considerable export business, largely of commercial vehicles.

Given the state of Daimler at the time, it must have been very difficult for Drake to distinguish frying pan from fire, even though company chairman E.H. Bayley had recently boasted of the 'highly satisfactory business' that had been done and claimed that 'orders had gone up, if not by leaps and bounds, at a rather surprising rate'. Bayley had also praised the changes in management made at Coventry and the London office and the 'wise expenditure on buildings, machinery and stock incurred in the year 1899–1900'. But that 'highly satisfactory business' had actually seen orders decline: 73 orders had been taken in the six months ending 31 March 1900 and 48 orders over the same period in 1901.

Meantime, in 1901 Arthur Meyrick was working to improve the design of Daimler's coachwork. 'He had many original ideas and several of his designs were put into construction in the building shops that year,' recalled Grahame-White. But new body designs could not prevent a crisis in the company's finances which was a major factor in a rapid turnover of company officials. John Ware, appointed company secretary in 1900, was sacked the same year and eventually replaced by George T. Grant in 1901, with Pedley filling the gap in addition to his other duties. Thomas Bayley MP resigned in February, along with H. Sherwin Holt, leaving just the chairman, E.H. Bayley JP, and J.H. Mace (last of the original 1896 board) as directors. The board, which claimed to be running the company within its means, had actually borrowed £3,000 in November 1900 without telling the shareholders, and taken out an overdraft of an extra £3,000 in order to carry on the business.

Part of the trouble could well have been the company's cavalier attitude to some of its high-profile customers. Wealthy Surrey land-owner Hugh Locke-King (who built the Brooklands race track in 1906–7) ordered three milk vans with Mulliner bodies for his farms but after repeated letters had failed to secure delivery, he had his £900 deposit returned; Count Eliot Zborowski tried to cancel the racing car he had on order in December 1900, but this time the company refused to cancel his order and instructed the works manager to 'put down a frame at once', though Zborowski continued to ask for his money back. A Major Howey stopped his cheque because his new car was unsatisfactory; Daimler refused to take the offending vehicle back unless Howey ordered a new 12 hp car. John Montagu threatened to cancel his order for a new Daimler unless the car could be delivered by 1 January 1901.

Obstinately, the company refused offers of help which had any strings attached, but continued going back to the seemingly eternally good-natured Evelyn Ellis for further £3,000 loans – two during the month of October 1900 alone. In 1900 John Davenport Siddeley and a consortium of friends offered to invest £30,000 in Daimler provided they received £100 debentures at 5 per cent annual interest and were entitled to nominate two directors; that came to nothing, though in September 1901 Daimler was to offer Siddeley the post of managing director. However, his conditions could not

be met and he went off to build cars under his own name with Rothschild backing.

Then on two occasions in 1900–1 Louis Tracey of 26 Maida Hill, 'a gentleman of great respectability' backed by a 'group . . . of the highest integrity and financial standing', offered to buy Daimler for £35,000 cash, £35,000 debentures, £20,000 to be put in as working capital 'to be taken or left, as under no circumstances will more favourable terms be offered'. Again, the offer was turned down. And when the overdraft was eventually paid off with cash in hand in April 1901, a new board took over at an extraordinary general meeting held in the Holborn Restaurant and found that there was not sufficient money left in the bank to pay the wages bill.

But the new board was determined to put the company on a sounder basis, though it was to prove more difficult than they had imagined. Most prominent of the new members was Sir Edward Jenkinson KCB, who had already been a Daimler director from January 1899 until he stood down through ill-health a year later. Jenkinson's return to the board was welcomed by the shareholders; it was little surprise when he was appointed chairman within a matter of days. Thomas Bayley also rejoined the board, while Captain C.C. Longridge of the Royal Artillery (a knowledgeable mechanical engineer, who was deputed to go down to Coventry to carry out an enquiry into 'the present condition of the works and the keeping of prime cost accounts' at a fee of £84 a month) and J.S. Critchley were voted in as directors.

With the appointment of Drake's successor, H.W. Bamber, Bayley remarked that Daimler had at last secured a works manager who, 'if he had a fair trial, will prove a great success'. Bamber had trained as an engineer with the great traction engine builders, Marshall, Sons & Co, of Gainsborough, Lincolnshire, and then 'had a varied experience in autocar design and manufacture'. He brought in W. Hemingway, 'conductor of the cycle class at the Battersea

Polytechnic . . . well-known for his advocacy of the bevel-gear driven bicycle', to take charge of the drawing office.

Product planning was, indeed, a little hit-and-miss. When the board drew up the specification for a 1901 type car, they asked for 'engine bonnet to be all aluminium if possible, with radiator in front of engine bonnet; pressure lubrication wherever practicable, ignition both electric and tube . . . with new worm gravity pattern carburettor below burners', revealing the dubious state of product development by asking for a sprag – a spike dropped into the road to prevent the car from running away backwards – 'to be fitted to front axle if found successful'. The new season's engines were to be a 'two-cylinder developing not less than 7.5 bhp, four-cylinder ditto 16 bhp, 2-cylinder to have present 12 hp gearcase; 4-cylinder to have new twin gearcase, both adapted for roller bearings. Lemoine type axles, brake pulley to be watercooled . . . a throttling arrangement to be used if found satisfactory'.

Daimler also sold secondhand cars on behalf of private owners, on the basis that if they fetched a higher price than the limit fixed by the owner, any surplus was handed over to the owner!

Reliability was now being taken (almost) for granted: in 1901 Watson & Company of Liverpool established a six times daily 'service of autocars' over an 8.5 mile route between Chester and Farndon and back and over a two month period noted that they had completed every journey, and that the cars had also covered 'close upon 50 miles . . . without the slightest mishap' while attending a wedding. Expectations were that low in the early days of motoring!

In January 1901 the president and chief engineer of the Daimler Manufacturing Company of New York visited Coventry on their way home from a trip to Cannstatt. The American company had been founded in 1888 by piano manufacturer William Steinway after a chance meeting with Gottlieb Daimler, who was visiting New York

as a member of a male voice choir. Up to 1900 it had built only engines and the occasional goods vehicle, but while the American duo, Graf and Moffat, were in Coventry they announced that 'our company is going to take right hold of the passenger car branch as soon as we are back' (though no cars were actually forthcoming until 1905, when the factory built an 'Americanized' version of the contemporary 45 hp Mercedes).

A new and more powerful model appeared in February 1901; this was the 20 hp (confusingly also known as '16 hp' and '18 hp') four-cylinder, and another of Sidney Straker's designs. This, it seems, was the first Daimler model not fitted with tube ignition, and had been built to the order of Clifton Talbot, who intended to enter it in the touring class of Continental races. Its hill-climbing powers, remarked a passenger on its test run, were 'magnificent'.

That April Daimler unveiled its Char-à-Bancs, a 'toast-rack' 11-seater designed by Straker which broke away from previous Coventry Daimler practice in using direct gear drive from spur wheels on the ends of the driving axle to an internally-toothed ring gear bolted to the spokes of the rear wheels, which revolved on the end of a separate dead axle. This transmission method – again, as used on Cannstatt-Daimler goods vehicles from 1896 – must have been fearfully noisy and the unsprung weight alarming; equally unsettling was Straker's clumsy attempt at single-pedal control, in which the first inch of movement of the pedal disengaged the clutch, and the remaining three inches applied the 'double purchase' countershaft brake; the ungainly machine must have really proceeded by fits and starts. Fortunately, the Nottingham Autocar Company had already offered to run the sole Char-à-Bancs built as a public service vehicle and pay Daimler half its earnings; it was hardly surprising that they failed to come back for more.

Another of Straker's consultancies was with the Motor Traction Company (of which Daimler board member E.H. Bayley, a well-known horse-bus operator, was also a director), and he designed a steam bus for them which turned out to be an abject failure despite its cost price of £1,000 ('not suitable for London work' was the verdict after trials with the first two built) and plans to buy a fleet of 40 of these buses ended in threats of litigation. Nevertheless, in June 1901 he resigned all his consultancies – Daimler had been paying him £500 a year – so that he could concentrate on his Straker Steam Vehicle Company, which was building steam lorries and buses.

If the Char-à-Bancs represented a blind alley, the company was also deaf to the pleadings of Frederick Simms, who had developed a low-tension magneto in conjunction with the German engineer Robert Bosch. Daimler's engineers were not fully convinced of the merits of electric ignition compared with the old hot-tube system, but agreed to carry out trials with it. When they announced the results, the response was far from what Simms had been expecting: 'We are NOT prepared to make Simms ignition standard – we shall only fit it on customer demand.'

Simms made things worse by billing Daimler for the magneto, and Critchley responded indignantly: 'You appear desirous that we should advertise your ignition and at the same time pay you for all the experiments that we have conducted on your behalf. We cannot see why we should be called upon in any way to pay for the expense of your engineer, seeing that we have been put to all the expense of trying the ignition, and the least that you could do would be to stand your portion of the expense, and also to supply free the experimental magneto machine, and forgo any question of royalty. We should have thought that you would have been so anxious to prove the efficiency of your ignition that you would have been willing to have paid for the whole of our experiments on your behalf.

'As regards the efficiency of the ignition,' Critchley pointedly concluded, 'we may as well state that we do not get the same result out of it as we do with the tube. An engine that will give $6\frac{1}{4}$ hp with tube will only give $5\frac{3}{4}$ hp with your ignition.' Undeterred, the persistent Simms tried again, and at Christmas-time was loaned a 6 hp wagonette to be fitted with a Simms-Bosch magneto on a trial basis.

In mid-1900, Frederick Simms had proposed a 'Daimler union' between Coventry and Cannstatt, but the Daimler Motor Company's identity was now firmly established and the board turned his proposal down. Nevertheless, an intriguing twist was to link the names of Simms and Daimler in the spring of 1901 when tramcar builders G.F. Milnes decided to enter the automobile market, making 'Milnes-Daimler' cars and lorries to the designs of the Motorfahrzeug & Motorfabrik Berlin AG of Marienfelde, Germany.

The Marienfelde company, founded in 1897, manufactured Daimler designs under licence and became a branch of the Cannstatt company in 1902. Its heavy vehicles used the internally-toothed drum drive first seen on 1896 Cannstatt Daimlers. Works manager of the new 'Milnes-Daimler' company was H.G. Burford, lately in partnership with Johann Van Toll; the company's London showroom 'Motoria' in Balderton Street, just off Oxford Street, had recently been vacated by the Simms Manufacturing Company – and Frederick Simms had been appointed consulting engineer, drawing up the specifications to which the Milnes-Daimler lorries were being built. Prominent in the early days of commercial vehicles in Britain, Milnes-Daimler faded away around 1907, as did other minor marques which sought to capitalize on the 'Daimler' name.

On 2 April 1901 George Foster Pedley, the newly-appointed Daimler manager, brusquely demanded the return of the 6 hp wagonette loaned to Simms. (Pedley, incidentally, was to leave Daimler in 1902; he joined his friend John Montagu's new magazine Car Illustrated and subsequently was

the host of the 'Master Builder's House' at Buckler's Hard on the Beaulieu Estate after its conversion into an hotel.) From the ensuing correspondence, it sounds as though the company was sorry to have got its wagonette back: 'The magneto ignition fitted by you on our wagonette recently has commenced to give very serious trouble,' Bamber wrote to Simms at the beginning of May. 'The cams amongst other things are so loosely fitted to the cam shaft that the whole thing gave way whilst taking a customer out last Saturday and caused us considerable trouble and expense to put right.

'We have succeeded in getting the car again on the road, but this mishap has caused us to lose all confidence in the car as now fitted for any lengthy run. We are surprised in view of the fact that you had the car with you for such a long time that you did not make quite certain that a mishap of this description was quite impossible. We might also say that one of the plug joints gave way at the same time and was only made good with the assistance of copper gauze and asbestos, as the face of the joint on the cylinder head was so badly grooved that any thin jointing material was impossible. We shall be glad to have your explanation of this.'

Explanation, it seems, was not forthcoming, for a couple of weeks later, Bamber told Simms: 'We are sorry to have to inform you that on Sunday night last [the magneto gear] entirely failed us some little distance from Coventry and we were put to the unpleasant necessity of leaving the car all night, bringing our passengers back by train and sending another car to tow it back in the morning. Under these circumstances, as our wagonette is urgently wanted at the present season of the year for customers' work, you will see that it is an impossibility for us to continue the use of this gear on this particular car. We have therefore taken it off and fitted one of our ordinary tube heads . . . Considering the way which the gear runs on this car we have no doubt whatever as to the reliability of the system, and the breakdowns which have occurred have been entirely owing to the unsatisfactory manner in which the gear is fitted. This, as we once before stated, very much surprises us considering that you fitted this gear yourselves and in view of the fact that you retained the car for such an extraordinary length of time in order to make a satisfactory job of it.'

It is, perhaps, hardly surprising that the Simms-Bosch low-tension ignition system was never standardized on the Daimler cars; fortunately, the company's enterprising chief draughtsman E.W. Lewis (who joined Rover in 1903 and designed its first motorcycle and its earliest cars) had patented his own design of contact breaker which proved successful enough to be fitted to the Royal wagonette.

The range was becoming increasingly complex: the Automobile Club Show in the Agricultural Hall at the beginning of May saw another new model, a 9 hp 'light frame car' with 'Marseilles tonneau body and double ignition – a car of particular interest to those who wish to have a fast but by no means heavy vehicle'. This was shown alongside two 16 hp fours, a 12 hp 'Coventry' wagonette, two 6½ hp twins and a 4½ hp Kimberley voiturette . . . and a launch engine.

Complained the new chairman: 'Two small cars were the only cars which we could send to the Reliability Trials in Glasgow and they broke down at the very commencement of the trials due to faulty design and bad materials. No less than ten types of car are under construction in the works, so that economy of production and punctual delivery of cars are impossible. It is difficult to obtain purchasers for the old 6 hp cars and the 9 and 10 hp cars which were designed in 1900 are faulty in design and of such excessive weight that the construction of them is exceedingly difficult and very expensive. Customers are becoming very dissatisfied and the Daimler company is losing its good name.'

But Bamber was out of his depth at Daimler, and lasted less than a year before he was sacked by the new chairman, Sir Edward Jenkinson, who remarked that not only had Bamber had a fair trial, but that 'in the opinion of some, we have been too long-suffering, and ought to have removed him sooner than we did . . . all I can personally say is that it was my desire to be just to him and to give him every chance of proving his fitness for the post, but I was convinced at last that he was not the man for the place. In justice to Mr Bamber, he undertook the management of the works at an extraordinarily difficult time and when the manufactory was in a disorganised and confused condition and worked hard and conscientiously to the best of his ability. He introduced order in many respects and made several improvements, but

he is not a highly trained engineer and has never had sufficient education and experience to fit him for so important and difficult a post as that of works manager in your manufactory at Coventry.'

The works were, indeed, in some trouble, and had been put on to three-quarter time (a 42-hour week) and, said Jenkinson, with a total annual expenditure of £77,400 – of which wages represented £28,560 and materials £29,000 – running well ahead of receipts, 'it is evident that economy is required in the working of our manufactory and that steps must be taken to obtain more orders and to increase our sales.'

Despite ingenious sales methods, which included deals with the proprietors of *Motor News* and *The Autocar* in which they took cars and Daimler guaranteed to take advertising space, the company was hardly realizing its potential. It was, however, raising its sights: the target selling prices for its 1901 models were based on the Panhard range, and a proposal by Bamber in February 1900 to build a twin-cylinder engine to sell to the trade 'for voiturette work' in competition with the popular 3½ hp De Dion-Bouton single was instantly rejected.

It would probably have made things worse, anyway: one of the problems exacerbated by Bamber's managership was the failure to convert the accumulated large stock of motors, frames and gear boxes built up during the summer of 1900 into cars that could be sold.

Complained Jenkinson: 'The motors and parts were left in stock, and when the new board took control there were no cars for sale, no new type of car to compete with cars manufactured by French and other makers had been designed and built and the consequence was that would-be purchasers went away from us disappointed and purchased cars elsewhere.'

There were desultory attempts at clearing the obsolete stock; in 1900 Drake had been asked to design a belt-drive car 'in order to secure the sale of the eighteen 6 bhp motors

French leave

The Daimler was one of the first two cars – the other being its great rival, the Napier – accepted by French authorities as meeting all the legal requirements for use in France. That was in 1903, and it had the great advantage that Daimler owners wanting to tour France only had to pass the French driving test (maybe not so easy, for there was no such examination in England until the mid-1930s) without having to submit their car to examination by the Ministry of Mines for official approval.

now in stock', and when in 1901 Critchley, sent to Paris to buy chassis frames for a new 10 hp model, ordered 20 frames from the Bail & Pozzy company through the London importer O.C. Selbach and they turned out to be both faulty and unsaleable, they were used the following year to create 20 light cars powered by obsolete 6 hp engines taken from a further stock of 55 which had been written off as unusable! Fitted with 'very light tonneau bodies' made in the Daimler works, these ill-starred hybrids had pneumatic front and solid rear tyres and were fitted with electric ignition (except for two cars used for hire work at Daimler's newly-opened London repair depot in Brownlow Mews, near Gray's Inn Road). Another crossbreed intended to use up surplus parts was created in 1901 by fitting a new 9/10 hp engine in a shaft-driven 'voiture Chainless' frame bought for £275 from a Parisian maker for experimental purposes.

And getting rid of surplus stock was not the only problem, as the Road Carrying Company of Liverpool, granted an agency in March 1902, discovered. The company was losing money in a pioneering road haulage operation with steam lorries, so took on a number of car agencies – Daimler and MMC among them – in an effort to improve its finances, only to find that the Daimler agency also involved a deal of financial commitment. Recalled the late Colonel E.A. Rose, former engineer of the RCC, in 1967: 'The Daimler Company was pretty much on the rocks, and many a time I had Ernest Instone ring me up and say, "For God's sake can you come and take delivery of a car, otherwise we won't be able to pay the wages next week!"' And we'd go up and take it and put it into stock; it wasn't everybody wanted to buy a big Daimler car!'

By such hand-to-mouth methods did Daimler come through its crisis.

* * *

At the end of June 1901 the Motor Manufacturing Company held what nowadays would be referred to as a facility visit, when it laid on a special train to carry some 200 journalists and shareholders from London to Coventry, where they were met by 'a fleet of the firm's motor carriages'. Since these all had Daimler chassis, it would have been impossible to tell which marque name they actually bore: but they made an impressive line-up and marked the watershed of the association between the MMC and Daimler.

MMC had been reformed in May 1900 after being threatened with closure, had spent all but £400 of the £37,300 raised putting its affairs in order and was running at a loss. For some time there had been an increasing sense of mistrust between the two companies; the regular conferences between MMC and Daimler had been discontinued by Daimler, and in November 1900 MMC employees were caught in Daimler's part of the works on a Sunday sketching 'portions of the machinery', which caused some serious correspondence.

The companies eventually began talking again in May 1901, and the question of an amalgamation was discussed. Jenkinson and Longridge met Gretton and Buckea of MMC, and after long discussions it was suggested that a new 'Daimler-MMC' company should be created, with Daimler increasing its capital to acquire the business, assets and goodwill of MMC, whose shareholders would be given one ordinary Daimler share for three MMC shares. The talks foundered on details in October – Daimler refused to take on any MMC liabilities in excess of £6,000 – which, said Jenkinson, 'is to be regretted because amalgamation on fair terms would be to the advantage of the companies.' Perversely, the MMC decided to plough a more independent furrow and immediately announced that it was to concentrate on light one- and two-cylinder cars and vans; 'high-powered and other cars' were to be dealt with in 'an entirely separate department' . . .

Works manager George Iden – a foreman on the London, Brighton & South Coast

Railway before taking over at MMC in 1898 – had very definite ideas on how cars should be designed, and there followed 'another period of costly experiment, with neglect of production . . . and more time and money wasted . . . Instead of settling upon a type and producing it, the manager was kept at producing new patterns, no less than nine different sizes and types of engines being got out.'

The scheme was an abject failure and by February 1902 Henry Sturmey – now acting as a freelance motor industry consultant – was pleading on behalf of MMC with Daimler, asking them to reconsider the question of amalgamation 'on the lines proposed last year'. Jenkinson turned him down flat, so Sturmey came back a few weeks later desperately asking whether Daimler would consider 'amalgamation on any terms'. But when Jenkinson asked him what he meant by that, no reply was forthcoming.

MMC – reformed yet again – continued for some time with intermittent success. H.P. Small remembered working on a grandiose 20/25 hp MMC saloon car which caused a sensation at the 1903 Paris Salon, but the cars were unduly heavy and, stated an MMC owner, 'I have never yet got the smallest spare part that would fit properly, and all other MMC owners I have come across seem to have had the same trouble: no two cars were exactly alike . . . things were done in a haphazard fashion by individually good workmen.' This ramshackle policy could only end one way: by late 1905 the company was in receivership and Daimler had taken over the whole of the Motor Mills for a modest £14,500.

MMC moved away to new premises at Parkside, Coventry, and was reformed in 1907 with plans to re-establish production in Clapham, London, but the end of Daimler's relationship with MMC came in January 1908, when Percy Martin and Edward Manville of Daimler met Tilden Smith of MMC and agreed to cancel MMC's outstanding debt of £155 7s 6d provided

MMC 'gave up all rights to the No 6 capstan lathe' in exchange for a cheque for £380. By December the same year the Motor Manufacturing Company, which had once been such an important part of Lawson's grand scheme to control the British motor industry, was in voluntary liquidation, having built just one car in its ultimate factory. Though the name briefly resurfaced in 1912 on a spare parts business run by its former manager, no more MMC cars were made.

* * *

Oliver Stanton was still initiating society 'into the mysteries of automobilism'. Among his pupils were publisher C. Arthur Pearson and the American Ambassador; he also drove the $6^{1}/_{2}$ hp wagonette laid on to carry technical journalists attending the 1901 heavy vehicle trials organized by the Self-Propelled Traffic Association in Liverpool (the S-PTA was shortly afterwards integrated into the Automobile Club). In August 1901 it was reported that Stanton and his wife had taken up temporary residence in Coventry so that he could supervise the construction of a new '30hp' Daimler christened Le Chat Noir – 'a giant machine, and its owner humorously asserts that he is going to carry a voiturette in davits at the stern as a tender'.

While he was in the Midlands, Stanton also organized the first-ever 'motor funeral' in August 1901, when the coffin of an elderly Daimler employee named William Drakeford (who had been caretaker of the Motor Mills building ever since it had been built in the 1860s and whose goat had famously eaten the flowers from the ornamental bed planted to improve the view from Pennington's office) was carried to the cemetery on a hearse based on an obsolete 6 hp Daimler chassis fitted with a flatbed body, painted black and hung with black drapery. It was followed by two horsedrawn coaches full of mourners and two Parisian Daimler cars, and the cortège was watched by a large crowd, who lined the mile-long road to the cemetery two and three deep.

Oliver Stanton's 30 hp Daimler Le Chat Noir *boasted a truly mindboggling dashboard layout, with three gear levers and 12 drip-feed lubricators.* [DBW]

A month later Stanton sold a 20 hp Daimler – a revised design with 'the new seamless or solid heads to the cylinders, equal wheels, and several other features of interest which will go to make it an extremely fine, powerful and comfortable carriage' – to Lord Craven of Coombe Abbey. 'So far as we know,' ventured *The Autocar*, 'this is the first automobile of the really luxurious type which has been ordered from a Coventry firm by a resident in the immediate district.'

It sounded good: but the truth was that Daimler, though showing a modest profit, was running out of working capital. Its policy

Miss Thornton from John S Montagu
April 1902.

Motoring monarch

'This was the first photograph of the new King in a motor car, and was taken at the Bungalow, my father's house on the Solent, in April 1902. He used it as the frontispiece of the first issue of his new magazine *The Car Illustrated*, which contained an article on "The King as a Motorist". The photograph is signed for Eleanor Thornton, his secretary on the magazine, who was the model for the Rolls-Royce "Spirit of Ecstasy" mascot. A few days later the King underwent an emergency appendix operation – he nearly died – which delayed his Coronation by six weeks.' **M**

of only building cars to order meant that business was highly seasonal, and to avoid this dead period Sir Edward Jenkinson proposed that the company should build up stocks during the winter ready for the spring and make sure that the works were run efficiently 'by appointing a good man – and paying him well – as managing director'.

A lucky chance brought the right man to London .

A skilled 30-year-old engineer named Percy Martin was on his way home to America from Milan, where he had established a new factory for the Union Elektricitaets Gesellschaft of Berlin, his employer since 1894. But a financial crisis had forced the German company to close down its Italian branch, and Martin was spending a few days in London before leaving for the United States to try and start a new career. While in town he met gear manufacturer Harry Orcutt, who also happened to be a friend of Sir Edward Jenkinson's. Orcutt told him of the vacancy at Daimler, an interview with Jenkinson was arranged, and on 23 October 1901 Martin arrived at Coventry as the new works manager at an annual salary of £500 plus a bonus of £200. It was an inspired appointment. Martin possessed great personal charm, allied to that rare virtue, the ability to listen. Jenkinson praised him as 'an able engineer, exceedingly keen and never tiring in his work.' Martin was flamboyant, too; his taste in cigars became an industry legend and a surviving order he placed with the Secretary of the Royal Automobile Club in December 1918 lists 2300 cigars of various types totalling £242 10s – the price at the time of a complete Model T Ford.

But it was Martin's abilities as an engineer and a leader of men which were to transform Daimler from an ailing giant into an industry leader.

* * *

Martin quickly set to work drawing up the specifications for the 1902 range, and just over a month after starting at Coventry, he proposed that the company should produce an 8 hp twin, and fours of 12 hp, 16 hp and

The King's new 22 hp 'Touring Carriage' at Windsor; its Hooper bodywork was designed by Arthur Meyrick to the King's personal specification. [NMM]

were new, and largely Martin's work. They were shown at the Agricultural Hall exhibition in late April, where they were inspected by the Prince of Wales, but regular production didn't begin until later in the year. The most immediately noticeable feature of Martin's new models was the design of the radiator, which had cast-aluminium water tanks at either end, heavily-finned to improve cooling.

One of the first customers for the new 22 hp was the King, whose new (and unfinished) car, with bodywork designed by Arthur Meyrick to the King's personal specification, was the centrepiece of the stand at the Agricultural Hall – and curiously, an identical car was ordered that summer by Sir William Gordon Cumming, the central figure in the 1891 Tranby Croft libel case which had so scandalized the nation when the then Prince was subpoenaed as a witness to attest to Cumming's having cheated at cards. Considering that the Prince had made him a social outcast, it seems odd that Cumming should copy his taste in cars now Edward had become King.

22 hp, all on wheelbases of 6 ft 6 in or 7 ft 6 in, at prices ranging from £450–£1,150 complete with bodies. The 12 hp and 22 hp

In July 1904 John Montagu's 22 hp light Daimler was used to transport King Edward VII from Hinton Admiral railway station to Highcliffe Castle, where he was staying with the Cavendish Bentincks. [NMM]

Between the initial sketch and completion, the King's new car had been fitted with a feature which for some years became as much part of the Daimler image as the finned radiator header; this was a capacious curved scuttle dash with copper 'shoulders' incorporating vertical cupboards at either side which gave extra storage capacity for small items.

At the time the King's car was being built, Daimler released details of its testing procedure, which was unusually thorough for the period, when the customer was often regarded as the experimental staff. Daimler engines were individually bench-tested and were not released for installation in a chassis until they were producing their designed horsepower. Gearboxes were also run-in on the bench, filled with a mixture of oil and fine emery powder to 'sweeten' the gears and the completed chassis was then road-tested for anything from 100–400 miles fitted with a test body ballasted to represent the weight of the coachwork.

Daimler placed great emphasis on the quality of its test drivers ('ordinarily good drivers are by comparison with good test drivers as plentiful as halfpennies compared with £5 notes'), who were rigorously supervised by the 'autocrat of the running shed', Alfred Bush, familiarly known as 'Uncle' – and it was 'Uncle' Bush who personally gave the King's car its 300-mile road test, with Ernest Instone as passenger, though the usual procedure was for the test driver to be accompanied by an intelligent apprentice.

Another client for the 22 hp Daimler was the famous tea magnate and yachtsman Sir Thomas Lipton, who had been converted to 'automobilism' by the ubiquitous Oliver Stanton (now confirmed as 'special representative' to Daimler), who had also sold a 22 hp Daimler, this time a long-chassis model with a seven-seat tourer body, to the Prince of Wales.

* * *

In January 1902, James Critchley decided that, since both electrical engineering companies by which he was retained as consultant – British Electric Traction and Brush of Loughborough – planned to make motor vehicles, retaining his seat on the

Tea tycoon and racing yachtsman Sir Thomas Lipton was among the many society figures who were enthusiastic Daimler owners. [NMM]

Daimler board might create a conflict of interest, so he stood down. By 1904 he was running a car repair shop in Chelsea, and also that year designed the first car to be built by the great Manchester gas-engine company, Crossley Brothers.

His replacement on the board was Edward Manville, a distinguished consulting engineer whose company Kincaid, Waller, Manville & Dawson had built tramways all over the world and worked on the electrification of London's southern commuter railway network. Though Manville's base remained in London, he worked very hard on Daimler's behalf, and his loyalty to Coventry was shown by the fact that he represented the city as its Member of Parliament from 1918–23. Manville was a man of many interests and sat on a number of boards: when the 1930 Companies Act at last compelled directors to reveal all their other appointments, Manville recorded that he was on the boards of some 27 companies, including the Baird Television Company. He was always a forward-looking man . . .

Manville was the ideal foil to Martin, and his appointment was shortly followed by the return from France of Ernest Instone, the final member of the triumvirate which was to establish Daimler as a sound and profitable company, building on the already substantial achievements of Sir Edward Jenkinson. Instone was appointed manager at the same meeting at which Manville joined the board.

The first task was to rationalize production, and the 1902 schedule, which had called for the construction of 25 22 hp, 40 12 hp and 55 8 hp chassis, was quickly revised to increase output of the larger (and more profitable) models, and the company now prepared to build 30 22 hp cars priced between £1,125–£1,200, 50 12 hp models (£725–£750), 20 9 hp cars (£500–£525) and 20 9 hp light public service vehicles (£500). A total of 120 vehicles in all: it seemed very little on which to build a world-wide reputation, but the policy was now to proceed cautiously and by mid-year, the board was already considering its 1903 programme.

Initially, a new 16 hp model was planned, using a more powerful engine in the 12 hp frame, but that idea was soon dropped and the successful 12 hp model continued in

The 1902 sanction of 22 hp chassis under construction at the Daimler works.

production, a wise move as it turned out, for demand far outstripped expectation. Originally 60 12 hp cars were scheduled and by February 1903, with the construction of 74 already sanctioned, the board authorized the manufacture of a further 45; production of 40 new-type 22 hp chassis had been approved, and by February another 10 were authorized. A new '14 hp' model had been added to the range, though at 2,324 cc it was actually far smaller than the existing 3,402 cc 12 hp; a run of 19 of these had been approved at the end of 1902; now another 45 were approved.

Only a dozen 9 hp twins were planned for 1903 and the board felt that the small future need for light cars could be met by buying in chassis from outside. Contacts were established with Belgica, a company from the Brussels suburb of Molenbeek-St Jean which, though it was making bicycles as early as 1885, had only begun building cars in 1901. However, it was anxious to break into export markets, had recently established a branch in Paris and was looking to export to France and Britain. Manville and the francophone Instone travelled to Brussels to investigate the possibilities – the Belgica company built a four-car range of two- and four-cylinder models of 6, 7, 10 and 20 hp – but nothing came of their negotiations. Daimler, it seemed, had no further need of small cars.

*　*　*

Like most manufacturers of any consequence at the time, Daimler entered its products in the reliability trials that were organized by the Automobile Club of Great Britain & Ireland, and protested vehemently to the ACGBI's trials committee in 1902 after the January Welbeck Speed and Brake Trials that 'two-seated cars stripped for racing were

Montie Grahame-White instructs the Countess de Carrié, prima donna of La Scala, Milan, in driving her new 1902 16 hp Daimler. [NMM]

permitted to compete as touring vehicles' (while privately noting that attention should be paid to fitting special tyres and lighter bodies for speed trials in future).

But when in November 1902 the ACGBI invited the company to build a racing car for the Gordon Bennett Race, the most prestigious international event of 1903, it was told point-blank that Daimler was not prepared to do so; and thus the honour of representing Britain eventually went to the company's principal rival Napier, whose 1902 victory had brought the 1903 Cup race to the British Isles where, for legal reasons, it was held in Ireland, because road-racing was not permitted on the mainland. However, Daimler touring cars *did* perform with distinction in the supporting events to the 1903 Gordon Bennett, where the 22 hp Daimlers of Instone, Manville and John Montagu scored a clean sweep in the hill-climb for cars costing between £650–£1000 (though confusion with the timing made it unclear whether Instone or Montagu had actually won) and were faster than the big Napier of John Hargreaves which won the next class up.

Another 22 hp car was supplied to King Edward through the offices of Oliver Stanton – this time a solid-tyred 22 hp wagonette – and it had been shown at the Crystal Palace Show in February 1903 alongside the king's old 1900 12 hp car, which had 'been very extensively used, running several thousand miles with complete satisfaction to its owner'. At the request of the King, Stanton had become a naturalized Englishman so that he could serve in the newly-formed Motor Volunteer Corps, in whose first official outing as a car-borne support group to the British Army early in July 1903 he drove his 22 hp Daimler 'Sunny Jim' in connection with the state visit of French President Loubet.

And then, a couple of months later, came the bombshell: Stanton had left Daimler and joined the Clement-Talbot firm, who were building a spectacular new factory in Ladbroke Grove, Notting Hill. He claimed

he had made the change after a trial run on a new 18 hp Talbot car driven by the silver-tongued Danny Weigel, and found it so silent that all he could hear was the clicking of the ignition spark and the buzzing of the ignition coils, while the car 'obeyed the accelerator pedal like a charm'. But there must have been more to his sudden change of allegiance than mere infatuation with a new car; perhaps he fell out with Daimler over the size of his commission. Frustratingly, the board minutes covering that period no longer exist to clarify the mystery: what is certain is that none of Stanton's illustrious clients followed him. Daimler was still the Royal car, and within a few days of Stanton's departure that fact was underlined by the news that Daimler had been awarded the Warrant of Appointment to the Prince of Wales too.

And then, early in 1904, Stanton was back at the wheel of a Daimler, though the press no longer referred to him as 'His Majesty's motor expert'. By then, Buckingham Palace was dealing direct with the company through the unforgettably-named Undecimus Stratton. He had taken over Daimler's London depot when Percy Richardson had resigned to become general manager of the new Brotherhood-Crocker company – which was to develop into the Sheffield-Simplex, another rival for the luxury car market whose prospects seemed boundless in those golden days of 5 per cent income tax.

Stratton, a remarkable young man, had made his fortune early in life in the brewing industry and retired in his early thirties, taking up motoring as a hobby and acquiring his first Daimler in 1898. He had married one of the three beautiful Thompson sisters and his brothers-in-law were both peers of the realm. He was a close friend of the Hon C.S. Rolls, with whom he often went ballooning – together they set an altitude record of 7,000 ft in 1905 – and when Rolls decided to go into the motor car business professionally he had asked Stratton to be his partner. After consideration, Stratton had decided against this move, and Claude

Johnson joined Rolls instead, late in 1903 and shortly before Rolls met Royce. But soon afterwards Stratton was driving down to Bexhill-on-Sea and stopped to help a stranded motorist mend a puncture. 'My name is Jenkinson of Daimler,' said his new acquaintance. 'You seem to know a lot about

cars: we need someone like you to run our London depot. Why not come along for an interview?'

Competition for the job was intense, but Stratton proved to be the outstanding candidate. He clinched his appointment by saying: 'I don't need a salary. I'll just take

Daimlers dominated hill climbing contests in the early years of this century: this is pioneer Daimler agent Albert Farnell on his 28 hp car which came fourth in the July 1904 Sunrising hill climb, the steepest ascent in the Midlands. [JDHT]

Undecimus Stratton at the wheel of a 35-hp Daimler supplied to the King in December 1905. [DS]

commission on anything I happen to sell.'

His society connections served him well, and he soon built up an impressive list of royal and noble clients for Daimler at home and abroad. Stratton's unique social position played a pivotal role in establishing the company's image, for what other car salesman had a house on the Old Mile at Ascot, maintained a stable of racehorses and trotters, and was so highly-regarded a courtier that on occasion he rode to Royal Ascot as a guest in the King's landau?

* * *

The company's more rational product programme was paying off; when Daimler

Ernest Instone walks the course before competing in the 1904 Frome's hill climb. [JDHT]

called its annual general meeting at the end of 1903, it was able to report a net profit of over £15,300 despite the cost of a debenture issue. 'Of course,' commented *The Autocar*, 'no dividend is suggested, as last year's deficit is not entirely wiped out, but we are extremely pleased to record the fact that the pioneer company has apparently come to the end of its lean years, and having now secured a substantial balance, it should soon be placed upon the list of dividend-earning concerns.'

But old habits died hard, and within a matter of weeks the company announced that it 'had arranged to turn out a limited number of 7 hp light cars' which, though they had the new radiator with the finned side tanks, were powered by the ancient vertical twin engines which had already been written off as obsolete (but were then uprated from 1,551 cc to 1,773 cc), while their under-pinnings were manifestly from another age. 'The engine, we believe,' remarked *The Autocar* coyly, 'is of the same type as that which was so thoroughly tested in the first 1,000 miles trial, when the Parisian Daimlers so greatly distinguished themselves . . .'

It was, perhaps, a shade cheeky to list these as new cars, but there was nothing obsolete about the rest of the 1904 range, announced in February, particularly the new 28/36 hp model, at 5.7 litres by far the biggest model that Daimler had built up to then.

Like the continuing 22 hp (now known as the 18/22) and the new 3.3-litre 16/20 (the company also offered to fit this engine in existing 14 hp cars), the 28/36 had the new radiator with the finned top tank. The distinctive cast finning, a feature that survives in stylized form on Daimler cars to this day, gave the Daimler a unique identity, making it one of that rare elite, a luxury car that could be instantly recognized despite its having no radiator badge, like the American Packard and Pierce-Arrow and the French Delaunay-Belleville.

Cooling on earlier models had been a problem, implied a coded remark in *The Autocar*, which referred to the engine's 'ample water jackets of a type not previously associated with the Daimler productions'. Some other features of the new car were downright peculiar, like a totally-exposed camshaft for 'ready accessibility . . . and its removal in cases of necessity' (which says a lot about 1904 standards of maintenance) and a complex chassis frame which combined a short channel subframe carrying the engine within a full-length steel flitch plate bolted to the wooden chassis frame, which had side extensions to carry the bodywork. 'Push pedals' replaced the old organ pedals 'and everything had been done to ensure the comfort of the driver and a ready control of the car'.

A neat change to the Daimler dash was also possibly a world first on a production car: the acetylene sidelights were now built into the corners of the dash rather than carried on separate brackets, 'a marked improvement upon the projecting lamps which obtain at present'.

Once again, King Edward had ordered a new Daimler, which was shown in facsimile at the Crystal Palace Show in February 1904: this was a Hooper limousine of 'magnificent proportions and quiet finish', delivered to the King in July, and praised as 'a splendid example of the progress which has been made of late in the designing and upholstering of expensive cars'.

But behind this apparent success, the Daimler Company was again in trouble, for it was desperately short of working capital, and had again lost sales by not being able to build up stocks during the winter. So a scheme of reconstruction was drawn up under which the old Daimler company was voluntarily wound up and a new company with a capital of £200,000 was formed in the name of Ernest Instone as trustee. The new company was to acquire the old one, pay the costs of winding it up and discharge all its debts, which included a substantial £60,000 debenture contracted in 1903 with the Hon Harold Plantagenet Mostyn and the Hon George Edwyn Hill-Thomas.

The reconstruction was not a minute too soon; in the same issue of *The Autocar* which carried the official notice of the formation of the Daimler Motor Company (1904) Limited, the Hon C.S. Rolls – who had once been fined for infringing the Daimler patents – announced that his motor sales agency would be launching a new all-British car at the Paris Show, and that it would be known as the 'Rolls-Royce' . . .

* * *

During 1905 Daimler began investigating the possibility of building its cars in the United States and sent one of its employees, Oliver Bush – son of the autocrat of the running shed – to America, where one E.W. Sutphen, owner of a 35 hp Daimler, proposed to set up an American manufacturing company. In January 1906 Sutphen's agent in London, E.B. Koopman (who represented various American companies from offices in Great Windmill Street), suggested that Daimler might like to supply him with a free car instead of any commission due to him if such a company were formed, but his proposal was refused. Late the next month, Edward Manville met Koopman in London and proposed terms for a joint venture, which Koopman passed on to Sutphen. Percy Martin told Koopman that as the mahogany used by Daimler Motor Company was unsuitable for the American climate, Sutphen should arrange to have the bodies built in America from drawings supplied by Daimler.

Discussions gathered pace, and Manville and Koopman talked about the supply of engines and gearboxes for the USA; provisional arrangements were agreed in principle in July, but there seem to have been problems over payment. Daimler called for a minimum royalty of 5 per cent if the manufacturing company went ahead, Sutphen asked to have the payment of his deposit on his order of components for 1907 deferred for six months, and it all ended with a terse cable to Koopman the following May demanding 'the return of the car which is now in the customs house'.

Meantime, towards the end of 1905 the English Daimler Company of New York City had begun importing Coventry-built Daimlers into the United States. The firm was, it seems, part of a larger organization which also sold French CGV and Decauville cars, though virtually every mention of the English Daimler in American directories in the 1906–7 period gives a different importer's name and address – including the impressively named triumvirate Wyckoff, Church & Partridge – possibly implying that the agency was not altogether successful and that the licence was handed around rather like a game of 'pass the parcel'. The cars were exhibited at the 1906 New York and Boston Shows, but sales seem to have ended around 1907, when E.W. Sutphen – who seems to have been behind the importing agency too – was informed by Daimler that he would be sent no further cars until his draft for £2,000 was met.

Certainly the Daimler, with its flitch-plated wood chassis, was behind the times compared with its rivals on the American market, which by that time had changed to pressed steel frames, though the fact that every engine option in the Daimler range – 28/36 hp, 30/40 hp and 35/45 hp – was available in each of the three available wheelbase lengths was praised by the American press: 'A great many of the component parts are interchangeable for the nine types of chassis, which enables the company to offer a large variety of cars without sacrificing the benefits arising from standardization and concentrating work as much as possible.'

But to the Americans, standardization meant lower prices, and that was far from the case with the Daimler, which – hindered by a swingeing import duty – was significantly more expensive than its competitors, costing up to $8,600 for a fully-equipped 30/40 hp tourer. A 40/45 hp Pierce Great Arrow touring car, in comparison, was just $5,000 –

and it had a pressed-steel chassis into the bargain, while a 45 hp American Mercedes cost $7,500.

However, if the manufacturing plans foundered and Daimler did not make a great impression on the sales front, the 40/45 proved a remarkably successful competition car in the hands of racing driver Hugh N. Harding. On 26 January 1906 he won the Ten-mile Corinthian Handicap on Ormond Beach from an 80 hp Darracq driven by S.R. Stevens and a 35 hp Mercedes driven by James L. Breese, then in May competed in the inaugural Giant's Despair Hillclimb at Wilkes-Barre, Pennsylvania.

Giant's Despair was a twisting climb of just over a mile up Wilkes-Barre mountain, with a steep hairpin predictably named 'Devil's Elbow' about half-way up and gradients estimated at between 16–27 per cent which proved too steep for several of the competitors, who were watched by a crowd estimated at 20,000 despite a chilly drizzle. In the absence of the Pennsylvania State Constabulary, local miners acted as course marshals. Harding, who had driven all the way from Springfield, Massachussets (with three passengers and 400 lb of baggage) started second, after the favourite, a locally-built Matheson 60 driven by Ralph Mongini, had 'got out of order 200 yards from the finish' and plunged off the road.

The event had a 200-yard flying start; Harding made a 'bold dash' for the summit, crossing the starting line at high speed, and reached the summit in 2 min 11.2 sec, which turned out to be fastest time of the day. Harding also won the 'free-for-all' class. Other victories for Harding's Daimler that season included the Foreign Car Race at Atlantic City and the Amateur Stock Car Class of the splendidly-named Dead Horse Hill Climb at Worcester, Massachussets.

But coming events dictated that Daimler would not make a serious attempt to return to the American market for over half a century.

* * *

One of the most remarkable achievements by Daimler cars was their performance in the 1905 Herkomer Trophy, a combined touring and speed international rally held in Bavaria and named after the Bavarian-born Royal Academician Hubert von Herkomer (renowned for having painted Queen Victoria on her death bed) who had not only donated the trophy but also designed it. The Daimler team of five cars (four 35 hp and one 28 hp) represented the ACGBI and had come out from England by road fully laden and carrying 17 passengers. It was very much a works entry: Manville headed the team and drove one 35 hp and his wife Maud – 'the most expert of lady drivers' another; 'Uncle' Bush was in charge of a private owner's 35 hp.

Maud Manville's brother-in-law, the journalist H. Massac Buist (known unkindly as 'the massive beast') was one of the

Daimlers dominated the touring car classes in the 1905 Bexhill speed trials – these are some of the competing cars. [JDHT]

A 35 hp works-entered Daimler races a 28 hp at the 1905 Bexhill speed trials. [JDHT]

Weighing Ernest Instone's 30 hp Daimler before the June 1905 Broadway hill climb organized by the Midland Automobile Club. [JDHT]

passengers, and he wrote: 'From the purely spectacular point of view, the Coventry-built cars, that ran so silently and had proportionately the smallest bonnets of any machine in the competition, gave one the best idea of speed as they came swinging around the corners one after the other . . .

'The point that particularly impressed the onlookers in connection with the performances of the British team was that

Driving one of the mighty works 35 hp racers, Instone wins the Holder Cup for fastest time of the day at the 1905 Shelsley Walsh Hill Climb. [JDHT]

The 35 hp Daimlers built in 1905 were considered too powerful for amateur drivers and only four were released to private owners, including John Montagu. [JDHT]

each car carried its complement of passengers, though there was no definite rule compelling them to do so, nor did any foreign make of car take more than three . . . Suffice it, therefore, that the British team, consisting of Mr and Mrs Edward Manville, Mr Philip Dawson, and Mr Frank Rundle, with his driver, Mr Alfred Bush, on their 35 hp Daimlers, and Mr Herdman Ash on the gallant little 28 hp, continued to enhance the favourable impression on the opening day of the proceedings.

'Among the party Mr Ash's car has come to be known as the "hanger-on", because on the tour from London here, and in the 100 miles unofficial excursion made in the mountains after the hill-climb, it was impossible for the speedy 35 hp machines to lose sight of it around the bends in the rear for more than three minutes at a spell. It is a pleasure to be able to record the well-earned tribute paid unhesitatingly to the British workmanship and design, when the judges inspected the cars as to beauty and general suitability.

'They were a shorter time discussing the Coventry-built machines than any other car seen in the exhibition, and gave maximum marks for all mechanical features and for simplicity and for accessibility, while, despite the fact the cars had come from London by road in extremely dirty weather, only four marks were docked from the highest possible number awarded for the condition of the coachwork, in connection with which it should be pointed out that more than half the cars there shown had come straight from the carriage-builder to the exhibition.'

Despite the fact that he had been born in the Bavarian village of Waal, Herkomer had left Germany with his parents in 1849 at the age of two and had lived in England since 1857. His face lit up when he saw Manville's party at the official reception before the trial: 'Oh, if only you knew how honoured I feel, such a splendid band of motorists having come over here to try for my trophy, and with cars of the very make that I have always used myself,' he enthused. 'I should so like to see you win it, I should indeed!'

While the Daimlers failed to win the Herkomer Trophy, they did dominate the speed trial in the Forstenrieder Park, in which Maud Manville came first and her husband second, beating Willy Poege's 60 hp

Mercedes, a thinly-disguised racing car, into third place. Bush was fourth and Dawson fifth. Though the Trophy went to Edgar Ladenburg's Mercedes, Dr Levin Stoephling of the German Automobile Club went out of his way to praise the performance of the Daimlers, which had come so far and only been held back by tyre trouble: 'No other team's performance has surpassed that of the Coventry-built Daimlers, the speed, simplicity and regular running of which has been the subject of general remark and admiration among those who have followed the competition.'

But perhaps the finest compliment was paid by Professor Herkomer, whose drawing

Daimler used Sir Hubert Herkomer's bizarre painting 'The Future' in their 1905 advertising. [DBW]

for the cover of the menu for the closing banquet featured a Daimler limousine with a near-naked lady lashed to its radiator. 'The Future' was the enigmatic title of the painting (now in a private collection in Texas) and Daimler used it in their advertising, even though they couldn't think of a more sensible caption to this decidedly strange image other than 'the car depicted here is obviously the Daimler . . . because it is the representative British car . . . because of its strength, its simplicity, its scientific construction, its effective transmission of power and the interchangeability of its parts'.

But the company must nevertheless have been taken with Herkomer's work, for when Sir Edward Jenkinson announced that he would be retiring from Daimler on 1 June 1906, the board decided to have his portrait painted by Herkomer 'to be hanged in the boardroom'. The astute Herkomer, who had known abject poverty while he was a student in the 1860s (and even played zither with the Christy Minstrels to pay his way) agreed, but set his fee high: he demanded a new long-wheelbase TJ 35 hp car worth £1,000 in exchange for the portrait.

* * *

'I seem to hear time and again in dreams the gradually increasing clatter of boots on the pavement which started every weekday at 5.30 am outside my bedroom window as I got up, and which grew to a steady roar just before I joined in. It was the men going to work at the Daimler,' recalled Sidney Charles Houghton Davis – known universally as 'Sammy' – who joined the company as an apprentice in 1906.

Though Sammy Davis was to become the most distinguished motoring journalist of the heroic age of motoring and a highly successful racing driver, in those days he was just a teenage enthusiast who wanted to gain experience of his beloved motor vehicles by working with 'the greatest of all British firms manufacturing cars at that time [when] the spirit that started the motor industry – in fact, through the Daimler Motor Company – was an overriding enthusiasm for motoring, an absolute conviction that cars had come to stay'.

At 'the Daimler', Sammy's circle of friends included a plump and dreamy young staff artist named Freddy Gordon Crosby who enlivened his daily routine in the Daimler drawing office as a 'draughtsworm' by making dramatic little thumb-nail sketches of motor cars: the two would eventually work together on *The Autocar* where the talented Crosby achieved fame as one of the finest motoring artists of all time.

The company which Davis joined was a very different concern from the ailing giant of a couple of years earlier; at the end of 1905 Sir Edward Jenkinson had told the first annual meeting of the new Daimler company that the net profit for 1904–5 had been £83,167, compared with £7,334 a year earlier. Martin's share in this success was recognized by the award of a colossal bonus of £3,400, while Instone received £1,747; an additional £2,267 was shared out between 15 members of the works staff.

Public confidence in Daimler had been restored at a crucial time, for investors were more likely to look kindly on such a well-established business than the heavily-capitalized new companies which were coming to market at that time in a manner which, said the new trade magazine *Motor Trader*, 'out-Hooleyed Hooley'; even so well-connected a company as Rolls-Royce was regarded with suspicion by those whose fingers had been burned by the now-discredited Lawson-Hooley organization. Daimler, by contrast, was able to raise £81,000 in preference shares, more than £100,000 in debentures and £137,000 in ordinary shares in the six years following its reconstruction at a time when many of the other Coventry-based car makers were seriously undercapitalized, and actually paid 10 per cent dividend on its ordinary and almost 14 per cent on the preference shares, a dramatic contrast with the previous situation.

The Company set the broad outlines of its next season's production by mid-year, and planning for 1906 was completed by November 1905 – a far cry from today's 'product planning cycle' in which it can take upwards of four years for a new car to come to market – when Martin was authorized to lay down 50 more TJ 28 hp and 50 TJ 30 hp cars (at this period, the codes 'TH' and 'TJ' signified normal and long wheelbase models) to bring the total planned to 420; shortly afterwards a further 230 were added. The allocation of these gives some idea of the relative popularity of the various models at the time: 15 TH30 (7,247 cc), 15 TH35 (8,462 cc), 75 TJ28 (6,787 cc), 110 TJ30 and 15 TJ35. An extra 60 cars – 15 each of the TH and TJ 28 and TH and TJ 30 hp models – were added in April.

At that meeting, the board also approved the 'design and construction of a car with a 50 hp engine such as can be handled in exactly the same way as the 35 hp car was handled in 1905'. At 10.6 litres, this was to be the biggest private car ever built by Daimler, and its selling price to 'a few selected customers' was a surprisingly modest £800. This additional model, the 45 hp, represented a considerable change in policy for Daimler, for it had a pressed steel chassis instead of the old armoured wood pattern, a monobloc cylinder casting (all the previous fours had the engines cast in two blocks of two) and roller-bearing crankshaft. It featured Daimler's ingenious combined throttle and ignition control in the centre of the steering wheel, which was supposed to be more sensitive than the new-fangled foot throttle. The gearbox had been redesigned, and had three speeds; most importantly, reverse was now engaged by the same lever as the forward gears instead of the old arrangement with a separate lever.

'It is probably the finest vehicle that has ever been turned out from the Daimler works,' enthused *The Autocar* (though ex-Daimler apprentice 'Sammy' Davis recalled 40 years later that 'magnificent though it was

Rare and powerful, the 45-hp Daimler was one of the fastest British cars of its day; Undecimus Stratton supplied this one to his friend the Sultan of Johore in 1906. [DS]

John Montagu, who had succeeded his father as Lord Montagu of Beaulieu in November 1905, drove the fastest of the works-prepared 45 hp Daimlers in the 1906 Herkomer Trophy. [NMM]

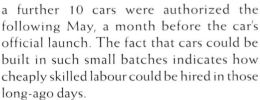

when travelling, that enormous machine could only be started if somebody of Sandow's power was available at the starting handle'). There were probably 10 customers for the initial batch (including John Montagu) and advance interest was such that

a further 10 cars were authorized the following May, a month before the car's official launch. The fact that cars could be built in such small batches indicates how cheaply skilled labour could be hired in those long-ago days.

Nine of the first batch of 45 hp Daimlers ran in the 1906 Herkomer Trophy, but stood no chance against Continental gamesmanship – including the entry of a 'faked 90 hp Mercedes racer' by that marque's Viennese agent – which was so blatant that the Kaiser's brother, Prince Henry of Prussia, apologized to Maud Manville: 'I have been struck by the consideration with which all the English competitors have been handling their machines throughout, and my only regret is that I am unable to say the same concerning the majority of the others who are figuring in these runs. I exceedingly regret the scorching that has been taking place and have heard many complaints about it.'

Though one of the 45s had finished tenth and Maud Manville had finished eleventh, her husband was not impressed by the way his Continental rivals had bent the rules: 'We shall not compete again. Once bitten, twice shy.' John Montagu, driving the fastest of the

45 hp Daimlers, was certainly not 'scorching': after crossing the starting line each day, he drove back to his hotel for breakfast, picked up his luggage, 'then pursued the road in peace and quietness'. It was, after all, supposed to be a touring event for amateur drivers . . .

The financial crisis had not affected Daimler's status as the Royal car (although King Edward also had a couple of Mercedes and a Renault in the Royal Mews) and in September 1905 the King had ordered his seventh new Daimler, on the new 35/50 hp chassis – which had shown itself to be a stunning performer in the July Blackpool speed trials – to replace his previous 28 hp car, which had proved to be underpowered with the heavy limousine body. By now he had his own 'in-house' motor expert, C.W. Stamper, recruited from the Lacre Motor Car Company (which had recently supplied Queen Alexandra with a Wolseley car) by Undecimus Stratton of Daimler. Stamper helped to train the new royal chauffeurs seconded from the Metropolitan Police; he acted as intermediary between the Royal Mews and Stratton, who had up to then personally trained the royal chauffeurs.

The body for this latest Royal car was built by Daimler's own coachwork department, which bodied most of the cars sold by the company (most other luxury car companies merely supplied bare chassis to outside coachbuilders) and in March 1906 Daimler consolidated this stylistic lead by appointing Ferdinand Charles head of its coachbuilding department. Charles, formerly with Rothschild of Paris and an accomplished fine artist famed for his mezzotint engravings, was at that time probably the world's most fashionable body designer, for in 1902 he had created an elegant body-style for the powerful new Panhard & Levassor of King Leopold of the Belgians. Charles had patterned its curvaceous seats on the pretty easy chairs in the apartment of Cléo de Merode, the King's *amie intime*, where his interview with the fabulously wealthy monarch (he had paid for the Belgian Congo out of his own pocket) took place, and the 'Roi des Belges' body style was copied all round the world.

At Daimler, Charles was in charge of an elite group of craftsmen, 'true to traditions handed down to them through the old Coachmakers' Guilds'. As one of that group recalled 50 years later: 'Many considered the Daimler as the first in its class. Some might consider the Rolls-Royce superior, but it was not a finished product as a factory unit. While Rolls made the complete chassis, the bodies were built and fitted by some outside firm of coachbuilders. Therefore the Daimler held a rare place in the market, and was esteemed

The young Lord Howard de Walden – nephew of Evelyn Ellis – prepared two 40 ft Daimler-powered motor boats for the 1906 International Cup Race in Southampton Water. Powered by three 90 hp Daimler engines mounted in arrow-head formation, Daimler II came third in the eliminating trials but failed to start in the race itself, which was won by John Montagu's Yarrow-Napier. The next year it raced at Monaco with the similar Daimler III. [JDHT]

alike by kings and commoners.

'The Daimler bodybuilder was a gentleman mechanic. In those days you would see him turning up to work dressed in a cutaway coat and striped trousers, with spats, silk topper and kid gloves, which he put away carefully in his cupboard before donning his apron. As overwhelming orders began to pour in, they worked extra long hours, from six in the morning until nine-thirty at night, weekends often included – and woe betide the sluggard who arrived late for work. But no bond could stem the demand for Daimlers, and the Honourable Society of Coachmakers had to consider admitting men of other crafts to help with the production of cars. Wheelwrights were accepted as belonging to an allied trade, then came an influx of railway carriage builders, cabinet-makers, makers of golf clubs, tennis racquets and suchlike.

'But the idea of engaging ordinary carpenters seemed to debase the entire coachmaking tradition. On one well-remembered occasion every man in the workshop sat upon the benches from 10 am to late afternoon because carpenters were engaged by the company . . .'

* * *

There were teething troubles with the new Royal car, shown unfinished at the November Olympia Motor Exhibition and delivered to the King at Sandringham in time for Christmas 1905, and Stamper seems to have ruffled a few feathers at Coventry with his criticisms. The King's car had been returned to Coventry for attention in early January 1906, and the Crown Equerry, Sir Henry Ewart, wrote to Percy Martin enclosing a letter he had received from Stamper complaining about bodywork details and problems with the steering and engine. Daimler countered by suggesting that the way to ensure that such problems did not arise was to appoint a Daimler employee to have entire charge of the 35 hp and that anyway the Royal Mews were running it on

the wrong fuel: 'Carburine or Carless Capel oil should be used – Pratts Motor Spirit is not suitable'. A Daimler mechanic was despatched to Windsor to work on the car; whether the Royal Mews heeded the advice on its choice of petrol is unrecorded.

The Daimler car was also finding its way into other Royal stables. In 1906 the Lacre Company shipped a 28 hp Roi-des-Belges tourer to the King of Siam in a tin-lined wood crate that was so substantial that it had to be built up round the car in the street 'by permission of the police'. Just imagine trying that in central London nowadays! Undecimus Stratton was also a prime mover in supplying Daimlers to the young King Alfonso XIII of Spain (for which he was appointed a Chevalier of the Royal Order of Isabella the Catholic) and to Kaiser Wilhelm of Germany. He supervised the Kaiser's fleet of Daimlers when the All-Highest was a guest staying at Highcliffe Castle, near Christchurch, Dorset, in 1907. Consequently, Daimler was awarded the German Royal Warrant early in 1908, as 'Motor Car Manufacturer to the Court of Prussia'; the Spanish Royal Appointment followed soon after.

With its finances now increasingly healthy, Daimler set about an ambitious programme of plant extension, including the construction of new machine and erecting shops and the refurbishment of the old Motor Mills building. The programme involved the purchase of some 28 acres of additional land from a local charity and, remarked Manville to the 230 guests – who ranged from the newly-elected Liberal MP for Coventry A.E.W. Mason (better known as the author of that splendid adventure yarn *The Four Feathers*) to industry rivals like S.F. Edge of Napier – attending the opening of the new extensions at the beginning of May 1906: 'The area occupied by the works three years ago is exactly one-third of that occupied today by buildings which have been erected during the past two years.'

A further £30,000 was invested during

In December 1907 Kaiser Wilhelm II (left) took a rest cure at Highcliffe Castle in Dorset, where Undecimus Stratton arranged a fleet of four Daimler landaulettes to take the Imperial party around the New Forest: in gratitude, the Kaiser gave Stratton a gold scarf pin with the initial 'W' inset in diamonds. [DS]

1907 in buying into the Coventry Chain Company, run by Martin's friend Alick Hill; this enabled Coventry Chain to build a new factory at Spon End and gave Daimler the right to appoint two board members. This move ensured not only steady access to a source of driving chains – like most powerful cars of the period, Daimlers relied on chain final drive – but a guaranteed supply of nuts and bolts of consistently high quality. This would prove to be the more lasting benefit; the dictates of fashion meant that by the end of 1908 Daimler had abandoned chain drive entirely.

Daimler's status as one of Britain's leading makers was emphasized by the appointment of Edward Manville as the president of the Society of Motor Manufacturers & Traders in June 1907; though it had been founded only five years earlier – by Frederick Simms, whose Simms Manufacturing Company was now making high-tension magnetos and trying to break into the luxury car market with a car called the Simms-Welbeck, chiefly notable for the use of pneumatic bumpers – the SMMT had become the unchallenged voice of the motor industry, and its

presidency was far from being a sinecure.

The Daimler company had established its own laboratory for testing bought-in parts as early as 1902, and in many cases had come to the conclusion that it was more reliable to make its own components; from 1906, the Daimler laboratory was run by Mr Picking, and under his supervision pioneered such now-commonplace techniques as microphotography of the crystalline structure of metal and testing components to destruction.

Underlining this reputation for technical excellence was the establishment in 1908 of an engineering scholarship scheme which led the industry and offered one major and five minor scholarships, which lasted for two years and were the practical equivalent of a university course. Successful candidates received cash grants and the guarantee of employment 'at a salary of not less than £150 per annum' at the end of their course, which guaranteed the company an intake of highly-qualified young engineers. It was a remarkable proof of the value of the scheme that the first winner of a major scholarship, Joseph Aloysius Mackle of Liverpool, was to play a major role in the Daimler story.

Daimler was also investigating new markets and products, and by the end of 1907 could report agencies in such far-flung markets as India, Australia, China, Canada, British Columbia, the Straits Settlements and Spain. The company also announced in December 1907 that it was 'inaugurating a hire department on modern and novel lines . . . Only first-class motor carriages of the latest pattern, indistinguishable from a modern carriage, are supplied. Drivers are in smart uniforms.'

At the end of 1905, the company had held a two-month trial of two petrol-powered railcars on the London, Brighton & South Coast Railway, which proved so satisfactory that the company proposed to build a single 100 hp engine for railway coaches instead of the twin-engine arrangement on the experimental coaches. Design and construction of this 100 hp railway coach began at the end of January and Daimler declared that it was ready to take orders; but none, apparently was forthcoming. Nevertheless, this experience with oversize power units was to prove invaluable to the

company, which was expanding into the manufacture of commercial vehicles. Recalled Sammy Davis: 'We built fire engines, a cab with front wheel drive, all sorts of oddities including a farm tractor steered by chains, steam-roller fashion.'

In April 1906 the company acquired the UK rights to make road/rail vehicles using the system of the SA Auto-Mixte, a Belgian company based in Herstal producing petrol-electric vehicles devised by Henri Pieper, in which the engine was linked to a dynamo, which charged a bank of accumulators during normal running but then became an electric motor for starting and hill-climbing. Daimler agreed to pay a royalty of £20 per Auto-Mixte chassis it sold with an engine of over 20 hp (and £10 a chassis under 20 hp), optimistically guaranteeing a minimum payment of £10,000 by 1 January 1908.

The Auto-Mixte transmission, it seems, was temperamental: an Auto-Mixte omnibus ran into the wall of the finishing shop in November 1907 and knocked part of it down, damaging two cars. In January 1908, Percy Martin was authorized to pay a deposit of £2,000 to M Pescatore, general manager of

The testing department at the Daimler works, circa 1908. [DBW]

Auto-Mixte, on an order for thirteen omnibuses; in consideration of placing of this order, Daimler also paid £5,000 royalties to Auto-Mixte. It looked like a one-way traffic and the venture doesn't seem to have been over-profitable, though a Daimler Auto-Mixte bus built for the Gearless Motor Omnibus Company of London was shown at the 1908 Olympia Commercial Vehicle Exhibition.

The final appearance of the Pieper transmission seems to have been on the 1910 KPL (Knight-Pieper-Lanchester), the first bus (and, indeed, the first motor vehicle) to use full all-steel monocoque construction with no separate chassis. It also had four-wheel brakes and two separate 12 hp engines, one driving each rear wheel through a separate petrol-electric drive and Lanchester worm gearing. It was a bold project, but only a few prototypes were built.

Another unorthodox commercial developed by Daimler was the Renard Road Train, a sesquipedalian device with a tractor unit powering the centre axle of multiple six-wheeled steerable trailers through a series of cardan shafts from a power take-off behind the rear axle. Originally invented by French airship pioneer Colonel Renard, the Road Train was first seen on the Darracq stand at the 1903 Paris Salon, but the good Colonel had gone where he had no need of flying machines by the time the Road Train found its way to England, in 1907. Percy Martin, by now a board member and managing director, agreed to put £2,500 into the Renard Road Train Syndicate, 'conditional on agreement to manufacture'. He subsequently picked up the Italian rights as well by taking over the contract held by one Mme Tzikos for an Italian motor transport scheme, though Daimler had to take her to court when her promissory notes amounting to a total of £1,500 bounced.

Daimler got a £300 'first and final' dividend out of this joint venture, and actually built and sold a few Road Trains, mostly powered by a monstrous 16.1-litre engine that seems to have been an enlarged version of the 45 hp. Daimler used one to carry components between Birmingham and Coventry and claimed it only cost half as much as rail freight. Lord Kitchener of Khartoum ordered a Road Train for service in Egypt, and sales were made in Europe, North and South America, India and Australia, where a derelict Road Train, once used by the Union Copper Company of South Australia to carry ore

An early Daimler-Renard Road Train which carried visitors around the 1908 Franco-British Exhibition at the White City. [NMM]

The 1905 shaft-driven experimental 3,308 cc Daimler built for (but not entered in) the Isle of Man Tourist Trophy race. [DBW]

from the Yudnamutna Copper Mines 80 miles to the nearest rail head, was found in the early 1970s in the ghost town of Farina and rescued, along with its powered trailers, for preservation. This particular Renard Train was run intermittently until the Second World War, but gave trouble crossing irregular ground, when the central driving wheels were lifted up by the outer wheels and lost traction. Another minor drawback was a fuel consumption of one gallon per mile . . .

Sammy Davis worked on the Daimler-Renard train, which he thought was 'an appalling machine . . . The theory that the trucks would follow accurately in the path of the tractor proved altogether wrong, the rear truck taking short-cuts which endangered such houses as occupied the peak of the corner . . . Certainly the thing progressed, but the row as the [universal] joints went over to fantastic angles had to be heard to be believed . . . Anyway, we swore that you could hear that train going along St Nicholas Street to the London Road while down a pit in the erecting shop.'

* * *

During 1905 Daimler had built a couple of experimental 3,308 cc cars, one shaft-driven, the other chain-driven, with a view to entering them in the Tourist Trophy race in the Isle of Man. They were curiously snub-nosed vehicles, with low-set radiators and

coal-scuttle bonnets, the idea being to eliminate the fan belt by mounting the cooling fan directly on the end of the crankshaft; but the disadvantages of the layout proved too great. Having built the cars, Daimler decided that they were not powerful enough for the TT, so they were used instead as experimental hacks by the design office over a four-year period before being sold to private owners.

Extended running tests showed that the chain-driven version was faster (but noisier and thirstier), but the gear-driven model was more efficient overall, so Daimler produced a batch of the shaft-driven design in early 1907 under the designation 17/21 hp. They had conventional radiators, but broke with precedent by having a all-indirect four-speed gearbox which was claimed to be 'practically noiseless', and were essentially a long-wheelbase version of the 1905 TT racer. Just 25 of this 17/21 hp chassis were built and, said *The Autocar*, 'it may not be out of place while discussing this little-known but much-prized pattern to say that its estimation among Daimler owners is that of a rare edition among book owners.' However, a board minute also records that Percy Martin 'reported regarding the disposal of the 17/21 hp cars now being completed and it was resolved that they should be sold with discretion'.

The shaft drive had proved a mixed blessing: Sammy Davis recalled in 1965 that 'the universal joints worked at such a wide angle that they lasted about a month!' However, that series of 25 had been the pilot run for a new cooperative venture which Daimler began discussing with Neapolitan company promotor Roberto de Sanna in November 1905. De Sanna proposed that Daimler cars should be built under licence by a prominent Italian engineering company, Carmine de Luca of Naples.

Founded in the mid-1800s, by the turn of the century De Luca had become one of the leading companies in Naples, with a 650,000 sq ft (60,000 m²) factory in the Via Arenaccia

In April 1906 King Edward VII visited Naples aboard the Royal yacht Victoria & Albert and went by 35 hp Daimler to see the eruption of Vesuvius: it may have been no coincidence that Percy Martin of Daimler was in Naples at the same time to sign the contract establishing the De Luca Daimler joint venture. [JDHT]

with its own foundry and a workforce of around 800, specializing in the manufacture of Schneider torpedoes and launching tubes. The four sons of the company founder – Vincenzo, Salvatore, Guiseppe and Raffaele De Luca – decided to diversify into automobile manufacture and in April 1906 De Luca Daimler SA was established with a capital of Lire 2,250,000 to build Daimlers under licence. Percy Martin, who had conducted the negotiations personally, went down to Naples to sign the agreements and

In 1907 Daimler sold three 30 hp racing cars to De Luca, who entered them in the 1907 Targa Florio; this car was driven by the French ace Victor Hemery. [JDHT]

the Coventry company contracted to take a fixed number of De Luca chassis from the Neapolitan company. One reason why Daimler was so keen to establish a foothold in the Italian market was almost certainly that its great rival Napier was simultaneously setting up an Italian joint venture with the San Giorgio company to manufacture six-cylinder cars of between 5 and 8 litres in Genoa.

Three Coventry-built 30 hp racing cars were sold to De Luca for £400 each and entered in the 1907 Targa Florio without notable success, driven by Daimler employee George Ison and French drivers Le Blon and Hemery. Riding on the back of one of the racers during practice, Swiss-born F.J. Rueger, 'a member of the Daimler staff and an exceptionally accomplished linguist', who had gone down to Sicily with Ison, was thrown out of the car and killed, so the directors subscribed 100 guineas for education of his infant son Karl at 'some suitable institution . . . when he is old enough to go there', and paid his salary to his widow for six months after his death.

The De Luca company exhibited at the Turin and Milan Shows, but though a four-car

In his short reign, King Edward VII owned ten Daimlers: this one would seem to be a 35 hp of 9.2 litres; the Prince of Wales owned a very similar car. [JDHT]

range – 3,308 cc 16/24 hp, 6,786 cc 28/40 hp, 7,964 cc 32/55 hp and 10,604 cc 42/65 hp – was offered, probably only the 16/24 hp (ex-17/21 hp) was actually made in Naples. Certainly three 45 hp cars were sold 'at a special price' of £750–£800 to the Italian company by Coventry, which refused its consent to De Luca building 30 hp cars 'whilst this company is making them'. De Luca also introduced an 'Auto-Mista' petrol-electric using the Pieper system in 1908.

Apart from the shaft drive, the 3,308 cc De Luca differed from its English prototype in having a pressed-steel channel frame instead of armoured wood and hub caps which only bore the name 'De Luca'; Coventry began importing De Luca chassis in the Spring of 1908 and fitting them with in-house bodywork as a lower-priced running-mate to its own productions (chassis price was £447 against £495 for the British-built 30 hp). Two of them were entered in the 2,000 Miles' Trial in June 1908 and one came second in its class behind the redoubtable 12/16 hp Vauxhall; the other – which had snapped a dumb-iron *en route* – still managed to finish sixth (and last) in class, no mean achievement in a real machine-breaker of an event.

At the November 1908 Olympia Motor Show, three De Luca-Daimlers were displayed, two conventional 20 hp cars 'of the 1908 type' and a 'highly-finished plated chassis, showing the 22 hp pattern, which is introduced for 1909'; it was powered by Daimler's new slide valve engine, which implied that relations between the two companies were still flourishing. But the following year the English Daimler company suspended the order for De Luca chassis, forcing the Italian company to rely entirely on home market orders. Consequently, the Neapolitan factory gradually wound down car manufacture, which ceased in 1910. The San Giorgio Napier had gone out of production a year earlier.

* * *

Apart from that unsuccessful attempt on the

King Edward took delivery of this 35 hp landaulette in 1907 and used it when he stayed with Lord Saville at Rufford Abbey during the Doncaster race meeting. [MBRT]

Targa Florio, the highlight of Daimler's international racing career came in 1907 when a team of cars was built for the Kaiserpreis race, an event whose trophy had been presented by Kaiser Wilhelm II of Germany in order to promote 'medium-powered cars' (by which the All-Highest meant cars of under 8 litres which were nominally touring models).

Daimler's attitude to the race was probably typical, for while the rules of the event were framed in such a way as to eliminate out-and-out racing cars, they did not prevent manufacturers from building cars specifically for this event, so that few of the competing cars – and there were plenty of those, for the organizing Imperial Automobile Club only limited entries to three cars per manufacturer, with no upper limit on the total number from all makers combined – bore much resemblance to normal production models.

Recalled Sammy Davis: 'It was the [Kaiserpreis] racing cars which were the highlight of our existence, the whole atmosphere of the works changing when news of their design leaked through. My instructor in the gang of fitters actually swore off drink to ensure that our "gang" would have

one of these chassis to build. Never was more care lavished on any cars Daimler had built to date, not even on the cars for the Herkomer Trophy . . . These Daimlers were limited to an engine capacity of eight litres, were low-built two-seaters with no body at all to speak of, a huge fuel tank behind the light seats and chain final drive. Since the four-cylinder engines were revving faster than ever before but still had splash lubrication for the big-ends, the mechanic was given two glass bowl drip feed lubricators which he could control personally.'

With a free choice on engine dimensions, it's revealing that the Daimler designers went for a considerably over-square bore/stroke ratio for the Kaiserpreis cars, whose 150x112 mm configuration (giving a swept volume of 7,917 cc) had no counterpart in production, where engines tended to be long-stroke units or, in the exceptional case of the 1907 45 hp, had identical bore and stroke measurements (150x150 mm, giving 10,603 cc).

Given the enthusiasm with which the Daimler racers had been built, it's sad to report that they failed to distinguish themselves in the event itself. The actual race was preceded by two eliminating races which

The low-slung Kaiserpreis racing cars were built with care, but proved no match for their Continental opponents. [NMM]

Kaiser's Cup. 1907
Daimler.

cut the vast entry list down from 80 to 40 cars which would run in the final; unfortunately, two of those eliminated turned out to be Daimlers. Lubrication and clutch troubles plagued the Coventry cars, which 'as a desperate remedy' had been fitted with long levers with which the mechanics could apply extra pressure to the huge cone clutches (which slipped at the slightest pretext). The only Daimler to make the final was driven by George Ison, a 'brusque he-man', and he only lasted for one lap of the 73-mile Homburg circuit before engine troubles put him out of the running. *The Autocar* explained this disappointing result by remarking that 'the Latin temperament is better suited to

Stripped of its bodywork, A.H. Moreing's 38 hp Daimler 'Billy' finished third in the August Trophy race at Brooklands on August Bank Holiday 1908. [NMM]

automobile racing than the slower moving and thinking Anglo-Saxon . . . presuming that the Daimler Company . . . were to turn out a racing car or cars capable of holding their own with the best, it would be necessary to give men who would steer them as much practice as is enjoyed by [the Italian drivers] Nazzaro and Lancia'.

Instone won a purse of 500 golden sovereigns driving this 10.6-litre Daimler at the very first Brooklands race meeting in July 1907. [JDHT]

The height of elegance: a 1908 30 hp limousine with Daimler coachwork. [JDHT]

Ernest Instone and friends followed in the wake of the South-Bound Car by taking this 45 hp tourer to Madrid in 1908. [JDHT]

* * *

Ernest Instone had an excellent eye for publicity. In 1907 he put up a hundred road signs bearing the name 'Daimler' in the Coventry area. He wrote articles extolling the virtues of the Daimler, 'the motor triumph of the Edwardian era'. When the new Brooklands race-track opened in Surrey, Instone persuaded the Daimler company to rent a garage at £40 a year to house its racing cars (and won a purse of 500 golden sovereigns at the wheel of a 10.6-litre Daimler in the Gottlieb Daimler Memorial Plate race at the very first meeting in July 1907). And when Percy Northey – who had come second in the 1905 Tourist Trophy driving a Rolls-Royce – asked for the loan of a car for a tour of Spain with his friends, the writer O.J. Llewellyn and the Punch artist L. Raven-Hill, Instone agreed on condition that 'Mr Percy Northey and his friends give the company as much publicity as possible in connection with the trip'.

Northey and Llewellyn (who wrote the 'Owen John' column in The Autocar) responded magnificently; not only was an account of their journey published in Motoring Illustrated but Llewellyn produced a splendid book entitled The South-Bound Car, largely illustrated with drawings by Raven-Hill. The car, a 30 hp tourer, behaved magnificently by all accounts, and The South-Bound Car, quite apart from being one of the best early motoring travel books, was a splendid advertisement for the Daimler car, which had successfully travelled where no car had gone before. 'We used to get out and look at the Daimler sometimes and threaten to get her canonised,' wrote Llewellyn, 'for her behaviour was simply marvellous. By every right of rhyme and reason . . . she should have given up the ghost somehow or somewhere long before. But she did not and . . . on her last day put in almost the fastest work of the whole course. She was English and she looked it, and she behaved in the English manner which is so annoying to others.'

Chapter 4

SILENT KNIGHT, WHOLLY KNIGHT . . .

One of the strangest publicity campaigns ever carried out by a leading motor company must have been the publication by Daimler in February 1909 of a little booklet entitled 'Some Letters of Appreciation'. Every page was headed with a glowing quote taken from a letter reproduced beneath it in facsimile: 'for its quietness and smooth running it has no equal', 'perfect satisfaction in every way', '15,000 miles without the least bit of trouble' were typical examples. But the curious thing was that most of the testimonials in the little book had been written by owners of another make on another continent. A make, moreover, that had gone out of production over a year earlier.

But there was a strong and logical rationale behind the booklet, for Daimler had just taken a huge commercial gamble by adopting a totally novel power unit, rejoicing in the suspiciously fey name of 'Silent Knight', and the only group of owners with substantial experience of operating the new machine was a handful of motorists in the United States who had bought one of the few Silent Knight cars that had actually reached the public. 'In this booklet,' said Daimler, 'will be found testimonials from some very well-known people in the United States which will, it is hoped, help to dispel the idea that the Knight Motor was in an experimental stage when adopted by the Daimler Motor Co.'

Ever since Gottlieb Daimler and Carl Benz first got their prototypes running with simple power units derived from gas engine practice, manufacturers have been looking for the miracle engine that will free them from the nineteenth-century Daimler-Benz legacy that is still evident in today's highly evolved power units. Mostly they spend large sums of money on a prototype programme, make grandiose and premature announcements of the engine's capabilities and lapse into silence again when further use brings unforeseen problems to light. Ford's recent flirtation with the Orbital two-stroke engine was only the latest in a long line of high-profile dalliances with alternative power units that failed to make the grade. Remember the Stirling 'hot-air' engine that the Dutch Philips group trumpeted so loudly in the 1970s and which vanished on its own thermals like a dream? Or the Wankel rotary which was all set to sweep away the reciprocating engine in the 1960s yet which only survives in a limited – and highly specialized – range from Mazda?

In dramatic contrast to this long litany of unfulfilled expectation, Daimler made the idiosyncratic Silent Knight – paradoxically, a 'valveless' engine that was nearly all valve – a viable proposition that powered some of the finest luxury cars of their day for a quarter of a century. And, indeed, changed the face of warfare too.

Remarkably, the man behind the Silent

Knight engine had no formal training as an engineer (which is probably why he persisted with it so long). Charles Yale Knight, born in Salem, Indiana, in 1868, was a journalist and printer who, after working for the *Minneapolis Tribune*, moved to Chicago and founded the magazine *Dairy Produce* in 1894, campaigning against the fraudulent sale of yellow-dyed margarine as butter. So that he could travel to the mid-west farms that provided his editorial copy, during 1901 Knight bought the fifteenth 'Waterless' Knox to be built, but found the air-cooled engine of this high-set three-wheeler distressingly noisy. A couple of years later he bought a Searchmont automobile – a Lee Sherman Chadwick-designed twin-cylinder – at a knockdown price after the failure of the Philadelphia-based company, and found it prone to valve spring breakages. This combination of events led Knight to start a quest for a silent, trouble-free valve gear – and he recalled repairing the slide valve mechanism of the steam engine that had operated his father's saw-mill back home in Indiana.

Slide valves had been outmoded by the adoption of the poppet valve for petrol engines, not least because the mushroom-shaped poppet valve was ideally suited to the early system of automatic inlet valves that just snapped open against the suction of the descending piston to admit the explosive mixture of fuel and air without the complexity of a mechanical operating system. After reading 'practically all the technical works printed in the English language treating the subject of internal combustion engines', as well as all the valid patents available in the Washington Patent Office, Knight decided that a modified slide valve system positively opening and closing ports cut in the cylinder wall at precise points in the four-stroke cycle of 'suck-squeeze-bang-blow' was what he was looking for in his search for silence and reliability. Financed by a Chicago merchant named Lyman Bernard Kilbourne, he began experiments with slide valve engines, patenting each step along the way.

By 1904 he had devised an engine in which the piston was surrounded by double concentric sleeves whose rise and fall was

Charles Yale Knight at the wheel of a 'Silent Knight'-engined Daimler touring car. [JDHT]

controlled by a subsidiary crankshaft; slots cut in the walls of these sleeves coincided with the inlet and exhaust ports in the cylinder walls and the top of the cylinder was sealed by a separate cylinder head which – without the need to accommodate poppet valves – could have an uninterrupted hemispherical combustion chamber with the spark plug at its apex, a near-ideal configuration. Knight later dished the piston top to give a near-spherical chamber for even smoother burning of the gas/air mixture. Since all the moving parts slid on a film of lubricant and there were no 'impact members' like the tappets and valve stems of a conventional engine, the result was great mechanical silence.

Port timing was positively controlled: this was probably the first 'desmodromic' power unit, though the advantages of this were not fully understood until Delage and later Mercedes-Benz used desmodromically-controlled poppet valves on their racing cars.

Anyway, the weight of Knight's double reciprocating sleeves precluded dramatically high engine speeds.

Knight's first double sleeve-valve engine was finished in October 1904; it was a 2,523 cc four-cylinder unit and was installed in 'a Panhard-type car' – actually his Type VI Searchmont – which Knight drove some 4,000 miles that winter. The following spring, the prototype 35/40 hp Silent Knight car, with an enlarged, 3,707 cc version of that original engine, was on the road, and Kilbourne ('not a car driver and not an admirer of the motor car') covered some 15,000 miles on it that year without any problems from the power unit.

From the start, Knight's aim was to sell licences for the production and use of his 'valveless' engine to established car companies, but both he and Kilbourne realized that it had little market value until it had been thoroughly proved in the hands of the public. So they set up a factory in

Knight demonstrates the inner mysteries of his sleeve-valve engine to a party of visitors.
[NMM]

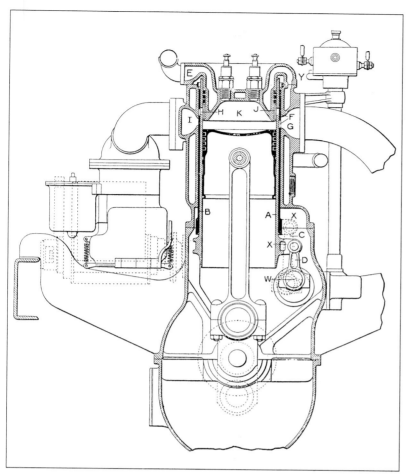

Inside the Knight engine: (A) inner sleeve; (B) outer sleeve; (C) link controlling inner sleeve; (D) link controlling outer sleeve; (F) slots for exhaust; (G) exhaust port; (H) slots for intake; (I) intake port; (K) separate cylinder head; (J) wide 'junk' rings sealing intake and exhaust slots; (W) half-speed crankshaft controlling sleeves; (X) lugs for control links; (Y) ignition distributor (note twin spark plugs). [DBW]

completed later. They were high-priced at $3,500 (£719) but sold without any high-powered advertising campaign, largely, it seems through people being impressed by seeing them on the streets 'invariably quiet and smooth, running along like rubber balls'.

But no American manufacturer seemed interested in taking up the licence: a general sales boom in the United States meant that American manufacturers could sell all the poppet-valve cars they could make without wasting time fitting a new type of engine that might give trouble. And then, recalled Knight in a celebrated lecture at the Royal Automobile Club in Pall Mall in October 1908, 'a friend of mine, who was familiar with what we were doing in America, chanced to be associated with Mr Manville, chairman of the Daimler Board, in a business transaction in London'. This mysterious friend told Manville about the Silent Knight engine, and found him unusually receptive, for Daimler were feeling threatened, particularly by Napier, which had gained considerable kudos with its launch of the first successful production six-cylinder car in 1903 and was now a strong contender for the luxury trade.

Based in new works at Acton since 1903, Napier copied Daimler in publishing lists of noble customers and using a slogan that would subsequently be used by another up-and-coming luxury car: 'The Best Car in the World'. Despite certain technical deficiencies – the six-cylinder engine had a severe natural vibration period which the ever-ingenious S.F. Edge attempted to sanitize under the name of 'power rattle' – the Napier was certainly trespassing on what Daimler had regarded as its own rather exclusive territory and could now even boast a Royal client: Arthur, Duke of Connaught, brother of the King. And then the Rolls-Royce company, though only a couple of years old, had just staked its own claim to the luxury market with its new 40/50 hp, the famous 'Silver Ghost' line.

Manville wrote to Chicago for details of the Silent Knight engine, but was only sent a

Chicago late in 1905 and publicly launched the Silent Knight car at the Chicago Automobile Show early in 1906. Following their 'softly, softly' approach, 1906 production was restricted to seven cars – a demonstrator plus six to be sold, minimizing the risks of bad publicity arising from mechanical problems.

Even this cautious policy got off to a shaky start when a Silent Knight car entered for the 1906 Glidden Trophy tour fell out on the first day, nor did Knight's proposed royalty of $100 per engine attract prospective manufacturing licensees. Nevertheless, the cars in private hands proved a 'mechanical success', and parts were laid down for the production of 50 cars, 38 of which were built during 1907 using chassis and transmissions supplied by Garford (also responsible for the first petrol-driven Studebakers) and the rest catalogue ('We were very busy at the time,' Knight later apologized.) Despite this rather half-hearted response, Manville wrote again, this time requesting Knight to send a sample engine that could be tested at Coventry. By now, 'our mutual friend' (was this perhaps E.B. Koopman, then involved in the discussions on American manufacture of Daimlers, whose role as a representative for American companies makes him an ideal candidate as go-between?) had sent Knight 'very flattering reports' about Manville and Daimler, and Knight – all thoughts of being too busy suddenly put aside – set sail for Liverpool with a biscuit-coloured Silent Knight tourer and drove down to Coventry. The young Sammy Davis saw him there, 'a queerly silent little man whose own car was almost wrapped in felt to demonstrate how silent a car could be, the felt being used to stop brake rods, controls, and such-like things producing their usual rattle'.

Obviously, Knight was going to get a sympathetic hearing from Percy Martin, a fellow American and a qualified engineer, and when Martin had tried the car, Knight offered Daimler the engine rights 'for England and the Colonies' (they later acquired three-fifths of the European rights too, the remainder going to Minerva of Belgium) and a deal was struck. On 1 April 1908 Daimler became sole licensee for Knight & Kilbourne.

As Knight later admitted, the engine as it then stood was 'a diamond in the rough', but Daimler had the great advantage of having Dr Frederick Lanchester as consulting engineer. Lanchester, who had been working as a consultant for companies like Daimler since he had lost his post as general manager of the Lanchester Engine Company when it was reorganized after going into receivership at the end of 1904, was perhaps the most original mind working in the British motor industry at that time. He was also helping Daimler with the Renard Road Train and the sheer unconventionality of the Knight engine would hardly deter him from refining its design. It was, after all, no more complex than the twin-cylinder Lanchester engines of a few years earlier, which had two crankshafts and six connecting rods in the interests of smooth running.

Work on the new engine went on in great secrecy, and what few references there were to it in the company minutes were laconic in the extreme ('Mr Martin reported progress on Knight silent engine') but it seems as though a fairly major redesign took place. Among the changes were the elimination of an auxiliary exhaust port at the bottom of the stroke and the addition of dual ignition, with twin plugs at the apex of each combustion chamber. However, not everyone at 'the Daimler' was happy about the new venture, recalled Sammy Davis: 'We were asked to believe in an American engine which had valves of which we did not approve. It was even rumoured that "Uncle" Bush, autocrat of the running shed, had poured a little sand into the experimental engine in the hope that it would fail, though the darned thing survived.'

Charles Knight, all pretence at being a motor manufacturer now at an end, moved to England late in 1907 and took a house on the outskirts of Coventry, promising to 'remain indefinitely where I can be within easy reach of the concerns which will in future exploit the new motor . . . I having made arrangements with the Daimler Company to carry on my experimental work at Coventry.'

Unveiled in September 1908, the new engine caused a sensation. Writing in *Motoring Illustrated*, Wilfred Gordon Aston remarked: 'In the course of over 12 months' critical testing at the Daimler works in Coventry, the new engine has shown itself to be, in every respect, far and away superior to tappet valve type of engine hitherto made as standard, so that the company have no hesitation in nailing this particular flag securely to their mast, having thoroughly satisfied themselves as to its superiority for their purpose over any other type. We were afforded an opportunity of seeing one of these motors running upon the test bench,

Flight of fancy

Some time around 1910–11, Daimler built an aero-engine designed by Frederick Lanchester. 'It was,' noted the redoubtable Charles Grey Grey, editor of *The Aeroplane*, 'a cross between the Knight slide-valve type and the ordinary Anzani [which had three poppet-valve cylinders set fanwise]. A considerable sum was spent on those experiments, but for some unexplained reason the engine was a failure and never succeeded in making a machine fly. Professor Lanchester was then an advisory engineer to the Daimler Company, so one assumes that he did not pay for the experiments himself.'

and we can certainly testify to its wonderful quietness and smooth-running qualities; moreover, it seemed to possess the power of rapid acceleration under load in an extraordinary degree.'

Though the Knight engine looked complicated, it was, said Percy Martin, 'a prettier proposition to tackle with the machine shop that they had at their command . . . as a manufacturing proposition, he would rather build the new engine than the old . . . the chief beauty of the manufacture was that they got more round work in building that engine than one did in the old type engine.'

The Daimler company was so sure of its ground that it dropped poppet valve engines altogether and launched a range of three four-cylinder engines – 3,764 cc (96x130 mm), 6,280 cc (124x130 mm) and 9,236 cc (140x150 mm) – promising that if any owner

'Mr Chas. Y. Knight surveys his masterpiece' – a cartoon from the company magazine.

was dissatisfied with his sleeve-valve engine within two years of buying his new Daimler, they were prepared to replace it with 'one of the company's late mushroom-valve types'. *The Autocar* test-drove a prototype sleeve-valve car and praised its 'extraordinary combination of silence, flexibility and power . . . the engine is not only extraordinarily quiet and very powerful, but pulls well from dead slow upwards'. Because of its peculiar design, it was, however, also a voracious consumer of oil, using a gallon every 450 miles, and a faint blue haze of oil smoke following astern became as much a Daimler trademark as the finned radiator header tank.

At the company's invitation, John Montagu was the first man from outside the Daimler organization to drive the new sleeve-valve model, and early in October 1908 took a 38 hp to France in company with the Rolls-Royce 'Silver Rogue'. The party included his wife, Sir Charles and Lady Seely and Montagu's biographer Archibald Marshall. They drove from Boulogne to Beauvais, spent several days in Paris, where Montagu and his friend Charles Rolls represented the Royal Automobile Club at the first International Roads Congress, then headed south to Le Mans to watch Wilbur Wright fly from the racecourse at Les Hunaudières. After driving the Daimler for 529 miles on all kinds of roads, Montagu admitted: 'I could find no fault, critic though I wished to be.'

Indeed, when later that month the Royal Automobile Club held a special meeting to discuss the new Daimler engine, he was able to speak with authority as the only man present – apart from Charles Knight himself – who had actually driven the car. Moreover, during his French trip he had carried out a head-to-head trial against the 40/50 hp Rolls-Royce (admittedly, one of four experimental specially-tuned '70 hp' chassis with overhead inlet valves) and 'found the difference in silence and flexibility at high speeds negligible. I can say honestly that the Knight engine is the more silent of the two. As regards the trial for speed,' he added with a twinkle in his eye, 'possibly I ought not to give the figures lest it should be thought that I am a road-hog, but they would understand that it was in France.'

When the laughter had died down, he continued: 'It was on an absolutely straight and empty road, without any hedges and without any traffic whatever. On the road between Chartres and Le Mans I let the car out for forty-five minutes consecutively on a hot day on a somewhat undulating road and I covered in that time about thirty-two miles. By the end of it the tyres were so hot that I deemed it advisable to slow down. Such a test would not be possible in England, naturally! There was no sign of heating in the engine, and the radiator was certainly cooler than with an ordinary Daimler, such as the one I had driven for a great many years – cooler than a 45 hp or 40 hp or any other existing Daimler type. On another occasion, between Argentan and Bernay, I ran eighteen miles in 20 minutes. Allowing for two slacks past cottages, a speed approximating to a mile a minute was kept up for the whole distance. The engine seemed to gather power on those long trials, and to be working almost better at the end than at the beginning.'

Moreover, Montagu's timing had been absolutely impeccable: the Daimler arrived at Les Hunaudières on 16 October, when Wright (whose historic first flights in Europe had been interrupted for four or five days because of engine trouble) flew higher than he had ever been, 'perhaps 50 or 60 feet up in the air'. Montagu was spellbound by the sight of Wright's Flyer in the air: his opinions of the Knight-engined car were equally favourable: 'The characteristics of the engine seem to be great flexibility, exceeding that of any other four-cylinder engine with which I am acquainted; noiselessness, especially marked when under way and running at high speed, and great power of picking up when a hill had to be negotiated, or when, after a slack of traffic, speed had to be attained again to get out of traffic. Those were the results of my

quite unbiased tests and experience. I think it is a remarkable engine. Whether it can attain the great success that some people prophesy is not for me to say; all I can say is that I was charmed with the running of the car that I took to France, and I think that it is, for a four-cylinder engine, the best I have ever handled.'

The Daimler factory had been working 18 hours a day to build up a sufficient stock of Knight engines for the launch of the new range, and by the end of October had around 600 on the stocks, plus some 60 complete

'Silence is Golden'.

Flying visit

'My father was the first man outside the Daimler company to drive the new sleeve-valve model. Early in October 1908 he took this 38 hp tourer to Le Mans to watch Wilbur Wright fly and later commented in *The Car Illustrated* that "the silence and smoothness of running were very remarkable for a four-cylinder engine . . . The speed attainable on the level was very high indeed, the hill-climbing powers were remarkable and the consumption of petrol, considering the power developed, not excessive."' M

cars. But was it because these cars were ready too late or a fear of the unknown by that most conservative of bodies, the coachbuilding profession, that the only sleeve-valve Daimlers at that year's Olympia Show were on the Daimler and De Luca stands?

Knight's aim had been to licence the leading companies in the main car manufacturing countries, and Minerva of Belgium came out with a sleeve-valve model simultaneously with Daimler; they, too, had modified the design, but phased the Knight engine in gradually, only dropping their poppet-valve models late in 1909, once their 'Sans Soupapes' 38 hp model had proved itself. In France, former racing driver turned luxury car manufacturer Léonce Girardot tried a 35 hp Knight-engined Daimler and was astounded: 'In my long career in motoring, I have never known an engine that runs so regularly and strongly. These different qualities make it a power unit of the first order which bears no comparison with anything that has so far been done. Please give my congratulations to Mr Knight on having been the prime mover behind this marvellous invention and to the Daimler

Company for having realized it industrially in so perfect a manner.'

Naturally, Daimler's whole-hearted conversion to the Knight engine had provoked quite a controversy, and to answer the criticism which had been made of the design, in May 1909 the company submitted two engines – a 22 hp and a 38 hp – to the Royal Automobile Club for testing. After 132 hours of continuous bench-testing (equivalent to well over 8,000 miles on the road), the engines were fitted in four-seated touring cars which carried a full load of passengers to Brooklands, where the cars were run for 2,143 miles non-stop, averaging 41.8 and 42.4 mph, before returning to Coventry, where the engines underwent a further five hours' bench-test and were then dismantled. The RAC examiners noted that 'no perceptible wear was noted on any of the fitted surfaces . . . the cylinders and pistons were found to be notably clean . . . the ports of the valves showed no sign of burning or wear'. Daimler challenged its competitors to match this performance, depositing a stake of £250 with the RAC for a three-month period: but there were no takers.

Love is — explaining the sleeve-valve engine to your sweetheart . . . [MBRT]

The Daimlers had successfully passed a most demanding test and in recognition Daimler was awarded the RAC's coveted Dewar Trophy, an honour which severely rattled the Rolls-Royce Company, which bought a 38 hp Daimler for testing against their 40/50 hp model. Henry Royce examined the Silent Knight engine and claimed: 'The design is all wrong; with a petrol engine it is essential to get the heat away from the piston and into the water jacket to be dispersed as quickly as possible, but with this sleeve-valve arrangement the heat is transferred from the piston to the two sleeves first.' Royce's right-hand man, that same Claude Johnson who had surveyed the route of the 1900 Thousand Miles' Trial in a Critchley Daimler, had been a motoring journalist in the period between leaving the Royal Automobile Club and joining Rolls-Royce, and was inspired by his master's verdict on the Knight power unit to contribute an anonymous article to *The Autocar* in 1910 under the heading 'Some Criticisms of the Slide Valve Engine'.

But he went too far in this long and humourless piece, damning the sleeve-valve engine under the headings 'Power', 'Silence', 'Fool-Proofedness', 'Fuel-Efficiency', 'Engine Vibration', 'Simplicity', 'Smokelessness' and 'Durability'. Knight's tongue-in-cheek riposte was a masterly demolition job, which, after hinting that the anonymous article might have been a publicity stunt by Ernest Instone to draw attention to the Daimler engine with 'a conglomeration of insinuations and suppositions deliberately wide of the mark', showed that he was fully aware of its authorship by making the Rolls-Royce company look excessively foolish, even illustrating an inordinately complex piston valve engine patented by Royce which claimed all the advantages of the Knight engine, and demolishing Johnson's arguments by using published quotes by Henry Royce (who had warned against the publication of the article).

This forced Johnson to break cover (prompted, one feels, by an irate Royce) with a long reply to Knight, though its effect was dampened by an accompanying article by Frederick Lanchester defending the sleeve-valve engine against Johnson's original criticisms and concluding: 'The manufacturers of the poppet valve will need to compete with the sleeve valve by maintaining a high degree of excellence of their own product and not by anonymous running down their competitors' goods.' Johnson had been made to look a fool, and he never forgave Daimler, which he would henceforth only refer to as 'The Unmentionable Car'.

* * *

The sleeve valve gamble certainly paid off for Daimler in terms of sales; in 1910 the company built some 2,000 vehicles which, according to Frederick Lanchester, was 'approximately one-quarter of the total output of Great Britain'. There were already sleeve-valve Daimlers in the Royal Mews, for the Prince of Wales had taken delivery of a 38 hp Hooper-bodied limousine in October

1909 and followed this with a 57 hp limousine the following June, the month after he had succeeded his father. The new King George V's stud of motor vehicles, commented *The Autocar*, 'is characteristic of an English gentleman, to whom unnecessary display and any sort of ostentation are averse'. Apparent was the fact that the Mercedes which King Edward VII had frequently used was no longer in evidence, just 'four fine Daimler cars'. Another 57 hp followed in September.

In 1910 Undecimus Stratton stayed at York Cottage, Sandringham, where he taught the new heir to the throne, Edward Prince of Wales, to drive on one of the Royal Daimlers: he supplied the Prince and his sister Princess Mary with their first cars, too.

Democratization of the sleeve-valve came when Daimler granted a licence to Rover, which unveiled a single-cylinder 8 hp and a twin-cylinder 12 hp – the smallest Knight-engined cars yet built – at the 1910 Olympia Motor Show. The press was awash with drawings of new engine designs with every conceivable sort of slide valve, all trying to circumvent the Knight patent, though only the Burt McCollum single sleeve-valve engine fitted by Argyll of Scotland actually saw any serious production. In Charles Y. Knight's native country, manufacturers who had scorned his engine a couple of years earlier now sent their representatives to England to examine the sleeve-valve engine, for which, said Knight, just four American licences would be issued.

The 'three Ps' which constituted the real summit of American luxury car manufacturing all sent representatives. Peerless president L.H. Kittredge and his chief engineer Charles Schmidt came to Coventry in company with the English-born chief engineer of Pierce-Arrow, David Fergusson (and later arranged for Fergusson to visit the Panhard-Levassor works in Paris where licensed production of the Knight engine was also beginning). On his return to Cleveland, Kittredge sent data on Knight

A dozen KPL petrol-electric buses were built in 1910 to the designs of Frederick Lanchester. They had four-wheel brakes, unitary body/chassis construction and a separate sleeve-valve engine for each rear wheel, but commercial pressures killed the project. [MBRT]

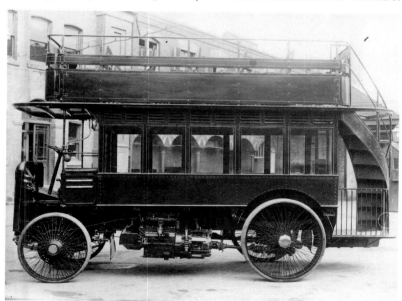

sleeves to his friend Colonel Clifton at Pierce-Arrow, but neither company adopted the sleeve-valve engine. Packard were more interested: their chief engineer Russell Huff was given the run of the Daimler works and full technical details of the Knight engine in the expectation that his company would take out a licence.

Indeed, so keen was Daimler that Packard become a Knight licensee that it shipped a sample engine to Detroit at cost in January 1909. Packard were indeed delighted with the engine; but the suggested royalty of $100 an engine proved a major stumbling block. It would, said Packard, add 20 per cent to the cost of an engine, which was quite out of the question. So they set about trying to obtain by guile what they were not willing to pay for, and sent their patent attorneys Watson & Tibbets to Washington to try and find some patent that anticipated – and therefore invalidated – the Knight & Kilbourne patent.

All they could find was a valve mechanism for steam-driven engines and compressors patented by Sidney A. Reeve in September 1901, but they agreed to purchase it provided that Reeve would agree to a re-write that would, in effect, retrospectively anticipate the Knight engine, changing words like 'ring valves' into 'sleeves' and implying that this was some kind of internal combustion power unit. Armed with Reeves's revisionist '1901' patent, Packard claimed a half interest in the American Knight royalties and a free licence for themselves, and when this ploy proved unsuccessful, cut their demand to 10 per cent and a free licence. Knight & Kilbourne refused them point blank.

Packard now tried a head-on assault, publishing claims that the Knight engine infringed the 'basic patents' which they held; Knight & Kilbourne called their bluff, inviting them to sue for infringement, and challenging them to a similar test to that carried out by the RAC in 1909. Though Packard failed to rise to the bait, laboratory tests were subsequently carried out by the Automobile Club of America on a six-cylinder Packard poppet valve engine which showed it to be markedly inferior in most respects to the Daimler-Knight power unit.

* * *

Though they had successfully fended off attacks by two of their most prominent rivals, Daimler still had work to do in perfecting their new engine. Knight may have made light of the Knight engine's tendency to smoke in his response to Johnson's criticisms, but it was a very real problem and various ways of reducing it were employed.

The first Daimler-Knight engines had oil feeds to the upper part of the sleeves but when a revised 22 hp chassis was introduced in September 1909 these were replaced by petcocks: now the chauffeur could apply a few drops of oil from a can before starting so that the sleeves were lubricated before the splash from the crankcase, flung up by scoops on the big-ends dipping into troughs constantly filled by the oil pump, reached

Young 'Sammy' Davis, a talented artist, drew the Daimler sleeve valve as Salome dancing round the broken head of a conventional poppet valve.

them. This system, soon adopted on the rest of the range, was further refined on the new 12 hp model introduced a year later, in which the troughs were hinged so that they moved up and down in response to a lever linked to the throttle pedal and the scoops dipped deeper as the engine went faster.

Another problem arose when Daimler launched their first six-cylinder engines, a 5,646 cc 33 hp and a 9,420 cc 57 hp, at the end of 1909. Periodic vibration was no respecter of valve systems, and the six-cylinder Knight engines were as prone to 'thrashing or harshness' at critical engine speeds as any poppet valve six, and the cars were only marginally saleable. Down in the running shed Alfred Bush attempted to cure the problem by fitting a wider fan belt and adjusting it very tight. This makeshift certainly worked for a while, but as the belt wore and stretched, so the vibration inevitably came back.

Frederick Lanchester was called in and,

after spending many hours in the running shed, he devised a crankshaft damper consisting of a secondary flywheel at the front end of the engine driven by a multi-disc friction coupling; at critical speeds, it slipped slightly, damping out the crucial first critical period and, recalled Lanchester, 'immediately released something like £20,000-worth of frozen assets.' The urgency with which he worked reveals the seriousness of the problem: the detail drawings were made on 14 September 1909 and the first Lanchester Vibration Damper was fitted to engine 10920 two days later by Bush's foreman Alfred Hensman, who found that 'the objectionable thrash or vibration disappeared'.

It certainly saved Daimler from considerable embarrassment, for in November 1909 campaigning began for a General Election as a result of the rejection of Lloyd George's 'People's Budget' by the House of Lords. Recalled Lanchester in 1921:

The new King, George V, was a devoted user of Daimler cars. [JDHT]

'Mr Steel-Maitland, MP for one of the Birmingham districts, purchased a six-cylinder 57 hp car from the Daimler Company . . . He wanted a car at once, and the only car that the Daimler could deliver at once was 'the big white elephant', that is to say the 57 hp before the days of the damper

. . . it was important for him to have a car of prominent British make in connection with his election campaign.

'After having won his seat, he discovered that the car was not all that he could wish and wanted the Daimler to take it back: the fact was the thrashing points owing to the

This chain-driven 10.4-litre 58 hp limousine was first used by George V when he was still Prince of Wales. [JDHT]

The impressive 57 hp Daimler Hooper Limousine delivered to the Royal Mews in 1910. [JDHT]

The Kaiser's younger brother Prince Henry of Prussia was a great motoring enthusiast and in February 1910 he paid a private visit to the Daimler to see the new engine before returning to London in the 38 hp Daimler belonging to the secretary of the RAC. [MBRT]

crankshaft vibration were very severe, and the noise and drumming at certain speeds were intolerable. Instone called me in to interview him and I managed to keep him quiet – I admit mainly by bluff. He thought he had a trump card in telling us that he should make us replace the engine with one of the valve type, under the old Daimler guarantee to do so if required. He was persuaded, however, to keep the car . . . we subsequently fitted him up with a vibration damper.'

More serious problems threatened in 1911, when Rolls-Royce started fitting a 'slipper flywheel' to its Silver Ghost engines. Claude Johnson asked to see Frederick Lanchester, who vividly described the encounter – long thought apocryphal – in a 1921 letter unearthed while researching this book: 'He [Johnson] held out his right hand with a smile on his face and presented a pistol with his left: in brief, he said he should be very glad to make an arrangement with me to

recognize my patent, but at the same time informed me that he was in a position to prove prior user on behalf of Messrs Rolls-Royce. I enquired as to what he meant by "recognizing my patent" and it turned out to be that he would work under my patent on a peppercorn royalty. I declined both the hand and the pistol.

'Speaking from memory, I believe Claude Johnson showed me, or sent me, a blue print illustrating something that Rolls-Royce had used some two or three years prior to my patent, but which they had certainly not adopted and there was no pretension that it had been used other than experimentally. There was no evidence to show that the article in question was a damper, or whether it was a friction-driven pulley in order to prevent injury to the fan belt. At a date subsequent to this the Rolls-Royce patented a damper which appeared to have been a resuscitation of this alleged old device and commenced to fit same to their output of cars . . .

The

Daimler

Bulletin

VOL. III.   JANUARY, 1913.   No. 3

— THE PIED PIPER — OF COVENTRY

been first in the field. Said that great engineer Sir Harry Ricardo, the Lanchester crankshaft damper 'proved completely successful in eliminating torsional vibration and thus laid the ghost which hitherto had haunted the six-cylinder engine'.

* * *

But now there was a new ghost haunting large cars like the big six-cylinder Daimler, for a major component of the Liberal Chancellor David Lloyd George's controversial 'People's Budget' (which had forced the February 1910 General Election when it was thrown out late in 1909 by the House of Lords after months of vitriolic debate), was the taxation of cars on their RAC horsepower rating (which was based on the bore and number of cylinders) rather than on weight, as they had been hitherto. Lloyd George promised that the new car tax would be devoted to road repairs and the building of village bypasses and

FAR LEFT Manufacturers came to Coventry from Europe and America seeking a licence to build the new engine.

'My view at the time, with which Mr Martin agreed, was that it was no use bringing an action against Rolls-Royce until the damages were sufficient to justify the action. A win would have meant that one would have been out of pocket so far as a portion of one's costs was concerned, and to lose would have meant the opening up of the damper to the public. But I should think that today substantial damages of the order of £10,000 could be claimed, and I propose to open up negotiations . . . with the Daimler company with a view to bunging in a writ if Messrs R-R will not come to terms.'

But that action never came to court and it has never been adequately decided whether Royce had actually independently devised 'a supplementary flywheel on the front end of the crankshaft with a suitable friction attachment' as Johnson had claimed in November 1910; certainly Royce had not patented anything prior to Lanchester, whose invention was subsequently repeatedly ruled by legal judgments to have

Stand No.
54

Stand No.
54

Daimler Guarantee.

In presenting the 1909 type Daimler Engine, the Daimler Motor Company (1904) Limited beg to state that although it is manufactured under Letters Patent, and consequently, in common with all patented articles, carries no guarantee whatever as to its suitability for the purpose for which it is sold, the Company have no desire to evade responsibility on this purely legal ground. On the contrary, the Company **guarantee in the fullest terms** the 1909 type Daimler Engine in respect of its principle of working, the material of which it is composed, and the workmanship employed in its construction. The only condition the Company make is that their responsibility is limited to doing the following things at one or other of their Depots, within a period of **two years** from the date of the sale of the Engine:

(1) Thoroughly repairing any such Engine, which, after proper examination by the Company, is found not to be working satisfactorily.

(2) Replacing any parts found to be defective in breach of this guarantee by the Company.

(3) Replacing, at a customer's option, any such Engine with one of the Company's late mushroom-valve type Engines.

The Company do not take responsibility for any contingent or resulting liability or loss arising through any defect, and the guarantee is not to relate to defects caused by wear and tear, dirt, misuse or neglect.

Daimler

The Daimler company confidently guaranteed to replace any sleeve-valve engine which proved unsatisfactory. [DBW]

By the end of 1910, Daimler had delivered over 3,500 sleeve-valve engined cars; five Royal houses were among the customers. [DBW]

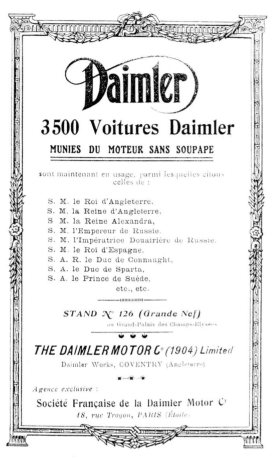

Daimler

3500 Voitures Daimler

MUNIES DU MOTEUR SANS SOUPAPE

sont maintenant en usage, parmi lesquelles citons celles de :

S. M. le Roi d'Angleterre.
S. M. la Reine d'Angleterre.
S. M. la Reine Alexandra,
S. M. l'Empereur de Russie.
S. M. l'Impératrice Douairière de Russie.
S. M. le Roi d'Espagne.
S. A. R. le Duc de Connaught,
S. A. le Duc de Sparta,
S. A. le Prince de Suède,
etc., etc.

STAND N° 126 (Grande Nef)
au Grand-Palais des Champs-Elysées

THE DAIMLER MOTOR C° (1904) *Limited*
Daimler Works, COVENTRY (Angleterre)

Agence exclusive :

Société Française de la Daimler Motor C°
18, rue Troyon, PARIS (Étoile)

The King's four 57 hp Daimlers and Queen Mary's personal 45 hp lined up for inspection in the Royal Mews. [MBRT]

established the Road Board to administer it. While taxes on smaller cars up to an RAC rating of 16 hp were either cut or remained much the same, taxes on the larger cars increased out of all proportion. At the upper end, cars of 60 hp rating or over had their annual duties increased eightfold, from a total of five guineas (£5.25) to 40 guineas (£42), roughly equivalent to more than £2,000 in modern terms. At 57 hp, the biggest Daimler narrowly escaped that top tax band and was now subject to an annual tax of 20 guineas (£21), but like all rapid tax hikes, Lloyd George's budget – which also imposed duty on petrol for the first time, at the rate of 3d a gallon, bringing the cost of a gallon to 1s 9d (8.75p) – hit sales badly.

A deputation from Coventry went to argue their case with Lloyd George in July 1909 and Ernest Instone acted as their spokesman, representing an industry that was just clawing its way back to prosperity after the disastrous trade slump of 1908 in which six out of Coventry's eight leading motor manufacturers had made substantial losses (Daimler recorded a net loss of £49,286 and paid no dividend – indeed, recalled Sammy Davis, at the time of its annual audit, Daimler had dismantled many of the cars the company had on hand because they represented greater worth as spare parts than they did as complete chassis).

Asked by Lloyd George whether the world industry was recovering from a very deep depression, and whether the recovery was

steady, Instone replied that it had been steady until it was affected by the Budget proposals, and showed the Chancellor letters which had been received by various Coventry manufacturers from customers cancelling orders. All Lloyd George could say was: 'Probably the motorists feel the effect of other taxes.' Even though Lloyd George

This magnificent six-cylinder Daimler drophead coupé carrying an AA committee member's badge is a participant in the 1911 Prince Henry Tour. [NMM]

This remarkable Daimler 57 hp six-cylinder with Prince Henry-type sports bodywork was supplied to M. Conill of Paris late in 1909. [NMM]

Beaulieu's 40 hp Estate car dwarfs the 6 hp De Dion-Bouton acquired by the Montagu family in payment of a bad debt in 1910. (42 years later it became the first exhibit in the National Motor Museum!) [NMM]

claimed to be 'a most enthusiastic motorist', he insisted, with that curious inverted logic that only politicians seem to possess, that his new taxes would only have a temporary effect on the recovery and 'would, in the long run, have a very beneficial effect on the growth and the development of the motor industry'.

Inevitably, the industry reported a slump in sales of high-powered cars, even before the new taxes came into force on 1 July 1910, following the re-election of the Liberal government in an administration which only held power with Labour support. Fortuitously, at the start of the year Daimler had begun production of a new 2,614 cc 15 hp car. Like all the 1910 models, it had Lanchester worm final drive, adopted in the interests of even greater silence, and its long-stroke engine was ideally-suited to the RAC horsepower formula, which only took account of piston area.

* * *

The 57 hp Daimler may have been redeemed by Lanchester's vibration damper, but nothing could save it from Lloyd George's budget, and it was withdrawn from the range after 1911, though in November 1912 a lone example – his fourth – was delivered to King George V; presumably it had been built from parts on hand. By the time the King's car was delivered, Daimler had once again been reformed, though this time out of strength rather than weakness, by amalgamation with the Birmingham Small Arms Company.

Founded in 1861 by an association of 14 master gunsmiths 'to make guns by machinery', BSA had diversified into the cycle fittings trade in the 1880s to keep that machinery – unprofitably idle thanks to an unwarrantably long spell of peace – turning over, with machines designed to spin shell-cases producing cycle hubs, the foundries turning out frame lugs, the forges stamping chainwheels and pedals, and the workshops

Even the tramp in the cloud of dust salutes as King George's Daimler goes by. [MBRT]

The year is 1913, the car is not hers, nor does Royalty usually stand on the seat: but Queen Mary is watching manoeuvres in Northampton. [MBRT]

One of the very first Daimlers to be made in Coventry, this 1897 4 hp tube ignition twin-cylinder is now owned by the Jaguar-Daimler Heritage Trust. Thistle emblems cast in its steps suggest its phaeton body may have been built by Stirling in Scotland. In 1961, driven by its then owner Ted Woolley, it crossed the 6,834 ft high Mont Cenis pass unaided, still using tube ignition heated by petrol-fired bunsen burners. (Christine Burgess-Wise)

One of the most instantly recognizable marques thanks to its finned radiator tanks, the Daimler often featured in early motoring cartoons, like this c.1902 lithograph by Tom Browne featuring a 22 hp tourer. (DBW)

DEAF OLD LADY —
"AH! I CAN DISTINCTLY HEAR A BEE HUMMING, SOMEWHERE."

Similar to the car delivered to King Edward VII in February 1903, this 22 hp wagonette won a gold medal in the 1903 1,000 Miles' Reliability Trial. (DBW)

This 1911 Daimler 12 hp four-seater tourer belongs to the Coventry Museum of British Road Transport. (Automobile Quarterly *photograph by Neill Bruce*)

Typical of the Daimler lorries produced during the Great War is this 1915 CB-type 40 hp 3-tonner. After war service it was used by a South Wales mineral water bottler. (Automobile Quarterly *photograph by Neill Bruce*)

LEFT Built on the 45-hp chassis, this 1920 Daimler convertible saloon with reputed Royal connections survives in the United States. (Automobile Quarterly photograph by Roy Query)

BELOW LEFT AND RIGHT Reputedly carried out of the Indian jungle slung between four elephants after its discovery in the 1970s, this spectacular 1926 Barker-bodied Daimler 45 hp all-weather tourer, with twin sets of folding side windows (one layer clear, one fitted with dark purdah glass to conceal its owner's two wives from public gaze), was commissioned by Gulab Singh, Maharajah of Rewa, ruler of a kingdom whose two million inhabitants were snake worshippers and whose fortunes were founded on shellac garnered from its jungles. With a unique radiator inspired by Lanchester practice – a glass window in the header tank revealed the water level – the Daimler was panelled in burnished German silver, an odd choice since it was used for tiger hunting by its 23-year old owner. (Automobile Quarterly photograph by Roy Query)

RIGHT This 1928 Daimler Double-Six 30 Touring Saloon was originally delivered to the Chinese Embassy in London. (Automobile Quarterly photograph by Roy Query)

This imposing Double-Six 30 Hooper Limousine was supplied to Queen Mary in 1928, the first of the new V12 Daimlers to enter Royal service. (DS)

Stratstone's publicity department waxed lyrical over the 1930 Double-Six Touring Car: 'The glories of earth and sky attend the happy owner of a Daimler open car,' enthused the catalogue. 'And if the shadows gather and clouds threaten, shelter is at hand – immediate, complete . . .' (DS)

With spectacular Corsica bodywork, this 1931 Daimler Double-Six 50 is one of the handful of low-chassis models designed by Reid Railton and built by Thomson & Taylor of Brooklands. (Automobile Quarterly *photograph by Neill Bruce*)

Discovered in a chicken coop before restoration, this stylish 1931 Daimler Double-Six-50 Formal Saloon is now part of the Merle Norman Collection of antique cars, housed in a purpose-built Art Deco building at San Sylmar, 'nestling like a precious jewel in the shadowed foothills of the San Gabriel Mountains, Southern California'. (Automobile Quarterly *photograph by Roy Query*)

LEFT *James Young of Bromley, whose coachwork is more usually associated with Rolls-Royce cars, built the saloon body on this elegant 1937 Daimler. (Automobile* Quarterly *photograph by Roy Query)*

RIGHT *Powered by a 7-litre five-cylinder Gardner diesel engine, this Daimler COG5 Saloon Coach dates from 1938. (Automobile* Quarterly *photograph by Neill Bruce)*

BELOW *The Light Straight Eight was Coventry's response to the Derby Bentley, certainly in terms of performance, though production – a total of just 180 cars between 1936–38 – was small. (JDHT)*

The 6th Marquess of Bath owned this 1938 Daimler DB 18 Drophead Coupé, seen in front of his family seat, Longleat, in Wiltshire. (Automobile Quarterly photograph by Neill Bruce)

One of the most advanced fighting vehicles produced during the Second World War, the Daimler Armoured Car featured all-wheel drive and disc brakes on all four wheels. This 1943 example is preserved, appropriately, in the Coventry Museum of British Road Transport. (Automobile Quarterly photograph by Neill Bruce)

American author Clive Cussler features his 1951 Hooper-bodied Daimler DE 36 — one of the exclusive 'Green Goddess' series — as the oceanographer hero's car in his Dirk Pitt adventure stories. (Automobile Quarterly photograph by Rick Lenz)

With its idiosyncratic glass fibre bodywork and Edward Turner-designed V8 power unit, the Daimler SP250 – unofficially known as the 'Dart' – was even used by the British police in the early 1960s. (Automobile Quarterly *photograph by Neill Bruce*)

LEFT *One of the quickest luxury cars of its day, the Majestic Major was capable of 120 mph, powered by Edward Turner's fine 4,561cc V8 engine. (JDHT)*

ABOVE RIGHT *A late (1968) example of the Daimler V8-250 four-door saloon specially created by Sir William Lyons to compensate Daimler agents Stratstone for relinquishing their Volkswagen franchise after the Jaguar takeover. (Automobile Quarterly photograph by Neill Bruce)*

RIGHT *The most devoted Daimler owner in the Royal Family, Her Majesty Queen Elizabeth the Queen Mother has had several Daimler Limousines, including the penultimate example (1992); this is her 1987 Limousine at Browns Lane. The lion mascot was originally fitted to one of King George VI's Lanchesters. (JDHT)*

143

In 1972–3, the Daimler saloon was available either as the Sovereign, with the classic Jaguar XK six-cylinder engine, or as the Double Six, with the new light-alloy V12 engine. This is the extended wheelbase Vanden Plas version of the Double Six.

Recalling the classic lines of the XJ6 series designed by Sir William Lyons in 1968, the 1995-launched Daimler XJ model represented an investment of more than £200 million.

that normally produced firing mechanisms making freewheels. After the first few years, the company ceased making complete cycles (it had turned down Harry Lawson's designs for a 'safety' bicycle in 1884) and until 1908 produced only components for other manufacturers as an adjunct to the production of the Lee-Metford rifle, adopted as the standard weapon of the British Army in the 1890s.

In 1908 complete bicycles once again began to leave the BSA factory at Small Heath, Birmingham – appropriately built in the shape of a hollow square – followed by motor cycles in 1910. An attempt was made to break into the motor car market in 1908 with a three-car range (four-cylinder 14/18, 18/23 and 25/33 hp models) made in a former government arms works at Sparkbrook which had begun pilot build of the 18/23 the year before. This venture only achieved moderate success, and BSA began looking around for a more experienced partner in the car field.

On 1 September 1910 it was confirmed

that BSA and Daimler were discussing an amalgamation of the two companies and on Monday 26 September shareholders in the two companies received circulars setting out the terms of the merger. The 1904 Daimler company was to be wound up and replaced by a new company, whose shares would be held by BSA, while existing Daimler shareholders would receive 25s (£1.25) plus any accrued dividend in exchange for each £1 preference share, and five full-paid BSA shares for every four ordinary Daimler shares.

The merger, though described by the *Financial Times* as 'one of the most important ever effected in the motor industry', went through with exemplary smoothness. BSA assumed responsibility for Daimler's liabilities, outstanding debts and debentures (which, at £51,000, were anyway well within Daimler's overdraft limit of £65,000) being cleared out of Daimler's assets and a new Daimler Motor Company took over the assets and undertakings of Daimler Motor Company (1904) Ltd from BSA under an agreement dated 22 September. For its final

The King's 57 hp Daimler – and Queen Mary in one of her famous hats. [MBRT]

year the old company recorded a profit of £100,000.

At the time of the merger, Daimler had a payroll of 4,116 workmen and 418 staff. Chairman of the new company was Edward Manville, at a salary of £1,000 a year. Manville, widowed at the very end of 1909, was now a very considerable figure in the motor industry, for he had been chairman of the Society of Motor Manufacturers & Traders since 1907: his vice chairman was Sir Hallewell Rogers of BSA. As expected, Percy Martin became managing director of the new combine, Ernest Instone continued as Daimler manager and the name of industrialist F. Dudley Docker – deputy chairman of BSA and engineer of the Daimler takeover – appeared on the board.

Docker, whose fortunes had been founded on his varnish business (another company established in workshops underneath railway arches) had been a Daimler owner since 1906 and knew Martin and Manville. 'Shrewd and ruthless to a degree', he had become famous for merging five great manufacturers of railway rolling stock in 1902 and was

renowned for agreeing deals worth millions with 'a short "yes", more often with a grunt and a kind of hiccough'. Though he resigned from the boards of BSA and Daimler at the beginning of 1912 to 'loaf for a year on a Scottish estate', and later organized the Metropolitan-Vickers combine, his son Bernard (born in 1896) would be a key player in the later history of both companies.

One by-product of the merger was an

Single-deck Daimler 40 hp buses in company livery brought workmen to the factory from outlying districts. [MBRT]

A Daimler bus gingerly negotiates Cook Street Gate in Coventry. [MBRT]

order from BSA for the production by Daimler of an initial batch of 500 sleeve-valve cars during 1911: launched at the Motor Show that November, this 2,015 cc four, which had the peculiar combination of semi-elliptic front suspension and transverse rear springing, was subsequently built at Sparkbrook where from 1912 the body shop, directed by Max Buch, was one of the first to build all-metal bodywork.

Daimler laid down a 1911 sanction of 1,153 cars, consisting of 250 15 hp chassis, 400 20 hp, 250 25 hp, 100 30 hp, 127 38 hp four-cylinder and 26 38 hp six-cylinder cars; the 57 hp was not included in this list in the company minutes, and it may be that all the engines for this model had been completed the previous year and put into stock against future orders. Continuing demand saw the development of the new factory site at nearby Radford from 1912.

A wonderful picture of the sort of client Daimler was serving in that vanished age was given in a 1962 interview with that great motoring enthusiast John 'Jumbo' Goddard in *Motor Sport*, for before 1914 Goddard's father

147

kept a stable of six Daimlers at the family seat at Pease Pottage, Sussex: an ancient (possibly pre-1900) car used as a luggage tender; three chain-driven poppet-valve cars; and two Knight-engined Daimlers, a 15 hp four and a 33 hp six with that most amazing of

A 1911 Daimler limousine waits outside the medieval shops of Coventry's Butcher Row. [JDHT]

Daimler's elaborate stand at the 1912 Olympia Motor Show with 28 hp four-cylinder and 39 hp six-cylinder limousines on display. [JDHT]

Vast crowds cheer the King in Port Sunlight on his 1913 visit to the North-West of England. [MBRT]

The Royal Daimlers on tour, circa 1913. [MBRT]

headlamps, the 'Diva', a huge globular unit fitted with four external mirrors, which projected five blinding white beams ahead of the car. These cars were tended by a staff of four – chauffeur, under-chauffeur, mechanic and washer – in a tiled motor house which had central heating (which the house did not), a six-inch lathe, drills and grinders, all driven by a 110-volt electric motor taking its current from a 10 hp Ruston hot-bulb engine/generator unit which also lit the house, pumped the water and powered the pipe organ.

In 1912 a man who had once played a major role in Daimler history surfaced briefly from the obscurity and poverty which had overtaken him. Oliver Stanton, one-time motor instructor to King Edward VII, had 'fallen on evil times' after attempting to promote the German-built Beaufort car and tried to re-establish himself in California, where the climate might benefit his consumptive wife. But the Californian authorities would not let her remain in the USA and the Stantons returned to England in 1911, where Oliver Stanton drove a taxi to earn a living: in 1912 he appealed to 'motorists who knew [him] in his palmy days' for £50 to help him buy his own cab. He died in 1915, a forgotten man.

At the beginning of 1913, the Daimler board was joined by Neville Chamberlain – scion of one of the great Midlands political dynasties and a future prime minister – and Colonel H.C.L. Holden, a civil engineer famed not only for having built a pioneer four-cylinder motor cycle in the 1890s but also for designing the world's first purpose-built race circuit, the banked oval track at Brooklands, Surrey.

At a lower level within the company worked a young Swiss engineer named Georges Roesch, who had left his job at Renault in Paris, determined to explore 'a quality of engine design . . . which was largely ignored in France: the quality of refinement

Out in the mid-day sun: a 1912 30 hp cabriolet in India, with an alfresco seat for the chauffeur. [JDHT]

Edward Manville welcomes guests to the new Radford factory with a celebratory dinner. [MBRT]

Chassis were assembled on the spot and lifted out by overhead crane. [NMM]

Crating a tourer for export, circa 1911. [MBRT]

Coventry Chain. It gave him the grounding he needed for his post-1916 job as chief engineer of Clement-Talbot in London, where he would design some of the most refined sporting cars of the 1920s and '30s.

And Cadillac's epochal V8 was created by ex-Daimler engineer D. McCall White . . .

Daimler's fame was now worldwide: Daimlers were in the service of many Royal families, including those of England, Russia, Germany, Japan, Spain, Sweden and Greece; its list of owners among the British nobility read like a digest of Debrett; there was a branch company in Paris; and Stratton's friend the Marquis of Villalobar – one of many foreign noblemen with Daimlers in their motor houses – used a Daimler landaulette as his official car in Washington DC when he was appointed Spanish Ambassador to the United States in 1910. The agent in Bombay had sent five cars to the 1911 Delhi Durbar and sold cars to a number of Indian princes. There was even a Japanese agent, Okura, whose company also handled sales in Manchuria and Korea, presumably the same car-mad Okura who had come to England and raced his giant 120 hp 16.3-litre Fiat *Silver Flyer* at the opening Brooklands meeting in 1907.

and smoothness which had been pioneered by Lanchester and brought to perfection in the Rolls-Royce Silver Ghost and the sleeve-valve Daimler, but in practically no other engines in the world.' Landing at Newhaven in February 1914 with just £10 in his pocket, Roesch was found a job in the Daimler design office by his friend Henry Wilfred Watts of

Ownership of a Daimler seemed almost inseparable from popular fame in that golden afternoon of an era that, though its central figure had died in 1910, would be known ever after as 'Edwardian': in Oxford a chain-smoking cycle and motor cycle agent named

Carriage à la mode – this astounding six-cylinder Daimler was the state carriage of an Indian prince. [NMM]

A sleeve-valve BSA coping with 'colonial conditions'. [MBRT]

This late Knight-engined Daimler-Renard Road Train was exported to Canada. [MBRT]

William Morris, who had begun manufacture of a new light car named the 'Morris-Oxford' in 1912, also ran the local bus service with a couple of single-deck Daimler coaches; the dashing and daring aviator Gustav Hamel, 'idol of the flappers' and winner of the 1912

An impressive fleet of Daimlers accompanying a Royal visit in the golden afternoon of the Edwardian age. [MBRT]

A 20 hp Daimler tourer
at Coventry's Cook
Street Gate circa 1914.
[JDHT]

Aerial Derby in his 70 hp Blériot, arrived at the Hendon and Brooklands flying fields at the wheel of an enormous open yellow Daimler; the future speed king Malcolm Campbell first went fast at the wheel of a motor car with his stripped 45 hp Daimler . . .

On a more utilitarian front, Daimler had developed a monstrous 105 hp 15.9-litre version of the sleeve-valve six for heavy haulage, which was used to power later versions of the Renard Road Train and monster tractors which Daimler had developed for the South American market in conjunction with William Foster & Company of Lincoln, the famous agricultural machinery makers. The company's commercial vehicle activities were booming, too: buses were being supplied to transport authorities all over the country, including a 1912 order for 350 double-deckers for the Metropolitan Electric Tramways of London. The same 40 hp Silent Knight-engined chassis was being used for lorries and drays, while a 12 hp model similar to the company's

Chassis on test in Sandy Lane, just outside the Daimler works, shortly before the Great War. [JDHT]

car chassis was an ideal base for a light 10 cwt delivery van.

Daimler also supplied sleeve-valve engines to the London General Omnibus Company. These were fitted in some of the chassis built at the Walthamstow works of the Associated Equipment Company (AEC), a manufacturing subsidiary of the LGOC established in 1909. This association resulted in Daimler's appointment in 1912 as sales agents for AEC chassis which were surplus to LGOC demand; AEC also built Daimler commercial chassis when the Coventry works was unable to cope with demand. The chassis produced by the two companies were anyway very similar, since Daimler had hired the former chief engineer of the LGOC, Frank Searle, to design their commercial vehicle chassis.

Things seemed much as usual in Coventry as the annual works holiday began in the afternoon of Friday 31 July 1914. There were distant rumours of trouble in the Balkans (but there was nothing unusual in that). Certainly Austria had accused Serbia of complicity in the assassination in Sarajevo of the heir to the Austro-Hungarian Empire in Sarajevo, setting off a flurry of diplomatic posturing, threat and counter-threat of mobilization,

Bringing in the last harvest of peace with a Daimler lorry. [JDHT]

The infinitely adaptable Daimler chassis fitted with ambulance bodywork for Birmingham's police force. [MBRT]

This 3-ton van is powered by a 40 hp sleeve-valve engine. [MBRT]

The Daimler works fire engine. [MBRT]

157

HIS MAJESTY
KING GEORGE V. has
graciously granted a Royal
Warrant of Appointment to
The Daimler Company, Ltd.,
Coventry.

across the Continent. But that was all safely across the Channel. Apart from a few who stayed behind working on plant renewals and repairs, Daimler's 3,824 employees cheerfully set off for their holiday destinations all over Britain.

In Europe events moved with bewildering quickness. The next day Russia mobilized and German troops crossed into French territory. By Sunday the Germans had begun a flanking movement through Luxembourg and Belgium. Britain called on the Kaiser to respect the 1839 treaty guaranteeing Belgian neutrality, but he dismissed it as a worthless scrap of paper. The British Government sent a telegram containing an ultimatum to Berlin: it was ignored.

On 4 August, Britain declared war on Germany.

'It will all be over by Christmas,' said Sir John French, newly-appointed Commander of the British Expeditionary Force . . .

Car of Kings

Daimler was the chosen car of rulers the world over: in 1912 Maythorn of Biggleswade were commissioned to build no less than five bodies for the Emperor of Japan's Daimlers. But the King of England, who ruled an Empire on which the sun had not yet set, was the marque's most notable client. His mighty cars rode on specially built seven-inch Palmer Cord tyres with an almost modern profile at a time when everyone else used skinny high pressure tyres, and his chauffeurs were ordered that they must obey the speed limit . . . unless a member of the Royal Family was on board . . . and they had a special card to show the police to prove it . . .

Chapter 5

SLEEVE VALVES GO TO WAR

'It seems to me that the Daimler people are running this war,' remarked the Prince of Wales on a visit to the front, noticing a sizeable fleet of Daimler military lorries. And certainly the company's involvement in the war effort had been instant, for as soon as war had been declared military officials – who had suddenly decided that maybe the motor vehicle was going to replace the horse after all – descended on the Daimler works and commandeered every car and commercial vehicle in sight: by the end of the week, over a hundred cars and lorries of all types had

been shipped out bearing the stencilled 'W↑D' symbol of the War Office on their bodywork. The company contacted all its depots, ordering them to send all the cars they had to London, and within three or four days some 200 cars – demonstrators, new and secondhand cars from the sales stock, cars awaiting delivery – had converged on Hyde Park, hastily converted into an assembly area.

Meanwhile, the military authorities had asked Daimler to supply a specific type of vehicle, a 20 hp chassis fitted with a utility box body. The company prepared drawings,

Daimler delivered over 2,000 lorries to the Army during the Great War. [MBRT]

In the autumn of 1914, Daimler built 50 wagonettes for the Army. [MBRT]

had them approved, built and delivered approximately 60 of these cars between 7–18 August. Then the War Office asked for wagonettes: by the end of October 50 of these had been built and delivered.

More orders followed. Some 150 'Inside Driving Limousines, suitable for the use of staff officers' were designed, approved, built and delivered in the space of three months: these had an ingenious interior layout, with large map tables folding out of the central division and seats which could be rearranged

The 20 hp 'Inside Driving Limousine' was a mobile base for staff officers. [JDHT]

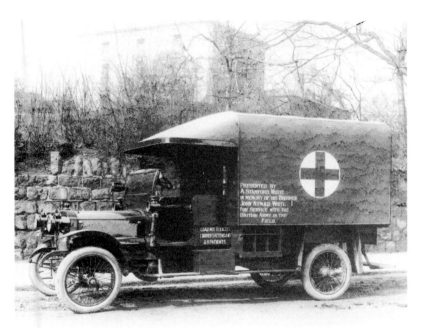

Daimler built well over 1,000 ambulances, many sponsored by private individuals. [MBRT]

The first type of box body built on the 20 hp chassis. [MBRT]

to make a double berth. 'Many a staff officer practically lived in his car for weeks on end,' noted the company. At the same time, Daimler had started building ambulances, and many of these were sponsored by 'well-known motorists, at home, in the colonies and in foreign parts', with the list headed by King George, Queen Mary, and the Dowager Empress of Russia. By the end of September

1915, a thousand ambulances had been completed and were serving on all fronts, even as far afield as India. By 1916, however, this aspect of Daimler's war work was drawing to a close and other makers took over the maintenance of the ambulances and staff cars.

Daimler lorries were widely used, too. Sales of these sleeve-valve chassis – built with load capacities of 2, 3, 4 and 5 tons and 30 or 40 hp engines – had increased so much that the company had planned for a weekly output of 50 chassis for 1915. When war broke out in August 1914, output was moving steadily towards this target and had reached 25–30 chassis weekly, but then quickly doubled in response to Government demand. Meanwhile, the 60 or so chassis awaiting delivery were impressed into government service and sent to Avonmouth to be shipped to France along with the original expeditionary force – French's legendary 'contemptibly little army'. Buses were taken off the streets of London at the rate of 10 a week and driven down to Coventry to be stripped of their double-deck bodies and converted into high-sided wagons.

At the beginning of March 1915 the War

Office ordered 50 two-ton trucks, which 'it was absolutely essential . . . should be delivered to a West Coast port the following Saturday'. Working round the clock for five days and nights, the Daimler employees despatched the last seven trucks to Avonmouth at 6.30 on the Saturday morning. These vehicles were off to the Dardanelles, where the Allied attack on Gallipoli had begun in a futile attempt to knock the Turks out of the war.

To maintain vehicles in the field, Daimler equipped a number of 3-ton chassis with travelling workshops: these were used along with store vans carrying stocks of Daimler spares. J.A.L. Gallard of the *Financial Times* (who was in charge of an ambulance column during the war) commented: 'One of the surprises – at any rate to the writer – was the way the sleeve-valve engine when fitted to heavy vehicles stood up to the hard work it was called upon to do in the war area. The war has proved that with a good regular driver a sleeve-valve engine may be run for years without any serious trouble developing; although of course it is not desirable to keep any internal-combustion engine going for a

long time without thorough decarbonising and attention to the wearing parts. I know a 30 cwt lorry which was run daily for a couple of years (excepting on a few occasions when springs or tyres had to be changed) and so far as I can remember the cylinders were never taken off during that period, though the heads were probably removed and these, with the tops of the pistons, scraped.' Compared with the average poppet-valve power unit of those days, that was a pretty remarkable record: engines were expected to need at least a decoke and almost certainly more serious attention every 3,000 miles.

An unexpected bonus of the sleeve-valve engine in those days when most engines (apart from the ubiquitous Model T Ford) had fixed cylinder heads was the ease with which the separate head over each cylinder could be removed for removal of the accumulated carbon. The sleeve valves, it was found, normally needed no attention during regular service.

On a more specialized front, Daimler supplied 18 specially-bodied vans to the Marconi Wireless Telegraph Company, for radio communications were beginning to be

Shelling out

During 1916, Daimler began producing high calibre (12-inch) shells for the Ministry of Munitions. The body, paint, trim, and upholstery plants were turned over to shell production, machining shell casings from rough forgings brought into the factory by train. At the peak of production, Daimler was making over 2,000 shell casings a day, which were then taken to the ordnance factories for filling in the same way that the raw casings had been brought in. It was, said the manager of the shell shop, the largest output of any private firm in the country.

The Daimler 3-ton travelling workshop carried a lathe, grinder, drill, vices and portable forge to maintain sleeve-valves in the field. [MBRT]

used in warfare: that was a collaboration which would bear fruit in peacetime.

Wartime production of Daimler lorries was more than 4,000.

* * *

'The position of Aeronautics in this country at the outbreak of war was very backward,' commented the BSA Group's official war history, *Munitions of War*, 'due mainly to the meagre pre-war inducements offered by the Government, which were totally inadequate to interest automobile manufacturers in the production of aircraft engines and insufficient to enable the few enthusiasts who were designing aeroplanes to increase their capacity for manufacture. The development of such aircraft engines as existed had been due to the French, the majority of aeroplanes being fitted with either the Gnome or Renault motors.'

Faced with a German front-line air force of 232 aeroplanes, the Royal Flying Corps and Royal Naval Air Service together could only muster 113 aeroplanes, and the military command, trained in an era when battlefield tactics were dictated by the requirements of

the horse, found it difficult to envisage any wartime role for the aeroplane other than as a kind of steerable balloon with limited capabilities for artillery observation. Commented R. Dallas Brett in his *History of British Aviation*: 'It was not until late in 1913 that the Government realized the futility of organizing an Air Arm which was entirely dependant upon foreign engines for its motive power, and it was not until early 1914 that any steps were taken to encourage the production of British engines. A competition, for an inadequate prize, was actually in progress at Farnborough at the outbreak of war, but, such was the inefficiency of the Royal Aircraft Factory, that months of invaluable time had been wasted through the inadequacy and frequent breakdowns of the plant which had been devised by the "experts" there for testing the engines submitted . . . Such was the muddled incompetence in official circles, with which the British aircraft industry had to contend.'

Despite the fact that its only experience of aircraft engine manufacture had been an unsuccessful experimental aero-engine – 'a cross between the Knight slide-valve type and the ordinary Anzani' – built to Frederick Lanchester's designs in 1910–11, Daimler was one of the first companies to attempt to counter this shortage of suitable engines. As soon as war broke out the company made arrangements with the Gnome Engine Company, London agents for the best-known rotary aircraft engine, the French Gnome *Monosoupape*, to build this idiosyncratic power unit in Coventry.

The Gnome Engine Company had been set up in 1913 by George Holt Thomas – a wealthy sportsman whose family owned the *Graphic* newspaper and who had inspired the establishment of Britain's premier aerodrome within the Brooklands race-track – to import power units for his newly-formed Aircraft Manufacturing Company, which built Farman-designed aeroplanes for the Royal Flying Corps. The 80 hp Gnome, which had the best power/weight ratio of the early aero-

Wartime fuel restrictions meant that civilian vehicles like this charabanc were forced to run on coal gas contained in roof-top gasbags. [MBRT]

This double-deck
Daimler bus used for
troop transport has been
fitted with special high-
traction solid tyres.
[MBRT]

engines, had its seven cylinders set in star formation, revolving around a fixed crankshaft which also acted as the inlet manifold. The fuel/air mixture in the crankcase passed into the combustion chambers through transfer ports in the cylinder walls uncovered by the fall of the piston in the cylinder, so that only an exhaust valve was needed – hence the name *monosoupape* (single valve).

There were no working drawings of the *Monosoupape* engine in England, so on Friday 7 August, the Gnome Engine Company sent an engine by road from Hendon aerodrome to Coventry, where it was dismantled in the Tool Room. A week later, all its 1,100-odd component parts had been measured, drawn and an illustrated specification made and issued. Working closely with the Physical Laboratory, the purchasing department acquired the necessary materials, and dies, tools, jigs and gauges were put in hand. Daimler had committed to building the first engine within eight weeks and by 30 September it was complete and waiting on its

test stand outside the Daimler works. All that was missing was the test propeller, which had gone astray on the railway.

Eventually it arrived, but by then it was dark, and the test had to be made by the lights of a motor car. Once the ignition system had been sorted out, the cylinders were primed with petrol and 'in response to a vigorous swing of the propeller, it suddenly burst into a roar of life. With flames issuing from the open exhausts it became a huge Catherine wheel, and the sight was both inspiring and satisfying to the crowd of its creators who had gathered to witness it. It wanted but an hour to the conclusion of the last day of the eighth week!'

It's apparent that Daimler's machining skills were particularly suited to the manufacture of the Gnome engine, for many of the operations – including making the cylinders – involved turning relatively large components, which of course Daimler had perfected in the manufacture of the sleeves for the Knight engine. After the usual teething troubles had been overcome, a 'steady output' of Gnome engines was achieved, along with large quantities of spares for existing engines, 'which considerably enlarged and complicated the programme'.

As is the way with aero-engines, the 80 hp Gnome – which powered planes like the little Sopwith Pup and Bristol Scout – was soon superseded; it does not seem that Daimler built the more powerful nine-cylinder 100 hp Gnome, for it had taken on an even more demanding job, producing the air-cooled V8 RAF 1 engine designed at the Royal Aircraft Factory at Farnborough to replace the 70 hp Renault (which it strongly resembled) in the Factory's BE2C biplane. Having awarded the contract to Daimler, the War Office declared that completed engines should be tested at Farnborough, but to circumvent this time-wasting procedure, Daimler developed its own test-bed, which turned out to be far superior to the Royal Aircraft Factory design.

The War Office then decided it needed far more RAF 1 engines than Daimler could supply, and contracts were issued to other companies, who sent representatives to Coventry for training.

As one of the few luxury car makers with its own body shop, Daimler had outstanding experience in woodworking, and soon took the obvious step from aero-engine manufacture to building the complete flying machine. With its blinkered views on aerial warfare, the War Office awarded Daimler a contract to build the BE2C, which Farnborough had produced as a standard type for the Royal Flying Corps in direct contravention of its official function as an experimental establishment. Daimler had actually built 100 of these machines as early as the end of 1914. Known familiarly as 'Stability Jane', the BE2C had been developed in accordance with the philosophy of providing 'eyes for the artillery'; 'Jane's' main

A 110 hp Le Rhône rotary ('a difficult engine to build') on the test stand at Daimler. [MBRT]

– and often fatal – fault was 'her inflexible sobriety', an inability to manoeuvre quickly if attacked . . .

Called as a witness during a 1916 judicial inquiry into the running of the Royal Flying Corps, Algernon Berriman of Daimler tried to justify this obsolescent machine: 'The RAF engine and the BE2C machine have their defects, but they form a combination that has been instrumental in enabling the Royal Flying Corps to perform invaluable service to the Army in France.' And certainly, when three Zeppelins were shot down over England in September–October 1916, the aircraft concerned were all BE2Cs fitted with RAF engines: however vulnerable she seemed in the daytime, 'Stability Jane's' after-dark performance was, it seems, outstanding. Nevertheless, the inquiry report did reveal some of the tensions involved in working with the Royal Aircraft Factory: 'We have not forgotten the complaints that, after the drawings of the BE2C and the 90 hp RAF engine were sent to the manufacturers, they were constantly being altered in detail, thus

causing delay and confusion.' But if the War Office's choice of aeroplane and engine was questionable, there was no querying Daimler's ability to meet the demand, several times extending its plant to provide the extra capacity for increased Government orders.

Again, the RAF 1, though developed into the 90 bhp RAF 1A, became outclassed, and a new 150 bhp V 12 design known as the RAF 4 was developed at Farnborough and went into production at the Daimler 'and was so widely useful as to be built in immense quantities'. An improved 159 bhp development, the RAF 4A, powered the next aeroplane to be built by Daimler, the BE12 single-seater 'Zeppelin buster', which was followed by the RE8 two-seater two-gun reconnaissance fighter, known familiarly as the 'Harry Tate' after a popular comedian of the day: official records show that Daimler built at least 300 of these.

With Daimler building aeroplanes in large numbers, the War Office decided that it might be a good idea to have an aerodrome in the Coventry area, which up to that time had lacked a proper flying field. The fields which

A wartime staff Christmas party saw Santa arrive in a scaled down BE2; but what was the fairy doing in the egg? [MBRT]

RAF 4A engines under construction. [MBRT]

The Daimler-built BE12 'Zeppelin Buster' was a single-seat development of the BE2C. [MBRT]

adjoined Daimler's Radford factory site were as suitable as any, so the company bought them, cleared the site using one of its 105 hp tractors and patriotically put the land at the

disposal of the Government for the duration of the war. Here King George V saw an entirely Daimler-built aeroplane fly when he visited the works in July 1915. The War

Office subsequently extended the site by compulsory acquisition under the Defence of the Realm Act and it became the main Royal Air Force testing ground for aircraft built in the Coventry district.

Government vacillation resulted in some frustrating false starts, like the programme to build the FE4 raider aeroplane, 'a huge bomb-carrying machine', which was cancelled just as Daimler had tooled up for production, and a programme to build an RAF 3A engine which was abandoned before the first engine was completed. Another contract, to build V8 Hispano-Suiza aero-engines, was converted to a contract to manufacture Sunbeam aeroengines – and then cancelled altogether.

Asked to explore ways of producing more power to give better rates of climb and greater weight-carrying ability, Daimler – which did a great deal of experimental research on aero-engines – developed a combination steel/copper cylinder which outperformed the aluminium cylinders devised by the Royal Aircraft Factory and raised power output of the RAF 4 to 220 bhp. However, this development, known as B.12.3C, came too late, for Daimler had been asked to revert to rotary engine production.

Once again, the brass hats revealed their blinkered outlook, asking Daimler to begin manufacture of the 110 hp Le Rhône rotary engine ('a difficult engine to build') for trainer planes after the War Office had wasted more than a year in comparison tests of the Le Rhône against the very similar Clerget. 'It was not,' dolefully recorded the company's war history, 'a job calculated to arouse enthusiasm, for the engine in question had long since passed the hey-day of its field service reputation, but it was a definite feature of the Daimler Company's war policy to set aside all considerations of personal preference in the firm belief that, by cheerful willingness to do anything that was really needed, the works would be contributing most to the winning of the war. It was on this account that no great effort was made to press

Daimler designs upon the Government, notwithstanding that an uninterrupted succession of plans was produced, partly in response to requests made by the authorities and partly in direct expression of ideas engendered by experience on the ground. Many different engines were designed in this way and any one of them might have been built with every chance of competing favourably with the corresponding motors of its day. The Daimler works and organization, however, always seemed to be placed first on the list for contracts to extend the production of some urgently required existing type.'

While Daimler's contribution to the Allied effort in those early years of the war that

Large numbers of women worked at the Daimler during the Great War in this 'maze of machinery and the hum of whirring wheels'. [MBRT]

Women assembling aircraft mainplanes in the Daimler body shop. [MBRT]

should have been 'all over by Christmas' were undoubtedly crucial, one wonders how much better it might have been had they been allowed to have a free hand – and if the War Office hadn't been so prone to changing its collective mind so very frequently. Nevertheless, there was a positive side to that wartime aero-engine building programme, for it gave Daimler unmatched experience of building V12 engines which would prove essential in peacetime. Moreover, the company trained mechanics for the air force in its works, and the Daimler training methods became a standard for all manufacturers instructing RAF mechanics.

Daimler's contribution to the war effort was fully recognized when, at the height of hostilities, Percy Martin was appointed Controller of Petrol Engines to the Ministry of Munitions and given a seat on the Air Board, while Algernon Berriman became Deputy Controller of the Technical Department at the personal request of the Minister of Munitions and the Secretary of State for Air.

The final warplane built by Daimler –

whose peak output was 80 aeroplanes a month around 1918 – was the DH10, a high-speed twin-engined biplane day bomber which was only just entering production at the time of the Armistice. Though there was a suggestion in July 1918 by oil magnate Sir Arthur Duckham, then at the Ministry of Munitions, that Daimler might manufacture the ill-fated ABC Dragonfly radial engine (which in the event was built by Clyno of Wolverhampton), the final aero-engine built by Daimler during the war represented, in some sense, the closing of the circle, for the company ended the conflict as it had begun, building a rotary engine.

Before the war, a young engineer named Walter Owen Bentley ('W.O.') had developed an aluminium piston (at that time pistons were mostly of cast iron, sometimes turned from steel) which he used to good effect in the DFP cars which he and his brother sold from a garage in Hanover Street in the West End. In 1914 he had been annexed by the Admiralty to promote the use of his 'Aerolite' pistons in aero-engines, and this had led him to design an improved rotary engine with steel-lined aluminium cylinders to minimize the risk of seizure through distortion. This 'Bentley Rotary' engine had been built at the Coventry Humber factory, but when a more powerful 'BR2' engine was developed, 'all this became too big for Humbers to cope with,' recalled 'W.O.' in his autobiography, 'so the Daimler factory was made the BR2 headquarters to coordinate the huge construction programme, and Crossleys, Humbers and several other firms all became involved. The BR2 was in production for the new Sopwith Snipe by the early spring of 1918, and output was running at more than 120 a week by the summer.'

Berriman was appointed 'Honorary Engineer-in-Charge' for the BR2 project, and the manufacturing drawings for the new engine were produced by Daimler draughtsmen. Daimler's first BR2 contract, for 1,000 engines, was signed on 5 April 1918 and by the end of June 36 engines had been delivered. Production peaked at 339 engines during October, and then tailed away and a new contract for 1,000 engines was curtailed by the signing of the Armistice on 11 November. By the time production of BR2s ended in December, Daimler had built 1,245 of these nine-cylinder rotaries.

But had the war dragged on into 1919, there could well have been a different ending to the story. Sometime in the spring of 1918 Frederick Lanchester was called in to help Percy Martin develop a more potent version of the BR2 (codenamed 'Rocket') as a private venture. No drawings or technical specifications seem to have survived, but the new engine promised double the 220 hp developed by the BR2, and it appears from Lanchester's referring to it as 'the new double rotation experiment' that it was either that most terrifying of concepts, a double-row rotary with no fewer than 18 cylinders or a counter-rotating engine in which the cylinders rotated one way and the propeller the other!

Lanchester was an uncompromising fellow, and his relationship with the newly-created Air Ministry seems to have been robust, to say the least. Writing to Percy Martin on 29 April, shortly after Lord Rothermere (brother of Lord Northcliffe) had resigned as Air Minister after five months in the job, Lanchester crowed: 'I feel sure you must be very much pleased with the turn of events that have taken place at the Air Ministry. The resignation of Rothermere, considered as an act of God, appears to show that the celestial powers are not so wholly on the side of the Huns as the Kaiser would have us believe.'

Though a prototype had been running in April, the development of the 'Rocket' seems to have been troublesome. On 24 September, Lanchester wrote to Martin at his home in Kenilworth trying to fix up a meeting in the Daimler company flat to discuss the Rocket, which he wanted to get into production to foil a threatened government attempt to coerce Daimler into building a Rolls-Royce

Most powerful rotary built by Daimler during the war was the 240 hp BR2 designed by W.O. Bentley. [MBRT]

Command performance

King George V's visit to Coventry on 22 July 1915 was the first by any monarch since the early years of Queen Victoria's reign. The royal party was collected from the station by 'several luxurious Daimler cars . . . of a special colour and character' and, after visiting the Coventry Ordnance Works, arrived at 'The Daimler' at noon. The King visited the entire factory, chatting to many of the staff. 'One son of Vulcan extended a grimy hand to His Majesty, who . . . shook it right heartily'. After inspecting motor lorries, gun tractors, the shell shop, and the aeroplane works, the King watched an all-Daimler aeroplane 'rise gracefully . . . showing much steadiness despite the heavy rain and tricky wind'.

engine: 'I was thinking of inviting you to take a sandwich and a glass of champagne with us at the flat when B [Berriman] turns up on Friday evening – the only difficulty is that it is your flat and your champagne!'

Replied Martin: 'I want to . . . make up my mind as to the advisability of putting through at least 10 Rocket engines incorporating in the design such detail alterations as our experience with the one engine suggests to us . . . Personally I feel that if we can succeed in building an engine that will satisfactorily give 330 hp at 1,020 revs of the propeller, the Government officials will undoubtedly find use for it, and after we have had a certain amount of experience with that engine . . . we ought to do much better than the performance above given. The manufacturing side will be relatively simple because of the resemblance it bears to the BR2 Engine which is turning out such a distinct success from the manufacturing standpoint. On the other hand, if upon examination of such evidence as I can get together by Saturday it looks doubtful, I should decide then to drop the engine for the time being – or at least drop any venture of putting it before the authorities.'

Lanchester's meeting with 'Uncle' Bush that Friday must have left the Daimler champagne tasting decidedly flat. After only 10 hours' running of the prototype Rocket engine, Bush had found 'formidable difficulties . . . the Rocket engine appears to suffer from a very excessive vibration in the event of any one of the cylinders missing fire. The extent of this vibration is reported to be of an entirely different order of magnitude to the corresponding vibration of the BR2 and is stated to have broken 3/4 inch diameter bolts in the very few minutes or seconds run . . . it appears to me to be one of the most serious unknown quantities in the behaviour of the Rocket engine. Mr Bush of the Test Shop certainly considers the engine is dangerous . . .'

Though Lanchester considered that all the problems could eventually have been overcome, the Rocket project seems to have

been shelved: certainly the next protracted correspondence between Martin and Lanchester, a couple of weeks before the signing of the Armistice made all thought of super-rotary engines redundant, concerned the purchase of a batch of cigars that Lanchester – converted to cigar-smoking by Martin and Manville – had discovered in a London shop. 'I was so pleased with a little purchase of cigars I made the other day at Savory's in Piccadilly that I bought 250 more from the same cabinet, the only ones of decent size that remained; 200 of these are for you if you care to take them. The price is £12-0-0 the hundred.'

* * *

On 24 March 1916 a cross-Channel ferry named the *Sussex* was torpedoed by a German U-Boat in an 'act . . . of sheer blood lust' which echoed the sinking of the *Lusitania* the previous year. Many of its 380 passengers died when the *Sussex* sank; among the survivors was a little man named Harry J. Lawson, who was badly enough injured still to be undergoing treatment when shareholders in the General Omnibus Supply Company met in August at the London Bankruptcy Court to prove that here was one old dog incapable of learning new tricks.

Said the Official Receiver: 'This company is one of a series promoted by Harry John Lawson. That individual is still in hospital, and we have therefore not been able as yet to obtain a complete history of the company or any account of the £40,000 subscribed by the public. The company never did any business and had no assets except unpaid calls (£4,000) and £100 in cash. There was nothing to show for the money of the shareholders and no hope of any dividend. There had been the usual ornamental list of directors, including the Marquis of Tweeddale and Sir G.H. Lacon, Bart, who had resigned after certain articles had appeared in *Truth*. In my opinion, the statements in the prospectus were absolutely misleading – this case calls for the attention of the Public

Prosecutor.' Commented *The Aeroplane*: 'The case bears a strong resemblance to the so-called Blériot prospectus issued by the same Lawson. His next attempt to float an aviation company would be well worth watching.'

Maybe there were still some working at the Daimler Motor Company who thanked heaven for a lucky escape when they saw this latest news of their long-departed founder in the press.

* * *

If Daimler was not actually running the war, there's little doubt that the company's contribution played a major role in securing the Allied victory in 1918, for its activities were not confined to the manufacture of cars, lorries, aircraft and aero-engines: from 1916 Daimler also made more 12 inch shells than any other company in the country, peaking at 2,000 a week. Each one was machined from a 990 lb forging down to a finished weight of 684 lb.

Then there were the massive artillery tractors built for Daimler by Fosters of Lincoln, developed from the 105 hp tractors that were being constructed for the South American market, and used to haul 15-inch howitzers built by the Coventry Ordnance Works. On 3 December 1914 the first machine completed out of an order for 97 tractors passed its acceptance trials at Lincoln in front of Admiral Bacon, managing director of the ordnance works, who suggested to William Tritton (his counterpart at Fosters) that what was really needed in a combat that was already settling into trenchbound stalemate was some kind of fighting machine that could cross trenches by laying its own bridge.

Tritton was called in by the Landships Committee recently formed by Winston Churchill, the First Lord of the Admiralty, and given the task of designing 'some new kind of engine of war, able to move across broken ground, which, without giving the enemy warning in advance, could break a way through the wire entanglements, penetrate the trench system, silence the machine-guns and effectively support the

Daimler made more 12 inch shells during the Great War than any other British company. [MBRT]

Built for Daimler by Foster of Lincoln, this 105 hp artillery tractor demonstrates its ability to cross a temporary wooden bridge to the assembled brass hats in Hatfield Park. [MBRT]

infantry in the assault'. All kinds of curious devices had already been projected, many seemingly devised by that man of the moment, William Heath Robinson, 'embracing sizes and weights of all degrees even up to lengths of 100 feet and weights of 300 tons'. Tritton began by experimenting with a curious modified Daimler tractor that had two front wheels set in line eight feet apart on an extended subframe to span a ditch while the machine dropped a 15 foot long bridge in front of the huge rear wheels so that they could follow across the gap, but the choice was quickly narrowed down to machines running on some kind of caterpillar track.

The basic idea of caterpillar tracks was nothing new and indeed tracked tractors had already been built in America: Tritton combined a pair of American-made 'Bullock' caterpillar tracks with an armoured hull and fitted this strange 'No 1 Lincoln Machine' with the only sufficiently powerful engine built in Britain, the 105 hp Daimler tractor unit, along with its gearbox and worm final drive. This makeshift prototype was built and running within the amazingly short period of 37 days in August–September 1915, but tests soon showed that it would not stay on the Bullock tracks. Various alternatives were tried: roller chains, wire ropes woven into a carpet, Balata flexible belting. But on 21 September Tritton sent the Admiralty a 'humorous and optimistic' coded telegram: 'Balata died on test bench yesterday morning. New arrival by Tritton out of Pressed Plate. Light in weight but very strong. All doing well, thank you. – Proud Parents.'

This new design of caterpillar track was used on a second machine nicknamed 'Little Willie', which was the first successful Tank (a name derived from Tritton's deliberate disinformation that he was working on a prototype water carrier for the Mesopotamian campaign). 'Little Willie' was followed by a larger design with lozenge-shaped tracks and guns housed in projecting sponsons either side of the hull, known as 'Big Willie' or 'Mother', this new design was also Daimler-powered and, after passing its preliminary tests with flying colours, was officially demonstrated in front of an impressive gathering of brass-hats in Hatfield Park in January 1916. Among the audience (whose most notable absentee was Winston Churchill, dropped from the War Cabinet

A Mark One Tank under test. [MBRT]

two months earlier) were Field Marshal Lord Kitchener of Khartoum, A.J. Balfour (the new First Lord of the Admiralty), David Lloyd George, Dudley Docker and a host of high-ranking officers including Major W.G. Wilson (who had helped Tritton develop the Tank) and Major H.O.D. Segrave, who was to achieve post-war fame as a racing driver and land speed record-breaker.

In February 1916 the British Army ordered a hundred Mark I Tanks, following this up with a further order for 50 Mark II models two months later, half of these armed with six-pounder guns and machine-guns ('Male') and half with machine-guns only ('Female'). Shipped to France in utter secrecy at the beginning of September, these Tanks were designed round the 105 hp Daimler-Foster power train – the existence of which was the crucial factor in the rapid development of this new weapon, which caused such a sensation when it was first seen in action a fortnight later during the Somme offensive.

A *Times* correspondent vividly described the battle debut of the Tank: 'Two days before they were used in the present advance I had an opportunity to see a lot of them – a whole herd – where they were resting before their first experience of real war. It was as incredible as a nightmare or one of Jules Verne's most fantastic imaginings. A slight hollow, a few acres in extent, in a level plain was full of the monsters, like cows in a meadow – huge shapeless bulks, resembling nothing else that was ever seen on earth, wandered hither and thither like some vast antediluvian brutes which Nature had made and forgotten. Painted in venomous reptilian colours, which made them admirably invisible against the dun background of dry autumn grass and bare soil, they were inexpressibly suggestive of living things – hybrids between Behemoth and the Chimera, toad-salamanders, echidna-dragons – anything you please which is mythical and fantastic.

'I was permitted to go inside one of the beasts and inspect its vitals in all their incredible details; and I watched the great things manoeuvre about the field, grotesque and unspeakable; and at each new antic which they performed, each new capacity which they developed, one could do nothing but sit down and laugh till one's sides ached. Were they only a preposterous joke, or were they a serious contribution to modern warfare? It was impossible to make up one's mind. But that they were appalling and hideous was certain as one saw them in the gathering dusk wheel off and, falling into single file, heave their huge bodies one by one up the sides of the hollow, and then go shouldering off outlined against the skyline, like a great string of mammoths, to take up their positions in the battle front.'

The element of surprise behind the tank attack against Prince Rupprecht of Bavaria's divisions at 6.30 the following morning was total: led by a tank carrying a dummy news hoarding that read 'Great Hun Defeat! Special!', the infantry had taken the town of Flers by 10.00 a.m., 'the garrison, which was hiding about in dugouts, surrendering in small, scared groups.' This first action of 'His Majesty's Land Ships' saw the biggest advance in one operation since the start of the Somme offensive in July: 'In the course of one day's fighting we have broken through two of the enemy's main defensive systems and have advanced on a front of over six miles

to a depth of over a mile,' reported Field-Marshal Haig, Commander-in-Chief of the British Army. 'All this has been accomplished with a small number of casualties in comparison with the troops employed. Our new heavily-armoured cars . . . known as Tanks . . . successfully cooperated with the infantry and, coming as a surprise to the enemy rank and file, gave valuable help in breaking down their resistance.'

A total of 49 tanks was under orders that day and 28 actually went into action: 'For once in the national life we had stolen a march on the astute German!' wrote an eye-witness.

All the early tanks were powered by Daimler engines, and though there were problems in their design, a report prepared for Sir Albert Stern, Secretary of the Landships Committee, concluded: 'The engines themselves were very reliable, and owing to their sleeve valves were easy to maintain, since the skilled work necessary for

Wartime Prime Minister David Lloyd George arrives by official Daimler to inspect the troops. [MBRT]

the adjustment of poppet valves was not required.' Weighing up to 28 tons, these early tanks were ponderous performers, with a maximum range of 23.6 miles and a top speed of 3.7 mph (at which they consumed two gallons of petrol per mile); for the Mark IV derivative, which had an 'overwhelming' success at the Battle of Cambrai on 20 November 1917, a more powerful 125 hp Daimler engine was introduced during the nine-month production run. Apparently developed by W.O. Bentley while he was based in Coventry working on the Bentley Rotary programme, this revised engine owed much of its improved power output to the introduction of aluminium pistons.

Various other Daimler-engined tank derivatives were produced, including a gun carrier (also used as a supply vehicle) which first saw action at the third battle of Ypres in July 1917, and salvage machines used to rescue broken-down tanks and heavy guns. Right at the end of the war tests were made with a Mark VII tank with Williams-Janney hydraulic transmission, but it never saw active service.

After the Armistice a 125 hp Daimler tank was manoeuvred into place in central Coventry as a war memorial: 'We heard the engine stop, and it was like the last heartbeat of a giant,' recalled journalist Ernest Appleby 19 years later when the tank was removed to make way for a statue of Lady Godiva – and found to be still capable of running.

There was one major problem with the Daimler-engined tanks: the inevitable oil haze from their sleeve-valve engines, which – once the enemy had realized what the blue smoke signified – made surprise attacks difficult; ultimately Harry Ricardo designed a dedicated six-cylinder poppet valve engine for the later marks of tank, but the 'war to end all wars' was almost over by then. It was the fact that the 105 hp Daimler sleeve-valve unit was ready and reliable at the start of the tank programme that ensured the early success of the Land Ships.

Crucial, too, was the use of the Lanchester

vibration damper on that massive Daimler engine, and Frederick Lanchester painted a typically forthright picture of a tank planning meeting in a letter written to Percy Martin in December 1916: 'Colonel Stern said he had decided to call a meeting at the earliest possible moment in London of the electrical firms which you agreed to take into our confidence in the matter of manufacture . . . Personally, I do not know why he wants a meeting; I should have thought that he could have left it to the Daimler to deal with the electrical firms and have dealt with the Daimler for the whole thing. Obtaining promises and estimates of delivery etc cannot be done at a meeting, and being matters of enquiry and calculation would be just as well

Ernest Instone shows his son Rupert the 125 hp Daimler-engined tank which served as Coventry's war memorial for 19 years. [MBRT]

The Bey of Tunis and his Zouaves with a 20 hp Daimler limousine. [JDHT]

done by correspondence; however all the Munitions people seem to like to get a lot of folks round a table and talk a little time away, probably the reason being that they have to educate themselves, which is of course a matter of no small importance . . .

'I had put before me a lot of gear schemes, involving epicyclics and various other devices. I did not think much of any of them . . . The gear systems struck me as altogether too experimental, and Wilson's design of an epicyclic gear was a rather horrible thing with cast teeth – it made me shudder . . . Tritton, who did not arrive until later, wanted to dismiss the internally driven spur off-hand

in his most Napoleonic mood. His argument was that it had been tried many times on heavy haulage work and always failed. He misses two points . . . that as tried it has rarely been given a fair chance . . . and what might be a ghastly failure in the ordinary commercial vehicle or tractor might yet be a thorough-going success in the case of the Tank; the standard of durability is different.

'The best point in Tritton is that when he makes up his mind he has the courage of his convictions. The worst of him is that when he makes up his mind he is as likely to be wrong as right. Put the two together and it is a living picture!'

Chapter 6

VEE-TWELVES AND FLUID FLYWHEELS

Even before the end of the War, Daimler was planning for post-war production. In between revising the design of the piston rings for the Bentley BR2 rotary engine ('in the ordinary way I should not mind the Tool Department working out its own salvation, but time is too precious for any flights of fancy'), Frederick Lanchester started work on a revolutionary new Daimler which represented a clean break with anything that Daimler – or, indeed, any other British company – had ever built.

On 28 August 1918 Frederick Lanchester was in Coventry to review future models with Percy Martin and the discussion was long and detailed. Lanchester, it seems, had already

Possibly a prototype for the post-war Light Thirty, this impressive coupé has a most unusual design of radiator. [NMM]

178

proposed a number of ideas to Algernon Berriman, and Martin decided to give Lanchester his head – not always a prudent course! It was agreed that a draughtsman named Milligan should be delegated to work under Lanchester's supervision, possibly in one of the new small offices (Lanchester referred to them disparagingly as 'loose boxes') that Berriman had recently had installed in the drawing offices. By 15 October – still a month short of the end of the war (though at that point Lanchester remained pessimistic about the outcome of the peace negotiations 'because broadly speaking the Hun has got to come off his perch and give an unconditional surrender') – his outline proposals were ready.

To put it mildly, they were sensational: Lanchester had conceived not only a post-war Daimler with all-round independent suspension but devised an ambitious forward-looking corporate philosophy for the company. Martin – who was convalescing from influenza at the St David's Hotel, Harlech – was bombarded with a succession of long memoranda bursting with Lancunian enthusiasm for both projects.

'The present establishment of the company, whether it be considered from the point of view of money, men employed or actual capital involved, is considerably greater than was the case prior to the war and the potential output of the company is correspondingly greater. On the other hand it is by no means certain that there will be any expansion after the war in the manufactures with which we have been hitherto engaged . . .: the manufacturing resources of the country, so far as concerns engineering products, have been considerably stimulated, and while we may endeavour to grasp more than our proportionate share of the after the war trade, there will be others likewise making the same endeavour and it does not altogether follow therefore that we shall be wholly successful . . .

'The Daimler Company was originally a Company for the manufacture and marketing of motor cars, and in particular pleasure cars, and for many years the market was almost exclusively confined to a pleasure vehicle programme. To this was added the commercial vehicle department which four years prior to the war was being run successfully, and various tentative feelers had been put out in various directions – such as the Renard train, the agricultural tractor, the railway coach – and, considered as a policy, the company's business was clearly tending to become a comprehensive one dealing with the petrol tractor.

'So far as I know there was no definite declaration of this as a policy to limit the activities of the Company, but it came about more or less as a logical fact, the various developments being those that individually recommended themselves as appropriate to the staff and to the managing director in particular . . . I am inclined to think that the position of the Company would be very much stronger if we were to take a wider view of the traction problems of the day and include other means of propulsion . . . such as steam and electrical.

'I regard the past limitation as less due to any essential limitations in our manufacturing resources or in the resources of the labour market than I do to the fact that our staff . . . has been petrol to a man . . . the main purpose of the present memorandum is that we should contemplate taking an altogether wider outlook and that we should strengthen our position by getting thoroughly capable, experienced men, in fact the best that we can get, to deal with steam traction . . . in addition to electrical . . . we should call ourselves and advertise ourselves as Self-Propelled Traction Engineers, and not merely the manufacturers and salesmen of particular articles . . . we should be prepared to take any problem in self-propelled traction whatever that is put up to us and work out the best solution, whether it be petrol, steam or electric, advise our clients, prepare estimates and recommend particular cars for particular services . . . in brief to replace the ideal of being manufacturers and sales men of particular motor vehicles by the ideal of being the leading firm – *the* one firm in fact – competent to advise clients of any kind without personal prejudice and to carry out and solve any problem in mechanical traction that may come our way.'

But for his post-war Daimler, Lanchester retained the petrol engine: it was about the only conventional feature of a design that in many respects would have seemed advanced several decades later – if it had ever been built. For a start, in an era when virtually every car on the roads had leaf-sprung beam axles fore and aft, Lanchester's design had no axles or metal springs at all, but independent hydraulic suspension units at each corner, their pressure maintained by a replenisher unit that automatically came into action when the suspension unit's oil fell below a predetermined level. 'All that is necessary for the attendant to do,' wrote Lanchester, who was obviously one of the old school who knew the difference between engineers and mechanics, 'is to see that the oil supply reservoir, containing about a pint, is duly filled when required.'

Both front and rear wheels were splayed outwards, a conventional enough practice in the case of the front wheels but unusual for rear wheels, one major advantage being that 'for the accepted standard of wheel gauge five inches of extra rear body width is available'. The front wheels were mounted on single vertical hydraulic pillars, which also acted as steering pivots in much the same way as the Macpherson Strut, which was to translate Lancunian theory into production reality nearly 30 years later, while the rear wheels were carried between dual guide pillars. They were driven by jointed cardan shafts in much the same way as the classic De Dion axle of veteran days, but with the shaft passing through the hub, with the outer universal carried on the hub cap so that the cardan was 'a foot longer than would otherwise be possible; the actual length of the coupling shafts is 22 inches,

which I believe is adequate'.

This enabled the worm final drive unit to be mounted direct on the chassis so that it became sprung instead of unsprung weight and gave increased ground clearance: 'The clearing away of all moving under-axles and axle work, torque tubes, etc, results in an enormous simplification of the whole design and, presuming everything comes off all right, will, I think be considered a very great advantage,' predicted Lanchester. 'It allows of the whole space between the two chassis members being utilised and I have arranged for a spare wheel locker under the floor of the rear body and a 20 gallon petrol tank under the driver's seat, the top of which only projects a couple of inches above the chassis members. There is no longer anything requiring access in the body work and no need to arrange for a hinged or lifting body . . .

'Practically speaking, the underneath of the car is a flat, smooth surface only broken by the protruding base chamber of the engine and the under half of the hydraulic gear box. This combination is of smooth streamline form. The exhaust box, which is being arranged on the inner side of the car directly under the chassis member, is a cylinder $6\frac{1}{2}$ inches diameter by about four feet in length. The floor level is approximately 24 inches but will vary with the state of the suspension. Thus, after long standing it would sit down somewhat, which is actually no disadvantage.' The patented 'hydraulic clutch gear box' was a drum-shaped flywheel bolted direct to the crankshaft and containing a three-speed and reverse mechanism controlled by a combined clutch and gear lever; 'the car will have a central control after the manner of some of the American vehicles, but if this is objected to, the control lever can be carried to the right hand of the driver. The transmission from the power unit to the worm box consequently becomes a straight tubular shaft about 7 feet in length and runs close under the petrol tank and spare wheel locker.'

More rococo ironwork on the 1919 Olympia stand: in evidence are the Saltley 45 hp limousine with Daimler's own bodywork (right) and the 'Windoveret' four-seater coupé. [JDHT]

Another advantage of the final drive layout was that inboard drum brakes were specified, mounted on either side of the worm housing. 'This disposition has other advantages of a more important kind,' noted Lanchester. The brakes . . . are controlled by two rods running longitudinally one on each side of the propeller shaft and are worked direct from a foot pedal. There is a hand brake lever fitted in the usual place also operating the same brake in order to hold same on when the car is left standing. The hydraulic gear itself can be used as a brake and it is contemplated that in the ordinary way it will be considerably used in this manner. Should occasion demand it, however, an additional brake may be provided, applied by either the hand lever or the foot pedal, in place of both operating the same brakes, as in the experimental design in operation.'

The chassis of the projected post-war Daimler was equally unorthodox. The side members were virtually straight, tapering uniformly outwards towards the rear and stiffened by four tubular crossmembers, three of them doubling as reservoirs for the hydraulic suspension units and the fourth, just ahead of the petrol tank, carrying the cross-shaft for the brakes. Lanchester had also designed a new kind of instrument panel and switch board 'with a view to more completely clearing up the obnoxious detail with which cars of the present day are encumbered'.

Though it was designed using the technology of 1918, the general layout had much in common with concept cars of 70 years later: 'I have designed a wheel on the lines used by the Humber company with a single tubular spoke,' Lanchester told Martin. 'If this is well made, it will not look amiss and it has several important advantages. The whole of the internal mechanism of the steering column becomes external mechanism. The steering pillar itself consists of a 4 inch tube through which the steering shaft passes, and in the space between the steering shaft and the pillar I am accommodating the various way-shafts to control the ignition timing, the throttle, the jet, the dual ignition and the conduits for the electrical connections of the switchboard and ammeter and voltmeter, also the shaft to drive the speedometer. The various functional connections can be made at the lower end of the pillar at any convenient points; they do not have to be carried through the middle of the steering shaft as at present and the whole design makes a clean sweep of all the objectional features with which we are only too well acquainted. The fixed dash with its instruments in all sorts of inaccessible and invisible positions disappears.

'In the detailed carrying out of this scheme I am designing the "instrument head" as we may call it in three pieces. There is one piece which I may call the Daimler section which includes and contains the throttle, jet and ignition levers, the electrical conduits and the speedometer driving shaft. There is the electrician's section, which is an independent unit secured to the Daimler section by a couple of screws, all electrical joints, etc, being made on the plug system when this unit is put into position. There is lastly the speedometer section which likewise is put on as a separate piece by a couple of screws and which contains in a straight line row the speed indicator, the mileage recorder, the trip indicator and a timepiece. The whole is being carefully studied with a view to making it weather proof and the idea is that the two separate components may be manufactured to our specifications and block drawing by a speedometer firm and an electrical firm, ready to put on the Daimler section without anything more than a couple of screws or bolts and unskilled labour.

'The key to this scheme, which I think you will consider very attractive, is actually the one-spoke steering wheel, since in order to carry the idea into effect the head fitting has to be under the wheel instead of above it . . . the worm steering transmission is able to be designed for its own sake and the worm does not have to be made of undesirably great diameter to include the various four or five concentric elements which have at present to come within it. My own opinion is that the 4 inch diameter steering pillar with the instrument head will look a strikingly attractive feature and will give a sense of strength and robust construction that will make the ordinary present day construction look like "back numbers".

'Admittedly the whole scheme contains so many novelties that it must be looked upon as including a large element of gamble, but I think you will agree that it is a legitimate one in view of the fact that no one feature definitely depends upon the other features. If we could win all along the line the success would be gigantic: it would pulverise people like Rolls-Royce and would paralyse the components business as it has developed in the United States. It is really an immense stake to play for.'

Lanchester asked Martin to release two or three members of the drawing office staff to work on the detailed plans so that he could go ahead with costing, 'although owing to the fact that there is hardly an existing feature of the present day motor car in the new design that has not undergone substantial modification, it will yet be some time, even with the assistance required, before complete drawings can be ready.'

A subsequent letter detailed some proposed features of the new engine: 'I rather presume that the forced lubrication experimentally adapted to the 30 hp will be adopted as our standard. Apart from the lubrication pump there have been altogether too many gear shafts . . . magneto, circulation pump, fan, lighting dynamo, starting motor and . . . distributor shaft . . . I have included the starting handle since it normally occupies the

Driven to drink

One of the more curious uses to which Daimlers were put occurred in 1922, when a fleet of five 30 hp six-cylinder Daimlers with van bodies shaped like beer bottles entered service to advertise Bass and Worthington ales. Daimlers were chosen because the fluting on the radiator echoed the shape of the crown stopper on the neck of the 'bottle'. The idea dated from around 1911, when the manager of Worthington, a Dutchman, had a round-radiatored Spyker (built in his homeland) turned into a bottle van.

end of the crankshaft, which might otherwise be used as a direct means of driving one of the necessary fitments . . . In a little experimental four-cylinder that we had on test just before the war, we had arranged the magneto to be driven from the tail end of the crankshaft direct and, owing to the small size of this engine, we had fitted the starting handle to the eccentric shaft. I am inclined to [use] the crankshaft end for driving the lighting dynamo direct and arrange the starting handle on gear a little to one side . . . possibly two revolutions of the starting handle to one of the engine . . . If we can embody a contact breaker and distributor in the dynamo itself, and assuming that the fan is driven by a belt off the damper, the number of extraneous driving connections is reduced to two, namely the circulation pump and the starting dynamo . . .

'I want to return to the practice of putting the chain drive on the front end of the engine. It is badly in the way in the rear position and interferes with the gear unit being bolted to the engine as is necessary in my experimental scheme.' Added Lanchester: 'I rather gather that the Lanchester Company would be open to associate themselves in this experimental work if you see fit to entertain a suggestion in that direction. It might be made an occasion to bargain with them to drop the worm manufacture and turn their plant over to us; the idea just passes through my mind as perhaps worth trying.' Or maybe Lanchester's brothers George and Frank, who still worked for the Lanchester Company but were working under a board they regarded as foolish, were anxious to broker an alliance between the two companies: coming events, as they say, cast their shadow before . . .

The letter concluded: 'I think we came to the conclusion that in introducing anything strikingly novel, it would be more effective if we could do it by a small group of companies under Daimler leadership than ploughing a lone furrow, as at first in the case of the Knight engine. Assuming success – and I always assume success – we should have to convince the public that the new thing is right, and the public take a lot of convincing if the rest of the trade (in self-protection) form what amounts to a conspiracy against us. It might be easily convinced if three or four of the leading firms were all to strike at once.'

The drawings were certainly completed around the first week in November – and indeed survive, in the possession of that great collector Peter Richley – but that seems to have been as far as Lanchester's scheme for the new Daimler car got: the war ended a few days later and the post-war models, announced in late 1919, were merely updated versions of the prewar 4,962 cc 30 hp and 7,413 cc 'special 45 hp' pair-cast six-cylinder models. In the fevered atmosphere of the post-war demand for motor cars, customers – as Lanchester had predicted – were not bothered about mechanical novelty: what they were after was reliable transportation.

Undeterred, Lanchester was still fizzing with enthusiasm, writing letters to Martin bemoaning the post-war inflation – 'all-round advances will have to be made . . . on the basis that thirty-three currency shillings go to the prewar sovereign or thereabouts' – and passing on industry gossip: 'I do not know whether you have heard that Pomeroy has given up his management of the Vauxhall and is going to the States. I do not know whether . . . there has been a disagreement between himself and his co-directors, but if I had shares in the Vauxhall Company I should sell them quick! . . . I do not know who they have got there capable of running the business. It was as nearly a one-man show as anything in the country.'

Ironically, Laurence Pomeroy – who had designed perhaps the first true sports car, the Prince Henry Vauxhall of 1912 – was to play a significant role in Daimler history in years to come, but for the next few years he would be working for 'people who do not allow financial considerations to interfere when they think that any line of investigation has a reasonable chance of leading to success' (the

Aluminum Company of America – 'Alcoa' – of Cleveland, Ohio, who reputedly spent several hundred thousand dollars to produce half-a-dozen Pomeroy cars, built largely of aluminium and with Vauxhall-like flutes in their bonnets).

In Lloyd George's post-Armistice 'Coupon Election' of 1918, Daimler-BSA chairman Edward Manville was elected Unionist Member of Parliament for Coventry: he was created a Knight in the New Year's Honours list of January 1923 'for services to the Board of Trade' and lost his seat in Stanley Baldwin's misjudged snap election that November.

Daimler's post-war range included a new variant which reflected the changed face of post-war society. This was the 'Light Thirty . . . expressly produced for the rapidly increasing number of owner-drivers who desire a comfortable and lively car shorn of unnecessary weight'. This was built on a 10 ft 8.25 in wheelbase (13.25 in shorter than the standard model) with a top gear of 3.78:1 giving nearly 29 mph at 1,000 rpm, and had a honeycomb radiator with the filler cap concealed under the bonnet, a tapered bonnet and lightened springs. Among the customers for the Light Thirty was Emperor Yoshihito of Japan, who bought a Maythorn-bodied tourer in 1920, most likely – in view of the Emperor's feeble health – for the car-enthusiast Crown Prince Hirohito who became Regent in 1921 (the same year that the Japan Automobile Company of Tokyo began fitting open and closed bodies on Daimler Light Thirty chassis).

It was, however, the commercial vehicle aspect that prompted another manufacturer of heavy vehicles, Leyland, to consider a merger with Daimler around this time, though the cash-short Lancashire company soon dropped the merger idea in favour of a share issue.

One of the most spectacular cars delivered in the immediate post-war period was a 45 hp limousine built for Sir Sarupchaud Hukamchaud of Indore: gold leaf covered the body panels, both sides of the wings, the wheel discs and springs, while the radiator shell and starting handle were gold plated. It

Motoring mountaineer George D. Abraham's 1919 Light Thirty on 'a curly bit of road above the shore of Crummock Water'. [MBRT]

A matched pair of 45 hp Daimlers for the Maharajah of Bharatpur, bodied at Hendon by Montie Grahame-White's aviator brother Claude in 1920. [JDHT]

cost £3,500 to build (and when it was returned to the works in 1936 for overhaul, it cost a further £1,450 to repair the car, the wooden body frame of which had been so badly eaten by ants that it had to be replaced).

Power outputs of completed Daimler chassis were tested on Froude brakes – much like the 'rolling roads' used in modern factories – and had to be 65 bhp or more at 1,400 rpm for the 45 hp and 45 bhp for the 30 hp. These were modest enough (around 9 bhp/litre) but there was obviously plenty of low-speed torque, for when in September 1919 motoring mountaineer George D. Abraham, author of several popular travel

Equipment of the Bharatpur Daimler included storage containers and a plumbed-in washbasin in the tail. [MBRT]

books, tried an early Light Thirty four-up over some of the notorious Lakeland hills, he was easily able to restart on the loose 1:4 gradient of Kirkstone Pass. Later the same day, the Light Thirty was the first car to cross the old mountain road to Fell Foot in Langdale, despite the warning of an old farmer that Abraham quaintly transcribed as: 'Nea car nivver yet went ower theer – on a gurt un like that it 'ud be daft to try!'

One narrow stone bridge nearly did defeat the 'gurt' Daimler, which was fractionally too wide to pass between its walls, and they only got through by removing the hub caps, but the Daimler finished the day by climbing the steep Dunmail Raise road on third gear. The next day Abraham and his party made a circuit of Lakeland using mostly mountain roads, and picked up a party of mountaineering friends, so that the car was carrying eight well-built passengers when they climbed the notorious old Honister Pass. Wrote Abraham: '[I have] never seen anything more wonderful in motor mountaineering. Up and up the trusty car climbed easily and so silently that the soft song of the neighbouring mountain stream could be heard distinctly, and soon we were out above the tree line and speeding towards the summit. The coolness of the engine after the heavy climb was surprising.'

The post-war Daimlers had been, as The Autocar quaintly put it, 'completely electrified', and the fitting of a CAV geared starter meant that this was one of the first English marques which did not have a fixed starting handle. Engine compartment access was excellent, as the bonnet was made in three pieces, with the side panels removable and the top hinged at the back and fitted with locking stays.

Another feature of the new cars was the 'special steel frame, designed to be an integral part of the body, on which the coachwork may be built without reference to the chassis . . . in order to facilitate the work of the coachbuilders.' In fact, this system had been devised largely to suit Daimler production

methods, for though Daimler chassis were bodied by all the leading coachbuilders to bespoke order, the company – unlike the majority of luxury car makers – also had its own large body shops where coachwork was series-built in relatively large numbers. A specialized ventilation system cleaned the air of dust, prevented draughts and maintained an even temperature while the bodies, each on its own sub-frame, were given their glistening 16-coat finish, carefully rubbed down between each coat and protected by a final coat of hard Copal resin varnish. 'It is,' claimed the company, 'an ideal method from every standpoint and gives ample time for each coating to become perfectly dry and hard before the next is applied.' And the verdict of The Autocar, when it described the cars at the 1919 Olympia Show was that Daimler bodywork was 'splendid' and added a little parody of the Vicar of Bray: 'And whatsoever King may reign, he still will own a Daimler.'

That message had been underlined when King George V used one of his pre-war 57 hp Daimlers, accompanied by a luggage brake, to return to London from Balmoral when the public transport system was paralysed by a national railway strike beginning on 27 September. The cars had been carried north by the London & North Western Railway in covered trucks but the King's driver, Oscar Humfrey (previously employed by Undecimus Stratton), made the long return journey in two days, resting overnight at Lowther Castle, approximately 250 miles from Balmoral, and covering the remaining 300 miles the next day. Noted The Autocar: 'The King was not in the least fatigued by his long trip and proceeded immediately to attend to his correspondence upon arrival at Buckingham Palace.' Sir Charles Wentworth-Fitzwilliam KCVO, Crown Equerry to the King, told Daimler: 'Both cars, which have been in constant service since they were delivered by you some years ago, ran the distance of 541 miles without the least trouble of any sort. The second car – a brake

– was for luggage only; so their Majesties depended entirely on the reliability of one of their Daimler limousines.'

The strike resulted in the government declaring a state of emergency and appropriating all available petrol stocks. Motorists volunteered the services of their cars to help break the strike and Daimler Hire – a newly formed company within the BSA Group which had taken over the activities of Daimler's hire department, operating a fleet of some 250 chauffeur-driven limousines from the old Princes Skating Rink in Knightsbridge – began running a shuttle service for 'business trips and journeys of importance in the national emergency' between London and Birmingham with 'high-powered Daimler limousines and landaulettes' at a one-way fare of 30 shillings (£1.50). Another Daimler service linked London and Manchester.

Like so many of their kind, the architects of the strike, which lasted only a few days before then collapsing, were ultimately

responsible for the decline of their industry, since the public, having been given a graphic demonstration of the 'enormous gain in the matter of adaptability to unforeseen and difficult circumstances that have been brought about by the progress of automobilism', began to desert the railway in favour of motor vehicles. And Daimler, with its regular car service between London and the Midlands, had played a leading role in creating that awareness of the vast potential of motor transport.

Realizing the growth potential of the motor industry, Daimler decided to change the way it did business. For a start, sales of cars direct from the factory would be stopped, and customers would have to obtain their cars through authorized dealerships. Then the number and efficiency of Daimler's service stations across the country was to be increased. The company also continued to emphasize the importance of training, offering an annual premium for the best paper presented by a member of the graduates'

This handsome 1919 Light Thirty coupé has a single door on each side for front and rear passengers. [JDHT]

section of the Institute of Automobile Engineers: in 1919, for instance, the premium was awarded for a paper on spark plug design.

Daimler was in a strong position in the British luxury car market as 1920 dawned, for there were few home-built rivals of similar calibre: the Light Thirty, for instance, cost £1,250 in chassis form, just £50 more than the 25/30 Crossley but considerably cheaper than comparable models from Sunbeam, Talbot, and Vauxhall, while the 45 hp Daimler Special, at a chassis price of £1,300, was £275 cheaper than the 40/50 Rolls-Royce and £450 less than the 40/50 Napier.

Owners of big luxury cars were – relatively – less badly hit than the owners of small cars by the taxation changes that came in the 1920 Motor Car Act, which altered vehicle tax from the broad band categories of Lloyd George's 1910 'People's Budget' to a rate of £1 per horsepower (tax on a 45 hp Daimler roughly doubled, from £21 to £45, while the increase on a humble Model T Ford was more than five-fold, from £4 4s to £23). Nevertheless, the rise in car taxation was at least leavened by the removal of fuel duty. Like turkeys calling for the date of Christmas to be changed, however, motorists campaigned for duty to be taken off cars and put back on fuel, and their ingenuousness was duly rewarded by the 1928 Finance Act, which duly reintroduced fuel duty, but also retained the horsepower tax unchanged, adding an extra burden to the ownership of motor cars in general and large luxury cars in particular.

In those days, purchase of a luxury car represented an investment in quality and precision, and the Daimler company was justly proud of its laboratory and tool room, probably the finest of their kind in the British motor industry, which featured in a little booklet issued around 1920. Entitled *The Daimler Way of Ensuring Quality*, it was enlivened by splendid full page illustrations in which that master of absurd inventions W. Heath Robinson fancifully depicted the design and construction of Daimler cars by intensely serious little men engaging in such intricately pointless activities as 'testing a micrometer by measuring a fly's leg' or 'testing engines before they are screwed on to cars'.

But the booklet had a serious message to impart about Daimler accuracy in manufacture: 'It will hurt no-one's feelings at this point to announce the fact, as an

This amazing 'dome back limousine' was produced by Park, Ward in the mid-1920s. [MBRT]

acknowledgment of achievement, that many of the master gauges issued through the National Physical Laboratory to the factories producing aeroplane engines during the War were products of the Daimler Tool Room . . . the Instrument Room . . . contains master gauges and instruments, some of which are the only specimens in existence and others which are only duplicated in the National Physical Laboratory. These instruments ensure a superiority of manufacture that must be reproduced in the products of the Daimler Machine Shops.'

As an example of the standards to which Daimlers were built, the company noted that it took four months to develop the special tools needed to cut a worm gear set for the Daimler back axle.

* * *

The first completely new Daimler to be unveiled since the end of the war appeared in July 1921. This was the Type TT 4-20, a 3,308 cc 20 hp model built on the 11 ft wheelbase and effectively a four-cylinder version of the Thirty, with which it had the bore and stroke measurements in common. Novel features included rear wheel brakes adjusted by an under-bonnet turnscrew and – since this car was intended for the owner-driver – a plunger which could be pressed while the engine was running to check whether there was sufficient oil in the sump (if there was, oil flowed into a tray 'neatly arranged to conduct it on to the road').

In November 1920 Ernest Instone's 21 years' service with Daimler had been celebrated by a dinner at the Piccadilly Hotel, London, at which he was presented with a silver tray engraved with the signatures of over a hundred of his industry friends, but within the year he had resigned and joined forces with Undecimus Stratton of the company's London office and Joseph Mackle – who had gone to Daimler in 1908 as the winner of its first engineering scholarship – to set up a new company called Stratton-Instone Limited to take over Daimler's

showrooms at 27 Pall Mall and handle Daimler sales within the London area. As that included sales to the Royal Household, this was a particularly important development and Daimler had a considerable shareholding in the venture (though this would be reduced to a nominal £1 in 1930, when the company's investment of £32,000 was transferred to a special 'Stratton-Instone reserve'). Stratton and Instone ran the new company with style: prompt at 11 each morning a butler in morning dress brought champagne and oysters up to the directors' room . . .

Late in 1921 the BSA marque, which had been in abeyance since the war, was revived for a sturdy-looking 1,080 cc air-cooled vee-twin-engined light car with the unusual refinement of a worm-drive back axle, priced at just £230 for the 'Popular' two-seater, its power unit allegedly 'embodying a great deal of practice which originated in the 90 degree RAF air-cooled aero-engine'.

Frederick Lanchester had proposed his own design for a new BSA light car: known as the 'HR3', it was a two-seater that would have been powered by a 585 cc flat-twin 6 hp engine weighing only 90 lb and capable, claimed Lanchester, of developing 20–21 bhp at 4,000 rpm; key features of Lanchester's concept were 'crank case scavenge [and] rotary valve direct driven by screw gear controlling all functions'. However, remarked Martin in a long-winded put-down, 'while fully admiring and giving credit for the cleverness in the conception of the car, at the present moment BSA does not think that it is a thing which they can interest themselves in to such an extent as to ask you to deal with the inventions embodied in the design as if those inventions came within your agreement' (though in February 1922 BSA did advance Lanchester £200 to build a rotary valve engine).

In April 1921 Lanchester also referred to 'a patent by Smith-Clarke of the Daimler that might be of use in connection with the new BSA car': this was Captain Thomas George Smith-Clarke who, after serving as officer-in-

charge of the Coventry area Aeronautical Inspectorate, had joined Daimler as assistant chief engineer in 1919. He left Daimler in mid-1922 and became chief engineer and works manager of Alvis, where he pioneered front-wheel drive: once again, a former employee of 'the Daimler' played a fundamental role in the automotive industry.

Soon after the new BSA went on the market there were rumours that Daimler was considering adding a smaller model to its range and in April 1922 the press speculated that the company was about to produce 'a 12 hp vehicle of the increasingly popular light family type'. This duly manifested itself at Motor Show time, though with a chassis costing £550 (£775 with an all-weather tourer body), the 1,542 cc 12 hp Daimler sleeve-valve six-cylinder could hardly be said to fall into the 'light family type' price bracket. It was just part of a massive expansion of the Daimler-BSA range that had begun in July with the announcement of a new 3,021 cc 21 hp six-cylinder Daimler,

which broke new ground with a monobloc casting for the cylinders (though there were still six separate cylinder heads, spigoted into the bores and fitted with compression rings for the inner sleeve) and coil ignition. The crankshaft ran in seven main bearings, the monobloc casting made the engine more rigid than the previous pair-cast units (and thus quieter and freer from vibration) and the cylinder heads eliminated a problem of the earlier design by incorporating a syphon tube connecting with the main water jacket so that they could easily be drained of water in frosty weather. In traditional Daimler style, the engine was mounted with the back end noticeably lower in the chassis than the front, so that the drive to the rear axle was as near a straight line as possible.

But a couple of new chassis in the earlier part of the year was no preparation for the full extent of the change revealed at the Motor Show. The combined 1923 Daimler-BSA range encompassed no fewer than 56 models, most of them introduced during the course of

1922. Admittedly, many of those 56 varieties were merely long- and short-wheelbase versions with a common power unit, and apart from the radiator the six-cylinder BSA Twelve was very similar to the smallest Daimler (though with quarter-elliptic springs all round and disc wheels, which economies were reflected in a chassis price of £450). But the 20 hp Daimler four had gone, there was a 1,446 cc 11 hp four-cylinder sleeve-valve BSA using the same chassis as the 10 hp vee-twin, and the overall impression was of a range that was being hastily expanded to make the most of the post-war boom . . . which was about to bust.

* * *

Daimler had become famous through sleeve valves: now it was to make history through thermionic valves, the amplifying device which had made practical wireless telephony a reality. In the summer of 1922, wireless had become an engrossing craze, for the Marconi-run 2MT station had begun broadcasting on Tuesday evenings from Writtle in Essex, and from 11 May more frequent broadcasts were made from Marconi House (2LO) in the Strand. Other companies followed suit with stations 2ZY (Manchester) and 2WP (London) and a few bold amateurs attempted to receive radio signals on sets fitted in motor cars. The equipment then available was clumsy and bulky, and an average set occupied the rear compartment of a car, but progress was unbelievably rapid – particularly considering that there were so few programmes available to 'listeners-in' – and in August 1922 the Cardiff & South Wales Wireless Society installed a set in an open car and claimed to have received Continental wireless programmes while their vehicle was 'travelling at touring speeds'.

Daimler was the first car company to

With 2MT Writtle coming in loud and clear over the Amplion horn and a chauffeur-driven TT 4-20 Daimler to waft you home after the concert, this was the ultimate in outdoor entertainment in 1922. [JDHT]

realize the potential of in-car radio as 'a means of relieving tedium on a long journey by the reception of speeches, messages and concerts', and in October collaborated with Marconi in a most remarkable experiment. Two Light Thirty saloons ('admirably suited for the work in hand since they ran quietly and were not responsible for any appreciable interference with audibility') were experimentally fitted with Marconi eight-valve receivers in their rear compartments plus large vertical frame aerials on their roofs and driven from Marconi House in London to the Marconi Works in Chelmsford, Essex, and, wrote one of the passengers, 'had perfect reception of messages from Marconi House and of Music from Writtle'.

The following month Daimler became the first company to produce a car with a factory-fitted radio set: a vee-fronted 45 hp saloon-landaulette was exhibited at Olympia with a 'Daimler-Marconi wireless installation' and another Light Thirty fitted with a wireless set took part in the Lord Mayor's Procession, which coincided with the last weekend of the Motor Show. This still had the clumsy frame aerial mounted on the roof, which had to be rotated by a hand wheel and gearing to locate the radio signal, but by the beginning of 1923 Daimler and Marconi had developed a far neater aerial, consisting of a flat copper plate suspended from the luggage grid ('this plate aerial,' noted *The Autocar*, 'will in future be built into the roof of the car . . . so it will not prevent full use being made of the luggage-carrying space [and] is capable of receiving signals from any direction with equal facility') together with an eight-valve receiver housed under the rear passenger seat, with a neat control panel mounted inside a little cupboard beside the left-hand passenger's armrest.

Another first for this January 1923 Daimler installation was the suppression of the ignition system so that the sparks did not interfere with reception, and the receiving set was powerful enough to pick up signals from Newcastle in the London area. That

probably inspired Daimler to take a wireless-equipped car to the Glasgow Show at the end of January, but the signals from London, where 2LO had been taken over by the recently-formed British Broadcasting Corporation, were too weak, so Marconi set up a temporary transmitter with the call-sign 2BP for the duration of the Show.

In March, the Glasgow Show car was the star attraction at the opening run of the Junior Car Club at Burford Bridge, in Surrey, taking parties of JCC members along the Guildford-Leatherhead Road to hear broadcasts from London, when they were 'delighted with the clearness of reception while being conveyed swiftly and silently over the open road, the tone increasing in volume as the car reached the higher ground towards Leatherhead'.

Daimler was, however, too far ahead of public demand: a dozen or so wireless-

Lupino Lane — famed for 'doing the Lambeth Walk' — listens-in to a built-in Daimler wireless set. [MBRT]

equipped cars were put into service with Daimler Hire, and a joint programme with Marconi resulted in the production of a two-valve portable wireless set for the small BSA which was designed to be used when the car was parked: studs on the running board engaged in holes in the base of the radio set to make the electrical connections and a 30 ft aerial wire had to be slung up into a tree for 'amply strong reception'. However, at £55 the set cost 25 per cent as much as the complete car, and even an economy version with a limited range and headphones was £25, which made wireless rather an expensive luxury. Few orders materialized for wireless-equipped cars, even though six British radio stations were available during 1923, and the option was dropped after a year. BSA, however, established a modestly-staffed subsidiary to make domestic wireless sets.

* * *

'Treading on the accelerator does not produce the familiar variations of sound or tremor,' wrote motor cycling canon Basil H. Davies, who covered the 1923 Scottish Six Days' Trial for *The Autocar* at the wheel of a Light Thirty tourer loaned by Daimler at short notice. 'The sole effect is that a smooth, invisible flow of power, which might well be compressed air, eases off or intensifies its secret pressure.' Sharing the driving of this works car with Davies (better-known as 'Ixion' of *The Motor Cycle*) was Joseph Mackle, proving the close relationship that existed between the Daimler Company and Stratton-Instone. 'The engine is more suggestive of steam than of petrol,' observed Davies. 'In its presence one would not mention such words as "revolution" or "exhaust", for it does not seem to possess either.'

A few months later, *Autocar* testers drove a 21 hp 'short coupé' through the night from London to Liverpool and found it 'a most delightful experience: nobody was tired, the passengers slept in comfort for a great part of the long journey and neither oil nor petrol replenishment was called for.' The fuel consumption of this heavy car was a commendable 23 mpg and even with closed bodywork, the occupants spoke of 'floating along . . . with no noise save for a gulping sound at the air intake of the carburettor as the throttle is opened'.

At this period, incidentally, Daimler were beginning to mount the gear lever in the centre, heading a trend away from right-hand change, though the push-on handbrake was still on the right; a unique feature was the interconnection of the carburettor jet control lever with a control valve in the cooling system header pipe, so that the valve was closed while the engine was cold and the mixture was rich. Once the engine was warm the mixture was weakened, automatically opening the water valve.

Daimler was always ready to pioneer new ideas and in July 1923 the company cooperated with the British Broadcasting Corporation in an experiment intended to prove the efficiency of wireless broadcasting in tracking down criminals. Daimler and BSA cars carrying the famous Radio Uncles and Aunts from the 2LO Savoy Hill station tried to escape from London, while a special announcement was broadcast warning the public to look out for them and give the thumbs-up sign if they recognized the 'criminals'. 'Had the hunt been in real earnest,' said the driver of the car containing Uncle Caractacus and Aunt Sophie, 'it is very doubtful if the car could have got any further than the city, for it seemed that half the inhabitants had turned out in response to the SOS from the London station.'

Foreign Royalty continued to use Daimlers: when Queen Wilhelmina of the Netherlands visited the Lake District with her Prince Consort and Princess Juliana in the summer of 1923, they used a pre-war Daimler sleeve-valve 45 hp six to visit local beauty spots, while the Crown Prince of Sweden was presented with a 21 hp coupé ordered from Stratton-Instone by the Royal Automobile Club of Sweden when he married Lady

Louise Mountbatten later that year. Stratton-Instone, in fact, were branching out into the supply of specially-bodied Daimlers, offering a short-wheelbase 21 hp owner-driver coupé as well as exclusive Charlesworth all-weather coachwork across the chassis range. The all-weather style combined the advantages of the saloon and tourer, with wind-down glass windows much like a modern convertible.

The early 1920s saw the deaths of two of the men who had been prominent in the early years of Daimler: Charles McRobie Turrell died in October 1923, while Harry Lawson followed in 1925.

There was a degree of 'cross-pollination' between the companies in the Birmingham Small Arms group: BSA Motorcycles annexed a brilliant young Daimler designer named Harold Briggs in the early 1920s and his first two-wheeler was a 75 mph sports 350 cc motor cycle with overhead valves and duralumin pushrods, followed by the best-selling 493 cc 'Sloper'. Sadly, Briggs later committed suicide as the result of a frustrated love affair.

For 1924, the Daimler-BSA line-up changed yet again, with the 12 hp six vanishing from both ranges and being replaced by a bored-out 16 hp. There were now 13 chassis of various capacities and a total of nine types of coachwork, which now took their designations from a new British Standard list, so that the former coupé was called a saloon de luxe and the old light coupé became a saloon, while the car that Daimler had previously catalogued as a saloon became the enclosed landaulette. A new 20 hp model was a larger version of the discontinued 16, while there was a 25 hp derivative of the 21 hp six: both were available on short and long wheelbase chassis.

Most interesting of the new models was a 35 hp, 'really in the nature of a Daimler express', and because it had been designed for high speed, with a large (5,764 cc) engine in a light chassis, was the first Daimler car to be fitted with four-wheel brakes (though these became optionally available on the 45 hp, too). Curiously, though the 21 hp model had a monobloc engine, this latest Daimler had its cylinders cast in three blocks of two. It also had light steel sleeves instead of cast-iron, a feature which had been standardized across the range by Motor Show time, and which gave increased power and speed as the engine could now rev more freely. The thinner sleeves also gave greater engine capacity within the same overall bore size. On the road, the new model was impressive: 'It gobbles up gradients as if they were non-existent, it swoops over roads fair and foul like a thing possessed, yet is controllable to a degree, creeping silently through town and village in that ghostlike fashion for which Daimler sleeve-valve engines are famous,' enthused The Autocar, adding 'with never a semblance of vibration or snatch, the engine responds with a perfect crescendo of speed, an experience as exhilarating as it is unusual.'

Stanley Baldwin's rash decision to call a general election in November to give his majority Conservative government a fresh mandate resulted in the loss of 90 seats for his party and the formation of a minority Labour government under Ramsay MacDonald in January: the new prime minister, who had no car, was 'reluctantly' presented with a Daimler (and £30,000-worth of shares in biscuit makers McVitie & Price, to enable him to run a car for the rest of his life) by his 'dear old friend' Sir Alexander Grant, who thought every prime minister should have a motor car.

In the spring of 1924, Daimler's body shops began building Weymann flexible-framed fabric bodies – which they listed as 'Construction Z' – for their 'natural silence, the entire absence of drumming and all those attributes which make for comfortable long-distance touring with a minimum of fatigue' and delivered the first example to The Autocar for the magazine's staff fleet. Though fabric-covered bodywork proved a short-lived fashion, the Daimler version was certainly one of the best-finished versions, with aircraft-style wicker seats elegantly button-quilted in Bedford cord. These Dryad 'basket chairs' were also used as occasional chairs in Daimler limousines and were fitted with pivoting mountings so that they could be turned round to face the back seats for picnic lunches.

Daimler's unique status as manufacturer of the King's motor cars resulted in the building of a special sanction of 57 hp four-wheel braked six-cylinder chassis during 1924 to replace the pre-war 57 hp cars: four of these cars (two limousines and two shooting brakes, all bodied by Hooper) were delivered to the Royal Household and the 'available balance' – almost certainly no more than half-a-dozen examples – of these 9,420 cc giants, which had little more than the bore and stroke in common with their 1910 predecessors, were bought by Stratton-Instone for sale to top-drawer clients. Riding on a wheelbase of 13 ft 6 in, the 57 hp Royal cars were initially shod with Palmer Cord 935x150 mm tyres, but the first to be delivered (one of the shooting brakes) suffered from tyre trouble and all four of the new Royal cars were fitted with the new straight-sided Dunlop tyres.

Improvements developed for the Royal 57 hp cars were incorporated in the production models, like the 'single point adjustment' for the four wheel brakes by an underbonnet handle: since the 57 hp was never officially catalogued, Daimler claimed that their 8,458 cc 45 hp was the largest production car in the world. However, Renault's antediluvian Type MC1 40CV actually had a greater displacement of 9,121 cc (but was 3.75 in shorter in the wheelbase).

Even without the extra complication of the 57 hp chassis, the Daimler-BSA range had become even more Byzantine by the end of 1924: there were now seven basic Daimler models varying from 16 to 45 hp, all available in 'two or more alternative models differing in respect to some important feature such as four-wheel brakes, body space, low entrance frame, or wider track (to suit low pressure tyres if required)', plus six basic BSA models with a choice of three engines from the 10 hp vee-twin to the 16 hp six, which in its more elaborate versions was a small Daimler in all but radiator flutes (and price).

Though Charles Y. Knight was now living

King George and Queen Mary inspect their new Daimler at Hooper's in 1924. [DS]

in Pasadena, California, he made a number of visits to England in the 1920s; when he came over in 1925, he bought one of George V's recently-retired 1910 57 hp limousines and had it shipped to America for exhibition purposes. But he had another reason for coming to England: he wanted Percy Martin's assistance in a claim he was raising for commission from Dr Lanchester (who, of course, had made the Knight sleeve-valve engine a practical proposition in the early days, and one wonders what justification Knight might have had for his action).

His scheme was that Martin, who had known both Knight and Lanchester for years, would act as a 'friendly mediator . . . in order to see if some arrangement could by any possibility be come to', but on reflection Martin decided to step back from the argument, since he 'came to the conclusion that Dr Lanchester's reply might be framed in the same – shall we say buoyantly fighting? – spirit as was shown in your letter. However, I thought that I ought to put your letter in front of Dr Lanchester to see whether there was any chance of my friendly service being of use to you both . . . I soon came to the conclusion that there is a wide difference of opinion between you and that if I continued to hold the position of a friendly mediator, I should probably be ground to powder between your two millstones.' Martin decided that discretion was the better part of valour and – sadly for history – handed all the correspondence relating to Knight's claim to Dr Lanchester to deal with in person, which he almost certainly did in the simplest possible manner . . .

In mid-1925, Daimler announced yet another range of engines, this time long-stroke units with dual coil and magneto ignition and full pressure lubrication of the crankshaft bearings replacing – at last – the old hinged troughs across the range, apart from the old 30 hp model. The light steel sleeves and split-skirt aluminium pistons were standardized, making the four new engines (16/55, 20/70, 25/85 and

35/120 hp units) particularly lively.

Joseph Mackle had a talent for devising dashing performance versions of the Daimler, whose image in some eyes had become associated with staid limousines: in 1925 he commissioned a sporting 16/55 two-seater which was good for 70 mph and 28 mpg, even though this chassis was the only one of the range fitted with a three-speed gearbox. It was probably the added spice given by ventures such as this which led novelist Dorothy L. Sayers to choose a Daimler as the preferred make of her best-known creation, Lord Peter Wimsey, whose suave butler Bunter worried in one novel about the effect of speed on a case of vintage port packed in the rear of his master's car: 'Great speed would render the wine undrinkable for a fortnight; excessive speed would render it undrinkable for six months.'

* * *

Daimler's commercial vehicle business had developed steadily during the 1920s. Its first post-war models, the 5.1-litre CJ and CK chassis, differed little from the company's 1914 products, though they were available with 'giant' pneumatic tyres and a built-in power-driven inflation pump as an alternative to solids from 1920. In 1925 two new chassis, the CL and CM, also powered by the 5.1-litre sleeve-valve engine, were launched; a new 3,568 cc six-cylinder power unit was also available. In June the following year Daimler and AEC set up a new joint venture known as the Associated Daimler Company to build chassis with a choice of Daimler sleeve-valve or AEC poppet-valve engines.

With headquarters in Southall, Middlesex, ADC manufactured a range of lorries, trolleybuses and buses up to the massive Model 802 six-wheeler, powered by a 60/120 hp 5,764 cc sleeve-valve six and costing £3,000 with a double-deck 68-seat body and Westinghouse air brakes, the final assembly of the chassis taking place at their respective engine makers' factories.

Despite this apparently equitable division

This 1929 six-ton forward-control ADC truck has pneumatic front tyres for comfort but solid back tyres for reliability! [LG]

This amazing Associated Daimler 'Sleeping Car' ran an express night service in 1928. [NMM]

of labour (and profits), this did not, however, prove to be a smooth relationship, as an internal memorandum to Martin revealed: 'The officials of AEC have rather regarded Daimler as being a very subordinate partner, and this feeling may have arisen from the fact that we were only supplying Sleeve Valve Engines when AEC were supplying all the Chassis and all the Poppet Valve engines which ADC required. In addition to this, a batch of engines which Daimler supplied

turned out to be unsatisfactory and wherever there was a complaint from a customer with regard to a vehicle in which there was a Daimler engine, that Customer treated all his complaints as if the whole vehicle was a Daimler Vehicle. This rendered the allocation of blame very difficult and possibly had the effect of again minimizing the value which AEC Officials placed in their association with Daimler. It is believed that the complaints with regard to Daimler

engines were very shortly entirely remedied as they were troubles which were likely to arise on the introduction of an entirely new Engine.

'To get over all these difficulties a suggestion has been made by Daimler to ADC that Daimler shall take over the entire manufacture of two types of vehicles so that responsibility may be adopted by Daimler for the types of vehicles which they build and responsibility may be clearly placed on AEC shoulders for their vehicles. If this proposition is accepted, and there is every reason to believe that it will be accepted, it will mean more work in the Daimler Shops but the actual date for the commencement of sharing the profits between Daimler and AEC on a basis of equality will be postponed from 1 January 1928 to 1 January 1929.'

But the ADC partnership only lasted until 1929, when the two companies separated again, and Daimler – which retained the 'Associated Daimler' trademark on a non-trading basis – brought out its own low-loader bus chassis, the CF6, available with 'superb examples of Parlour-Coach and All-weather body-work', at a comparable price to the equivalent AEC Regent.

* * *

Though the Associated Daimler combine proved short-lived, Percy Martin had expected much of it. He obviously thought Daimler would play a more dominant role in product development than turned out to be the case, for he set out to recruit one of the world's leading automotive designers as the chief engineer of ADC.

It was probably through his American connections that Martin learned that Laurence Pomeroy, late of Vauxhall, was looking for a new job: his work on 'all-aluminium' cars with Alcoa – latterly in conjunction with Pierce-Arrow – was grinding to a halt and the test programme would end inconclusively after some seven cars had been built. A month after the formation of Associated Daimler, he cabled Pomeroy in the United States to offer him the ADC post, 'position to include consultant work for Daimler Company, Associated Equipment Company and London General Omnibus Company', and asked him to name his terms. Added Martin: 'This proposal expresses my personal desire, therefore strictly confidential and naturally subject to approval of all concerned.'

Pomeroy's return cable was the response of a man thrown an unexpected lifeline but – knowing his rescuer was desperate to have

With an elegance to rival any contemporary sports car, 'Her Ladyship's Coupé' was available on both 16/55 and 20/70 Daimler chassis in 1926. [JDHT]

him – hopeful of obtaining the best possible personal advantage out of the affair: 'I greatly appreciate your offer. I shall accept it if terms are acceptable unless overwhelming inducements and offers here . . . consider it proper to discuss major terms before taking decisive action: these are £4,000 per annum after payment of income tax or £3,000 ditto plus commission with reasonable possibility of exceeding above sum, usual automobile facilities appropriate to official of your company and half expenses of return to start October First.' There was obviously no immediate response from the Coventry end, so two weeks later Pomeroy ventured: 'Arrangements here can now be satisfactorily concluded – could start about one month after receiving your advice.'

Fifteen days later Martin replied: 'Am personally anxious to advise your appointment but holidays have prevented me consulting all concerned. Strongly recommend you authorize me to advise appointment at £3,500 and bonus to be arranged at earliest possible date . . . The new company has most excellent prospects.' Pomeroy accepted Martin's terms instantly: 'If appointment can be made fairly soon it will avoid my being involved in the impending final commercial negotiations re the production of my car and considerably facilitate my departure.' The deal was quickly closed once the Daimler board convened and Pomeroy set sail for England aboard the liner *Carmania* on 2 October 1926.

His tenure at Associated Daimler was necessarily brief, though he designed a revolutionary Daimler coach chassis which made extensive use of aluminum alloys to achieve a high power-weight ratio, and in September 1928 he was appointed general manager of Daimler in Coventry. He brought in E. W. Hancock, one of his gifted pupils from Vauxhall (the brother of Vauxhall works manager and racing driver A. J. Hancock), who was to become Daimler's general manager after Pomeroy.

But overshadowing Pomeroy's return to England was the announcement of one of the most sensational new cars of the 1920s: Britain's first production V12, the Daimler Double-Six. News of this amazing car first leaked out in September 1926, when American sources reported that it was to be sold in the United States through Knight's oldest US licensee, the F.B. Stearns Company of Cleveland (Ohio), which had been building sleeve-valve cars for 'Mr Substantial Citizen' since 1911, but home market announcement did not occur until the following month, shortly before the London Motor Show.

The V12 configuration had actually been pioneered by the British Sunbeam company in 1913, when the company's brilliant Breton chief engineer Louis Coatalen had developed six-cylinder, V8 and V12 aero-engines and planned a V12 luxury car, but the outbreak of the First World War had meant that the only Sunbeam V12 car had been the aero-engined *Toodles V* Brooklands racer, shipped to America to continue its racing career. There it had inspired Packard chief engineer Jesse Vincent to develop the world's first production V12 automobile, the 1916 Twin-Six, and it might well have been Percy Martin's American origins which had led him to adopt the V12 layout for the giant Daimler which he designed to counter such rivals for the luxury car market as the new Rolls-Royce Phantom in his company's 'search along the avenues of progress for a design which will carry a large closed body from walking pace to hurricane speeds with the least possible noise or vibration'.

In fact, the engine of the Double-Six – a name obviously inspired by the Packard nomenclature – was essentially two 25/85 pair-cast cylinder assemblies set at an included angle of 60 degrees on a common crankcase, with forked main connecting rods running on a conventional seven-bearing crankshaft. The two halves of the power unit were virtual mirror images with a complex arrangement of helically-geared cross-shafts at the front of the engine. A lower cross-shaft

Olympia 1928, with a
Double-Six 50 to the
left and a 35/120
Limousine to the right,
both costing
substantially more than
a new four-bedroomed
detached house in the
Home Counties . . .
[JDHT]

drove twin water pumps, while the upper cross-shaft had a six-cylinder magneto at each end and also drove twin vertical shafts running in aluminium towers which carried coil ignition distributors for either block.

The induction arrangements, with a single Daimler seven-jet carburettor for each bank of cylinders, were unusual: 'From the water-jacketed mixing chamber, a passage leads up through the induction manifold to a cast aluminium jacket surrounding the water return pipe,' wrote Marcus Bourdon in the American journal *Automotive Industries*. 'The mixture passes through the induction manifold from the centre towards both ends, where it descends into the aluminium inlet manifold, which inclines slightly towards the centre. The advantages claimed for this arrangement are uniform distribution and effective vaporisation.'

The result was an engine which ran with uncanny silence and could idle at 150 rpm when, recalls Jack Fairman – who worked at Daimler in the 1930s – the only audible

sound made by a Double-Six ('if you opened the bonnet and went right up to it') was the almost imperceptible tick as the ignition points opened and the faint breathing of the carburettor.

One drawback of the engine layout was that the heavily-finned exhaust manifolds ran in the valley between the cylinder blocks, creating 'an embarrassing amount of heat' which was dissipated by roofing in the vee with an aluminium shield down which cooling air was forced by a four-bladed fan driven from the Lanchester vibration damper on the nose of the crankshaft. Some of that warm air passed through ducts cast in the crankcase walls to the carburettor intakes.

The replacement of the old splash lubrication by a full pressure system had meant that the sleeve valves were no longer given an instant oil bath as soon as the crankshaft began to revolve, so on the Double-Six a primer valve linked to the starter switch forced oil to the lower ends of the sleeves, while a second valve operated by the mixture control lever on the steering column sent oil to the upper end of the sleeves when the lever was in the starting position.

Because the engine filled the bonnet so completely, the Double-Six had an ingenious steering system, which the company had patented in the summer of 1926. This used a short steering column ending in a worm-and-sector gear in a casing bolted to the rear of the rigid aluminum dashboard casting. A 'drop arm' moving up and down actuated a vertical linkage connected to one end of a bellcrank mounted on the chassis frame; the other end of the bellcrank operated a conventional drag link connected to the steering arm.

This colossus of roads was built for prestige rather than profit: 'These great cars, with the largest, most powerful and most expensive of any touring chassis built in the British Isles,' wrote *The Autocar*, 'are for the lucky few who have the means to purchase them and to keep them in commission . . . We found that the petrol consumption taken over a distance of about three hundred miles worked out at approximately 10 mpg. To the private owner of a small car this may sound a great deal, but to a man who is able to pay the best part of £3,000 for a car, it is more or less

An impressive Double-Six 'Thirty' Seven-seat Vee-fronted Limousine; Daimler offered drivers of such cars special three-day training courses at Coventry. Additionally, it was claimed, 'in three weeks the instructors can make a proficient driver out of a man of normal intelligence who has, so far, done little else but gardening'. [JDHT]

a trifling matter, particularly when one considers that first-class travel for seven full-sized people is being provided.' In truth, as Sammy Davis recalled many years later, 'we had quite a time taking the Double-Six round the West Country and along the south coast, its fuel bill being fantastic, even for an expense sheet.'

Autocar's managing editor Geoffrey Smith, who shared that road-test with Sammy Davis, privately remarked: 'You must stop the engine if ever the fuel tank is filled from one of these new petrol pumps, otherwise the engine uses so much petrol that the pump cannot cope,' inspiring a memorable *Punch* cartoon in which a harassed pump attendant implores the driver of a gigantic car: 'D'you mind switching off, Sir? She's gaining on me . . .'

* * *

Little remains to record the story of one of the most fascinating industrial 'might-have-beens' of the late 1920s, which has remained secret for nearly 70 years, or to explain the rationale behind Percy Martin's 1927 plan to merge Daimler-BSA with Sunbeam of Wolverhampton, perhaps the weakest member of the

Dramatic sports convertible coachwork on a Double-Six chassis.

Sunbeam-Talbot-Darracq combine.

It may have been in response to various other moves which were taking place in the industry: General Motors of America had taken over Vauxhall in 1925 and would take over Opel of Germany in 1929 after flirting with companies like Citroën while Morris, which had come to dominate the British popular car sector took over the ailing Wolseley company in 1927 and gained an excellent power unit that had its roots in Wolseley's wartime production of Hispano-Suiza aero-engines. But the Daimler company was hardly in the same league, even with the backing of BSA, for the Coventry factory was woefully starved of investment and its ageing machine tools were in need of replacement. Moreover, its board of directors was of the old-fashioned sort: few of its members had any practical knowledge of the motor industry and many of them – including Manville, who became chairman of the entire BSA group in 1928 – held a multiplicity of directorships, which meant that they could hardly give their full attention to Daimler.

Nevertheless, Martin duly put out feelers to Louis Coatalen of Sunbeam-Talbot-Darracq (had Coatalen maybe advised Martin on V12 design during the development of the Double-Six?) and on 27 September 1927 the board of the Anglo-French combine met to discuss the proposed merger between Sunbeam and Daimler. In a handwritten note, Coatalen explained to Martin that he had put the Daimler offer of an amalgamation before his fellow directors: 'They are interested in the proposition and want time in which to think it over, so you will hear from me later on. I am returning to Paris tomorrow but will be back in a fortnight.'

Things seem to have moved slower than anticipated, for it was not until January 1928 that the principals of the two companies got together for a more detailed discussion over lunch. Coatalen and his chairman James Todd met Sir Edward Manville and various 'pleasing suggestions' were made. Martin, who was unable to be there, sent a confidential note to Coatalen suggesting that they should meet and try and reduce those suggestions to 'a definite first step to be taken'. The proposal was that a 'confidential man' from each company should be appointed to discuss what effect the proposed merger would have on the business of the various companies in the two organizations. 'I am assuming,' wrote Martin, 'that you feel that most can be gained by agreement on the subject of programme, prices and, if possible, merging to a certain extent the sales schemes of the different companies.'

Three weeks later, Martin wrote to William Iliff, joint managing director of Sunbeam, suggesting that he should meet Algernon Berriman to discuss 'possible arrangements whereby the sales policy of the Daimler Company and the Sunbeam Company can cooperate without coming into conflict'. Added Martin: 'A clear insight as to the possibilities as between the two companies would forward matters in connection with a future arrangement more than anything I can think of at the moment.'

And that, it seems, is as far as the proposed merger went. Had it gone ahead, it would probably all have ended in tears, for the two companies' model programmes were equally undisciplined, and would hardly have dovetailed comfortably at any point, while the uncompromising standards of their top men would probably have been equally incompatible. But the thought of a Daimler-Sunbeam car is still a fascinating one.

* * *

It was inevitable that King George V should have been given the opportunity to try the new Double-Six and in June 1927 Stratton-Instone put a 57 hp Daimler re-engined with the new V12 unit at the King's disposal 'for as long as may be required'. The immediate result of this extended loan was that the King had both his 1924 57 hp Limousines re-engined with Double-Six power units at the suggestion of Undecimus Stratton; the conversion involved considerable modification of the chassis, which required new radiators, bonnets, steering gear, final drive gearing and instrumentation, and were additionally fitted with the Dewandre power-assisted servo braking which had recently become available on production

Daimlers. The cost of the conversion – which took around six weeks to complete – totalled £1,000 for the two cars.

At the beginning of August 1927 Daimler responded to criticism that 'the size and price of the original Double-Six placed it beyond the reach of any save the very wealthy' by launching a 3,744 cc 30 hp V12 using two banks of cylinders from the 16/50 hp six and priced at £1,130–£1,430 in chassis form. 'While it lacks nothing in dignity,' commented The Autocar, whose accounts department was doubtless much relieved at the appearance of this more economical model, 'it creates the impression that it is light to handle and manoeuvre in confined spaces, and not difficult to keep in order; hence the prospective owner-driver can examine it with enthusiasm.'

So, too, did Queen Mary, who ordered a new Double-Six 30 Hooper Limousine, which was delivered by Stratton-Instone in February 1928. Because the radiator was (like that of most royal Daimlers until the Second World War) finished in black, the newly-introduced distinguishing feature of the Double-Six range – a vertical dividing strip down the centre of the radiator – was rendered virtually invisible.

While King George had used his Daimlers for long journeys at times of national emergency, it was an emergency of a very different nature that caused him to travel from Buckingham Palace to Bognor in Sussex by Daimler in February 1929. In November 1928 the King contracted a feverish cold, apparently from standing at the Cenotaph in chilly, damp weather on Armistice Day, and his condition worsened so rapidly that on 4 December a Council of State was appointed. On 12 December Sir Hugh Rigby performed an operation to drain the right side of the King's chest, but the Royal patient had a 'very narrow margin of safety' and his recovery was very slow.

It was only at the beginning of February that the King's health was considered to be sufficiently improved for him to travel and he was taken to Craigweil House, Bognor – the seaside retreat of Dunlop Tyre Company chairman Sir Arthur du Cros – to convalesce. The King travelled in a specially-adapted Daimler, apparently a 57 hp model, converted into an ambulance by Stratton-Instone and fitted with such equipment as an electric radiator: it scaled three tons. The route was lined with thousands of loyal well-wishers, and many of the vehicles on the road stopped and their occupants got out and stood bare-headed in respect as the royal motorcade of five Daimlers passed slowly and silently by.

The Queen, meanwhile, had seen the King off from Buckingham Palace and then followed a slightly different route in her Daimler so that she could overtake the ambulance and be in Bognor in time to welcome the King. Commented *The Autocar*: 'Thus passed off without a hitch what must justly be regarded as one of the most significant royal progresses in England. Road transport could not have proved itself more completely.'

It was not until May that the King was thought sufficiently recovered to return home to Windsor Castle – again, by Daimler – but he was still far from well, and it was not until the autumn that 'he was so much his old self that he could enjoy motoring, fishing and shooting at Sandringham'. By then, two more Daimlers had been added to the royal fleet, a 28/35 hp Hooper enclosed limousine for the use of the Royal Household and a second Double-Six 30, an enclosed Brougham for the King's official use.

* * *

Another early customer for the Double-Six 30 was Bernard Docker: his father F. Dudley Docker had been on the Daimler board from 1910–12 and was a great friend of Percy Martin's: a hint of the high style with which Daimler was run in the 1920s is given in surviving correspondence between the two when Martin sent Dudley Docker a case of champagne to sample: 'I suggest you try it and

if you have any use for more of it, we have a considerable stock here at Coventry which we would be very pleased to let you have at what it cost us . . . The price from our stock would be 74s [£3.70] for the 1911 and 97s [£4.85] for the 1915 and I believe we could buy more of the 1915 today for 102s [£5.10] per half dozen magnums.'

Bernard Docker, who would become Daimler chairman in 1941, was then in his early 30s and well-used to the champagne lifestyle himself. When he went north to his Scottish estate of Murthly Castle in Perthshire in September 1928, he drove his Double-Six 30 and complained to Martin by letter that the car had developed 'a very bad wheel wobble', despite the tyres having been changed round and checked before the journey. 'I do not know if there is anything you could suggest we could do to cure it before I come south, as I am not much looking forward to the drive down complete with wobble!' wrote Docker, who also complained of intermittent ignition trouble on both coil and magneto ignition.

In those days Daimler operated a nationwide chain of depots, though the nearest one to Perthshire was in Wallsend-on-Tyne. Four days after Martin had received Docker's letter, Daimler mechanic Purvis was despatched by the 7.12 a.m. train from Newcastle Central carrying a set of spring wedges, a tyre pressure gauge, an ignition change-over switch, a set of plug leads, a condenser and a coil, secure in the knowledge that a car from Murthly Castle would be waiting for him at Perth station. It wasn't; so Purvis caught a bus which took him the 10 miles to a crossroads which, said the bus driver, was 'but five miles, up side tracks' from Murthly Castle. Purvis trudged on through the rain, asking his way from the few people he met on the road, but few of them even knew where the Castle was. Suddenly a Daimler van carrying several passengers drove by without stopping, though the driver stared at Purvis. A few minutes later it came back, and turned out to be Docker's van, driven by his chauffeur, Lewis, though as by that time Purvis was only a hundred yards from the Castle, that was really immaterial.

Docker was not in that afternoon and Lewis had apparently been left in charge: Purvis easily fixed the ignition (it was just a loose switch spindle and took a few minutes to rectify) and then Lewis airily commented: 'That was really the only trouble; the wheel trouble is nothing. Anyway, you can't take the car out to try, as it has been washed and polished.' Asked to put on two new front tyres so that Purvis could test for wheel wobble, Lewis replied: 'Mr Docker will not permit me under any circumstances to put on the new tyres until we get down from the heights on to the main road. I went out with the car this morning and had no wheel wobble at all: this is such an insignificant matter that it can be fixed when we come down to Coventry.'

And so poor wet uncomplaining Purvis had to make the long journey back to Wallsend with his bag of spares, having made a round trip of some 220 miles for a few minutes' work. Bernard Docker may have been a rather special customer, but that was the degree of service that was expected – and

given – when Daimler built Europe's only 12-cylinder car. Only one other maker ever attempted a V12 sleeve-valve engine, and that was the French Voisin marque, and its production (1929–37) was both minimal and spasmodic.

The V12 Daimler could even be transformed into a stunning sports car: Reid Railton converted a Double-Six 50 into a low-built two-seater for a Captain Wilson, apparently supported by Laurence Pomeroy. Its engine was tuned to develop 150 bhp, the chassis was underslung at the rear and the radiator tapered from top to bottom; the conversion was carried out by Railton's employers, Thomson & Taylor of Brooklands early in 1930, towards the end of the Double-Six 50's production run, and at least three cars – the Wilson sports model, a Weymann sports saloon (later fitted with Corsica drophead coupé coachwork) and a futuristic sportsman's coupé commissioned by Stratton-Instone – were transformed in this exciting manner.

Joseph Mackle of Stratton-Instone – which had taken over most of the nationwide chain of Daimler service depots in 1928 when they were appointed Daimler-BSA

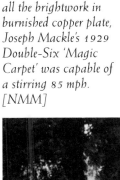

Finished in cream, with all the brightwork in burnished copper plate, Joseph Mackle's 1929 Double-Six 'Magic Carpet' was capable of a stirring 85 mph. [NMM]

distributors for England and Wales – also revealed the sporting potential of the Daimler Double-Six by commissioning a magnificent boat-tailed two-seater body on the Double-Six 30 chassis from the Hoyal Body Corporation. Largely designed by Mackle, this amazing car (painted 'a rich cream shade of cellulose, almost amounting to a mayonnaise colour, with bright copper metal fittings') was strictly a two-seater, with hood, luggage and spare wheels concealed in the long tail and tools carried in aerofoil-section running boards. Its leather upholstery had an antiqued copper finish and a combination of light weight and a higher-than-standard final drive ratio gave this car, appropriately named 'The Magic Carpet', a top speed of 85 mph.

Mackle's car was delivered in May 1929. A few weeks later his partner Undecimus Stratton, who for years had been the link between Daimler and the Royal Household, first as manager of Daimler's London depot, then as one of the founding triumvirate of Stratton-Instone, died at the age of 61. His 'sage advice and untiring energy' had created a unique relationship between monarch and manufacturer, and the King and Queen expressed their regret at the death of an old and valued friend.

* * *

In August 1929 Laurence Pomeroy was appointed managing director of Daimler in place of Percy Martin, who nevertheless retained his position as managing director of the BSA Parent Company. As his son (a distinguished technical journalist and bon viveur) recalled, Laurence Pomeroy was of that generation of chief engineers who 'lived on terms of financial and social equality with all but the richest of car users and could appreciate motoring from their customers' point of view'. He soon made his presence felt by introducing a new 30 hp model for 1930 in which much use was made of 'special tough alloys of aluminium in places where heavier metal hitherto has been used'.

Aluminium frame and spring brackets were fitted, and the cylinder block was a one-piece light alloy casting. This obviously saved weight but additionally enabled the engine to warm up quickly from cold. Moreover, it was claimed, 'aluminium alloy is very well suited as a material for the cylinders of a sleeve valve engine, inasmuch as no cylinder liner of special metal is needed, since the outer one of the pair of steel sleeves, rising and falling over a comparatively short distance at a relatively low speed can work successfully in direct contact with the aluminium cylinder bore. It actually is at work under more favourable conditions than an aluminium piston within a steel liner.'

The sleeves were now running in longer cylinder bores which supported them almost to the end of their working faces, and considerable attention had been paid to lubrication. Though the engine had full pressure lubrication of the crankshaft bearings, the big ends were also fitted with a modified form of splash lubrication to ensure that the sleeves were properly lubricated when starting from cold. When the oil was cold, it was extremely viscous and very little escaped from the bearings to be flung on to the sleeves, but the thickness of the oil forced open a pressure release valve which poured oil into the troughs below the big-ends, from which it was scooped by dippers. But as the oil became warmer and more fluid, not only did the release valve close, but carefully calibrated slots in the walls of the troughs enabled the more fluid oil to escape and the splashing ceased (and so, presumably, did the light oil haze that habitually followed in the wake of over-lubricated Daimlers).

The new Daimler was among the first road-going cars to be fitted with an oil radiator, in this case incorporated in the radiator housing, and designed to maintain oil temperature at a maximum of 130° F even in summer: oil was constantly circulated through this radiator by one of two submerged pumps in the sump, the other feeding the crankshaft, eccentric shaft and

Towed . . . in a hole . . .

Inspired to join Daimler by the sight of the motorcade accompanying a Royal visit to his mother's home town of Bristol during the First World War, a gangling youth nicknamed 'Lofty' England joined Daimler's main service depot as an apprentice in 1927. He paid his first visit to Coventry at the end of a tow rope, steering a bus chassis behind a breakdown truck (the rope broke in busy Hertford Street) but his later relationship with Daimler was at a loftier level, as chief executive of Jaguar after that company took over Daimler in the 1960s.

conrod bearings. It was also one of the first cars to pay attention to ergonomics, with lighting and manual throttle switches on the steering wheel boss, and dual horn buttons and headlamp dip switch on a stalk below the steering wheel rim, all within finger-tip reach without the driver removing his hands from the wheel. Evidence of Pomeroy's years in America was evident in the Art Deco design of the dashboard, which was finished in dull bronze and, remarkably, incorporated a warning light that glowed green if the oil level in the sump fell below the safety limit. And to a generation of motorists that was accustomed to decarbonize engines and grind-in valves every 8,000 miles at most (and often at much shorter intervals), the fact that the new Daimler would run up to 40,000 miles before it needed a decoke was little short of miraculous.

The launch of the new chassis – necessary to reverse declining sales and falling profits – was not the only sign that things were changing. The 1929 announcement that Daimler would be offering bodywork by outside coachbuilders as catalogue models cloaked the company's decision to close its own bodyshop, making a number of employees – several with 20 to 30 years' service – redundant. By the standards of the day, the company looked after its discharged bodyshop staff well, offering what might nowadays be termed 'golden handshakes' varying between £10 and £103 dependent on age and length of service, and even offering some 'old employees whose services are being dispensed with' modest weekly allowances if they were in difficult circumstances.

A rare surviving chassis progress report dating from November 1929 reveals that the new model was intended to play a prominent role in the company's typically complex production programme for 1930, which encompassed six engine types and some 17 variants on seven chassis types. It also shows that a significant part of the next year's programme was completed – and sold – early.

By mid-November, Daimler had completed 3,763 chassis out of a total 1930 sanction of 5,494 units and had advance orders for over 72 per cent of that sanction. Of the total, 1,180 were 16 hp chassis, 2,176 were 20 hp chassis, 1,735 were the new 25 hp, 236 were 30 hp Double-Sixes, 396 were 35 hp sixes and just 74 were the mighty 50 hp Double-Six. In addition, there were 129 of the old 'ADC' Types 423 and 424 (which were sold with a fluted-top Daimler radiator after the ending of the ADC link) and 531 of the new CF6 bus chassis, as well as 72 'old type' car chassis, of which 68 remained unsold in mid-November.

But by then Wall Street had already crashed, and Commander St John of Daimler Hire was reporting a fall in turnover, 'principally due to the smaller number of funeral orders and to the lack of orders from hotels . . . the serious fall in the prices of American stocks has caused the premature departure of a large proportion of the American visitors'.

It's easy enough with hindsight to claim that the effects of the Depression were exacerbated by over-reaction, but the panic repercussion that set in at the end of 1929 hit the motor industry hard. At first, Daimler tried to close its eyes to the crash. When Captain Pelham-Clinton of coachbuilders Hooper approached Daimler seeking financial aid for his associated company Maythorns of Biggleswade, he was turned down flat on the grounds that his chassis order for 1930 was insufficient. Pelham-Clinton then went to see Joseph Mackle and agreed to increase his order for the year to ten chassis.

Percy Martin's response was frosty: 'While the ten chassis would represent an increase on your business last year, it is not at all, to my mind, the volume of business that the Daimler Company have a right to expect from Hooper in view of our past association, and I feel that 20 should be the minimum number of chassis that you should undertake to sell if there is to be a continuance of the

Daimler directors visit the factory in 1930, including Percy Martin (second from left), Patrick Hannon (fourth from left) and E.W. Hancock (right). [JDHT]

friendly relationship between our companies. As, however, I do not expect you to make a definite contract to cover this full maximum number, I suggest that you revise your contract with Stratton-Instone to the increased total of 15 chassis and when this has been done I will be prepared to consider favourably the question of accommodating you, at the ordinary bankers' interest, up to £5,000 over a period of six months.'

Whether or not the loan was eventually made, Maythorns were beyond saving and closed their doors in 1932 after some 90 years of coachbuilding. In 1928 they had built what today would be called a 'hatchback' on a Double-Six 30 chassis for Lord Rosebery; it had doors in the back of its saloon body and was fitted with a pull-out ramp up which Rosebery could be pushed in his wheelchair. Some of Maythorns's last orders were for coachwork on Daimler chassis, including a spectacular streamlined Double-Six completed in January 1931, a Double-Six landaulette with tapestry-upholstered passenger compartment shown at the British Empire Exhibition in Buenos Aires in March 1931, and a 20/30 Daimler saloon commissioned by Henry Ford's son Edsel and shipped to Detroit in November 1930. This car was fitted with Pomeroy's tour de force, the fluid flywheel and preselector transmission, which aroused such interest on the far side of the Atlantic that Cadillac's chief engineer Ernest Seaholm came to London and bought a fluid flywheel Daimler off the Daimler stand at Olympia for technical investigation: it inspired his assistant Earl Thompson (inventor of synchromesh) to develop the Hydramatic automatic transmission.

The principle of the fluid flywheel was an old one, originally devised in 1905 by Professor Föttinger of the Vulcan-Werke Shipyard in Hamburg to drive the propellers of turbine steamships developing up to 15,000 hp. The 'Föttinger Coupling' basically consisted of a closed casing containing a flywheel (or 'driving member') and a driven member, both with cups around their rim. There was no physical connection between the two members, but the casing was filled with oil and as the engine revolved faster the driving member impelled oil into the cups of the driven member with increasing force until sufficient kinetic energy was developed to create the effect of a solid coupling with imperceptible slippage.

English engineer Harold Sinclair of Hydraulic Coupling Patents Ltd collaborated with Dr Bauer of the Vulcan-Werke to adapt the Föttinger Coupling to vehicle transmission, and in October 1926 he initiated discussions with the London General Omnibus Company. The first trials of Sinclair's 'Fluidrive' were made on an Associated Daimler bus chassis in February 1928 but it was not until Percy Martin of Daimler decided to apply the principle to a private car that real progress was made.

The engineering of the Daimler installation was due to Laurence Pomeroy and initially the fluid flywheel was launched, in May 1930, in conjunction with a conventional 'silent third' gearbox. However, the drawbacks with this system were shown in March 1929 when a Double-Six 30 fitted with an early example of this transmission ran away when it was left ticking over in gear at a Devon garage by Pomeroy himself, and demolished two petrol pumps and the cashier's kiosk before it could be restrained.

Dr Lanchester – who had frequent differences of opinion with Pomeroy, one of the few engineers who could match him intellectually – had warned that introducing this transmission as it stood would be 'a terribly big gambling risk': it was, perhaps, not surprising that Daimler chose to terminate his consultancy soon afterwards. But he was nevertheless proved right when in June, some six weeks after the unveiling of the fluid flywheel, Daimler unveiled the new 3.5-litre 20/30 hp which replaced the conventional gearbox with a 'self-changing' epicyclic transmission controlled by a 'finger-tip control' lever moving in a quadrant just below the steering wheel rim. This gave a virtually automatic transmission, for all the driver had to do to engage a gear was to move the lever to the appropriate notch on the quadrant and depress the 'clutch' pedal: gear-changing was made as simple as 'switching over from one station to another on a wireless set to pick up a palatable programme'. And if the driver was careless enough to leave the car parked with a gear engaged, a red warning light was illuminated.

And when the new transmission was fitted to the new Pomeroy-designed 30/40 hp Double-Six launched in September 1930, *The Autocar* described it 'unreservedly . . . as one of the finest cars yet designed in the "sovereign class" of automobiles'. When this was followed a month later by a new 40/50 hp V12 which like the 30/40 had an all-alloy power unit, the press was hard pushed for superlatives. Words like 'far-reaching' and 'of transcending interest' greeted the new models: and for once the hyperbole was something of an understatement.

Chapter 7

DAIMLER IN THE THIRTIES

Christmas 1930 was a bleak season for the British motor industry. The year had seen an overall fall in new car production from 180,426 to 167,287, making annual output only equal to the home market sales of 1929, and though the industry had escaped some of the more pernicious effects of the depression which had hit the Americans so badly, nevertheless there were several notable casualties around that time, often caused by panicking banks calling in overdrafts unnecessarily. One such victim was the Lanchester Motor Company, one of Britain's oldest manufacturers, whose bank called in their overdraft of just £38,000 at ridiculously short notice at the end of 1930 with the ultimatum 'amalgamate or go bankrupt'.

Though the luxury car market was at first remarkably little affected by the depression, Daimler was convinced that its future lay in extending its appeal downward into the middle-class sector, and the opportunity to acquire its old rival, whose Birmingham factory adjoined one of the BSA group companies, seemed heaven-sent for, as the official BSA announcement stated, 'the general character and reputation of the Lanchester car is in keeping with that of the products of the Daimler company'. Certainly Pomeroy, backed by Hancock, was strongly in favour, and when the BSA board offered the shareholders of the floundering Lanchester company 8s 3d (£0.41) for each share they held – issued capital was £64,321, making the cost to BSA just £26,371 – they accepted virtually unanimously, with just two briefly dissenting.

This was not the first time Lanchester's name had been linked with a take-over: in August 1929 there had been rumours in the press of 'a big amalgamation that is proposed between a group of well-known motor manufacturers' which involved Lanchester, but this had been vehemently denied by Lanchester chairman (and principal shareholder) Hamilton Barnsley, who had been on the company's board since its foundation 30 years earlier. 'Although it is true that our company is not unmindful of the great benefits obtainable from some such grouping of interests,' he said, 'we shall only be parties to any scheme in which Lanchester cars, of high power, will continue to be produced, of the same high quality material and workmanship for which we have always been so noted in the past, and where the interests of Lanchester owners and buyers will be carefully safeguarded in the future.'

Now there was no choice, and Percy Martin reported to the BSA board meeting on 16 December 1930 that the acquisition was likely to be finalized 'in the course of the next day or two'. It was, it seems, all too much for poor Barnsley who died on Christmas Day, less than a fortnight after the BSA board

Lanchester works test driver Archie Millership climbs the Crystal Palace steps in 1904. [JDHT]

meeting, ironically when he was making plans for his retirement to the south coast 'in the hope that the more genial climate than that of Birmingham would fully restore him to health'.

The news of the BSA take-over was made public early in January, a few days after the announcement of Barnsley's death, and was summarized by *The Autocar* as 'in the nature of an act of industrial rationalization, the

Lanchester's London depot at 311 Oxford Street was shared with coachbuilders Lawrie & Marner. [JDHT]

acquiring company being what is known as a parent, or holding, company, and the transaction just concluded not implying any particular important changes, nor any amalgamation in the ordinary sense of that term'. It proved to be a pious hope. Before the month was out BSA announced that the offices and production were to be transferred to the Daimler headquarters at Sandy Lane, Coventry, though 'it should be clearly understood . . . that while the proximity of the new production programmes will benefit both concerns from the standpoint of technical development and facility of manufacture, both cars will retain their individuality – in no way will there be any

Interchangeable bodywork was a feature of some early Lanchesters [JDHT]

25 hp Lanchesters used by the Royal Naval Air Service. [JDHT]

These 38 hp Lanchester armoured cars of the RNAS fought for the Czar of Russia during the Great War. [JDHT]

fusion of the Lanchester and Daimler cars'. George Lanchester, chief engineer and works manager, followed the family firm to Coventry; his brother Frank, a brilliant salesman, was appointed London Director of the Lanchester Motor Company and also joined the board of Stratton-Instone, which had acquired both the sole distributorship of

Tyre manufacturer Lionel Rapson used this monoposto Lanchester 40 hp racer for tyre testing at Brooklands. [JDHT]

Lanchester cars and their showrooms at 95 New Bond Street.

The Lanchester story went back to 1894 when gas engine pioneer Frederick Lanchester, backed by his friends James and Allan Whitfield, had formed a private syndicate to acquire the rights to his patents. Dissuaded from developing an aero-engine because his ideas were too far ahead of what the scientific establishment would accept, Lanchester began designing a motor car, which was first road-tested in the spring of 1896, but proved insufficiently powerful with its original single-cylinder 'balanced' engine. It was rebuilt with a twin-cylinder power unit and in 1897 George Lanchester joined his brother as assistant. However, the Lanchester did not go into production until 1901, largely due to Frederick Lanchester's refusal to compromise in any way in the design or construction of his car, with the result that when at last manufacture began his advanced ideas looked like eccentricity, for design had already settled into a broadly established pattern – engine in front, driving the rear wheels through a multi-ratio gearbox, and wheel steering.

While the Lanchesters' mid-mounted 'balanced' flat-twin engine with its twin crankshafts and six connecting rods may have been remarkably smooth-running, their side-lever steering judged more natural than a wheel, and their preselector epicyclic gearchange easier to use than a conventional gearbox, the end result was that their cars looked different from anything else on the road. So while Lanchester acquired a hard-core of dedicated enthusiast owners – most prominent of whom was Rudyard Kipling – who appreciated the brilliance of their design and construction, many potential customers, afraid of appearing 'counter, curious, strange' at the tiller of the determinedly unorthodox Lanchester, placed their orders elsewhere.

Sadly, Lanchester had the means at their fingertips to serve a far wider market, for Frederick Lanchester had devised a system of jigs and limit gauges that guaranteed complete interchangeability in production, and it's probably no coincidence that Henry

A 1915 Lanchester Sporting 40 tourer. [JDHT]

The Maharajah of Alwar's extended-wheelbase Lanchester 40 hp state landau had a gold silk brocade interior. [JDHT]

Ford bought himself a Lanchester to study in his early years of assembly-line production. It was only in 1913, after Frederick Lanchester had been replaced as chief designer by his younger brother George, that cars of more conventional appearance joined the range, the board having decided that it was no longer possible to attempt to 'educate the public to appreciate a car that is designed and produced strictly by adherence to the first logical principles of design'.

Nevertheless, the Lanchesters of the 1920s were very fine cars by any standards: the Forty, launched in 1919, had an overhead camshaft six-cylinder engine inspired by aero-engine practice, and was described by pioneer motorist S.F. Edge as 'the best suspended car in the world', while the 21 hp, developed as a counter to the new Rolls-Royce Twenty, was effectively a scaled-down Forty. Then, in 1928, George Lanchester's masterpiece, the 4,440 cc Straight-Eight, supplanted the Forty. Again it had an overhead camshaft and its crankshaft ran in 10 main bearings, and the general opinion was that with his new model George Lanchester had improved on perfection.

Certainly, the Lanchester was by now rivalling the Daimler for the affections of a very exclusive clientele who wanted a more discreet form of conveyance than a Rolls-Royce: most notable Lanchester owner was the Duke of York (later King George VI), whose first example of the marque had been a 1925 Forty in which his baby daughter – now Her Majesty Queen Elizabeth II – first appeared in public at the age of six weeks, while many Indian rulers also favoured the Lanchester, as did the reclusive tycoon Sir John Ellerman, 'the richest man in Britain'.

The acquisition of the Lanchester name had several advantages for Daimler. It was a marque of equal standing, catering to a very similar clientele, and the take-over not only turned Lanchester from a growing threat into an ally, but enabled Daimler to redefine the Lanchester production programme to plug its own middle-market gap, and to obtain the services of George Lanchester (as brilliant an engineer as brother Frederick but far more pragmatic) and gain practical experience of the design and manufacture of poppet-valve engines without undermining the sleeve valve, which was fast being rendered obsolescent by technical progress but whose silky silence still appealed to the carriage trade.

Indeed, the Knight sleeve-valve patent had fallen into such desuetude that the Knight & Kilbourne Patents Company was dissolved at the end of 1931, with Daimler receiving a final payment as stockholders of just $346.62, the equivalent of roughly £77. Even so, the sleeve-valve engine still had much to commend it. That connoisseur of fine cars David Holland recently restored a Barker-bodied Daimler 35/120 originally owned by Winston Churchill, to whom it had been presented in 1931 by a group of admirers led by Brendan Bracken at a time when Churchill was in the political wilderness; it was waiting at the foot of the gangway when he limped off the transatlantic liner in Southampton, having been knocked over by a car when getting out of a cab in New York during a lecture tour of America. David Holland had the Daimler fitted with new sleeves and drove it to Switzerland in the early 1990s, perhaps the longest tour made by a sleeve-valve Daimler in recent years: not only was it smooth and silent, but it did not smoke.

With Lanchester, Daimler had acquired perhaps the most technically-advanced poppet-valve engines of 1931, for they had pressed-in dry cylinder liners and a full-pressure lubrication system designed to keep the oil clean, with not only gauze filters on suction and delivery sides of the pump, but also a magnet inside the delivery filter to take out metallic particles from the oil. Another clever feature was a carefully gas-flowed multi-branch exhaust system which added some 8 per cent to the power output.

But Daimler had little interest in the Lanchester 21 hp six and 30 hp straight-eight: production of the six was quickly halted while limited manufacture of the straight-eight was transferred to the Daimler works. A new large car had been on the stocks at the time of the take-over, but only two engines were built. In the late 1930s Frederick Lanchester built up a third engine out of spare parts for a special Lanchester car for Major-General Sir Edmund Ironsides, Governor of Gibraltar.

The vacated Lanchester factory, Armourer Mills, was cleared of spares – post-war components were transported to Coventry and pre-war parts were scrapped, a decision

The stylish 1931 Daimler 16/20 hp foursome coupé. [JDHT]

that doubtless made a great deal of sense commercially, for the veteran car movement was then very much in its infancy – and turned over to another BSA subsidiary, the Burton Griffiths Machine Tool Company. Part of the factory was also used to store unsold bicycle frames; after the Second World War plastic macs were made there.

In parallel with the Lanchester take-over, Daimler had developed a new small sleeve-valve model, the 16/20, 'particularly suited to the owner who drives himself'. Apart from cast-iron cylinder blocks, this 2,648 cc six-cylinder model had many of the features of Pomeroy's larger sleeve-valve Daimlers, including the ingenious auxiliary trough lubrication for the sleeves when starting from cold. Of course, it had the fluid flywheel and self-changing gearbox, though one notable departure from Daimler tradition was the use of a pull-on handbrake: up till then, Daimler handbrakes had pushed on.

The preselector gearbox now had self-adjusting brake bands for the epicyclic gear trains. *The Autocar* devised a particularly brutal test of this, driving a 16/20 down the

1:4 Brooklands test hill using first gear as an engine brake and preselecting reverse, dipping the transmission pedal and simultaneously flooring the throttle pedal: 'The car slowed, stopped and finally climbed the hill backwards.' When, after several repeat performances of 'this form of butchery', the reverse brake band began to slip, it was restored to full health by dipping the pedal several times with the engine stationary and reverse selected. Another feature which appealed to the press was the construction of the bonnet which, apart from being made in three sections in typical Daimler fashion, was sound-insulated, with asbestos padding between double panelling.

The Daimler was still the favourite car of kings: in mid-April 1931 it was announced that the King of Siam had just taken delivery of a 20/30 hp Daimler sports saloon bodied by Arthur Mulliner of Northampton, while King George V, just recovered from a severe attack of bronchitis, took delivery of five new Hooper-bodied Daimlers, which he had ordered in October 1930 to stimulate British industry and alleviate unemployment during the winter. These cars – three 40/50 hp Double-Six limousines and a 30/40 'enclosed limousine' each for the King and Queen – were the first Royal cars to be fitted with safety glass, which the King had previously refused to have fitted in case 'discoloration might prevent people seeing him'.

In the mid-1930s Jack Fairman, later a distinguished racing driver with Connaught and Aston Martin, worked as an 'improver-fitter' in the Daimler service department housed in the old Motor Mills, where he developed the analytical skills that helped to develop the Aston Martin DBR1 which won the world championship in 1959. During his time at Daimler, Fairman became one of only two employees trusted to test-drive the Royal Double-Sixes when they were overhauled: 'When the Royal Cars came in for service, we didn't take the mudguards and body off, as we did with other cars; nobody except Charlie Lloyd (the head tester) and myself ever road-tested the Royal Cars. I gravitated on to road test because Charlie Lloyd said so! It happened like this: there was

a Daimler limousine that had had a compete overhaul, but Charlie was suspicious of a slight howl from the back axle, so he shut himself in the back of the car and got me to drive so that he could listen and concentrate on what he was doing, pulling the floorboards up while we were going along and having a look underneath. Everything was removable then . . .

'Charlie realized that I could drive a Double-Six 50 Daimler and I started doing the testing myself – this ability to control $2\frac{1}{2}$ tons of Daimler stood me in very good stead when I got mixed up with motor racing after the war, when I was employed by Connaught and Aston, not only to race their cars but test them first. The Daimler Double-Sixes didn't oversteer or understeer or go straight on at corners – they just steered! The steering wheel rim was hollow and was loaded with lead. The lead loading was all balanced and helped the steering; it didn't make the steering any heavier but gave you better control. Daimler intended the steering to be fairly heavy – after all, it gave you a feeling of

Commissioned by Mr A. Webber of Wandsworth, and built on the standard Double-Six 40/50 hp chassis, this low-slung coupé was built by Martin Walter of Folkestone in 1932. [NMM]

*This Mulliner-bodied
1931 Double-Six 40/50
was exported to Quebec.
[JDHT]*

confidence – and these cars were never meant for women to drive. When parking – yes the steering was heavy, but the cars were made to drive on the road, never mind the parking!

'You had a great tapering bonnet; there was a radiator cap with a flag on and you could see the top of the headlights. If you decided you were going to shave the kerb by two inches or pass a stationary car, you weren't doing it with your heart in your mouth, you could steer with just one hand on the wheel: the car went exactly where you wanted it to. The Double-Six 50 did about 8 mpg, there was a Double-Six 40, with a smaller engine, then there was a smaller one than that, a Double-Six 30, which was only 3.7 litres – it was a dead loss, because it hadn't got enough power.

'One day I got picked up by the police while driving the King's car, a Double-Six 40, which had been in for a general check. The engine of the King's car was still a little bit tight and wanted a couple of hundred miles' running in. Charlie trusted me to do that: I went out round Coventry and promptly got picked up by the police as the Double-Six

had no number plates because it was the King's car!'

* * *

Times were changing, and Daimler was changing with them. Under Laurence Pomeroy the Engineering Department was working on a range of projects as diverse as a poppet-valve bus engine and the new front-wheel driven BSA 9 hp model, effectively the popular BSA three-wheeler with a dead axle fitted at the rear (but nevertheless absorbing a fair amount of Daimler Drawing Office time).

The principal preoccupation was the new 15/18 hp Lanchester, which was intended as a solid bedrock of the 1932 programme, which anticipated production of 1,000 of the new chassis during the year, along with 200 16/20 hp Daimlers, 150 Lanchester Straight-Eights and 250 bus chassis, both the sleeve-valve CH6 and the new poppet-valve CP6. Oddly enough, the other Daimler models were not listed in the internal document circulated to group managing directors.

Presumably all necessary development had been completed and stocks of parts already laid down.

Launched in September 1931, and hailed as 'one of the most interesting cars in Olympia' at its Motor Show debut the following month, the new model was largely the work of George Lanchester. Remarks Jack Fairman, who often drove George Lanchester on test runs in heavily-instrumented 15/18 prototypes: 'His heart was still with the original Lanchester company . . . he didn't like this "small car disease" that was creeping up and his compromise was the 15/18.' Though it had been designed to sell at a very moderate price (£565 complete), this 2,504 cc six still possessed many original features in the Lanchester tradition, like self-lubricating ball-bearing spring shackles, a novel design of pushrod overhead valve gear which operated at very wide clearances (0.042 in instead of 0.004 in) but gave 'absolute quietness of running' and a fan belt whose tension could be adjusted by removing shims from the driving pulley so as to expand its effective diameter.

Daimler features were obvious, too, like the self-changing gearbox and fluid flywheel (it was the least expensive car so equipped) in conjunction with the Lanchester worm drive. A sign of the stylistic times intended 'to provide plenty of body space upon a conserved wheelbase' was the forward mounting of the engine with the radiator set well ahead of the axle, while in contrast the transmission brake behind the gearbox was a once-common feature that had dropped out of general use. It was certainly a package that was attractive enough to secure an order from the Duke of York, who took delivery of a Lanchester 15/18 in May 1932.

The all-round performance of the new Lanchester was dramatically demonstrated in March the following year, when Colonel A.H. Loughborough's 15/18 saloon was the overall winner of the first-ever RAC Rally, a 1,000-mile touring event ending in Torquay.

Second place in that event was taken by J. Mercer's 30/40 Double-Six Daimler (driven by a Daimler apprentice named Raymond 'Lofty' England), and cars fitted with torque convertor transmissions – including Armstrong Siddeley, which had been first with the preselector gear and had returned the complement by adopting the fluid flywheel – swept the board in the slow-running test. But no-one could match Loughborough's slow-running time of 5 min 7.8 sec over 100 yards, an average speed of just 1.5 mph.

Daimler had mounted a stunning display at the Olympia Motor Show in October 1931, by which time every car (and, incidentally, every bus) in the Daimler range was fitted with the 'fluid flywheel and preselective gearbox that a child can handle'; every car on the stand, from 16/20 saloon to 40/50 Double-Six enclosed limousine, was painted crimson lake, bringing a 'fine splash of colour' to a show that was noteworthy for its lack of stand dressing, a direct result of the recession that was now being felt more keenly throughout the industry.

Manufacturers exhorted the public to 'buy British' and hoped for 'the turn of the tide when the trade, which has faced extraordinary difficulties with great courage, finds that the sales curve has commenced its upward progress once more'. Ernest Instone, who had become President of the Society of Motor Manufacturers & Traders, spoke of his 'pride and gratification' in the way that the British motor industry had emerged from 'a year of unprecedented and worldwide commercial depression . . . with a degree of success far greater than that achieved in any other national industry'.

Nevertheless, though its association with BSA had acted as a shield from the worst effects of the depression, by the end of 1931 Daimler was feeling the need to cut costs and halt over-production, and when the group managing directors met to discuss the 1932 programme on Christmas Eve, Pomeroy proposed a drastic cut in output to reduce

First success for the 15/18 Lanchester: victory in the 1932 RAC Rally for Colonel A.H. Loughborough. [JDHT]

presumably the rest were stock in hand) and the bus chassis programme was reduced from 250 to 160, which, added to stock brought forward, 'brought the total sales possible to 216, and there is reason to believe that these will be sold'.

Among the commercial vehicle projects being undertaken was a research programme on behalf of one of Daimler's biggest bus customers, the Edinburgh Corporation, which was investigating the viability of a high compression sleeve-valve bus engine capable of running on creosote oil. Tests using normal petrol as a fuel showed a saving of 10 per cent at 2,600 rpm and 23 per cent at 1,200 rpm and, said Pomeroy: 'In my opinion the sleeve-valve engine is much more suitable for high compression than a poppet valve and there seems reason to believe, although the work done up to date is very limited, that we can show a saving to bus operators of £80 to £100 per annum per double deck bus in fuel costs alone.' Though the research programme continued, it was overtaken by Daimler's adoption of the Gardner 5LW five-cylinder 7-litre direct-injection diesel engine, which had one block of three cylinders and another of two cylinders and proved remarkably successful in conjunction

costs. The Lanchester Straight-Eight was dropped altogether, while the target for the 15/18 was cut from 1,000 to 800. Actual production of the Daimler 16/20 was revised downward from 200 to 174 (though the sales programme for 1932 called for 397 cars:

Young 'Lofty' England drove this 30/40 hp Double-Six in the 1932 RAC Rally. [NMM]

with the preselector gearbox, optionally available with five speeds for buses.

In his presentation, Pomeroy quoted development costs for various recent model programmes which, even allowing for the fact that they were quoted in Gold Standard pounds, seem remarkably cheap compared with the billions it can take to develop a new car in the 1990s. For 1928–9, the cost of developing the 25 hp, Double-Six and CF6 coach chassis had been £5,800, for 1929–30, when the 20/30, 30/40, 40/50 and CF6 coach were launched, development costs were £6,500 and for 1930–1, the cost of the Lanchester 15/18, Daimler 16/20 and CH6 and CP6 bus chassis had again been £6,500, making the cost of developing each new model approximately £2,000; annual supervision costs averaged £3,400. In addition, about £2–3,000 was spent annually producing experimental models.

However, the drawing office was working flat out, said Pomeroy: 'In general, the drawing office is regrettably behind with its normal work. No assembly drawings have been made for a year or so, being postponed while the department has been working overtime and Sundays in connection with the Q 16/20, Lanchester 15/18, bus poppet valve engine and Wilson gearboxes, all of which have been most urgently required. It will require approximately five to six weeks with the present staff to complete the work now in hand. Because of this extreme pressure of work for the last year, coupled with recent dismissals, there is no doubt that the morale of the department is low and the men concerned are not working efficiently. I propose to handle this department directly for the next few months and believe that a considerable amount of unnecessary scheming and designing can be eliminated and the situation relieved from the conditions which have arisen from the great pressure of the last year. Given that in a few months from now – if the Minimum Lanchester car goes on – it should be possible to reduce the Engineering Department cost by approximately £5,000 per annum.'

The so-called 'Minimum Lanchester' appeared in July 1932: a 1,203 cc four-cylinder 10 hp with the engine mounted well forward in its low-slung chassis, which passed underneath the rear axle, it was the smallest model yet built with the fluid flywheel and self-changing transmission, though it was joined just before the Olympia Show by a cheaper BSA derivative with a marginally smaller displacement of 1,185 cc. This had rod-operated brakes instead of hydraulics and spiral bevel final drive instead of worm, which bought the price tag down to just £230 with open tourer bodywork.

Diehard Lancunians may have condemned the 'Minimum Lanchester' as unworthy of the name, and Jack Fairman dismisses it as 'a doctor's car... couldn't pull the skin off a rice pudding, though it was well finished in the Lanchester style', but Pomeroy's decision to proceed with its production was fully justified by the results. Following the same line of reasoning, he developed a new 15 hp Daimler, effectively a six-cylinder de luxe version of the Lanchester Ten costing £450, with 'dignified' six-light saloon bodywork, whose overhead valve engine was described as being smooth, sweet and free from vibration. Not only was the Fifteen the first poppet-valve Daimler car since 1909, but it was also the first Daimler model to be marketed for less than £500 since the end of the First World War. The sleeve-valve Twenty, Twenty-Five and Double-Six models continued, with the Twenty-Five substantially reduced in price, indicating that the factory was anxious to clear unsold stock.

The Fifteen may have broken the sleeve-valve's long domination of the Daimler range, but it also played a role in creating a novel BSA motor cycle shown at the November 1933 Olympia Motor Cycle Show. This ohv 500 cc single had a Daimler fluid flywheel transmission which used the first three speeds of the Daimler 15 preselector gearbox and incorporated a fluid flywheel which replaced the nearside internal flywheel in the

The Daimler stand at the 1932 Olympia Show, with the old wrought-iron sign still giving good service. [JDHT]

specially-widened crankcase. Though the new model featured in the BSA catalogue for 1934, it never passed the prototype stage.

The decision to rely on outside body suppliers had not proved altogether wise. Daimler was becoming dissatisfied with the quality of some of the production bodywork coming from companies such as Mulliners and decided to resume in-house production. Among the designers it recruited at this time was Eric Neale (later a distinguished designer for Jensen), who worked on bodies for both Lanchester and Daimler and recalled that the company had a Heenan-Froude 'shaker' rolling-road machine, which tested wooden body frames for squeaks in Daimler's continual search for silence.

Pre-war production figures for most makes have always been difficult to determine due to the curious reticence of makers and the Society of Motor Manufacturers & Traders to publish detailed data. Daimler-Lanchester were no exception to this tiresome rule, but the magnificent leather-bound testimonial volume presented to Percy Martin when he

retired as managing director of the BSA Parent Company in 1934 actually gave detailed output figures for the previous year: 5,000 Lanchester Tens, 1,100 Daimler Fifteens, 850 Lanchester Eighteens (an uprated version of the 15 hp model) and 150 Daimler Twenties. Moreover, the launch of the Ten – available between 1933–6 in cheaper BSA guise, offering a fluid flywheel drive at prices between £210–£245 – had helped the BSA group turn a loss of £688,000 in 1932 into a profit of £245,000 in 1933. Pomeroy's cost-cutting programme really had paid off.

* * *

The fortunes of Daimler had been guided for three decades by a core of three strong men – Percy Martin, Sir Edward Manville and Ernest Instone – and within two years they were all gone.

Ernest Instone, chairman of Stratton-Instone and a council member of the Royal Warrant-Holders' Association, who had guided the sales fortunes of the Daimler marque throughout the 1920s, died in June 1932 aged 60, shortly after completing his year of office as president of the Society of Motor Manufactures & Traders (of which he had been five times vice-president since 1905) and only some ten months after his father. 'We have lost a great Englishman and a great friend,' said Leslie Walton, who had succeeded Instone at the SMMT. But Joseph Mackle, the remaining member of the triumvirate which had established Stratton-Instone, was strongly steeped in the Daimler tradition. He took firm control of the company (which had recruited a number of outstanding staff from Daimler) and renamed it 'Stratstone'; as a consequence, Frank Lanchester lost both his seat on the board and his directorship of Lanchester, and was appointed to the sales staff of Daimler-Lanchester-BSA, which he represented on several SMMT committees and whose board he duly joined in February 1936.

However, the Daimler company itself faced a more serious problem. In May 1933 Sir Edward Manville, who had been chairman of Daimler since 1905, died, aged 71, and was briefly succeeded by Sir Alexander Roger, who had been Director-General of Trench Warfare Supply with the Ministry of Munitions from 1915–17. He held the post for only eight months before he was in turn replaced by Percy Martin, who had just stepped down as managing director of BSA. Martin remained as chairman of Daimler until October 1935 when he finally retired, an event seemingly unnoticed by the press, which once had faithfully recorded every management development at Daimler. Remarkably, no chairman was officially appointed to the Daimler board until December 1936.

Martin's replacement was Geoffrey Burton, who had succeeded Martin as managing director of BSA in 1934 after managing the Round Oak Steel Works at Brierly Hill, Staffordshire, since 1930. Aged 43, Burton was the son of a Church of England Canon. He had trained as an engineer at Cambridge and served as a Captain in the Royal Engineers during the First World War (he was at Gallipoli and was twice mentioned in despatches) before taking up a career in industrial management in the West Midlands.

Even before his appointment became official Burton was acting chairman, and – having little knowledge of the motor industry – seemingly allowed himself to be persuaded by external 'efficiency consultants' that Pomeroy was taking the Daimler-Lanchester group down the wrong path and that the future really lay with larger cars, a theory seemingly borne out by the 56 per cent increase in sales of Daimler cars costing over £650 during 1935 following a reduction in car tax from £1 to 15s (£0.75) per rated horsepower.

Since the 'logical, rational' Pomeroy/Hancock scheme seemed to have stalled – Hancock had called for monthly production targets of 200 Lanchester Tens and 50 Daimler Fifteens before he left the company in 1935 to join Humber as works manager – there seemed to be some substance in the consultants' view (until you considered the inefficiencies built into Daimler's complex production programme). Certainly there were ample grounds to justify a clash of personalities between Pomeroy and Burton.

Pomeroy had a cutting wit – he once described the Rolls-Royce Silver Ghost as 'a triumph of workmanship over design' – and his published writings show that he did not suffer fools (or those, like Frederick Lanchester, who disagreed with his opinions) gladly. Matters finally came to a head in early May 1936. A *Midland Daily Telegraph* staffman named Porter had obviously heard rumours of a rift at the top in Daimler and spoke to Pomeroy, who stated categorically: 'I am still the company's managing director.' Porter rang Burton for confirmation. 'I can neither confirm nor deny this statement,' Burton replied haughtily. 'You must take your information from Mr

Made for a Maharajah

One of the most sumptuously finished Double-Six Daimlers was delivered in 1931 to His Highness the Maharajah of Bhavanagar. A Connaught enclosed-drive limousine, it was painted coronet red and black and all the brightwork – including the radiator – was silver-plated. The passenger compartment was upholstered in red and gold silk tapestry, with a gold pile silk headlining, all the woodwork was in macassar ebony, and the ventilation system, controlled by flaps concealed in the roof, incorporated cages containing scented cotton wool to perfume the air in the rear compartment.

Pomeroy and publish it at your own risk.'

Porter pressed Burton further and was told in confidence that Pomeroy's position as managing director was 'nominal'. By 15 May the news of Pomeroy's resignation was out, though in fact he had been sacked with immediate effect by the BSA board. He was paid £3,000 compensation in lieu of his 12 months' notice and in consideration of any assistance he might be called to give during the period to May 1937 in connection with the Daimler transmission patents. The parting seems to have been as amicable as it could have been, though Pomeroy did not in fact hand in his official resignation until July. He was succeeded as chief engineer by C.M. Simpson, who had joined Daimler from Sunbeam in 1919; significantly, the job no longer held board status.

Ironically, eight days after the news that Pomeroy had left Daimler became public knowledge in England, Ettore Bugatti sat down at his desk in Molsheim, Alsace, and wrote Pomeroy a letter, which only came to light during the research for this book. When Bugatti had been developing his high-speed railcars, he had decided to use the fluid flywheel transmission to link the quadruple 12.8-litre Royale straight-eight engines in the engine car to the driving axles, and Pomeroy had sanctioned this after a visit to Coventry by Bugatti's son Jean. Now Ettore planned another use for Pomeroy's transmission.

'I do not know how to express my gratitude for all the information which you have given me relating to your products and particularly to your hydraulic coupling,' he wrote. 'As you are aware, since our early relations, I have been using your hydraulic coupling on all my rail cars. It gives entire satisfaction and is probably one of the reasons which has allowed me to realize, with some cars, more than 150,000 km without repairs, and particularly repairs to engines. The transmission mechanism is certainly very much assisted by the use of such a coupling. I would like to make a few tests on some of my

vehicles and it is for this reason that I asked you for a small coupling. If I am not troubling you too much, I would very much like to receive the drawings of a coupling which could be fitted to an engine giving 200 CV at 4,000 revolutions for a very light sports car. I should be happy to put at your disposal any details concerning my products. To this effect I am preparing a list of the most important patents which I have had and which I still have. It may be that you will find some details of importance to you. I will then forward to you all the documents relative to the products.'

It sounds as though Bugatti was angling for a cooperative programme with Daimler, probably for a fluid-flywheel version of his Type 57S which was to be launched that October, but in the summer of 1936 France erupted in a series of left-wing strikes which paralysed industry and eventually even reached the feudal calm of Molsheim, where Ettore was locked out of his own factory. Cut to the quick by the disloyalty of a work-force that he had regarded as an extension of his family, Bugatti moved his office to Paris, leaving the running of the factory to Jean. With Pomeroy and Ettore gone, so was any hope of a joint venture between Bugatti and Daimler.

After leaving Daimler, Laurence Pomeroy went to De Havilland Aircraft as general manager of their engine division, but this was not a successful move and in November 1938 he set up practice as a patent consultant in London; he later joined the Claudel Hobson carburettor company. He died in 1941, aged 58, and was mourned as 'a brilliant engineer and also a brilliant wit, [whose] amazing quickness of mind would have won him fame as a KC if he had elected to try the law instead of engineering'.

* * *

Before his departure, Laurence Pomeroy had successfully overseen Daimler's transition from sleeve-valves to poppet valves. The first pushrod Daimler, the Fifteen, had given rise to an enlarged 20 hp derivative and then been uprated for 1935 with an engine increased in capacity to 2,003 cc, Girling rod operated brakes and a pull-on handbrake, but in May 1934 Pomeroy had demonstrated that the pushrod engine was truly suited to the traditional Daimler luxury limousine by launching his new 3,746 cc 'V26' straight-eight chassis. This was the result of a two-year development programme and Pomeroy stated that he had chosen the straight-eight configuration rather than the six because equal gas distribution from carburettor to cylinders was easier to obtain. A twin Stromberg down-draught set-up was used, with separate inlet manifolds for the inner and outer four cylinders.

An interesting verdict on this choice was given by Sir William Sleigh, head of Scottish Daimler distributors Rossleigh, in a private letter to Percy Martin at the time the model was introduced to the marque's dealer body in March 1934: 'As far as publicity is concerned, I don't think it would be advisable to emphasise the fact that it is an eight-cylinder. From an engineer's point of view, the eight-cylinder is the correct thing, but there have been so many failures in connection with eight-cylinder cars that I don't think it would help the new Twenty-Five to make that the feature we want to shout about . . . I don't think there is any chance of your making the chassis too cheap . . . I don't think you should market the new chassis under £850 to £900, probably £875, but see that you make it worth it. I want it to be . . . a keen competitor of the 25 hp Rolls, something on which we can give a roomier and perhaps a better body. With high-class bodywork it should not exceed £1,400. I think the cheapest Rolls you can get is about £1,550.' (In fact, the chassis price at launch was £900, £105 cheaper than the Rolls 20/25; with bodywork, the new Daimler cost from £1,425.)

Briefly testing an early V26 straight-eight, *The Autocar* noted that 'the engine really does run remarkably smoothly, really is exceptionally quiet and pulls with an even

flexibility'. With a crankshaft running in nine main bearings, the overhead valve power unit was flexibly rubber-mounted on 'a special bi-axial system employing five points' in a chassis frame that was boxed-in for rigidity at the front, stiffened at its mid-point by a massive combined scuttle, footboard and toolbox built up from elektron castings, and had a cross-stay running beneath the engine.

Pomeroy had been an early advocate of the 'harmonic stabilizer bumper', which he thought one of the 'mechanical achievements of the year' when it had been introduced at the time of the 1933 Motor Show by accessory company Wilmot Breeden, and now he specified harmonic stabilizer bumper bars 'to subdue any tendency to "frame twitching" at the outset'.

This was very much a car for the carriage trade, riding on a stately 142 inch wheelbase, but it still pioneered a number of features that were to become universal. It was, for instance, probably the first car – certainly in Britain – to have a blue warning light indicating whether the lamps were dipped or not; the Stromberg twin carburettor had a thermostatically-operated automatic choke; and festoon lamps were fitted under the bonnet. The smoothness of the ride was the result of a dedicated programme of road testing, including a high mileage over bad roads on the Continent, and short springs with self-lubricating bronze tips were fitted to minimize friction between the leaves; the powerful hydraulic dampers were identical to those fitted to the 10-ton Daimler omnibus.

Daimler's experimental staff carried out some of the most intensive testing of any company in the motor industry, every night carrying out a 12-hour drive in selected models to the West Country and back, during which notes were taken of air and water temperature, speed, elapsed mileage, oil pressure, and fuel consumption at hourly intervals. Racing driver Brian Twist rode as passenger in a seven-seat Straight-Eight limousine on one test run in the spring of 1934, when the stately Daimler easily coped with a number of severe trials hills, including the 1:3½ Doverhay near Porlock, prompting Twist to comment: 'If a car of such a size, weighing over two-and-a-half tons with five up, had climbed the hill in a trial, it would have been hailed on all sides as an altogether extraordinary performance, and so, indeed, it was. The small sports car would have donned competition tyres, lowered the pressures, tightened the shock absorbers and revved furiously all the way up. We had done none of those things. We had just taken the hill *in the dark* in the course of an ordinary run.'

Jack Fairman recalls the lighter side of road testing from his days working in the service department: 'When I was at Daimler on road test, Percy Maclure (a well-known racing driver) was road-testing for Riley. Going out from Coventry in a 15/18 on the long Kenilworth Straight, suddenly I found Percy Maclure on my tail in the latest Riley Monaco . . . In a straight line the Daimler was nearly as fast as the Riley – we went neck and neck down that straight. There was a roundabout

in the middle and we arrived together, so Percy went one side and I went the other!'

The company's dedication to testing ensured the exemplary reliability of the Daimlers, whose new poppet valve engines ran as long between overhauls as the sleeve-valve units which were nearing the end of their production life; only Minerva of Belgium persevered longer with the sleeve valve than Daimler. As Frederick Lanchester said around that time: 'In my opinion the sleeve-valve engine has served its purpose. It blazed the way to silence [but] would not admit of so high a revolution speed as would engines of the poppet valve type, and when, mainly by the more exact profile of the cam profile, the poppet engine had achieved a degree of silence practically equal to the sleeve-valve, the balance of advantage swung over to the poppet system.'

However, Jack Fairman, who test-drove all the final sleeve-valve models, thinks that the roots of the sleeve-valve's downfall lay in Laurence Pomeroy's espousal of aluminium

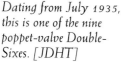

Dating from July 1935, this is one of the nine poppet-valve Double-Sixes. [JDHT]

cylinder blocks: 'One of the things that didn't do a lot of good was when Pomeroy came back from America and joined Daimler. He was all for everything being made of aluminium, saving a hell of a lot of weight and he got a lot more revs out of the engine – but the engines were rougher: when they were pulling hard you were conscious of a deep rumbling. There was no change in the noise or any vibration with the older Daimlers, with their cast iron cylinder blocks . . . the Daimler sleeve-valve engine was a complete master in its own class.'

The sleeve-valve Double-Six 40 and 50 were still listed at the end of 1934, but these were the very last of their line, and production had very likely already ended, for when the King ordered a new Double-Six – his 30th Daimler – in July 1934, 'the makers . . . put forward a petition, which was granted, to be allowed to install an engine of the Double-Six type, but specially built in accordance with their latest practice to incorporate the silent overhead valve system.'

This new Royal car, delivered in April 1935, in time for the celebration of King George V's Silver Jubilee, was a real anomaly, for its V12 pushrod engine had no equivalent six-cylinder production model and was only built to special order. Its bore and stroke (81.5x104 mm) were identical to those of the sleeve-valve Double-Six 50. It is believed that only nine of these chassis were built between 1935–8; two joined the royal fleet. One was the King's Jubilee car and the other – a similar Hooper limousine – was delivered to the Queen on New Year's Day 1936, less than three weeks before the King died at Sandringham after a brief illness.

Queen Mary retained her 'Jubilee Daimler' until after the War, when it was fitted with a new six-cylinder engine because spares for the Double-Six engine had become unavailable; in the 1960s it was displayed in the old Montagu Motor Museum at Beaulieu. After a spell on the liner *Queen Mary* in California, it was brought back to England and restored by the Museum of British Road Transport in Coventry, where it is exhibited

Queenly tribulations

'Queen Mary used her 1935 poppet-valve Double-Six until after the Second World War and in the 1960s it was exhibited at Beaulieu. It was subsequently loaned to the liner *Queen Mary* at Long Beach, California. I went over in the 1980s to make sure that it was all right, and found that the car was being displayed on the upper deck with the doors and windows closed, which in that humid climate was disastrous. To cap it all, a young docent was telling visitors: "This Mercedes was given to Queen Mary by Adolf Hitler before the War." Protracted negotiations and a law suit ensued, at the conclusion of which the car was brought safely back to England.'
M

alongside the correct poppet-valve Double-Six power unit and a later Royal Daimler from the reign of George VI.

* * *

Though production had ceased in the old Motor Mills many years earlier, the building housed the Service Department in the 1930s. Jack Fairman has vivid memories of his time working there in the mid-1930s, and of the very special aura that surrounded 'the Daimler' before the Second World War: 'As an improver fitter, I worked as fitter's mate with an experienced man and became an expert on sleeve valve engines. I went through all the departments before being persuaded to go back to the family business in Horley, Surrey.

'Bill Everitt, whom I worked with, was one of their top fitters and we worked very well together. When an engine came in for complete overhaul – perhaps a Double-Six 50 as used by the King – Bill and I would strip it down (it had all been cleaned off, they had people to do that) and lay everything on the bench, and the chief of that department would come round and decide what wanted doing. We could strip and rebuild an engine in an afternoon when it took anybody else in that department a day – sometimes two days.

'Every engine we built had to go for bench test. It was run gently on gas for a bit then for 2–3 hours at steady revs before it was given a final bench test. The engines that Bill and I did quickly never failed. Bearings had to be scraped and fitted to the crankshaft. You weren't considered as one of them by the other skilled engineers unless you could make your own bearing scraper, starting with a 12 inch bastard file.

'When a car came in for overhaul, the mudguards were taken off and stored. When it came to the road test, temporary mudguards were put on and we went out like that. If it had been a complete overhaul, we went out in chassis form. It was a common sight to see a bare chassis being driven over to Mulliners of Birmingham with a driver sitting on a soap box with a temporary screen in front of him in cold or wet weather. This also served as a final test drive, as he could see the axles. He'd leave the chassis at Mulliners and get in a finished car and drive it back, keeping an ear open all the time for something that shouldn't be there . . .

'Daimler was the big thing in Coventry then. It is difficult to describe the extraordinarily friendly, very happy atmosphere: I never saw anybody appear to be dissatisfied – there was no trade union. The head man was called Joe Mercer. He always wore a brown trilby hat; you never saw an executive, even on a hot day, walking around without a collar and tie or hat – not a flat cap, but a trilby – and no superior would dream of walking into the shop in his shirt sleeves. He was like the captain of a battleship: an order was an order and that was it! But as long as you played ball, there was no trouble.

'I remember that an electrician climbed in the back of some dowager duchess's Daimler limousine with Bedford cord upholstery with dirty overalls on and left marks on the upholstery, he was promptly threatened with the sack. There was no such thing as a shop steward, but two or three of his colleagues got together and got hold of Mercer and said: "You can't work on a car without getting your overalls dirty and they have to be washed. It costs money and it takes time and this chap hasn't got a spare set . . ." A scheme was thrashed out round the table. The company agreed to supply the overalls, three to each man – one on, one in the wash and one in reserve – so from then on there was never any excuse for a man climbing into a car with dirty overalls on.

'The toilets had been built for the original staff of the cotton mill in the 1890s. They were called the dungeon – they were downstairs in the basement. When Daimlers moved in, the toilets became inadequate for the number of staff. They got dirty and you had to queue. This was brought to the attention of one of the higher management who came and had a look at the toilets. Great horror was expressed that they, the Daimler company, should have put up with such a thing as this. Proper toilets were built, there was no more trouble; that was complete cooperation between the workers and the management. Nobody said: "If we don't get new toilets we're going on strike."

'There was no such thing as a works canteen; nobody wanted one. If you felt like a cup of tea at any time, you simply finished the job you were doing, got your billycan, heated it with the gas jets provided on the benches for soldering or an oxyacetylene torch and tipped in your tea, sugar and Nestlé's condensed milk.

'Quite a few of the staff had really old Daimlers, but they kept going. A 1910 Daimler would do 100,000 miles before it needed a decoke . . . those were the days when you were lucky if a Morris-Cowley would do 5,000 miles between decokes. If you had a Daimler or any other Coventry-made car, there was always room in the car park, but no foreign cars – particularly American cars – were allowed in at all. They had to be left outside.

'The prestige of Daimler was quite astounding. You never saw a Daimler man going to work unshaven or scruffy, even if he was only the chap who changed the wheels. There were at least twenty motor manufacturers in Coventry and when you went down to the pub on Saturday night you met chaps from all the different factories. When a Daimler man walked in, they didn't exactly stiffen to attention but you'd hear them whisper: "He's from the Daimler"!'

* * *

With the discontinuation of the sleeve-valve engine, the smaller Daimlers, the Lanchesters and the rear-wheel-driven BSAs became variations on a theme, differing mainly in radiator design and levels of specification. Lanchesters, indeed, adopted the Daimler-type three-piece bonnet at the end of 1934, at which time the Daimler

Fifteen acquired Girling rod-operated brakes in place of the servo hydraulics of the earlier model, a pull-up handbrake instead of the traditional Daimler push-on pattern and a larger-capacity power unit, in which an increased stroke of 105 mm (from 95 mm) gave a swept volume of 2,003 cc instead of 1,805 cc. An early customer for the new Fifteen was King George of Greece, with a stylish four-door saloon supplied by Stratstone in August 1934.

The following month a new Lanchester Eighteen made its debut. This had an ingenious lattice-girder boxed chassis, which combined stiffness and lightness, extremely flexible front suspension controlled by radius rods and a new overhead-valve engine with a fixed cylinder head. This, it was claimed, avoided complicated castings, improved cooling and thus reduced cylinder distortion, and eliminated gasket failure and water leaks. Though it appeared that this made it more difficult to attend to the valves and decarbonize the engine, Daimler-Lanchester stated that 'the official servicing charges of the company for these operations will be no greater than for the same operations on such of their engines as have detachable heads [because] the cylinder block by itself is not heavy; when clear of the car one man can lift it and carry it without difficulty; after the valve cover has been removed and the side plate taken off, it is not very bulky; and lastly, a simple form of jig can be used to enter the six pistons back into the cylinder bores without difficulty or fear of breakage of rings'.

Hard though that was to swallow, in July 1935 the company announced a bored-out 2,563 cc version of this design with vacuum-servo Girling mechanical brakes as the Daimler Light Twenty and it duly appeared after an interval of a few weeks and a change of radiator as an improved Lanchester Eighteen . . .

Nor was that the end of the changes: at the beginning of October Daimler launched the 3,421 cc Light Straight-Eight, a 'high-performance car for the owner-driver' claimed to be the fastest Daimler ever sold to the public, with a top speed of 90 mph. Lighter and more highly-tuned than the long-wheelbase Straight-Eight (which was simultaneously uprated from 3,746 cc to 4,624 cc), the new model went into production in January 1936. Among its features was a novel type of rear anti-roll bar, a cranked torsion bar linking the spindles of the rear shock absorbers (which were adjustable by a pull-out handle beside the steering column). In a wonderfully chauvinistic sentence, *The Autocar* summed up the typically Daimler silence and stability of the new model: 'It will be found that the fairer sex, youthful or not so youthful, occupying the rear seats, do not cease their conversation as the speedometer needle creeps quietly up to the 70 mark and beyond.'

This was also one of the very few cars in the world capable of going from a standstill to 90 mph on top gear, taking just 34 seconds to reach 60 mph in this mode. However, it also had a fixed-head engine, and it was now claimed as a virtue that the power unit would

run for 20,000 miles between decokes: the fact that the old sleeve-valves would travel at least twice as far between top overhauls had conveniently been forgotten.

Intriguingly, in 1950, one J. Lindsay Hatchett, who seemed to have a predisposition for building unusual specials, fitted a Light Straight-Eight engine and close-ratio preselector transmission into the chassis of the ex-Kaye Don Type 54 Bugatti.

One of the more remarkable instances of marque loyalty was recorded at the end of 1935, when it was announced that the Maharajah of Jamnagar had bought no fewer than 16 new Daimlers and Lanchesters during the year, consisting of a fleet of 13 10 and 18 hp Lanchesters plus three Daimler Straight-Eights.

In January 1936 George Lanchester resigned from Daimler-Lanchester and joined Alvis, working in the design department (headed by former Daimler employee Captain Smith-Clarke) where he updated the Silver Eagle and designed the 12/70 four-cylinder.

The Light Straight-Eight was Coventry's response to the Derby Bentley: this is a particularly elegant example. [JDHT]

The 1936 season was to see the discontinuation of the 'Daimlerized' BSAs; the marque then only produced small front-wheel driven cars, the sole front-wheel drive models available from a British company at the time. During 1936, too, Stratstone became part of the Thomas Tilling group, founded many years earlier by London's biggest jobmaster; the enterprising Joseph Mackle, whose genius for developing sporting versions of Daimler models was undiminished, commissioned a handsome Daimler roadster very much in the Mercedes 500K idiom, with chromed external exhaust pipes, from James Young of Bromley for his wife that spring.

The death of King George V had deprived the company of its keenest royal devotee: the new King, Edward VIII, had a more catholic taste in cars and in fact the first new vehicle he bought after his accession was a Humber Pullman limousine, while he used a fleet of Hillman Hawks for a visit to Cornwall in June. However, though his reforming instincts tempted him to leave his father's 'immense, sombre' Daimler (known irreverently to the royal princes as 'the Crystal Palace') in its garage and walk to his office, he realized that the sight of that massive limousine passing by had come to symbolize the institution of monarchy to many of his subjects, and in fact ordered a new royal Daimler limousine through Stratstone. Delivered in June 1936, it was the latest 4,624 cc Straight-Eight and its comprehensive equipment included an electric telephone with which the King could communicate with the chauffeur.

In fact, the King's brother Albert, Duke of York, had acquired his own Straight-Eight at the beginning of the year, though in deference to the Duke's enthusiasm for Lanchesters, this car was fitted with a Lanchester radiator and bonnet, one of several 'Lanchesterized' straight-eights built for very special customers, including Indian princes like the Maharajah of Jamnagar and the Jam Sahib of Nawanagar, who ordered a Vanden Plas tourer during 1936 and an all-weather from the same coachbuilders the following year. The Duke of York retained his affection for the marque after he became

The 1,378 cc BSA Light Six was a cut-price version of the equivalent Lanchester. [JDHT]

After the death of King George V, the first poppet-valve Double-Six was taken over by Queen Mary and given the registration 'CYF 662'. Chauffeur Oscar Humfrey also transferred to the Queen's service. [JDHT]

King George VI in December on the abdication of Edward VIII, and owned a further three of these Lanchester Special Straight-Eights up to the outbreak of war in 1939.

Improvements in the range for 1937, announced in August 1936, were mostly to the coachwork, with a new razor-edge sports saloon available on the Daimler Fifteen (with the engine capacity increased from 2,003 to 2,166 cc, which actually shifted it into the 17 hp tax bracket) and Lanchester Fourteen

The future King George VI – seen here with his wife (now the Queen Mother) and Princesses Elizabeth and Margaret Rose – owned four of these 'Lanchesterized' Daimler Straight-Eights: this was the first, a Hooper Landaulette delivered in February 1936. [JDHT]

Roadrider (a bored-out 1,527 cc development of the Light Six with a new design of radiator, soon adopted by the Eleven and Eighteen too). A month later, Daimler announced a new Twenty 'Light Limousine' with a detachable-head 3,317 cc six-cylinder engine in a cruciform braced double-dropped frame very similar to that of the Light Straight-Eight. 'Possessed of the dignity which a town carriage should have, nicely modulated into the modern clean-cut appearance of present Daimler practice', it was notable for a remarkably inaccessible battery carried within the chassis just ahead of the rear axle.

Early in 1936 the British Government had at last realized the potential menace to peace posed by the rise of the Nazis in Germany and instituted a scheme operated by Daimler, Austin, Humber, Standard, Rover, Singer and Wolseley to build government-financed 'shadow factories' to manufacture components for Bristol Hercules radial aero-engines against an outbreak of hostilities: Daimler began work on its shadow factory alongside the Radford Works at the beginning of September 1936 with the aim of going into production within 18 months.

Even though there were to be no more Royal orders for the Double-Six, the Lancefield Coachworks showed a spectacular Double-Six 'Saloon Limousine' designed for the carriage of wealthy invalids at the 1936 Olympia Motor Show. Fully 20 ft in length, it was the biggest car at the Show and had a large rear compartment panelled from the waistline up in burr walnut and containing a single removable stretcher bed, a wash basin, heater, cupboards for medicine and equipment and fixed and folding armchairs. It was designed to be as unobtrusive as such a huge car could be, with a dummy door on the off-side to give the illusion that it was just a private car.

Daimler's bus production had developed steadily during the 1930s. While the petrol-engined CP6 had been discontinued in mid-decade, a number of diesel-engined variants had been offered, with six-cylinder Gardner, 7.7-litre AEC and four-cylinder Armstrong-Saurer power units, while 1938 models featured brakes with automatic self-adjustment plus a Clayton Dewandre lubrication system which sent a tiny shot of oil to the chassis bearings every time the foot-brake operated. Additionally, in February 1937 a new company, Transport Vehicles (Daimler) was registered to build trolleybuses; an early order came from Belfast Corporation, which adopted the Type CTM6, which used Metro-Vick electrical equipment.

Despite his affection for Lanchesters, in April 1937 – shortly before his coronation – King George VI took delivery of another Royal Straight-Eight Daimler, a Hooper ceremonial limousine 'designed to be both a means of transport and a travelling office'. In June came a Straight-Eight Hooper landaulette, for the new King and Queen rode in the back seat of the car rather than using the central seats favoured by George V, and the open hood of the landaulette meant that they could easily be seen by their subjects. A third Hooper-bodied Straight-Eight, a shooting brake finished in natural wood, was delivered at the end of July that year in time for the King's summer holiday in Balmoral. The supreme role of the Daimler in affairs of state was shown by the chartering of a fleet of 150 Daimlers – mostly Straight-Eights – for the conveyance of foreign dignitaries attending the Coronation in Westminster Abbey on 12 May 1937; over a thousand privately-owned Daimlers were also used in connection with the Coronation.

For 1938, Daimler launched the 2,166 cc 'New Fifteen' which its makers claimed 'wedded to Daimler comfort the precision control and road-holding of a modern racing car', thanks to coil-spring independent front suspension developed from an André-Girling design. This had unequal-length parallel arms located by radius arms and damped by Luvax hydraulic shock absorbers linked by a torsion-bar stabilizer. An underslung rear

Testing times

Every night except Saturday, winter and summer alike, a small fleet of specially-instrumented Daimler and Lanchester cars set out from the Coventry works, and were driven to the West Country and back by members of the testing staff. Normally, they returned by 6 a.m. the following morning, though if it was foggy they were sometimes delayed until 3 p.m. If the cars were new, and needed miles put on them, another team took them straight out again to Wales, where they climbed the 1:5 Bwlch-y-Groes test hill before returning . . .

Some of the 150 Straight-Eights chartered to carry foreign dignitaries attending the Coronation of King George VI. [JDHT]

tests complained of vibration periods at just over 40 and 60 mph and slight transmission noise: 'A drone could be heard in neutral,' said the normally forgiving *Autocar*.

A similar chassis was used in the 1938 Lanchester Roadrider de luxe, launched at the London Casino at Motor Show time. This had an 1,809 cc six-cylinder power unit; a conventional gearbox with Borg & Beck single-plate clutch was available as a £25 cheaper alternative to the preselector transmission and – for the first time in Lanchester history – a spiral bevel back axle was fitted instead of the Lanchester worm.

An intriguing experiment was carried out during 1937 by a Coventry engineer named F.J. Tippen, who bought a new Lanchester Eighteen and replaced its power unit with a 2,245 cc Tippen 'Colt' four-cylinder diesel engine, which developed 42 bhp at 3,000 rpm and had a useful speed range of 800–3,600 rpm. Aided by the fluid flywheel transmission, it proved capable of 'smooth and even' acceleration and combined a top speed in the region of 60 mph with a fuel economy of 33.5 mpg.

At Christmas 1937 Queen Mary took

axle helped the handling, though signs of the times were pressed-steel 'easy-clean' wheels and lower-geared steering, while press road

The Lanchester Roadrider De Luxe was basically a 1.8-litre version of the Daimler DB18 with a different radiator shell. [JDHT]

King George VI's Royal Straight-Eights leave the Scottish palace of Holyrood House. [JDHT]

delivery of a new Daimler Straight-Eight from Stratstone, its Hooper body fitted with a number of special fittings requested by the Queen Mother; it carried her personal number plate A-3179 and broke with royal tradition in having chrome-plated radiator and lamps instead of the customary black or brass finish.

Visiting the five shadow factories in the Coventry area in March 1938, the King was shown his grandfather's first Daimler at the Daimler Radford No 1 plant and jokingly asked whether the 38-year-old veteran still worked – and was given a ride in the 1900 car. At the controls was chauffeur George Street, who had often driven Edward VII, and Air Minister Lord Swinton was among the passengers in the tonneau. Though the old Daimler had been modified over the years, Daimler would not part with it for any price, not even an offer of £2,000 from America, far in excess of anything paid for any veteran car pre-war. Eventually, the old Daimler would be presented to Queen Elizabeth II by the Daimler Company, along with three other former Royal Daimlers in their possession, to

form the nucleus of the Royal Motor Museum. Having been put into running order by the Veteran Car Club in 1968–71, the first Royal Daimler was eventually restored to 1900 condition by the National Motor Museum for the Queen's Silver Jubilee

King George VI visits Radford in 1938. [JDHT]

King George VI, at Radford in 1938, meets his grandfather's first Daimler. [JDHT]

A Straight-Eight competing in the 1938 Scottish Rally. [JDHT]

in 1977 and has several times completed the annual London-Brighton Veteran Car Run.

Daimler's move into the middle-class market was not altogether smooth, for some potential customers proved reluctant to buy a car which in their mind was associated with stately progress and high first cost, and took some convincing that a Daimler with 70 mph-plus performance could now be bought new for less than £500; but the fact that celebrities such as test cricketer Jack Hobbs were beginning to be seen at the wheel of the popularly-priced Daimler Fifteen did much to overcome this barrier.

And for those who recognized the superlative nature of the Daimler, there were triumphs in concours d'elegance like that which concluded the 1938 RAC Rally, where Colonel Rippon's Straight-Eight, bodied by his own company (which had built a carriage for Queen Elizabeth I as long ago as 1564), was voted the finest four-door saloon costing over £1,000. Rippon's Straight-Eight won the premier award for closed cars at the 1938 Scottish and Welsh Rallies, too.

The end of 1938 saw Daimler undertaking extensive alterations at Radford, which were intended to virtually double the output of standardized bodywork for Daimler and Lanchester cars to match the capacity of the recently remodelled main erecting shops.

Various modifications were made to the

Daimler-Lanchester range for the 1939 season, most notably the introduction of larger engines in the Daimler Fifteen and Light Straight-Eight; the Fifteen gained a 2,522 cc power unit (which was actually rated at 18 hp, though Daimler cumbrously called the new DB18 model the 'Fifteen 2½-litre'), while the Light Straight-Eight was uprated to 3,960 cc and became known as the 4-litre. There was also a new range of saloon and sports saloon coachwork for the Twenty-Four. The Straight-Eight continued almost unchanged: Stratstone announced that they were supplying King George with another Hooper-bodied Straight-Eight, for delivery on New Year's Day. This was a splendid machine, a landaulette with a glass panel in the roof to let in more light so that Their Majesties could be more clearly seen when bad weather compelled the hood to be raised: this literally bright idea had been suggested by the King, who enjoyed designing special features for his cars. Another royal client for the 1939 Straight-Eight was the King of Greece, who ordered a Hooper landaulette from Stratstone.

The 1939 models had only been on the market a couple of weeks when Prime Minister Neville Chamberlain – a Daimler director between 1913–22 but an Armstrong Siddeley owner since 1927 – flew to Munich to attend Hitler's Four-Power Conference on 29 September 1938 as threats of imminent war with Germany grew ever stronger. His return proclaiming 'peace in our time' was to prove only a temporary respite: but Daimler was already responding to the international crisis with work in progress on a second Shadow Factory on a 62-acre site at Brown's Lane, Allesley, Coventry. Scheduled to build 200 Bristol Hercules aero-engines a month in wartime, the Brown's Lane plant was to prove a vital factor in the survival of the Daimler marque in peacetime.

* * *

In March 1939, Daimler became the first British motor company to open a works museum, with a fine display of Daimler and Lanchester cars ranging from the prototype Lanchester of 1895–6 to a 1912 Daimler Sedan which had been in constant use by Colonel Orde of Bristol until 1936; among the cars on display were several Royal Daimlers, including the 1900 Mail Phaeton, and Rudyard Kipling's 1901 10–12 hp Lanchester, immortalized as the 'Octopod' in his short story *Steam Tactics* (inspired by an

Lady Roger, wife of group chairman Sir Alexander Roger, designed the coachwork on her 1939 Daimler Straight Eight. [JDHT]

Mrs Arthur Dennis had this stylish 2½-litre coupé specially built for her in 1939. [JDHT]

exploit by George and Frank Lanchester, who had 'kidnapped' a policeman who was attempting to book them for speeding in a Lanchester in 1902).

The museum opened at the same time as Daimler's new sports and social club, which had 3,000 members and 18 sections: the clubhouse, which had cost £2,000 to build, was on the old Radford airfield and the first pint was pulled by managing director E.H.W. Cooke, who had founded the Daimler Long Service

Association the previous year.

That summer, Stratstone supplied some outstanding coachbuilt cars to private owners, including a 2½-litre coupé with stylish rear wheel spats specially built for Mrs Arthur Dennis and a massive Straight-Eight nine-seater Gurney Nutting limousine 18 ft in length and weighing 2.5 tons for the radio talent scout Carroll Levis, who auditioned Daimler employees for his 'Discoveries' show in the new sports pavilion when he visited the factory in June. For his personal use, King

Bridging the gap between the Dolphin and the post-war Sports Special was this stunning 2½-litre drophead inspired by Frank Feeley's designs for the Lagonda Rapide. [JDHT]

239

George VI ordered a 2¹/₂-litre coupé and gave a similar car to his daughter Princess Elizabeth for her eighteenth birthday in 1944.

Daimler bodywork continued to collect concours awards during 1939: Colonel Rippon had built a new, more square-cut touring limousine which lived up to the slogan 'when fine cars are compared and judged, Daimler and Rippon form an irresistible Rally combination' by carrying off the premier award for four-door closed cars at the Blackpool Rally and Ramsgate Concours d'Elegance, but it was Daimler-built bodywork that attracted most attention.

In January, Sammy Davis came second in the over 1,500 cc class in the Monte Carlo Rally comfort competition with a Daimler Fifteen, with lockers in the front wings for spares and unditching gear, Hades 'central heating', screenwasher, and windscreen heater, and early in the year Daimler launched a series of cars based on the company's experience in rallying. First to appear, during January, was the 'Ritz', a limited-production sports saloon based on the 2¹/₂-litre Fifteen chassis but with higher overall gearing. 'Designed for arduous motoring and equipped and finished for

coachwork competitions', the Ritz was 'beautifully equipped and had just about every accessory needed to make motoring a pleasure in all weathers'. Standard fittings included a cedar-lined cigar box in the central

Production at Radford shortly before the outbreak of war was still very much a hand-assembly affair. [MBRT]

The 2¹/₂-litre Dolphin dual-cowl sports tourer was a natural concours winner. Oddly enough, the 2¹/₂-litre Daimler saloon which came second in the 1939 Monte Carlo Rally was also registered 'DVC 681': did the cars share the same chassis or was Daimler economizing on road tax? [JDHT]

The 3,317 cc ES24 launched in April 1939 had a new curved radiator shell. It also, apparently, has King George VI's radiator mascot, though no ES24 was supplied to the Royal Family. [JDHT]

rear armrest, while the side armrests held Thermos flasks; interior woodwork was in grey sycamore.

In April Daimler announced a 'Special Sports' 2½-litre with stylish dual-cowl tourer bodywork and a high-compression 90 bhp engine with a special light-alloy cylinder head, redesigned porting and twin carburettors. The top-gear ratio of 3.55:1 was effectively an overdrive ratio for 'exceptionally easy fast running'. Features not normally seen on a Daimler were a rev counter and a fish-tail exhaust and when *The Autocar* eventually road-tested one of these 'Dolphin' tourers the staffman noted with some surprise the 'slight but unmistakable exhaust resonance'.

An early example of the new model painted chocolate and cream was driven in the RAC Rally by Daimler employee Bob Crouch (whose father, John Crouch, a director of Daimler's bus division, had started his career at Daimler in 1899 and subsequently built the Crouch light car of 1912–28) and won first prize for open cars

from £600–£1,000 in the coachwork competition; a Ritz took second prize in the class for four-door closed cars from £350–£600 and the prize for four-door closed cars priced between £600–£1,000 was taken by the third of the new Daimlers, the 24 hp six-light saloon, driven by its designer Cyril Simpson. This 3,317 cc 'ES24' model had a new, curved radiator grille, an electric sunroof (possibly the first use of this feature) and an electrically-operated rear window blind; it also had a pipe rack on the steering column, three electric cigar lighters and thermos flasks in the rear armrests.

A similar result was achieved in the Welsh Rally in July, despite torrential rain: 'That proceedings were nonetheless lighthearted was due in no small measure to the presence of that most excellent tonic, Pimm's mixture, in Marjorie Eccles' Daimler,' noted *The Autocar*'s correspondent without being so ungallant as to suggest that the cargo of Pimm's had anything to do with Mrs Eccles' victory in the £351–£600 class for open cars . . .

Chapter 8

WAR AND
PEACE

When it became clear early in 1938 that German rearmament had a more sinister aim than the professed restoration of lost national self-respect and that the territorial ambitions of the Third Reich for more 'living space' posed a serious threat to international peace, as part of Britain's substantially-increased defence programme the Army commissioned Daimler to develop a fast armoured scouting vehicle which could travel across all types of terrain and climb gradients as steep as 1:2, yet be capable of cruising at high speed on normal roads.

Though this involved developing a vehicle of an entirely new type with few components in common with existing Daimler designs, the firm's engineers performed miracles and not only had the design completed by the beginning of June but were already at work on the first prototype, which was handed over for endurance testing early in September. The Army placed its first quantity order in May 1939 and the first batch of production vehicles was handed over in December the same year, just three months after the outbreak of war with Germany.

The basis of the Daimler Scout was a punt-type armoured steel hull with deep channel-section sides and inclined ends; at the rear end of the frame was the 2.5-litre six-cylinder engine, basically the same as that of the 1939 open rally car but incorporating dry-sump lubrication, a special three-stage Solex carburettor capable of maintaining constant petrol level at any angle, and a high-compression cast-iron cylinder head with inclined valves which developed over 70 bhp on the wartime 'MT80' petrol.

Considering that this was Daimler's first attempt at four-wheel drive – indeed, few British manufacturers had any experience of this type of transmission – the transmission arrangements of the new scout car showed that the company had lost none of its engineering genius. A new design of fluid flywheel which minimized slip at low speeds was used in conjunction with an epicyclic gearbox driving through a transfer box set across the hull; short propeller shafts linked to spiral bevel gear units within the side channels drove the four independently-sprung wheels through Tracta constant velocity joints. The transfer box enabled five speeds forward and backwards and, acting as the differential between the opposite pairs of wheels, eliminated 'diagonal wheelspin'. This gave the driver of the Scout the useful ability to reverse direction instantly, even when travelling at speeds of 35 mph, by simply preselecting reverse and dipping the gear-engaging pedal. After a brief flurry of wheelspin, the wheels would grip and the Scout would shoot away backwards at the same speed. Top gear was engaged by a multi-plate clutch rather than brake bands, while the coil and parallel link independent suspension units gave the remarkable displacement of 8 in at each wheel. Luvax hydraulic dampers were fitted in conjunction with rubber bump stops at either end of the suspension travel.

Since the Scout was virtually as fast in reverse as it was when going forwards, the driver's seat was set at an angle so that he could see backwards easily through the armoured trap doors in the coaming; when the car was 'closed for battle', the driver's forward vision was through triple bullet-proof glass-covered slots in the visor. And driver's and passenger's seats could be raised vertically, allowing the occupants to see over the lip of the turret when there was no danger of attack.

The main purpose of the Scout being high-speed reconnaissance, it was only armed with a Bren gun (later replaced with twin rapid-fire Lysander K-guns from the RAF on some Scout cars); despite a weight of three tons, it could travel at 40 mph in either direction across irregular ground, becoming airborne over grass hummocks 2 ft and more in height, climb gradients of 1:1.5 and had such good steering and road-holding that its test drivers – including former Lea-Francis racing driver 'Soapy' Sutton, who had partnered Bob Crouch in the 'Dolphin' in the 1939 RAC Rally – claimed that they could set 'lap records' on any roundabout ('not that they go round roundabouts habitually – if no-one is looking, the temptation to drive *over* the roundabout is exceedingly strong!').

Production of the Scout Car got under way in Coventry, but a foretaste of what was to come occurred in August 1940 when a couple of German bombs fell on the Radford site, causing minor damage to the Shadow Factory, which was hit again by a firebomb raid in October after the Luftwaffe, thrashed in the Battle of Britain, had switched its tactics to night bombing raids against industrial targets. But it was on the night of 14 November that the Germans unleashed their main attack against Coventry, when 600 tons of bombs and thousands of incendiaries fell on the city, reducing the medieval cathedral to a shell, devastating the historic city centre and causing severe damage to the Daimler factory.

In a second big firebomb raid on Coventry on 8 April 1941, half the factory was wrecked, including body-building and erecting shops, the stores, toolroom and the venerable Motor Mills building. However, since May 1940 Daimler had been setting up a network of 'dispersal units', which would bring the company's wartime work-force up to a peak of some 16,000 people. These were properties away from the factory area which had been requisitioned by the Government to provide additional production, testing, storage and staff accommodation – and eventually these totalled over 40 sites, including a skating rink, a slate quarry, several hosiery works, a bus garage, an ironmonger's shop, the Pirelli factory at Burton-on-Trent, a deer park, and the J.C. Bamford agricultural machinery works at Uttoxeter, which assembled Scouts after the production facilities at Radford had been destroyed.

George Hally, appointed managing director on Cooke's resignation in February 1941, took up residence in a requisitioned house being used as a store at Dudbury, Derbyshire, in order to be roughly in the centre of these dispersal units; his wife organized the surgeries, canteens and welfare units at the main, shadow and dispersal factories, working for a nominal salary of £1 a year (increased to a guinea after two years) and in the process inventing safety headwear for the female operatives in the factories who came under her care.

Also destroyed in the April raid were two armoured Daimler Straight-Eights being built for the War Office and intended for the King's use. These were the idea of speed ace Sir Malcolm Campbell, who was a tireless advocate of the merits of armoured cars built on conventional chassis (and engineered by his self-effacing mechanic Leo Villa): two replacements were immediately put in hand and similar cars were subsequently built for

the protection of other public figures, including Prime Minister Winston Churchill.

In mid-1941 Daimler chairman Geoffrey Burton (who would be knighted in 1942 and joined the board of Lodge Plugs in 1946) was appointed chairman of the Tank Board, Ministry of Supply, and on 22 December he was succeeded as chairman of Daimler by Sir Bernard Docker, who had joined the BSA board in 1939 and become a Daimler director in July 1940. The son of former BSA deputy chairman F. Dudley Docker, Sir Bernard became managing director of the BSA group (which took over the Hooper and Barker coachbuilding companies during the war) in 1944 and – already a wealthy man in his own right – inherited the bulk of his father's £890,000 estate (largely accumulated though the skill of 'DD' in arranging large-scale mergers) when Dudley Docker died a few weeks later.

The Daimler Scout, described by the Canadian journal *Motor Truck & Equipment* as 'a British-built box of tricks on wheels, which resembled nothing ever before attempted and the most unorthodox armoured car', played a major role in the war in North Africa, Sicily and Italy, and in October 1942 appreciation of its virtues came from an unlikely quarter. Field-Marshal Rommel was said to have escaped capture by General Montgomery after the German defeat at El Alamein by using a captured Daimler Scout as his 'getaway car' . . .

During the air raids on Coventry, the Daimler engineering staff had been working from dawn to midnight, weekends included, on a larger fighting vehicle along similar lines: this, too, was designed in the remarkably short time of six months. While the suspension and transmission were very similar (prototypes had incorporated extra – lockable – differentials between front and rear wheels on either side, and four wheel steering, but these features had proved unnecessary and not gone into production), the Daimler armoured car had also to provide a stable gun platform in the roughest

The Radford works were severely damaged by the Nazi Blitz on Coventry, but that didn't halt Daimler's contribution to the Allied war effort. [MBRT]

Four-wheel drive, all-round independent suspension and disc brakes – the Daimler Armoured Car was a most advanced design! [MBRT]

conditions, carry a considerable load of shells and equipment and be so shaped that projectiles would tend to glance off its armour-plating. Moreover, its turret had to be capable of traversing a complete circle without any obstacles in the way of the gun barrel, even at full deflection.

A refined version of the four-wheel independent suspension designed for the Scout had the remarkably long travel of 16 in – 10 in upwards and 6 in downwards – with the springs acting through cranks to increase resistance during upward movement. The suspension was so effective that with one wheel lifted to the full extent of 16 in, the other three remained in contact with the ground. Power was provided by a 100 bhp 4,095 cc six-cylinder engine with inclined overhead valves, twin Solex 'non-spillable' carburettors and dry-sump lubrication; this was built in unit with an improved design of fluid flywheel and five-speed preselector gearbox. Because the seven-ton armoured car needed an extremely low bottom gear, extra reduction was provided by epicyclic gearing within each wheel-hub.

Another remarkable feature of the design was the employment of four-wheel disc brakes, probably the first time this characteristic had appeared on any vehicle. This was an ingenious concept by Girling in which a movable pressure plate was forced against a revolving disc on the hub by twin hydraulic plungers; steel balls in conical seatings in the pressure plate forced it into closer contact with the disc, creating an automatic servo action.

During his Army career, David Holland drove both types of Daimler armoured fighting vehicle: 'When I went into the army, my main ambition was to get as near as I could to vehicles; the war was coming to an end and we'd been starved of any form of motoring. Soldiering for me meant vehicles; I took every possible opportunity of serving in units which were equipped with tanks or – better still – armoured cars. Over the next five years or so I had a lot of fun: tanks and armoured cars of all descriptions. Of the armoured cars, my love was the Daimler: it was sophisticated, a tremendous performer in its environment and technically very, very advanced indeed.

'They were remarkable vehicles, designed for their active service role of reconnaissance with the need to be highly manoeuvrable; sometimes if you poked your nose round the wrong corner, you needed to get the hell out of it! Therefore, the Daimler armoured car had its five speeds available in reverse gear as well, which made for a great deal of fun. The suspension was extraordinary – something like 9 or 10 inches of rise or fall at each of the four wheels – and its geometry was such that it was just as stable – which didn't mean it was tremendously stable! – in reverse as it was forward. Road cars which had all their gears available in reverse, like those equipped with the French Cotal transmission, were sometimes quite unmanageable, and it was a challenge to get into second or third in reverse.

'It was truly designed to be driven either way. It had a steering wheel at the back, which would be taken over in emergency by the commander, whose only other control was a hand throttle. Thus the driver would be left using all the pedals and the gearbox, while the commander would do the steering and shout when he wanted the gears changed up or down. This made for a highly manoeuvrable and very effective armoured car, equipped with a high-velocity two-pounder gun. This met with a certain amount of derision later in the war, but in fact was an extremely fine weapon of its size and calibre. There was also a co-axially mounted machine gun in the fully-traversable turret.

'Both the armoured car and the scout had dry sump lubrication, and remarkable cross-country performance in terms of gradients; you could virtually hang them upside down and still have some lubrication to the crankshaft.

'The little scout car – familiarly known as the Dingo – was a very rapid vehicle, and

David Holland with his Daimler Dingo. [DH]

extraordinary AEC heavyweight armoured car, a massive 4x4 diesel device which had a 75mm gun. Our job was patrolling the East Zone border with the Russians on the other side and this was a very serious programme; every other day we were doing 12-hour patrols. I left that wonderful regiment and those lovely armoured cars to go to Korea where I had a troop of Centurion tanks.'

During the war, Daimler built over 6,600 Scouts and some 2,700 armoured cars in Mk I and Mk II form, though the first batch of armoured cars produced was destroyed in the Blitz of April 1941. Subsequently Daimler and Humber collaborated in the production of the Coventry armoured car, which was designed to supersede their individual designs of armoured fighting vehicles. Powered by a 175 bhp six-cylinder Hercules engine, it incorporated the best features of the Daimler and Humber designs, though at 11.5 tons it was considerably heavier than either. However, it did not arrive on the scene until 1944 and only a few were built.

The considerable showing by Daimler Scout and Armoured Cars in the victory parades in London and the conquered German capital Berlin testified to the major role these vehicles had played in the hostilities. The company also supplied components for other armoured fighting vehicles, including epicyclic gearboxes which controlled the speed of tank tracks differentially to provide steering; these were fitted in some 2500 Crusader, Covenanter and Cavalier tanks.

could be whacked up to about 60 mph under conditions of either no roads at all, pockmarked roads or roads that had been blown to bits by landmines. I remember achieving an incredible average – we set a record from Brunswick to Hanover in one of these little things. It turned round completely twice on the journey because of its incredibly short wheelbase!

'When the Cold War was coming to a height in 1949–50, I spent a year with a marvellous regiment, the 11th Hussars – the 'Cherry Pickers' – who were using Daimler Scout Cars and Armoured Cars and the

Daimler, which had been making parts for Bristol aero-engines since 1929, again played a vital role in the provision of fighting aircraft in the Second World War, though this time their work was restricted to components rather than complete aeroplanes, most notably 50,800 aero-engines – Bristol Mercury, Hercules and Pegasus radials – plus full sets of parts for a further 9,500 engines and nearly 7,200 'power eggs' (replacement engine nacelles which simplified the repair of combat-damaged aircraft).

Over 10 million aircraft parts were also produced by the company during the hostilities, ranging from the massive propeller shafts for Rolls-Royce aero-engines down to tiny brake components.

Since 1929, Daimler had also been building aeroplane gun-turrets for the Government as a sideline, and in 1937 the company began making gun-turrets for the new Bristol Blenheim day bomber. Once the shadow factory scheme was in operation, orders flowed in from the Ministry of Aircraft Production, and by the end of hostilities, a total of 14,356 turrets had been produced for such front-line aircraft as the Blenheim, Beaufort, Lancaster, Stirling and Sunderland, latterly in dispersal sites including a former cafe and two underwear factories. The armament for these turrets consisted of 0.303 in Browning machine guns which were partly made (in a hosiery factory) and – up to the first major air raid – also reconditioned by Daimler.

Daimler also machined nearly 74,000 main bodies and over 184,000 other components for the ubiquitous Bren gun, initially at Coventry and, after the Bren gun shop suffered a direct hit in the April 1941 raid, at the euphoniously-named Eatcough Boot & Shoe Factory in Burton-on-Trent.

In March 1942 Daimler began producing double-deck buses for the Ministry of Supply, which replaced buses destroyed in air raids or which had simply worn out; many of these were assembled in a Courtauld textile factory in Wolverhampton, which also produced armoured cars. Though the company had begun development work on a diesel engine of its own in 1936, this had been shelved on the outbreak of war and existing power units such as the AEC and Gardner 'oilers' were used; Daimler resumed development of its own engine in the latter stages of the war, and this 8.6-litre six-cylinder unit went into production during 1944 and formed the basis for post-war bus production. Renowned for its longevity, the Daimler bus diesel engine was capable of travelling up to 250,000 miles between major overhauls.

By November 1944, when Daimler held an exhibition for its employees showing the extent of its war work, development of the post-war Daimler and Lanchester models was already under way on a limited basis, though in George Hally's opinion preparation for the re-establishment of industry in peacetime was 'long overdue'.

* * *

Though Daimler had been officially requested during the closing stages of the war to supply a fleet of large cars for the use of ambassadors and senior military personnel in anticipation of the occupation of Germany, the 30 or so cars shipped to the Continent at the very end of 1945 for the use of Ambassadors, British Embassy officials and British Consulates (plus new official limousines for the Lieutenant-Governors of Jersey and Guernsey) were mostly pre-war type Straight-Eights, presumably assembled from parts which had survived the Blitz. The 24 hp Windover-bodied limousine delivered to President Benes of Czechoslovakia around the same time was probably an example of 'new old stock' too.

It was not until September 1945 that Daimler was able to outline its post-war programme. The first model to go into production was the Eighteen, an updated version of the Fifteen with the 2.5-litre engine that had been so successfully used in the Scout Car. Wartime developments – notably a new high-compression cylinder head with inclined valves – had made it more powerful and, remarkably, more economical, partly because the engine improvements had allowed a 10 per cent higher final drive ratio.

Standard bodywork was a six-light saloon offering more space than the pre-war Fifteen: it was luxuriously equipped, with the expected leather and walnut interior trim, but a feature which might well have been a production 'first' was the use of curved side windows to increase interior width. Unusual,

Frustrated exports

Daimler buses were popular in Empire markets: there was already a large fleet in Cape Town when in 1940 the company received an order for a further 30. However, the war caused several of these export orders to be diverted to the home market; buses intended for Southern Rhodesia and Johannesburg ended up in South Monmouthshire and Birmingham in 1941.

too, at that time was the use of chromed metal channels to carry the side windows rather than the thick pillars which were then customary.

A sign of the times was the use of aluminium panelling for doors, bonnet and boot-lid instead of steel. This wasn't for lightness but because the supply of steel panelling to the motor industry was restricted by the post-war Labour government's Ministry of Supply, which effectively robbed Peter to pay Paul by diverting much of the steel needed to build cars to other industries like housing and office furniture, while the industry was exhorted to 'export or die', which left relatively few new cars for the home market.

The first new post-war Lanchester was the Ten, a pleasant little car which had been designed by chief engineer Cyril Simpson before the war and looked rather like an oversized Ford Prefect. This was hardly surprising, for its bodywork was manufactured at Dagenham by Briggs Motor Bodies which, though its factory was built on the Ford estate, remained an independent company supplying bodywork to Riley, Jowett and BMC until it was taken over by Ford in 1953 after the death of its founder, Walter O. Briggs. The engine of the Lanchester Ten was a 1,287 cc three-bearing four-cylinder unit designed along similar lines to the six-cylinder Daimler Eighteen and developing a very creditable 40 bhp at 4,200 rpm: 'It is very smooth running,' noted *The Autocar* after a preliminary run with an early example, 'and a stranger would hesitate to say if he were behind a four or a six.'

Both these models came on the market shortly before Daimler marked its golden jubilee with a lunch at the Savoy where the guests included many pioneer motorists: guest speaker was Lord Brabazon, who remarked that the whole history of the British motor industry could be written round the Daimler Company: 'It is a national institution, its history is national history in which we all feel national pride.' And then

caused great amusement by likening Britain's ascetic Trade Minister Sir Stafford Cripps, who dictated export targets, to the Red Flag Man of 1896. George Hally later revealed the pre-tax prices of the new models: the 10 hp Lanchester would be £525, the Daimler 18 would be £925, the 27 hp would be £1,200 and the 36 hp £1,500; a Lanchester 15 was also under development. 'Early deliveries,' he informed the guests, 'will be to the Government and overseas.'

The two largest Daimlers, massive eight-seater limousines which went into production in March, were the 4,095 cc DE27 six (using the detachable-head engine developed for the armoured car) and the new 5,460 cc DE36, which proved to be Britain's last production straight-eight. The DE27 chassis was also used for the affectionately-remembered Daimler Ambulance, one of the most handsome public service vehicles of its day, with elegantly practical bodywork by Barker and Hooper. The DE27 and DE36 were almost certainly the first series-built cars fitted with electrically-operated windows and central division. There were also automatic interior lights actuated by opening the rear doors and the bootlid; warning lights on the rear wings came on automatically when the boot was open.

These two cars, which differed chiefly in wheelbase length (11 ft 6 in on the six, 12 ft 3 in on the eight) also made Daimler history by being the marque's first models since 1909 not to be fitted with worm final drive, the company's new hypoid bevel axle being used instead. New, too, was the design of the radiator shell, which, though it retained the traditional fluting, now had a curved profile which blended better with the latest designs of coachwork.

Even though the Straight-Eight was shorter than the pre-war Double-Six, it was still the biggest British – and, it was claimed, world – production car of its day, both in terms of length and engine capacity. It offered a matchless standard of ride and comfort in those cheerless post-war days when harsh petrol rationing applied largely on doctrinaire grounds restricted the monthly allowance of such cars to a fraction over 10 gallons of 'pool' petrol a month – equivalent to around 200 miles or so, at a time when many European countries were lifting such restrictions. All Britain got was an increase of 50 per cent in the allowance in July.

'Driving or riding in this car,' said a member of *Autocar's* technical staff after driving one of the big Daimlers, 'the smooth comfort of the suspension and the general quietness give one the odd sensation of sitting in a comfortable lounge seat in a cinema and seeing the world roll by on a screen . . . the great degree of comfort at low speed is maintained at high speeds, and to cruise at 70 mph seems nothing when one is sitting in the back . . . they hold the road to perfection and have the sureness on fast curves of a speed car. Despite their size they are exceptionally light and untiring to drive and they steer to a hair line.'

But even as these new models were announced a pre-war type 4½-litre Straight-Eight limousine finished in jewelescent green

was shipped to India as a Diamond Jubilee present to the Aga Khan from his followers (who presented Daimler with a replica of the Aga Khan's jubilee medal in appreciation of its work). Delivered at the same time was a '3½-litre' dual-cowl tourer – looking rather like an oversized 1939 Dolphin and painted in two-tone brown – which had been bought by his playboy son, Prince Aly Khan.

And on 8 March, after being in failing health for some time, Dr Frederick Lanchester died at the age of 77: 'In every sense of the word he was a great man,' wrote his friend Montague Tombs. 'Large in intellect, large in physical stature, large in heart and large in sense of humour. In subjects which interested him, he was wholeheartedly interested.'

Though manufacturers were being forced by Government edict to export a large part of their production, in June Stratstone reopened their Berkeley Street showrooms, which had been requisitioned during the war. That month, too, the Emperor of Ethiopia ordered a new DE36 Straight-Eight patterned on the British royal cars (though as Buckingham Palace had not yet even ordered

A DE36 Straight-Eight, this time a streamlined sports saloon by Freestone & Webb, for a customer in the West Indies. [JDHT]

Fall of the mighty – the post-war Lanchester LD10 was bodied by Briggs of Dagenham and looked like an overblown Ford. [JDHT]

its first Straight-Eights, the Lion of Judah was presumably referring to a body style rather than a chassis type); similar orders were placed by the Queen of the Netherlands, the Prince of Monaco and the Kings of Thailand and Afghanistan.

The first British Royal DE36 Straight-Eights – a brace of State Landaulettes – were ordered in August 1946 (and fitted with 'semi-bucket' front seats in case the King wished to drive the cars): it was around this time that Robert Cracknell of Stratstone's was awarded the MVO for his work in supplying the Royal cars for so many years, much to the chagrin of his employer, the punctilious Joseph Mackle, who coveted (but never received) such an honour, despite his company's unique position as supplier of the Royal Daimlers.

The truth is, however, that 'Crack' Cracknell (who had begun his career before the Great War as the chauffeur appointed by the Daimler works to drive the Kaiser's Daimler) enjoyed the particular respect of

King George VI – who would sometimes invite him down to the Royal Mews to talk cars and discuss the need for any replacement vehicles over a glass of whisky – and is still well remembered by Her Majesty the Queen.

* * *

The scene was set for a colourful stage of Daimler's post-war history in 1946 when Sir Bernard Docker added the chairmanship of Hooper's to his corporate responsibilities; newly appointed chief designer and assistant works manager of the old-established coachbuilder, which had just undergone a comprehensive management shake-up, was the gifted Osmond Rivers. Barker, too, was being revived as Daimler's in-house bodybuilder after its acquisition in 1940, with 250,000 sq ft of the No 1 Shadow Factory at Radford being specially converted to provide production facilities for the production of up to 200 bodies a week by some 1,000 workers. Both Hooper and Barker were under the managing directorship of Allan Hally; Barker's chief stylist was E.J. Skelcher, responsible for styling the 1947 Daimler and Lanchester ranges.

An important order completed at the end of the year was a fleet of five 36 hp Hooper-bodied Straight-Eights – two limousines, two landaulettes and an open tourer – for the South African government, to be used by the Royal Family during their 1947 tour of South Africa, Bechuanaland and Rhodesia. These impressive vehicles were painted royal blue and black with fine red coachlines, and an unusual feature of the landaulettes was a sliding roof with a fixed transparent panel beneath. There were also seven official 2½-litre saloons, which were bought by the South African government at the end of the tour, while a further Straight-Eight for the use of the King and Queen on their tour was a black Windover limousine bought by the Transvaal Administration.

The twelve official cars covered a total of some 80,000 miles during the tour and, despite the fact that none of the South Africa drivers had previously used the Daimler fluid flywheel transmission, the cars had no

mechanical breakdowns and the all-pervading dust only caused the electrically-operated roof and windows to stick a couple of times. Despite temperatures reaching more than 100° F, none of the cars suffered from overheating or vapour lock, and they coped with road surfaces ranging from hard corrugated dirt surfaces to deep mud which cut the average speed to 10 mph for 40 miles.

Vanden Plas, a coachbuilder not normally associated with Daimler products, produced two of the more unusual special-bodied Daimlers of 1947. Built on the 27 hp six-cylinder chassis, these 'gracefully-proportioned' all-weather four-seat convertibles must have been among the last 'outside' orders produced by the Kingsbury-based coachbuilders, which had become a subsidiary of the Austin Motor Company the previous year to provide bodies for the new Princess luxury car. Commissioned by the Maharajah Jam Sahib of Nawanagar, these cars were fitted with Lanchester radiators, as His Highness (who was in the news at the time as a potential saviour for the financially-troubled Kendall minicar) had a

Twelve Daimler cars were used by the Royal party on the 1947 Tour of South Africa by the King and Queen, Princess Elizabeth and Princess Margaret. [JDHT]

252

huge Hooper-bodied Daimler Straight-Eight roadster, at £7,001 the most expensive car at Earls Court. Painted a greeny-turquoise shade which earned it the nickname 'Green Goddess', it incorporated such elaborate conceits as head and pass lights sheltered behind Perspex covers within bezels shaped like miniature headlamp shells set into the long front wings. *The Autocar* was open-mouthed: 'There is a broad front seat for three . . . behind are folding seats for two, but even these are armchairs. When the two rear seats are folded, the space is equivalent to the carrying capacity of a small van! . . . There is not space here to tell fully of all the intriguing detail design such as the speedometer trip which can be switched to operate in miles or kilometres; of the tool-kit which includes hand-cleaning equipment, and of the arrangement of handles and levers which lift the rear wheel covers.' Other features of the big, but beautifully-proportioned Daimler were a power-operated hood (which on one inauspicious occasion burst its piping and

sprayed Lady Docker's pigskin luggage with hydraulic fluid) and an instrument panel which followed the curve of the exceptionally wide windscreen with its triple wipers.

There was nothing as spectacular from Hooper in 1949 or 1950 when Daimler launched an up-dated DB18 with the curved radiator grille and hydro-mechanical brakes of the 'Special Sports' under the name 'Consort' (there was also a new Lanchester, the four-cylinder 1,968 cc 'LJ200' with torsion-bar independent front suspension and Daimler-like bodywork). Originally intended principally for export, the Consort had steel bodywork by Mulliners of Birmingham and had a top speed of 82 mph. However, there was a splendid 'Empress' saloon with the same 'mini-grille' headlamp surrounds which the Dockers demonstrated to Princess Margaret at the Paris Salon: and then the redoubtable Norah Docker got the bit between her teeth and, she claimed, told her husband to rethink Daimler's marketing policies.

A 'Docker Daimler' before Norah Docker came on the scene, the Green Goddess was breathtaking in every respect. [JDHT]

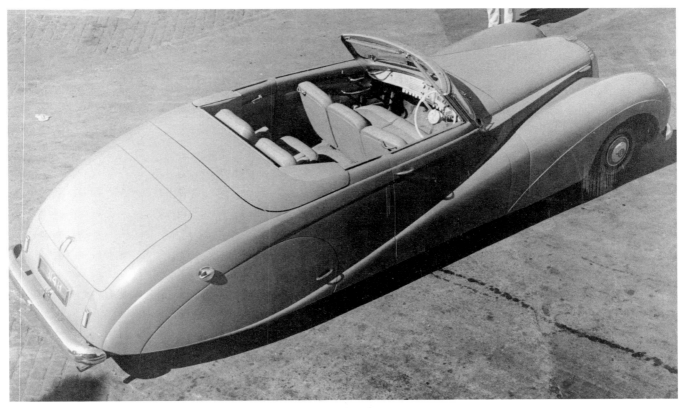

'The only people who know about the Daimler are the Royal family,' she said. 'I know you couldn't find better customers, Bernard, but Daimler can't survive on status alone – it's got to sell to the masses. Look what happens when we go abroad with our car. Whenever it's admired by the Italians, or French, they call it a "Delahaye". I'm fed up with repeating, "No, *Daimler*, please!" We shouldn't have to correct them, Bernard. There's no reason why anyone in the world should mispronounce "Daimler". It's because so few people know about the damn car! Why can't you manufacture a smaller Daimler, suitable for the family?'

As the opening shot in her campaign of popularizing Daimler, Norah Docker was appointed a director of Hooper's and set up a drawing-board in their Mayfair flat. Hooper's chief designer, Osmond Rivers, was summoned to help her Ladyship sketch a Straight-Eight show car (though it's obvious from the end result that it was mostly Rivers's work), which she intended to symbolize a grand campaign for the launching of a small, popular, competitively-priced Daimler car for the mass-market, yet 'still containing the same standard of workmanship to be found on any Royal or VIP model'.

What Lady Docker – who recalled that 'my enthusiasm was unbounded, and a fresh meaning had came into my life' – added to Rivers's flowing lines was a touch of honest vulgarity. Only she could claim that 'it was out of necessity that we came to consider gold leaf [for the brightwork of the show car] . . . for, in the early days of 1951, it was practically impossible to obtain chrome. Because of this deficiency, we had to consider a substitute finish for the fittings. My first idea was that the bumpers, radiator, wing-mirrors and other fittings should be brass. This, however, proved to be impractical, as brass dulls and the fittings would have required constant polishing. [Gold] was a suggestion from one of our design assistants, and it got my immediate stamp of approval.'

It was, apparently, a chance remark made

by Sir Bernard's personal assistant Harry Barker aboard the *Shemara* which inspired Norah Docker to add the final over-the-top touch to 'her' design. She was wearing a black cocktail dress, studded with gold stars, and Barker joked: 'Still thinking about that car of yours? Why don't you cover the bloody thing with gold stars, like those on your dress, and have done with it?'

So, recalled Lady Docker, 'our basic limousine began to take on lines of grandeur never before encountered in the automobile world: gold leaf was sprayed on to all the fittings, even the exhaust pipe, and petrol cap and wheel-hubs were tinselled in gold. A multitude of gold stars embellished the bodywork and door panels in an uninterrupted streamlined sweep, from bonnet to rear. Against the velvet-toned black, the effect was quite dramatic!' Interior fittings on this first 'Docker Daimler' included a cocktail bar, 'tea-cabinet' and folding tables in Australian camphor-wood, black leather upholstery with gold piping in the front, embroidered 'Coteline' gold silk brocade in

Corbishley's Lanchester LJ200 returned a fine performance in the 1953 Monte Carlo Rally despite the loss of its windscreen. [JDHT]

the back, and a gold vanity set; luxury items which were probably the first of their kind were the rear-window demister, double-glazed side-windows and electrically-operated glass sunroof.

The car was built under strict security at the Hooper works in London's Western Avenue (where a permanent scent of toffee hung in the bodyshop air thanks to the art deco building's location next to Callard & Bowser's confectionery works) and completed only a few hours before the 1951 Motor Show opened. Heraldic artist Geoffrey Francis stayed up the entire night applying the last of the 7,000 gold stars – or 'mullets' – to the panel work.

The unveiling of the 'extraordinary' Golden Daimler, which 'sent the pale wraiths of austerity far into limbo', caused a sensation at Earls Court, where it dominated the coachwork section of the Motor Show, totally eclipsing such serious opposition as a six-light Park Ward sports saloon on the Rolls-Royce Silver Wraith and the Radford Bentley Countryman. Recalled Norah Docker: 'The Golden Daimler not only stole the show, but it also stole the headlines of almost every newspaper throughout Britain and across the world. Every penny of the £8,500 we spent on its production now

seemed worthwhile. I am sure that the record attendance at Earls Court that year was the measure of its success.'

Coming as it did on the heels of the resignation of the Attlee government (which was replaced midway through the Motor Show by a new Conservative administration led by 77-year-old Winston Churchill), the Golden Daimler seemed to symbolize the start of a new era in which England confidently expected to be freed from 'the shackles of Socialism and muddled mismanagement' (though the reluctance of the Treasury to rescind the 66 per cent purchase tax on new cars indicated that behind the scenes the spirit of change was not encouraged). Wherever it was shown, crowds queued to admire it; when Lady Docker went shopping in the West End with it, she 'returned home with her ears ringing with the ecstasy of the crowd . . . and we didn't get one rotten tomato thrown at us!'

The Golden Daimler – which won its class in the annual coachwork competition organized by the Institute of British Carriage & Automobile Manufacturers – was not the only novelty unveiled by the company at Earls Court. The new 3-litre Daimler Regency was effectively a 2,952 cc derivative of the Consort which, despite claims that it

7,000 gold stars were applied to the flanks of the first Docker Daimler, Stardust, unveiled as the 1951 Motor Show opened. [JDHT]

Sir Winston Churchill campaigning in what appears to be a pre-war DB18, though as the registration dates from late 1944, presumably this one was moth-balled during the war.
[JDHT]

'represented values unprecedented in Daimler history [with] extreme docility and easy handling in traffic, flashing acceleration and speed that is all you will ever need or can safely use anywhere outside a race-track', never really got into its stride. Though the company made optimistic statements that 'considerable production is planned', that first Regency proved to be the post-war Daimler model with the smallest output – just 51 were built in two years. Also shown was a De Ville Convertible version of the 2-litre Lanchester launched in 1950, though few, if any, of these seem to have actually found their way into private hands. It had a power-operated hood and power windows, still very much novelties on British cars.

In August 1950, Princess Elizabeth told her mother that there was an unusual small car at Stratstone's and Bob Cracknell was requested to bring it for the Queen to see. Queen Elizabeth's association with the Daimler marque had been a long one: her father had a large Daimler which she drove at Glamis. 'It was very heavy to steer and

excessively noisy.' Since her marriage she had owned a succession of Daimlers and found them to be excellent vehicles: the car at Stratstone's was a particularly rare DB18 2½-litre Sports Convertible bodied by Hooper (only six were made) with a power hood and electric windows. It had, indeed, originally been intended for Princess Elizabeth, then the order was transferred to the Duke of Edinburgh and the car was eventually delivered to the King, who both liked it and drove it often. In the summer of 1951, it was altered by Hoopers to give more rear leg-room and delivered to Balmoral for the Royal Family's summer holiday in August.

Sadly, it was to be the King's last holiday at Balmoral. For some time his health had been a matter for concern and in September he underwent surgery for the removal of a lung affected by a malignant growth. His daughter and her husband were to take his place on a visit to Australia and New Zealand, for which Hooper-bodied open Straight-Eight Daimlers had been fitted with one-piece moulded Perspex tops made by the Triplex glass company, and on 31 January the King saw them off at London Airport on the first leg of their flight, to East Africa.

And then, on 6 February, came the news that shocked the nation: the King had died in his sleep at Sandringham. In its tribute, *The Autocar* recalled: 'King George VI had . . . displayed a special interest in the motor car . . . He shared with motorists . . . the fascination that is exercised by all intricate mechanical devices – motor cycles, motor boats, aircraft and locomotives – and evidence of this, which he constantly displayed, was one of the many endearing attributes of a well-loved sovereign.'

The lofty state Daimlers that awaited the new Queen at London Airport as she stepped out of the BOAC Argonaut that had brought her home represented the peak of Daimler domination of the Royal fleet: in 1950, after the disappointing gearbox problems with the 'wedding present' Daimler, the Duke of Edinburgh had taken delivery of a very special Rolls-Royce, the Phantom IV fitted with the 5.7-litre 'Scalded Cat' straight-eight engine of military origin. Just 17 of this type were built: 16 were destined for Royalty or heads of state, while the seventeenth was for the chairman of Rolls-Royce, the future Lord Hives.

And during the period of state mourning this car was transformed from personal conveyance to state limousine, reupholstered and repainted royal claret over black – the work being carried out by Daimler's associate company Hooper – so that when the Queen distributed Maundy Money on 10 April 1952 she rode to the ceremony at Westminster Abbey in the Rolls-Royce, the first time a car of this make had been used by a reigning British monarch on an official engagement. The 50-year reign of Daimler as Britain's car of state was drawing to a close.

* * *

The end of 1952 saw another new model, the 3-litre Sports Special Convertible Coupé; it replaced the 2½-litre Sports Special (which it broadly resembled) and was built on a modified Regency chassis. Extra performance came from an alloy cylinder head which boosted power output to 100 bhp plus an overdrive fourth gear, while windows, hood and boot lid were power operated. Rare and handsome, it came in a carefully-chosen range of 'duo-colour' paint schemes which enhanced its 'modern and speedy lines'

But of course what everyone was really

Built on a modified Regency chassis, the 3-litre Sports Special was launched at the end of 1952. [JDHT]

waiting for was the 'Docker Daimler' that would be a star exhibit at Earls Court not only for its styling but also because Lady Docker's exploits had become notorious. She had made the headlines in no uncertain manner during the year when she was asked to leave a charity cabaret being held in the Casino at Monte Carlo in aid of the Red Cross after making loud disparaging remarks about the quality of entertainment. Her protests resulted in the withdrawal of the Dockers' casino membership cards; in retaliation the Dockers sued the Sporting Club de Monte Carlo and the newspaper *Nice-Matin*. And then the Dockers were involved in another fracas, this time with a harbour guard in Capri, which culminated in a costly court case. Such events caused more comment than they might nowadays, for Britain was still suffering under the pernicious foreign travel allowance regulations which restricted the amount of money holiday-makers could take out of the country to £25 a head.

And then came the Motor Show car that starred on the Hooper stand: it did not disappoint the sensation-seekers. A much sleeker design than the Golden Daimler, with side windows as elliptical as Spitfire wings, it

was known as 'Blue Clover' and was finished in two tones of powder blue with tiny painted four-leaf clovers dappling the side panels. The seats – three in the front and two in the back – were covered in lavender blue leather piped in dark blue, while the interior trim borders and steering wheel were covered in blue lizard-skin, as were the cabinets on either side of the foldaway rear seats. The cabinets contained cut glass flasks and glasses, silver Thermos jugs, sandwich boxes, cups and saucers and linen – everything that was needed for a genteel picnic or cocktail party – while recesses above the rear seats held an 8 mm cine-camera and field-glasses. In the left-hand door was a fitted manicure set (covered, of course, in blue lizard-skin), while a shallow tray under the instrument panel held a mirror, comb, clothes brush, two silver-topped jars and a powder compact. The side windows were both double-glazed and electrically-operated, the curved windscreen was glazed with heat-reflecting Triplex glass and the head- and spotlamps were housed beneath Perspex covers flush with the front wings.

It was, exuded *Motor*, 'the most elegant thing at Earls Court.'

The wraps come off Blue Clover *to reveal the tiny four-leaf clovers dappling the side panels and the lavender blue upholstery . . . [JDHT]*

In January 1953 Sir Bernard Docker took over the additional post of managing director of Daimler from James Leek, who had been forced to stand down after undergoing an operation. Leek, who retained his seat on the BSA board, was also managing director of BSA Cycles and BSA guns, and had recommissioned the Small Heath gun works in 1937 in response to the government rearmament drive. Working under Docker was the newly-appointed general manager of the Daimler group, Dick Smith, who just happened to be married to Norah Docker's sister Bernice.

At that time Daimler sales were stagnating due to the excessively high purchase tax of 66.6 per cent on new cars, which the change of government had done nothing to alter. The situation was so bad that production of the 3-litre Regency was suspended at the beginning of 1953 and so, 'to enable the planned production to be maintained, to protect the employment of the 4,000 workers involved in car production and also to maintain activity throughout the Daimler dealer organization', it was announced that between 4 February and the next budget, due in April, Daimler would reduce the price of all

Consorts delivered by £239, equivalent to a cut in purchase tax to 33.3 per cent.

The company had sufficient orders in hand to cover this period; the problem was that customers were reluctant to take delivery in case the anticipated reduction in purchase tax took place; those who took advantage of the offer must have blessed their foresight (and Daimler) when Chancellor R.A. Butler cut the tax, but only to 50 per cent. Lanchester then responded by cutting the basic price of its Fourteen (also known as the 'Leda') by £153, making the saving to the customer £353: again, the stated aim was to stabilize production.

In fact, Daimler had another trick up its sleeve: in May it unveiled its new Conquest, apparently developed in the space of four months, which used a short-stroke six-cylinder version of the Lanchester Fourteen engine in a slightly modified version of the Lanchester chassis and bodyshell with a Daimler radiator and bonnet. The independent front suspension used laminated torsion bar springs with a neat vernier adjustment to compensate for loss of tension with age, and the car took its name from the fact that it cost £1,066 before tax.

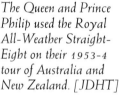

The Queen and Prince Philip used the Royal All-Weather Straight-Eight on their 1953-4 tour of Australia and New Zealand. [JDHT]

Launching the new model to the dealers at the Daimler works, Sir Bernard Docker announced that 'armaments work undertaken by suppliers' had disrupted the production of bodies for the Regency, but that the car would be re-launched with a larger engine and new bodywork early in 1954. When, following her Coronation in May 1953, the Queen was at last able to undertake her visit to Australia and New Zealand, a dozen Conquests were shipped to Australia to act as back-up to the four Straight-Eights already there.

But there seemed to be a certain lack of purpose about the Daimler group's new model policy. At the time of the 1953 Motor Show it was announced that Lanchester was launching a new 2½-litre six-cylinder model known as the Dauphin, 'specially produced to carry Hooper coachwork'. Panelled in light alloy on an ash frame, the Dauphin saloon was a dedicated four-seater with 'English half knife-edge' lines, priced at nearly £3,000 and looking very much like a scaled-down version of the Golden Daimler. Two Dauphin saloons were shown at Earls Court – one right-hand drive, one with left-hand controls – but that seems to have been the limit of production.

Deliberately exclusive was the 'Docker Daimler' built for the Hooper stand on the 'Special Series' Regency 3-litre chassis. With just two seats (the space behind them was occupied by two red crocodile leather suitcases), this sleek coupé was panelled in light alloy and fitted with a 'Sundym' glass roof; with green leather seats piped in red and red crocodile dashboard and door cappings, this car had the usual vanity drawer under the dash containing silver accessories. As built, it was finished in green but the colour clashed with the interior trim and 48 hours before the show was due to open Lady Docker telephoned Osmond Rivers and told him to re-spray the car in a metallic silver. When asked what the car should be called, Norah Docker responded 'Silver Flash', taking her inspiration from the famous BSA 'Golden Flash' motor cycle.

The third surprise at the Motor Show was the Conquest Roadster, a low-slung sports two-seater with slightly confused 'modernistic' lines and a 100 bhp twin carburettor version of the 2½-litre engine; intakes in the Roadster's rear wings were intended to direct cool air on to the back brakes. It won second prize in the Earls Court coachwork competition, but there were no

The Royal Straight-Eights were magnificent cars by any standards. [JDHT]

Silver Flash *was named at the last minute because of an eleventh-hour colour change.* [JDHT]

similar honours for *Silver Flash*.

But then it hadn't been the best of years for the Dockers: the inevitable publicity attaching to his wife's antics had forced Sir Bernard's resignation from the board of the Midland Bank in January and two weeks later he had been fined £50 for a technical offence against the currency regulations (he had combined the £25 a head allowance for the 32 members of the *Shemara's* crew to form a pool from which each man drew £2 a week). Though the fine was nominal and the whole affair summed up as a 'trivial infringement of the regulations', it cost Sir Bernard £25,000 in legal fees. It can have been no compensation for him that the allowance was raised to £50 during the year!

Inevitably, the 100 bhp engine was soon being tested in the Conquest Saloon and the result was unveiled in March 1954 as the 'Conquest Century', with marginally larger brake drums to cope with the near-90 mph performance. The new variant ultimately proved more popular than the £1,066 original, with sales of 4,818 against 4,568, though it took slightly longer to reach that

Daimler's first sports car for decades – the 1954 Conquest Roadster. [JDHT]

total (1954–8 compared with 1953–6). Among the customers for this agreeable small Daimler was Viscount Montgomery of Alamein, who took delivery of an ex-works demonstrator in 1954 and kept it for 13 years, usually driving slowly down the centre of the road followed by a queue of impatient drivers unable to get past.

There was also a drophead coupé version of the Conquest Century, with a hood that was power-operated as far as the 'de ville' position (halfway up or halfway down, depending on whether you were an optimist or a pessimist) and had to be manually extended the rest of the way. Less attractive than the earlier Barker Sports Special, it was also less successful, and only 234 were built during its short production life, which was all over in 1955.

The end of Straight-Eight production in 1953 had left a gap in the Daimler range which the company was slow to fill, and when a replacement finally materialized in the autumn of 1954, it was only a warmed-over version of the abortive Regency, slightly longer and lower and now available with either 3.5- or 4.6-litre six-cylinder power units. Despite its claims to be a full production model, it was still a rarity, available as standard with a six-light saloon body, or with four-light Mulliner (Birmingham) Sportsman bodywork in conjunction with servo-assisted brakes and a transmission with an overdrive fourth speed.

There was also a seven-seat limousine variant, the Regina, built on a 10 ft 10 in wheelbase (the normal Regency had a 9 ft 6 in wheelbase) and with a slightly wider track; this had direct drive in top and formed the basis of the by-now traditional Hooper 'Docker Daimler'. This year's offering was 'Stardust', finished in royal blue and silver with six-pointed silver stars on the side panels and the usual lavish interior treatment. This time the rear compartment was upholstered in hand-woven silver-grey silk brocatelle and the 'cabinet work' (which was actually made of aluminium alloy) was covered in blue crocodile skin and contained cut-crystal decanters and Wedgwood china cups. The double-glazed side windows and central division were all electrically-operated, as was the sliding shutter which could be drawn out beneath the fixed glass roof panel above the rear seats. In the spacious boot was a set of four tailored crocodile-skin suitcases.

The rare (234 built) Conquest Century drophead coupé had a top which was only power-assisted to the halfway 'de ville' position. [JDHT]

The Dockers go to a fancy dress ball – and Norah's fancy dress was specially tailored by Madame Fanny Chiberta . . . [JDHT]

Vacillating model policy again revealed itself in the fate of the Regina, which in 1955 it was decided to offer as a standard eight-seated Carbodies steel limousine with in-house trim, known as the DK400. Only a few 'custom' bodies were built on this chassis, including a Hooper-bodied car based on 'Stardust' (but less ostentatiously equipped) built for the Queen Mother in 1955.

During 1954, the Golden Daimler – still a crowd-puller after three years – was sent on an international publicity tour, and Norah

Docker was able to get her own back on those Continentals who had so annoyed her by mistaking Daimlers for Delahayes: the car was shipped first to Paris, once the civil servants at the Board of Trade had been persuaded that the Golden Daimler was the spearhead of Daimler's export drive and approved the release of sufficient funds for the company to exhibit the car in its new Paris showrooms on the Avenue Montaigne. Naturally, Norah Docker added her own special touch to the event, 'a whole new range of clothes . . . designed by my own dress designer, Madame Fanny Chiberta, to match the Golden Daimler'. They included an all-gold dress, a black dress covered in gold stars and a mink stole.

The popular illustrated magazine *Picture Post* followed the Daimler to Paris to take cover photographs, and featured the car in a special supplement. A Hollywood production crew filming location shots for the 20th-Century Fox comedy *Gentlemen Marry Brunettes* used the Golden Daimler as a 'prop' while Norah took lessons from the film's stars Jane Russell and Jeanne Craine on how to pose with the car. It was all wonderful publicity – 'certainly worth well over half a million pounds', thought the extravagant Norah – but inevitably there were rumblings of discontent.

Certainly the size of Madame Fanny Chiberta's bill for the special range of clothes designed to match the Golden Daimler horrified the grey souls of the Inland Revenue: an expenditure of £7,910 for a wardrobe just to accompany a motor car to Paris was obviously not a legitimate business expense, and they rejected it out of hand. When the expense account was returned to the BSA group board, they declined to support it, and sent it back to Lady Docker, who was incensed.

Never mind the fact that it had cost nearly as much to clothe the lady as it had to build the car: 'If a famous film star had been engaged to pose for publicity purposes with the show Daimler, and to attend the ceremonies that I did, on behalf of the company, they would have had a staggering bill to meet,' she fulminated. 'The least they could do, in my opinion, was to pay for my clothes on a promotion tour of this kind.'

* * *

One of those group board members who had failed to back the Dockers' expense account was James Leek, characterized by former BSA employee H.D. Corben as 'a ruthless, vain and arrogant man, obsessed with getting his own way'. Like his near-contemporary Harry Bennett of Ford-US, Leek sought to control the company of which he was an executive by appointing 'yes-men' to positions where they could report back on their colleagues, who were liable to summary dismissal or redeployment.

Though the gentlemanly Sir Bernard was, apparently, incapable of thinking the worst of a fellow-director, Lady Norah was, as they say nowadays, 'streetwise' and realized what the mild-looking Mr Leek was up to; she called him up to the Dockers' Claridge House flat after the BSA board had voted against a scheme proposed by her husband to build £6 million-worth of tractors for Massey-Ferguson and told him that 'there was going to be a lot of strong resistance to a *coup d'état* if one was being planned'. Leek's response was dramatic: 'Damn you!' he swore at Lady Docker. 'I am not going to have you around any more!' 'Just get out,' she retorted, adding as he stormed past her, 'Now we know the arch-enemy.'

The aftermath was bizarre: Norah Docker secretly hired a private detective agency to investigate the activities of every group executive, even her brother-in-law Dick Smith, now a board member and the recently-appointed managing director under Bernard Docker's chairmanship of the long-established Carbodies company, taken over by the BSA Group in June 1954, and already supplying Lanchester Fourteen bodyshells. 'Their report to me was quite astonishing, and I was now in possession of all the facts,'

recalled Lady Docker in her autobiography. 'These included a clandestine affair between one of the senior directors and a company secretary, which I had long suspected.'

Mark you, the fact that James Leek's private secretary had the use of a company Daimler to transport her between her home in Redditch and the Coventry works might have made anyone suspicious in those days when car ownership was still in the minority and certainly seemed at odds with Leek's declared view that 'what was wanted in this world was a sense of responsibility which would get to grips with realities'.

Reality was certainly still lacking from the group's model policies. In October 1954 Lanchester had announced the 1.6-litre Sprite, which broke new ground by using a specially-developed Hobbs Mechamatic automatic gearbox instead of the fluid flywheel preselector transmission, and was the smallest British car available up to then with automatic transmission. The four-cylinder engine was special, too, developed from the six-cylinder Conquest unit with the aid of Harry Weslake.

The unit-construction bodyshell was a first for Lanchester, and had light-alloy bonnet, boot lid and door skins; Vynide upholstery and a washable PVC headlining positioned the Sprite well down the social scale, but it didn't matter very much, because Lanchester was on the way out. The Sprite was listed throughout 1955, but couldn't be bought. The Lanchester engineers, it seems were busy trying to sort out the Hobbs transmission, the body had been totally redesigned, and the engine had undergone considerable detail modification. By mid-1956 just 13 Sprites had been built and the ancient Lanchester marque had simply faded away, its passing marked in *The Autocar* by no more than a letter from motoring historian St John Nixon.

Though it expressed an interest in building the 616 cc Czech Aero Minor economy car under licence in 1946, BSA stuck to two-wheelers post-war, despite persistent rumours that it was planning a return to the small car market, which were strong enough in 1954 for the company to declare 'it is unlikely that anything will be offered for sale for at least a year or two'.

In late 1955 Daimler unveiled a 100 mph variant on that erratic Regency theme, the One-O-Four, with a twin-carburettor 137 bhp engine. It took its name from the 104 mph achieved by a prototype during testing and there was a special 'Ladies' Model' (one strongly suspects Norah Docker was behind this variant) available in a choice of five single and three two-tone colour schemes. This model had burr walnut window surrounds and fascia panel and 'little name plates' to identify the minor controls and warning lights. A drawer beneath the fascia contained a torch, cigarette case, notepad and pencil (the finish on these only looked like gold), while other items of equipment intended to attract the feminine market included a folding umbrella, vanity case (with cosmetics by Max Factor), motoring rug, sheepskin mat, ice flask, shooting stick, picnic hamper and four fitted suitcases. It was a short-lived model in its standard form: by the spring of 1956 the 'special Lady's items' had become optional extras.

And then of course there was the Hooper show car, and 1955's offering was perhaps the most amazing of all: it was the 'Golden Zebra' DK400 two-door fixed-head coupé, whose fluid lines Michael Brown of *The Autocar* thought 'voluptuous'. Painted ivory all over, with all the external and internal brightwork gold-plated, and ivory leather trim, it had heat-reflecting glass in its windscreen and roof panel and of course there were the cocktail cabinet, vanity box and built-in picnic basket that Norah Docker regarded as essential. There was even an ivory-handled folding umbrella. Lady Docker's initials were inscribed in gold letters on the door, and the mascot was a golden zebra.

'But,' recalled Norah Docker, 'the *pièce de résistance* was the real zebra-skin upholstery.' And when journalists asked 'Why zebra?', Lady Docker replied: 'Because mink is too hot

to sit on.' She later claimed that she had used zebra-skin upholstery, instead of mink, because 'it was more practical' and would not moult on to passengers' clothes, but its publicity value could not be denied. When Prince Rainier of Monaco married Grace Kelly in April 1956, the Dockers were invited, and flew *Golden Zebra* and *Stardust* to the south of France as their transport during the wedding festivities.

But though they were definitely attracting publicity, it was the wrong kind. Once Rolls-Royce had breached Daimler's monopoly of the Royal fleet, its advance seemed unstoppable and though Sir Bernard Docker and Joseph Mackle cooperated in building a pair of DK400s – a limousine and a landaulette – in 1955 with the hope that they might replace a couple of the older Royal Daimlers, the cars were not taken on to the Buckingham Palace strength. Instead, they were retained by Stratstone as 'Royal Stock', cars to be used for relief work if other cars were not available. Their service was short: Stratstone was informed at the end of 1958 that the 'Royal Stock' Daimlers would no longer be needed, nor would the existing Royal Daimlers be replaced by cars of the same make. And by the end of 1960 all the State Daimlers had been sold and replaced by Rolls-Royces.

By then, Daimler had changed fundamentally, too. While the Dockers were in Monaco, the board's attempt to unseat them had been orchestrated. On 30 May 1956, Sir Bernard was asked to attend a special board meeting in the office adjoining his flat in Claridge House to discuss 'the future conduct of the company' and was voted out of office by six directors against three. His replacement as chairman and managing director was Jack Sangster of Triumph Motorcycles, a company acquired by BSA (along with its associate Ariel) in 1952 for £4.5 million: Sangster, coincidentally, had known the then Norah Turner at school and she had once gone out with his brother Harvey.

Fearing the disintegration of the company, Sir Bernard fought to expose what he saw as the motives behind the coup, claiming that: 'The circumstances which have led to the passing of a certain resolution by the board of the Birmingham Small Arms Company, by a narrow majority, affecting my position, involve personal disagreements and do not concern the stability of the Company.' He sent out telegrams to over 10,000 shareholders, promising that they would know the full and honest facts behind his dismissal. Norah, typically, sent photographs of herself to another 17,000 shareholders along with a signed letter demanding that the shareholders should be consulted. Sir Bernard even took advertising time on the new independent television network to argue his case, a step which was regarded as such a dangerous precedent that such 'opinion advertising' was to be barred in 1958. He claimed: 'Under my leadership, from 1940 to 1955, the available profits of BSA have risen from £560,000 to £2,693,000. Is this a sign of incompetence?'

It was all in vain. The board's refusal to pay Norah Docker's dress bill was followed by a claim that the five show Daimlers had been made for her own personal amusement, and not for the benefit of the company, and that the £50,000 cost of making them was nothing to do with the company. The Inland Revenue pounced: Sir Bernard was sent a £20,000 tax demand for the cost of making, running, and maintaining the cars. At first, he refused to pay, but after taking legal advice, agreed to settle at a reduced figure (and also paid Fanny Chiberta's near-£8,000 bill for Norah's frocks).

Dick Smith resigned as Daimler managing director and Norah Docker's brother Royce, who ran Spink's, the Daimler distributor in Bournemouth, also handed in his notice. The Dockers managed to force an extraordinary meeting of the company at Grosvenor House in London, attended by 1,300 shareholders, but they were outvoted when the Prudential Assurance Company, one of the larger corporate shareholders, backed the board. Eventually, after having spent some £20,000 on their campaign, the Dockers admitted defeat.

They revealed their bruised feelings for the make whose image they had done so much to promote by buying a brace of Rolls-Royces and registering them 'ND 5' and 'BD 9': the Docker Daimler days were over.

The show cars were 'decommissioned', stripped of their glamorous trim and sold: the Golden Daimler, the £900-worth of gold leaf which had given the car its name removed to comply with export regulations, was bought by Californian motor cycle distributor William E. Johnson Jr, of Pasadena (whose Johnson Motors company held the West Coast agency for Ariel and Triumph) and shipped to Los Angeles in January 1958 aboard the MS *Loch Ryan*.

Golden Zebra, for which six zebras had died in vain, and which had cost £12,000 to build, was for sale by Daimler distributors Henlys of Chester in 1966 for a mere £1,400 with 25,000 miles on the clock.

Stardust, found abandoned on a Welsh farm with a frost-damaged cylinder block, was restored to show condition in the early 1980s. Mr Francis came out of retirement to once again dapple its flanks with golden stars though, since crocodiles had become a protected species in the meantime, the interior fittings had to be retrimmed in blue lizard-skin. It was an economy of which Norah Docker would surely have approved.

Chapter 9

UNDER NEW MANAGEMENT

Though Daimler was no longer exclusively the British Royal car, there were still foreign rulers keen to buy the marque's products. When Hooper's celebrated their 150th anniversary in 1957, they were working on a Daimler with a moulded Perspex roof and Sundym side windows for the Ameer of Bahawalpur (its interior fittings included a housing for a pistol) and an open state Daimler for the King of Afghanistan. But though Hooper's had successfully made the transition from wood-framed bodywork to bodies built over a skeleton of cast or extruded aluminium, their days were numbered, for changing methods of production were hastening the end of cars with separate chassis. Within five years there would be no separate coachbuilding section at the Earls Court Motor Show.

The new management at Daimler made no immediate changes: the Century drophead was discontinued late in 1957 and the DK400 was now available in two versions, the DK400A, with three occasional seats and the DK400B, intended as a chauffeur-driven car, with a drop division, two occasional seats and more luxurious trim in the rear compartment than the other model.

Significantly, the long reign of the fluid flywheel and preselector transmission was obviously drawing to a close, for the three-speed Borg-Warner automatic transmission was now available as an option on the soon-to-be-withdrawn Conquest and the One-O-Four. The DK400 would be the last production car with preselector transmission, though it would survive on the company's commercial vehicles and armoured cars.

It seems that the ousting of Sir Bernard Docker had one side effect that the conspirators had not foreseen: many of the important European purchasers of BSA products were personal friends of his, and with his departure they did not renew their orders. Moreover, with the Dockers out of the picture, the Daimler name was no longer headline material.

There were troubles on the two-wheeler front, too. In 1943, BSA had bought the famous Sunbeam company from Associated Motor Cycles and hired Erling Poppe to design a 'super de-luxe machine'. The result, the S7 shaft-drive in-line twin, was the first all-new post-war British motor cycle and went into production at the BSA Redditch factory. The first batch was shipped out to South Africa as the escort for the Royal Daimlers during the 1947 visit by Their Majesties and Princess Elizabeth and proved inadequate to the challenge: only half the 50 Sunbeams sent finished the tour, excessive engine vibrations and broken forks having eliminated the rest. Moreover, the bronze worm final drive had an unacceptably short life, and the cost of rectifying the faults added to the already high cost of the machine, which proved a sales disaster and was discontinued in 1957, effectively ending the Sunbeam marque (though BSA did use the name subsequently on a rather dismal little scooter). And though the position of the BSA and Triumph marques seemed unassailable in the late 1950s, the story was quite different in the 1960s when Japanese bikes took over the market and the British motor cycle industry, weakened by poor management and complacency, simply melted away in the heat of the Rising Sun.

Oddly enough, although the Dockers were gone, the tradition of showing a special Hooper-bodied car at Earl's Court continued with the display of an eight-seater Hooper limousine on the company's stand, though no exotic fauna had been asked to surrender their hides to upholster it and this time the headlines on the coachbuilding front were snatched by an extravagantly-equipped Rolls-Royce bodied by Freestone & Webb. Though the model was consistently listed in buyers' guides, the Hooper-bodied Limousine was one of just seven in this style built on the DK400 chassis between 1955–9 and was acquired in 1959 by C.F. Anderson & Sons, passed to the Birmingham Cooperative Society in 1961 (who used it as a wedding car) and eventually returned to its manufacturers.

In fact, Daimler's old role as furnisher of official limousines had been taken over by the North London coachbuilders Vanden Plas, which in association with Austin had begun producing the Princess luxury saloon in 1947, reaching an output of five a week in 1948 and ten a week the following year. Inevitably, a limousine version followed in 1952 and the first two off the production line at the Vanden Plas Kingsbury works were bought by the Queen even before her Coronation, and the model became a permanent feature of the Royal fleet.

The lacklustre nature of the Daimler products at Earls Court had fuelled rumours that the company was about to cease car production, and these were intensified by the closure of one of the Daimler foundries and a number of redundancies. At the group AGM in November 1957 Jack Sangster was compelled to reassure BSA shareholders that these rumours were untrue and that 'intensive development work has been proceeding with all speed on our Daimler products'. Now in charge of the Automotive Division of the BSA Group was famed motor cycle designer Edward Turner, who backed Sangster, saying that the remaining level of foundry production 'appeared to be assured' for the next 12 months and that 'no further substantial redundancy was contemplated'.

Turner was, of course, the creator of such classic two-wheelers as the Ariel Square Four and the famed Triumph Speed Twin, which equipped practically every police force worldwide; for many years he had declared that he wanted to build 'equally good cars'. He backed his statement with the launch the following July of the Majestic, a development of the One-O-Four with a 3.8-litre engine which gave a genuine 100 mph top speed. It was the first British-built limousine fitted with servo-assisted disc brakes on all four wheels and came with Borg-Warner automatic transmission as standard, the first Daimler model since 1931 not available with the 'self-changing' gearbox. The critics were impressed; testing the new car for the *Sunday Times*, Stirling Moss wrote: 'There is no wallow even when cornering fast. Steering is light and accurate . . . You can make 80 or 90 come up on the speedometer very quickly and the maximum is over 100 mph.' More alarmingly, he added: 'I simply touched the brake pedal with my fingers at 70 mph and slowed the car to a halt.'

By the end of 1958 the news was out: Turner – one of the best engine designers in the motor cycle industry – was working with Cyril Simpson on a new 2½-litre V8 power unit for future Daimlers. Models under development, it was revealed, were a sports car and a saloon car, 'of strikingly modern conception and in the medium price range'.

Fortunately, the proposed DN250 – the 2¹/₂-litre V8 engine in a Vauxhall Cresta bodyshell with a Daimler radiator shell – never made production. [JDHT]

Sadly, the planned saloon, codenamed 'DN250', showed a considerable lack of understanding of the needs of the Daimler customer, for, despite claims that it was 'entirely new', it was to have been based on the bulbous bodyshell of the Vauxhall Cresta: fortunately, this ill-conceived hybrid never reached production.

Change was apparent elsewhere in the organization: the company's bodybuilding associate Carbodies was not only producing convertible bodies for Ford Consuls and Zephyrs but had also just launched the famous London black cab. And though Daimler Hire had been independent for many years, it still marked the end of an era when at the beginning of 1958 it was announced that the company – whose chauffeurs covered 2.3 million miles a year, with self-drive clients accounting for a further 7.5 million – had been acquired by the Hertz Group of America as their first inroad into the British car hire business.

* * *

The 2,547 cc Turner V8 engine made its debut in the spring of 1959 powering a new sports car, the SP250. This was aimed directly at the American market – its public announcement was at the New York Show in April, where a red pre-production car was exhibited – and was initially known as the 'Dart' until representations from Chrysler, who had registered the name, forced its abandonment by threatening to sue.

Just as Vanwall had taken the 500 cc Norton motor cycle engine layout for its 1959 Grand Prix car, so Turner had also looked to a two-wheeler power unit for his inspiration, in this case his Triumph Speed Twin. The new engine was patterned on the motor cycle unit's top end, though unlike the long-stroke Speed Twin it had a very oversquare bore-stroke ratio. The camshaft was set high between the cylinder blocks, operating inclined valves in hemispherical combustion chambers through short duralumin pushrods and valve-gear like that on the Speed Twin. Given the engine's air-cooled antecedents, the water-cooling

273

appeared to be a bit of an afterthought, with numerous short hoses to the inlet manifold and heater which showed a tendency to split on early models until a stronger material was used.

Other than that, there was nothing but praise for the engine when the SP250 began to find its way into the hands of the motoring press as production got under way later in the year. Conversely, road test reports criticized chassis design, handling and the 'original and distinctive' styling of the glass fibre bodywork with its heavily swaged wheel arches and prominent tailfins, which was entirely built in the Daimler works. 'How lucky it is that Daimler have chosen to use a plastic body,' commented *Autocar* artist Gordon Horner acidly, 'for it will be so easy to reshape the moulds!' Gordon Asbury remembers another problem that was not widely publicized: 'There wasn't a lot of experience in glass fibre body building at that time and Daimler didn't make the drain holes in the doors large enough. The result was that whenever it rained, the door pockets filled with water on the early examples!'

The car normally came with a manual gearbox, though automatic transmission was available as an option. This was mainly with an eye on the American market, for which the car was principally intended, but sporty American drivers rejected the automatic option as a 'stigma' and it was soon dropped. However, among the British customers for the SP250 were several British police authorities, who put the model (in its improved 'Specification B' form) into service from the summer of 1961 and preferred the automatic transmission because it gave a quicker getaway. The 120 mph car also gave the police an unfair advantage in areas like Surrey, where speed cops normally used upright Wolseleys, for not only did the low-slung SP250 fail to show up in the rear view mirror when it was close on a car's tail, but the Wolseleys always gave themselves away at night because of their easily distinguished light-up radiator badges.

Summing up the appeal of late 1950s open-top motoring – an SP250 on location in Wales. [JDHT]

One of the features that made the SP250 suitable for police work was that lovely engine, which had excellent bottom-end torque in true V8 tradition, yet revved freely up to the redline limit of 6,000 rpm and beyond, giving the car genuine 120 mph performance. This was matched by four-wheel disc brakes and, should the worst happen in spite of that superior stopping power, Daimler claimed that the glass fibre bodywork was easier to repair than metal. However, it was also less rigid, and the simple ladder-type chassis was prone to flexing, which not only gave rather twitchy handling characteristics but could also result in the doors flying open if the car was cornered too hard.

The BSA Group's motor cycles had an

excellent reputation in America, where the 650 cc Triumph Trophy dominated the long desert races which were then fashionable, and the SP250 was actually imported by the Triumph Corporation of Baltimore, which set up a special Daimler Division to handle the new model under the ambitious slogan 'Fine English cars since 1896; sports and personal cars of exceptional merit.' 'It is hoped,' commented *Sports Cars Illustrated*, tongue seemingly firmly in cheek, 'that the two-wheel supply and servicing experience will serve the Daimler Division well.'

The SP250 went on sale in the United States in November 1959, though the newly-organized distribution network was sketchy, to say the least, with just four dealers handling the entire country. The New York agency was Fergus Imported Cars, Inc, which could trace its roots back to a company formed during the Great War to market the Irish-designed Fergus 'owner-driver' car, and which also handled Morgan and Borgward imports. Sales, however, were disappointingly slow, for in the SP250's first year of production just 110 cars were built, and only 77 of those were exported to the USA, which meant that those dealers were carrying considerable spare parts stocks for a handful of cars.

The 1959 Earls Court show had seen the surprise launch of the Majestic Major, code-named DQ450, which was powered by a 4.56-litre version of the SP250 engine, which gave this massive luxury saloon – which tipped the scales at 1.8 tons – a top speed of over 120 mph, the ability to accelerate from 0–100 mph in 28.9 seconds and a standing quarter time of 17.1 seconds, making it Britain's fastest six-seater. 'Formidable,' said *The Autocar*.

Another showtime surprise was a strange-

Some 1,200 left-hand drive SP250s are believed to have been built, but the model hardly took export markets by storm. [JDHT]

DAIMLER

V8 2·5 LITRE

CLOSE COUPLED SALOON

WITH THE NEW DAIMLER V8 2½ LITRE ENGINE

The Daimler, V8 2·5 litre close-coupled saloon is strictly for the discriminating enthusiast. For him (or her ') this brilliant car has all the answers: vivid acceleration and performance with disc-brake safety, featherlight handling, wonderful roadholding . . . . and a practical ultra-modern saloon body for all-weather comfort and convenience. It blends the best of both worlds - in the best possible fashion.

Hooper's last gasp was this weirdly-styled 'close-coupled saloon' on the SP250 chassis. Mercifully, it never went into production. [JDHT]

Ease of entry

One of the many features of the 1995 Daimler range was a steering wheel with a memory. As part of an automatic 'entry/exit mode', the electric motors tilted the wheel upwards, retracted the steering column and moved the driver's seat backwards. But then hadn't that first Royal Daimler featured a tilting steering column back in 1900?

looking fastback saloon built by Hooper's on the SP250 chassis, with its own special radiator grille (divided down the centre like a BMW's) and peaked headlamp surrounds; upswept edges to the roof eliminated the need for gutters at the expense of appearance and had winking turn indicators in their rear ends. It was a sad little swan-song to the 150-year history of Hooper's, for it had already been announced that they were to close down: when production ended two months later, they had built 691 bodies on Daimler chassis since 1929. The toffee-flavoured Hooper works on Western Avenue became the London service depot for Standard-Triumph and Osmond Rivers joined Daimler as chief designer; the company name was subsequently revived by Hooper Motor Services at nearby Kilburn, though London black cabs proved to be their prosaic mainstay.

The demise of Hooper's was, perhaps, inevitable, for the number of cars with separate chassis on which bespoke bodywork could be fitted was diminishing rapidly, and the market for luxury cars was also shrinking – one of Daimler's closest rivals, Armstrong Siddeley, was about to pull out of car production after 55 years. Since the withdrawal of the Century in 1958, Daimler had offered no mid-market model: there was a crying need for a saloon of about 2.5 litres which the company had singularly failed to develop after the ludicrous plan for the Vauxhall-bodied V8 had been shelved.

Indeed, Daimler production had been allowed to fall to a level that was more appropriate to the turn of the century than the 'never had it so good' late 1950s, for those 110 SP250s represented the totality of Radford's private car output; the six-cylinder Majestic was already dead and not a single Majestic Major actually left the factory in 1959. Stratstone, the company's principal dealer, had already diversified by acquiring a more profitable agency, and was now marketing the popular Volkswagen; Gordon Asbury recalls selling horse-boxes and

tractors to the Royal Household in order to keep the company's Royal Warrant alive. It looked as though Daimler was just fading away. And then, on 26 May 1960, a preliminary announcement confirmed that negotiations between BSA and Jaguar over the sale of the Daimler name and factory were close to fruition.

The deal was concluded between Jack Sangster of BSA and Sir William Lyons of Jaguar at 11 a.m. on 18 June 1960, and Sir William commented: 'I do not recall a more amicable deal with anyone.'

* * *

He had good reason to be pleased. The acquisition of Daimler brought much-needed additional production facilities to Jaguar, which was hugely profitable (it had paid a 20 per cent dividend in its previous financial year) but bursting at the seams despite a considerable expansion of their plant (a former Daimler shadow factory) at Browns Lane, Coventry, after a disastrous fire in February 1957 had damaged half the buildings. Moreover, Sangster had forgotten to include £10,000 worth of outstanding pension rights in the £3.4 million deal, and Lyons tossed him for it – and won. Not only that, but this was the era when the motor industry was being reluctantly forced by government policy to locate new production facilities in areas of high unemployment, usually with disastrous results.

The ill-fated factories which Rootes, Triumph and Leyland had reluctantly established under government pressure in 'development areas' at Linwood, Speke and Bathgate became bywords for industrial unrest before their protagonists eventually lost patience and closed them down. By taking over a functioning factory with a skilled work-force on his home ground in Coventry for a fraction of the cost of building on a greenfield site (Linwood had cost the Rootes Group over £25 million), Lyons astutely sidestepped the ill-conceived government diktat that was to prove so ruinous to the Big Four and avoided all the problems of training and recruitment that would plague all those 'development area' factories. Proof that he had made the right decision came at the end of the next financial year, when Lyons announced an all-time production record of 25,224, over 15 per cent higher than the previous 12 months.

He also became by default a manufacturer of commercial and military vehicles. The excellent Daimler buses were acknowledged leaders in their field, with engines capable of running up to 500,000 miles between major overhauls (though with the expansion of package tours in the 1950s, the Daimler coaches of at least one tour company had failed *en masse* on mountain passes due to the forward-mounted transmission oil pump sucking air instead of lubricant on prolonged steep gradients). The company also had a current contract to supply the Army with the Ferret scout cars that had replaced the

wartime scout car. But when this expired in the early 1970s, the contract went elsewhere.

In 1963 Sir William had been approached by W.J. Semmons of the Fighting Vehicles Research & Development Establishment at Chobham, Surrey, to see if he would be interested in quoting for 200–250 6x6 10-ton general service vehicles, but turned the job down after several months of indecision due to 'other programmes which, for reasons outside our control, we have been unable to determine speedily'.

Though Jaguar had categorically declared that 'the company's long term policy envisages not only the retention of the Daimler marque but the expansion of its markets at home and overseas', it was difficult to see how that was going to be possible with the existing model range. And, recalls former Stratstone chairman James Smillie, 'Sir William bought the company to gain extra capacity; he didn't really expect to sell many

With Edward Turner's splendid V8 engine in the Jaguar Mk II bodyshell, the V8 250 was one of the finest sports saloons of the 1960s. [JDHT]

Peter Westbury's Felday-Daimler, winner of the 1963 RAC Hillclimb Championship, had a supercharged 2½-litre Daimler V8 engine in a Formula Two Cooper chassis. [JDHT]

Daimlers. But we pressed him very hard for a new model.' The result was that Sir William bluntly told Stratstone to get rid of their VW agency, which he thought inappropriate to their new image as combined Jaguar and Daimler dealers. 'Give up Volkswagen and I'll give you a small Daimler,' he promised.

The result was the splendid 2½-litre V8, which married the Turner engine from the SP250 with the automatic transmission and bodyshell of the small Mk II Jaguar. Over 17,600 were built between 1962–7, making it the most popular Daimler of all time. Yet at first there was so little enthusiasm for the project in Coventry that Jaguar's experimental department were only allowed an old 'absolutely rotten' Mk I bodyshell to build the prototype. The much modified Mk I had been used for air suspension experiments and then dumped outside the factory mill building for so long that all the tyres were flat and 'it was practically welded to the ground!'

The compact Turner V8 fitted into the Mk II's engine compartment with ample room to spare and easily outperformed Jaguar's 2.4-litre XK six-cylinder unit. 'The Daimler 2½-litre V8 was a tremendous success,' says James Smillie. 'Sir William Lyons didn't appreciate the value of the marque, but it was soon outselling the 2.4-litre Jaguar. The main

trouble we had was that the V8 engine was so quiet that people could hear the back axle, and we had to repair more back axles on the Daimler than we did on the equivalent Jaguar, even though the units were exactly the same.' S.C.H. Davis, once a Daimler apprentice and now one of the most respected motoring writers, praised its 'marked character' and declared: 'This is not a Jaguar with a Daimler radiator grille and name plate. It can stand on its own.'

If Sir William was not over-enthusiastic about Daimler, nevertheless the marque had a friend at the highest level of Jaguar, whose assistant managing director F.R.W. England, universally known as 'Lofty', had begun his distinguished career as an apprentice at the Daimler between 1927–32, inspired to apply for the job by the boyhood recollection of a cavalcade of Royal Daimlers during the First World War.

Despite the success of the 2½-litre V8, there was a strict upper limit on production of these small Daimlers: the extremely cautious level of tooling investment. Maximum output of the 2.5-litre V8 engine had been set at 140 per week, and, though production never remotely approached this figure, that upper limit precluded the development of any incremental model, though a marine version of the power unit was announced a

279

few days before Christmas 1961.

It was decided to continue building the SP250, which was offered through the Jaguar sales network in America, though many of the dealers were reluctant to take on a new model line. Foreign car dealer Bob Grossman thought the SP250 'a funny car', with 'horrible' steering and an 'abominable' chassis, but nevertheless liked it, and sold an estimated 375, 'more . . . than any other American dealer', for which the model's track exploits may have been partly responsible: 'In their SCCA class they were a hands-down winner.'

Sir William Lyons did subtly restyle the idiosyncratic SP250 bodyshell, but the timing was wrong, since in March 1961 Jaguar launched the dramatic E-Type, which the SP250 undercut by some 25 per cent. Had the proposed 'SP252' sports two-seater gone into production, the development costs would have meant that its price would have been closer to that of the E-Type, making it a potential rival. Inevitably, the Daimler project remained firmly at the prototype stage.

An odd feature of the SP252 was the omission of the traditional fluted Daimler radiator grille – it just had a low intake to match the higher bonnet line – but since the SP250 had been most un-Daimler-like and carried its name in script on its nose, that feature was carried over on to the two examples of the SP252 that were completed.

Another, unofficial, variation on the SP250 theme was a glass fibre coupé created in 1962 by David Ogle Ltd, a coachbuilding offshoot of an industrial design company. David Ogle himself was killed in a car accident when the job was still unfinished and the design was completed by Tom Karen. The Ogle company, which had previously built a rather italianate fastback on a Riley One-Point-Five floorpan, made a few Ogle SX250s before selling the design to Reliant, which built it as the Scimitar.

* * *

Styled by David Ogle, the SX250 was a dead-end for Daimler, so the body design was sold to Reliant! [JDHT]

By now the 120 mph Majestic Major was beginning to find its way into the hands of the public: 'It was a wonderful car,' comments James Smillie. 'Lord Brabazon, who was a director of the Tilling Group (which owned Stratstone), received a graph from Bill Argent of Mercedes-Benz – another Tilling Group company – showing the performance of the latest Mercedes compared with its rivals. But the Majestic Major wasn't included. Brabazon added its figures, and the Daimler was a far better performer than any of the rest . . . including the Mercedes!' (It also outperformed the bigger Jaguar saloons.)

A limousine version of the Majestic Major was launched in September 1961, riding on a wheelbase increased by 2 ft to 11 ft 6 in and weighing over 2 tons. With seating for eight when the occasional seats against the division were in use, the Limousine had a top speed of 110 mph allied to impressive acceleration; again, journalists praised the

Aviation pioneer Lord Brabazon of Tara – first Briton to hold a flying licence – with his appropriately-registered Majestic Major. [JDHT]

quietness and smoothness of the engine (which must have been galling to Jaguar engineers, who were already working on a 60 degree V8 of their own, which was noticeably lacking in the latter virtue and was consequently abandoned at the prototype stage).

Daimler car final assembly now took place in the Jaguar Browns Lane factory, though Daimler and Jaguar engines were built at Radford where, wrote William Boddy of *Motor Sport*, 'rows of machine tools in closely-serried ranks are redolent of an older regime . . . and the engines come together in an unhurried atmosphere that spells competent efficiency.' Since the closure of the Daimler foundry, engine castings were bought in from outside suppliers, though they were still left outside to weather in the classic tradition.

The bodies for the 4.5-litre Daimlers, supplied by the Coventry specialists Carbodies and Park Sheet Metal, were also finished at Radford, and an interesting social distinction was that while Jaguar bodyshells were given an 'opal synthetic' finish, Daimler bodies were still cellulosed ('to enable Daimler customers to have a choice of the older shades of colour not always available in the synthetic finishes'). There were separate, hand-moved lines at Browns Lane for the big Daimlers.

There was also progress on the passenger vehicle side, which had been an incidental of the Jaguar purchase, yet which within two years made the group second only to Leyland in the British heavy commercial vehicle industry. Launched at the 1960 commercial vehicle show, the Daimler Fleetline was powered by a rear-mounted Gardner Diesel and was soon outselling the broadly similar Leyland Atlantean: it was a fitting swan-song to the career of Cyril Simpson, who had joined Daimler in 1918 and stayed on beyond retirement age to see the Fleetline safely into production. His successor as chief engineer, Peter Windsor-Smith, came from Coventry-Climax, acquired by Jaguar in March 1963.

Eventually nearly 30 Fleetlines were being built at Radford every week, making Daimler the biggest producer of double-deck bus chassis; a new Roadliner rear-engined single-decker followed in 1965. Front-engined buses were still being made, too, though changing regulations – especially the introduction of one-man buses – meant that these were on the way out, the last batch being delivered to Hong Kong in 1971.

There would have been a new lorry too, for Lyons had recruited Dodge truck engineer Cliff Elliott to design a new Daimler commercial shortly after the takeover, but then the old-established Guy company went into receivership, and in 1961 Jaguar bought that, too (for a typical Lyons bargain price of £800,000) and with it a well-regarded range of heavy trucks – plus, incidentally, the moribund Sunbeam Trolleybus Company,

acquired from the old Sunbeam car company by Guy in 1948 – and the Daimler lorry project was stillborn, with the Daimler truck engineering department being transferred to the Guy factory in Wolverhampton.

* * *

The DR450 Limousine of 1961 was the last 'all-Daimler' car to be introduced, and by 1965 the lack of any new Daimler models was beginning to affect sales. While the V8 Saloon was continuing to attract 'trade-up' sales from other makes like Rover, Ford and Wolseley, there were few instances of customers trading an old 2½-litre Daimler for a new one.

'While there have been improvements to the car since its inception,' James Smillie of Stratstone told Sir William Lyons that October, 'our customers are reluctant to exchange one car for another which looks exactly the same. This is quite contrary to our experience with Jaguar, where we can offer a

This special DR450 landaulette was built for the King of Thailand in the early 1960s. [JDHT]

The original Daimler Sovereign was launched in the autumn of 1966. [JDHT]

range of 14 models; 60 per cent of the cars we take back when selling Jaguar, are Jaguars, a much higher percentage than with Daimler. In each one of these sales this year, the customer has exchanged for a different model . . . our Daimler sales for the past two months have been very poor, and our stocks are building up . . .'

Sir William's response was rapid: Smillie and his managing director John Olley were summoned to Coventry and shown a prototype for a Daimler version of the forthcoming Jaguar 420 by Lyons and Lofty England. 'What shall we call it?' Sir William asked the Stratstone executives.

'Royale,' suggested Olley. 'Sovereign,' said Smillie.

'Royale – that's what we intended to call it

ourselves,' replied Sir William. However, two months later, he phoned Stratstone and said: 'We've decided it shall be the Sovereign'.

'I should have asked for a royalty!' said Smillie.

The new Sovereign – which was a de luxe version of the 420, launched in October 1966, fitted with a Daimler grille – came with overdrive manual transmission as standard, automatic as an optional, and neatly filled the gap between the V8 saloon and the Majestic Major. There were voices of dissention from people like former Daimler designer F.T. Alexander-Prebble, who condemned it as 'merely a Jaguar in disguise' and marque enthusiast Tim Ward, who complained 'with great sorrow . . . that it had the good, but rather outdated "XK" engine and not a great torque-developing vee-8', but most Daimler customers were happy to have the new model, which sold a healthy 5,824 units in its four-year production life.

In the meantime, in the prevailing atmosphere of 'biggest is best' that was pervading the European motor industry, Sir William Lyons had been approached by a number of companies – Standard, Rolls-Royce, Leyland – but after 40 years of autocracy, Lyons (who held over 54 per cent of the Jaguar voting stock), was not about to relinquish control. But he was near retiring age and his only son John had been killed in a road accident in France in 1955: he was anxious to ensure the continuity of his company.

Then, in the wake of a failed attempt to merge with Leyland, Sir George Harriman of the British Motor Corporation (whose Pressed Steel subsidiary supplied Jaguar bodyshells) offered Lyons a 'logical and beneficial' merger deal, which would leave Jaguar operating under Lyons's chairmanship as 'a separate entity and with the greatest practical degree of autonomy' within a new organization called British Motor (Holdings) Limited. The idea was to create a group capable of matching the Leyland-AEC-Standard-Triumph combine, particularly on the commercial vehicle side: but Lyons had unwittingly boarded the motor industry's equivalent of the *Titanic*. BMC, formed in 1952 by merging the Austin and Morris organizations, was a partnership at war with itself, with many of its marques and models competing for the same slice of the market. Moreover, the corporation's cost controls were notoriously lax, and Harriman wasn't prepared to listen.

Famously, when Allen Barke of Ford told him in 1960 that there was no way that BMC's new Mini, launched to compete with the Ford Anglia 105E, could possibly be making any money (and the Ford engineers had carried out a careful cost analysis to prove it), Harriman just replied with the enigmatic phrase 'the product will push the price'. In other words, it would all come right if enough customers bought the car (but it didn't, because BMC had priced the Mini against the obsolescent 100E Anglia launched in 1953). Moreover, the same seat-of-the-pants pricing strategy ruled the products of the corporation's popular Austin and Morris lines, which sought to undercut each other regardless of the fact that they were supposed to be working in unison. The folly of this policy was shown by the mounting losses of BMC.

It was as well that Lyons had retained control of Jaguar-Daimler, for his cars' value-for-money image was based on tight costing and his company had been consistently profitable. Though the Daimler commercial vehicle activities would be lost in the BMH labyrinth, there were definite benefits on the car side: Daimler was given the task of developing the successor to the Austin Princess, dropped after the merger, while BMC shelved plans to build a sports car designed to rival the Jaguar E-Type.

But overall BMH group model policy was irrational, with its core marques fighting one another for market share and the marketing department too much in awe of the idiosyncratic chief engineer Alex Issigonis to dare tell him when his brilliance had led him

into an error of judgment. It was as well that Jaguar-Daimler was operating apart from this, though the new BMH-Jaguar sales network in the USA dropped the Daimler line because there was not enough money in the advertising budget to cope with the multiplicity of marques in the group's line-up.

Sadly, the motor industry was now under the spotlight of the Industrial Reorganisation Corporation, a quango set up by the ardently interventionist Wilson government, which convinced itself that the British motor industry was too fragmented and that a merger between BMH and Leyland was essential. With their chief executives Sir George Harriman and Sir Donald Stokes cajoled into acquiescence by smooth-tongued prime minister Harold Wilson – who flattered their egos by inviting the pair to dinner at Chequers, then persuaded them that a merger would be in the national interest – the two groups came together in 1968. As *The Autocar* commented at the time: 'Put bluntly, BMH are in a mess, with a reduced share of the market and little to look forward to in the near future. Even Triumph cannot be held up as a shining example of product planning or marketing, and their car production is comparatively small.'

The only apparent attribute of the new group was its sheer size. The combined BMH and Leyland-Triumph ranges, built in 60 production centres across Britain, overlapped terrifyingly – there were 42 basic car models bearing seven different marque names between 1- and 2-litres alone – but at least there were only Daimlers and Jaguars above the 4-litre mark, and Sir William Lyons, now chairman and chief executive of Jaguar, again managed to retain a high degree of autonomy for Jaguar-Daimler . . . in the beginning, anyway.

Indeed, the first new model to emerge from the vast new conglomerate was a Daimler, the new DS420 limousine built on the 420G platform with a 21 inch section let in behind the front seat by Motor Panels of Coventry (acquired by Jaguar in 1939 and rapidly sold

Parliamentary occasion

'On 3 July 1969, exactly 70 years after the famous incident in which my father became the first man ever to drive a motor car into the House of Commons yard, I drove the very same car (now registered AA-16) through the yard, this time without let or hindrance. I was led in by Sir Gerald Nabarro MP, chairman of the House of Commons Motor Club, in his Daimler Majestic "NAB 1" and accompanied by Margaret Thatcher (then Shadow Minister of Transport), MP for the New Forest Patrick McNair-Wilson, and Lord Strathcarron.' **M**

again, to Rubery Owen); this very strong floorpan was also available as a 'drive-away chassis' as a basis for specialized bodywork (mainly hearses built by companies like Startins of Birmingham, which was to build 300 bodies for the funeral trade on the DS420 chassis over the next 26 years).

To compensate Vanden Plas for the loss of their Princess replacement, they were given the task of finishing, final assembly and trimming the interior of the Daimler-styled limousine bodywork (developed in the best Jaguar tradition, under the keen eye of Sir William Lyons), which arrived at Kingsbury in the bare metal. The combination of the Jaguar 420 chassis and power-assisted Varamatic steering resulted in a stately limousine with above-average road-holding

and performance (0–100 mph in 43.5 sec, top speed 110 mph, 19.5 sec for the standing quarter-mile) for which Dunlop had developed a dedicated low-profile SP41 tyre. Significantly, power came from the 4.2-litre Jaguar XK six-cylinder engine. The two excellent Turner-designed V8 engines were early victims of the merger, the larger unit (never produced in sufficient numbers to make economic sense) disappearing during 1968 and the 2.5-litre engine vanishing a year later.

With the disappearance of the 2.5-litre V8 and the first-generation 420 Sovereign in 1969, just one Daimler saloon remained in a newly rationalized Jaguar range. This was a new Sovereign announced at Motor Show time and based on the XJ6 launched the previous year, with a Daimler grille and fluting above the rear number plate, and available with 2.8- or 4.2-litre XK six-cylinder power units.

In 1972 a new V12 engine developed by Wally Hassan and Harry Munday went into production and the Jaguar XJ12 duly won the coveted Car of the Year Trophy. Of course there was a Daimler variant and Lofty England – who had recently succeeded Sir William Lyons as Jaguar chairman – recalled his days as a Daimler apprentice and declared that this new model should be called 'Double Six'. It had luxury trim by Vanden Plas and maintained the Daimler tradition of exclusivity, and *Motor* magazine declared that it had better handling and high-speed cruising ability than the Rolls-Royce Silver Shadow which cost almost twice as much. Though a proposal to produce a Daimler version of the 1975 Jaguar XJ-S coupé only produced a prototype, the two-door coupé derivative of the XJ saloon was produced in Daimler guise between 1974–8.

Nevertheless, before long the Daimler and Jaguar identities were being subsumed in the British Leyland body corporate as the Jaguar Division of British Leyland. With the fuel crisis that followed the Yom Kippur war of 1973 posing a threat to sales of large cars, and the early retirement of Lofty England in January 1974 when the new management structure proved unworkable, the future for Daimler looked bleak, particularly when the Jaguar management board was abolished under the disastrous recommendations of the Government-backed Ryder Report on the future of BL. There was talk at that time as to whether there was any point in continuing with the Daimler or Jaguar names. Daimler was felt to have little or no relevance and there was, anyway, an attempt to try and establish 'Leyland' as a brand name – for instance, the Broadspeed racing Jaguar 'Big Cats' were prominently badged 'Leyland'.

What kept the Daimler name going, as much as anything, was the profitable business fleet market. The retention of the marque enabled a company chairman to have his Daimler and the other directors to keep their

To celebrate the revival of the Double Six nomenclature, Daimler photographed this 1973 two-door coupé alongside a low-chassis Double Six. [JDHT]

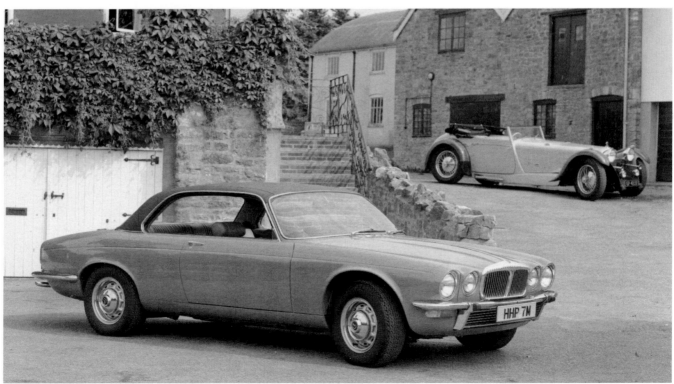

A 1973 Series I Double Six in Switzerland. [JDHT]

Jaguars: the hierarchy was important for fleet sales. The stubborn independence of the Jaguar men was a major factor, too, for they continued to develop a replacement for the XJ saloon, even though the Ryder Plan had debased the marque to a component in BL's 'specialist' Jaguar-Rover-Triumph car division (Daimler was not even granted the courtesy of inclusion in the title). An attempt to rename the project 'LC40' (for 'Leyland Cars'), was ignored at Browns Lane, infamously referred to by JRT as the plant of 'Large/Specialist Vehicle Operations', rather than Jaguar-Daimler.

As none of the proposed replacements – fortunately, in most cases – materialized during the BL era, the old XJ shape soldiered on through two face-lifts (and the introduction of a long wheelbase version in 1972 to head off the threat of a projected Rover luxury car) to become a much appreciated design classic. The DS420 limousine also soldiered on at a gentle pace of three or four units a week throughout the

difficult years, for it was a product with no obvious rival.

The Stokes management had gone from BL after the Ryder Report and autonomy began to seep back to Browns Lane after Sir Michael Edwardes took over as executive chairman of British Leyland at the end of 1977 on a five-year contract. As part of his massive programme of reformation and retrenchment that was aimed at bringing BL 'back from the brink', he began re-emphasizing the identities of individual marques like Jaguar (though he also closed down 19 of BL's 55 factories, including the Triumph works at Speke and the MG factory at Abingdon). By 1979 Edwardes was able to declare that JRT was 'only a holding company with Rover and Triumph still separate identities . . . and Jaguar quite rightly looking for greater independence', and in fact JRT was dissolved the following year.

Edwardes had lobbied for £100 million of investment in Jaguar, whose fortunes were at their lowest ebb; 1980's sales of 13,988 were

half the 1979 figure and the lowest since 1957 when the factory burned down. The new body shop at Castle Bromwich could only supply cars in red, yellow and white – and they had to be repainted in the factory because the quality was so poor.

In 1980 Jaguar-Daimler slowly began to climb out of the trough with the appointment of its first full-time chief executive since 1975, John Egan, who proved very supportive of the Daimler marque and expressed his desire to 'maintain and enhance the reputation for luxury and elegance which was first established last century.' Nevertheless, the Daimler name was dropped in Continental Europe during a period of two to three years in the early 1980s and the hiatus meant that Daimler lost the 'Sovereign' designation to Jaguar. However, Jaguar was forced by popular demand to bring the Daimler marque back to those markets at the end of 1985, for European dealers were making a fortune importing conversion kits of Daimler body parts to convert Jaguars to Daimler specification.

On the other hand, in the USA British Leyland used the 'Vanden Plas' designation on its flagship models, with the odd result that cars that were recognizably Daimlers, with fluted radiator shells and number plate lamp housings, were sold as 'Jaguar Vanden Plas' models.

The election of Margaret Thatcher's Conservative government in 1979 had heralded the break-up of the heavily state-subsidized British Leyland group and the readying of its more viable components for privatization. Significantly, the man put in charge of improving Jaguar-Daimler quality, which had slipped badly in the dispiriting JRT era, was Bill Stanton, who had joined the Daimler in 1937 at the age of 14. The turnround was dramatic: from a loss of £47 million in 1980 and threatened with closure,

The Chief Scout with his Limousine. [JDHT]

Jaguar was back in the black in 1982, with a profit of £9.4 million, rising to £50 million the following year.

In 1984, the year before the death of Sir William Lyons, Jaguar was returned to the private sector: the share flotation raised £297 million. The £0.25 shares were eagerly snapped up at a starting price of £1.65, though the Government retained a 'golden share' which they said would remain valid until at least 1991 to prevent an unwelcome takeover of the company. There was record group output that year, too, though less than five per cent of the 36,856 cars produced were badged as Daimlers. However, that percentage had doubled to 11.5 per cent two years later (and was nearly 23 per cent if you included the visually similar 'Jaguar Vanden Plas').

The new XJ40 range was launched in October 1986, a new car with the new 'AJ' six-cylinder engine (which had been experimentally installed in 74 Daimler and 53 Jaguar saloons during 1984–5) and a Daimler version was available from the start. The 36 year-old XK unit was only retained in the Daimler Limousine, used mainly for weddings and funerals, where fuel economy was not a consideration. However, since the XJ40 bodyshell had been designed while Jaguar was still part of BL, there was no provision for a V12 version, so to meet continuing demand the 12-cylinder engine continued to be fitted to the classic series III bodyshell designed by Sir William Lyons in the 1960s and face-lifted by Pininfarina in 1979. The V12 Series III remained in production in the Browns Lane pilot build facility until December 1992, just over 24 years from the launch of the original XJ6. Appropriately, the last Series III of all was a Daimler Double Six, which went straight into the company museum.

* * *

Since the war, Ford had flirted with just about every other major (and many minor) motor manufacturer in Europe, from Mercedes and BMW to Lotus and Ferrari, but had never managed to bring these negotiations to a positive conclusion, apart from its 1987 takeovers of Aston Martin and AC (and only Aston Martin was to remain within the fold). Then, with the perversity that seems to accompany such events, in 1989 Ford of Europe found itself involved in simultaneous takeover discussions for two respected names, Saab and Jaguar.

Recalls Bruce Blythe, former vice-president of Ford's European business strategy office: 'We realized that in order to take on both Saab and Jaguar would have been a monumental management task, and we faced the decision of trying to either buy both and manage both or having to choose between one and the other. The fact that Britain's oldest marque, Daimler, belonged to Jaguar was obviously a consideration in Ford's interest in acquiring the Jaguar group.'

The choice proved relatively easy: 'Jaguar was a much stronger name; it would provide something that we could take pride in, whereas Saab would have been hard work.' Nor did Saab's location in central Sweden – the last place that Ford needed additional capacity – aid its chances, and the decision was taken to make an all-out assault on Jaguar. As Blythe says: 'Jaguar is more distinctive, they're the only company in the world that still makes beautiful cars.'

Ford's interest in Jaguar-Daimler went back to June 1987 when Alex Trotman, then Chairman of Ford Europe, contacted Sir John Egan to discuss a possible Ford stake in Jaguar. By October Trotman felt that there was 'sufficient lack of discouragement' from Jaguar for him to refer the matter to the Ford Board, which recommended acquiring Jaguar stock 'in the most friendly manner that we could mutually devise'. However, the ensuing talks grounded, to the particular disappointment of the Ford family members on the board, keen car enthusiasts

determined that their company should be Jaguar's successful suitor. The most senior of them was William Clay Ford, a Jaguar owner since his college days and a strong advocate of the retention of the Daimler marque; he was the last surviving son of Edsel Ford, who had owned a Daimler saloon in the early 1930s.

Jaguar-Daimler suddenly became vulnerable when the dollar – which represented 40 per cent of Jaguar sales – slipped against the pound in 1989, and the company's half-year profits plummeted from £22.5 million to £1.4 million. Nevertheless, launching the new 4-litre XJ6 at the September 1989 Frankfurt Motor Show, Egan bravely declared: 'Jaguar will be much more profitable next year.'

Ford moved quickly, for Jaguar had been talking with virtually every major car maker about possible alliances, but had been unable to find anyone prepared 'to offer the assistance that we require without taking away the independence that we have'. Conscious that General Motors were interested in taking a 30 per cent stake in Jaguar, Ford filed its intention of buying Jaguar stock with the US authorities to deter GM and called Egan to tell him it was about to begin buying shares.

After the Trade and Industry Secretary, Nicholas Ridley, was informed of Ford's intentions for Jaguar, signals began to emanate from those suavely anonymous 'Whitehall sources' that the Government might not exercise its 'golden share' rights limiting potential bidders to a 15 per cent stake in Jaguar. Prime Minister Margaret Thatcher endorsed Ford's interest in Jaguar, and the price of Jaguar shares promptly rose by 38p to 548p. Trading in Jaguar stock continued unabated, and by 5 October the shares were trading at 700p. The next day, the US authorities gave Ford permission to buy up to 15 per cent of Jaguar: 13 million Jaguar shares changed hands on the London Stock Exchange and 4.5 million more were traded in New York.

Eye of the beholder

One of the select few who bespoke an Ogle SX250 – the coupé derived from Daimler's SP250 by designer David Ogle – was Boris Porter of Helena Rubenstein. He ordered his car painted 'opalescent golden sand', then had the interior trim colour-matched to the French Violet scheme of his Knightsbridge flat. Ogle Design weren't complaining: they got a contract to package Rubenstein cosmetics, while the publicity Mr Porter's gaudy car generated inspired Reliant – best-known for sub-utility three-wheelers – to buy the design rights to the SX250 and relaunch it as the Ford-powered Reliant Scimitar, a car trendy enough for Princess Anne . . .

Then fate stepped in on Ford's behalf. Late the following Friday afternoon – ominously, it was Friday the 13th – the New York stock exchange plunged dramatically and an hour before the market closed, Ford had bought more than five per cent of Jaguar's stock. The New York collapse on Friday affected prices in London on Monday and Ford's stake increased to 10.5 per cent. On Tuesday, over 19 million Jaguar shares changed hands; prices gradually stabilized, and Ford moved steadily towards a 13 per cent stake.

At a secret meeting, Ford agreed with Egan that it would bid for the whole company within a two week period. But at what price? While Jaguar's book value was around £300 million, the 'magic of the name' added a considerable – but intangible – premium, so among the papers helping the Ford board members in their deliberations were short 'heritage histories' of the Daimler and Jaguar marques prepared by the Ford Corporate History Office. It came as a surprise to both parties when, the evening before Ford was due to make its bid, the Government announced that it was prepared to waive its golden share, and Jaguar share prices soared above £9, while Ford had already structured its bid around an initial offer of £8 a share.

When it emerged that the Ford view of the future of Jaguar largely coincided with the view of the Jaguar board, a deal was thrashed out which proved acceptable to both sides, and after some detailed negotiation, Jaguar accepted the price of £8.50 and, at a press conference the next morning announced unanimous support for the Ford bid. 'So,' comments Bruce Blythe, 'despite having taken 18 months of stalking and 18 months of laying out game plans and 18 of theorising, the actual face-to-face negotiations took about 24 hours.' Egan was adamant that the first people to know should be the Jaguar-Daimler employees, not the press or the City, so he returned to Coventry at midnight; the news of the Ford takeover was made public at 9.30 a.m. the next day.

The cash-rich Ford company had paid £1.6 billion for Jaguar and Daimler, a figure deemed too high by some commentators, though when you consider that for the cost of developing a new popular car range Ford had acquired two of the greatest names in the British motor industry plus a sizeable manufacturing complex in Coventry, maybe that price didn't look so excessive after all.

* * *

October 1992 saw the launch of a new Majestic range at the NEC Motor Show, though now both Jaguar and Daimler variants were available. The new model had a 5 in stretch in the wheelbase to improve rear legroom, and 3.2-litre and 4-litre models were announced first off the production line, with V12 variants following in February 1993. These were powered by a new 6-litre development of the V12 engine first seen in 1971, with an increase in stroke from 70 to 78.5 mm adding mid-range torque and increasing maximum power from 260 to 318 bhp. A new four-speed overdrive automatic transmission was also specified, and top speed, as a consequence of the alterations, increased to 155 mph from 139 mph for the last Series III Double Six. The changes to the bodyshell involved in accommodating the new powertrain meant that nearly 20 per cent of all the panels making up the body-in-white had to be modified or replaced. The new Daimler Double Six was expected to account for some 75 per cent of sales of the new V12 range, and had such sybaritic features as Autolux leather seating, inlaid veneer rear picnic tables and a six-disc autochanger CD unit unique to its specification.

At the same time, a new 'Insignia' range was launched, which allowed Daimler and Jaguar customers to specify distinctive hand-finished versions of the range, with a choice of ten special paint colours and unique interior leather and wood veneer trim options; Insignia models were prepared by the Special Vehicle Operations department, staffed by many of the craftsmen from the Daimler Limousine Shop, which had proved

The return of the Daimler Double Six, February 1993.

an early casualty of the Ford takeover.

The 'fast but ponderous' Limousine was the last of the Jaguar group products to use the classic XK engine, whose 44-year production life is one of the longest in automotive history. The last Startin hearse built on the DS420 chassis (which briefly outlived the Limousine) was handed over to its owner, a Cheshire funeral director named Slack, on 9 February 1994.

In September 1994, the first new Jaguar-Daimler range to be announced since the Ford takeover was revealed. The new XJ series, topped by a new 6-litre Double Six Daimler, was unashamedly inspired by the classic Series III XJ saloons: the more square-cut lines of the 'XJ40' series had been criticized by many for departing from the spirit of Sir William Lyons's original design. Modern yet traditional, the new XJ was hailed as one of the most beautiful luxury cars in the world, its feline elegance a dramatic contrast with its increasingly bland (and sometimes downright ugly) European rivals. Indeed, one of the first Ford specialists to work at Browns Lane after the takeover had been ex-Ghia designer Manfred Lampe, classic car enthusiast and Ferrari owner, who

participated in the early stages of the design process of the new 'X300' under chief designer Geoff Lawson. Among the traditional 'XJ' features which had been lost with the XJ40 bodyshell had been a boot designed to pass the famous 'two golf bag' test, a feature revived on the new model. Maybe that was the influence of Bill Hayden,

The Daimler Limousine was the last production car to use the immortal Jaguar XK-series power unit. [JDHT]

who took over as Jaguar-Daimler chairman after Sir John Egan left in 1990.

Bill, whose passion for golf led to the building of a personal golf course in the grounds of his Essex home during his spell as manufacturing vice president of Ford-Europe, was one of Dagenham's great production experts and used his many years of experience to transform Jaguar-Daimler manufacturing methods before his retirement in 1992. He was keen to preserve the individuality of Daimler and actually proposed a new Daimler model using different sheet metal pressings to distinguish it from the equivalent Jaguars. Though that project failed to reach fruition as a separate model as planned, nevertheless some of Bill Hayden's Daimler proposals did see the light of day in the 'X330' long-wheelbase derivative of the new Jaguar-Daimler bodyshell.

Hayden's successor, Nick Scheele, is committed to continuing the proud Daimler tradition into the marque's second century, commenting: 'The long-wheelbase Double Six launched in June 1995 is just one of the ways we are seeking to use the Daimler name more effectively. All our current saloon car

projects – including the new compact "X200" range scheduled for 1999 – incorporate a Daimler variant, and that's important, for in many Continental European markets, the Daimler marque is considered to be very chic. In Germany and the Benelux countries, for instance, Daimler has a particularly strong following.' So that second century looks good for Britain's oldest marque. The Royal Family still treasures its Daimler connections and displays many of its old Daimlers at Sandringham, while there have been Daimlers at Beaulieu since 1898, making the Montagu family the marque's oldest customers, with one of the very first examples of the new 1996 model the latest addition to the fleet.

John Montagu's 1899 Daimler – the oldest British four-cylinder car – was preserved by the Science Museum for many years. It returned to Beaulieu in the late 1960s and was restored to its original configuration to become a star exhibit in the National Motor Museum. It remains remarkably active for a near-centenarian and added another achievement to its long roll of 'firsts' when it participated in the Rally inaugurating the Channel Tunnel in 1994 and rode beneath

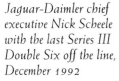

Jaguar-Daimler chief executive Nick Scheele with the last Series III Double Six off the line, December 1992

Based on the 4-litre Daimler saloon, this extended-wheelbase six-door Limousine was launched by Eagle Specialist Vehicles in 1994.

the Straits of Dover aboard 'Le Shuttle', typifying the way the marque has always been able to combine tradition with progress.

Today, Daimler is justifiably proud of its heritage and of the fact that, as well as being Britain's oldest motor manufacturer, it is one of the three oldest marques in the world, born 1896 and still going strong.

And, though the pioneers who founded the Daimler Motor Company a hundred years ago might find the appearance of today's Daimlers bewildering, they would surely applaud the way that, against the pressures of a changing world, the Daimler still retains its essential qualities of craftsmanship and exclusivity.

This 1996 long-wheelbase Double Six is the latest in a long line of Daimlers to be seen at Beaulieu since 1898.

Appendix

THE PRE-WAR ROYAL DAIMLERS

Preserved among Undecimus Stratton's papers, the first part of this list of Royal Daimlers was compiled in 1926 and gives chassis numbers of most of the early cars. Body types, where they can be correlated, are taken from a list compiled in the early 1940s by Stratstone, whose principals had supplied these cars.

KING EDWARD VII

Delivered	Chassis No	HP	Cyls	Capacity	Bore/stroke	Valves	Final Drive	Body
1899*	1566	6	2	1,527 cc	90x120	Poppet	Chain	Mail Phaeton
1900	—	6	2	1,527 cc	90x120	Poppet	Chain	Brake
1901	—	TA12	4	2,324 cc	86x100	Poppet	Chain	Wagonette
1903	2012	TB22	4	5,733 cc	105x130	Poppet	Chain	—
1903	2015	TC22	4	5,733 cc	105x130	Poppet	Chain	—
1904	2177	TB28	4	6,786 cc	120x150	Poppet	Chain	'Motor body'
1905	2867	TK35	4	8,462 cc	134x150	Poppet	Chain	Limousine
1907	4270	TO30	4	4,942 cc	110x130	Poppet	Chain	Brake
1907	—	35	4	9,236 cc	140 x 150	Poppet	Chain	Landaulette
1908	4570	TC58	4	10,431 cc	154x140	Poppet	Chain	Landaulette
1908**	—	TL58	4	10,431cc	154 x140	Poppet	Chain	—

* The date is queried on Undecimus Stratton's original list. Though its chassis may have been laid down that year, this car was actually completed in March 1900.

** This car was delivered to Queen Alexandra.

THE PRINCE OF WALES (KING GEORGE V)

Delivered	Chassis No	HP	Cyls	Capacity	Bore/stroke	Valves	Final Drive	Body
1904	2175	TB22	4	5,702 cc	110x150	Poppet	Chain	Limousine
1905	3038	TK35	4	9,236 cc	140x150	Poppet	Chain	—
1905	3048	TJ30	4	7,246 cc	124x150	Poppet	Chain	—
1906	3083	TK35	4	8,462 cc	134x150	Poppet	Chain	Limousine
1908	4644	TC42	4	7,964 cc	130x150	Poppet	Chain	—
1909	5074	TC57	6	9,420 cc	124x130	Sleeve	Bevel	Brake
1909	5224	TC57	6	9,420 cc	124x130	Sleeve	Bevel	—
1909	5641	TC38	4	6,281 cc	124x130	Sleeve	Bevel	Limousine

KING GEORGE V (*The latter part of this list is based on information supplied by Stratstone*)

Delivered	Chassis No	HP	Cyls	Capacity	Bore/stroke	Valves	Final Drive	Body
1910	6314	TD57	6	9,420 cc	124x130	Sleeve	Bevel	Lim/landaulette
1911	—	TA23	6	3,921 cc	80x130	Sleeve	Bevel	—
1912	10509	TG57	6	9,420 cc	124x130	Sleeve	Worm	Limousine
1914	12283	TB45	6	7,412 cc	110x130	Sleeve	Worm	Brougham
1914	13069	TO20	4	3,308 cc	90x130	Sleeve	Worm	Ambulance
1920	15432	TL30	6	4,962 cc	90x130	Sleeve	Worm	—
1923	18971	TJ45	6	7,413 cc	110x130	Sleeve	Worm	Brake
1924	22628	C20	6	2,648 cc	73.5x104	Sleeve	Worm	Limousine
1924	21411	G57	6	9,420 cc	124x130	Sleeve	Worm	Limousine
1924	21412	G57	6	9,420 cc	124x130	Sleeve	Worm	Limousine
1924	21414	G57	6	9,420 cc	124x130	Sleeve	Worm	Brake
1924	21415	G57	6	9,420 cc	124x130	Sleeve	Worm	Brake
1925	24553	N45	6	8,458 cc	117.5x130	Sleeve	Worm	Limousine
1926	27046	R35	6	5,764 cc	97x130	Sleeve	Worm	Limousine
1929	30440	V25	6	3,568 cc	81.5x114	Sleeve	Worm	Limousine
1929	30671	V30	12	3,744 cc	65x94	Sleeve	Worm	Brougham
1931	32348	OP40/50	12	6,511 cc	81.5x104	Sleeve	Worm	Limousine
1931	32349	OP40/50	12	6,511 cc	81.5x104	Sleeve	Worm	Limousine
1931	32336	V30	12	3,744 cc	65x94	Sleeve	Worm	Limousine
1935	39901	50	12	6,511 cc	81.5x104	Poppet	Worm	Limousine
1935*	38438	25	8	3,746 cc	72x115	Poppet	Worm	Limousine

* Royal Household Car.

QUEEN MARY

Delivered	Chassis No	HP	Cyls	Capacity	Bore/stroke	Valves	Final Drive	Body
1911	—	TH38	4	9,420 cc	124x130	Sleeve	Bevel	Limousine
1928	29440	V30	12	3,744 cc	65x94	Sleeve	Worm	Limousine
1931	32347	OP40/50	12	6,511 cc	81.5x104	Sleeve	Worm	Limousine
1931	32335	V30	12	3,744 cc	65x94	Sleeve	Worm	Limousine
1935	39700	50	12	6,511 cc	81.5x104	Poppet	Worm	Limousine
1937	43728	EL24	6	3,317 cc	80x110	Poppet	Worm	Limousine
1937	44254	32	8	4,624 cc	80x115	Poppet	Worm	Limousine

According to Stratstone the 1914 TB45 no.12283 and the 1925 N45 no.24553 were also delivered to the Queen.

KING EDWARD VIII

Delivered	Chassis No	HP	Cyls	Capacity	Bore/stroke	Valves	Final Drive	Body
1936	41326	32	8	4,624 cc	80x115	Poppet	Worm	Landaulette

KING GEORGE VI

Delivered	Chassis No	HP	Cyls	Capacity	Bore/stroke	Valves	Final Drive	Body
1936	41289*	32	8	4,624 cc	80x115	Poppet	Worm	Landaulette**
1936	41290*	32	8	4,624 cc	80x115	Poppet	Worm	Limousine**
1937	43584	32	8	4,624 cc	80x115	Poppet	Worm	Landaulette
1937	44209	32	8	4,624 cc	80x115	Poppet	Worm	Limousine
1937	44235	32	8	4,624 cc	80x115	Poppet	Worm	Shooting bus
1939	43615	32	8	4,624 cc	80x115	Poppet	Worm	Landaulette
1939	43617*	32	8	4,624 cc	80x115	Poppet	Worm	Landaulette
1940	43616*	32	8	4,624 cc	80x115	Poppet	Worm	Limousine
1941	44282	32	8	4,624 cc	80x115	Poppet	Worm	Limousine***
1941	48327	32	8	4,624 cc	80x115	Poppet	Worm	Limousine***

*   Fitted with Lanchester radiator.

**   Delivered while he was still Duke of York.

***   Armour-plated.

ACKNOWLEDGEMENTS AND SOURCES

ARCHIVES AND INDIVIDUALS

Her Majesty the Queen; His Royal Highness Prince Philip, Duke of Edinburgh; Her Majesty Queen Elizabeth the Queen Mother.

Gordon Asbury; Stephen Bagley, Museum of British Road Transport, Coventry; Bruce Blythe; David Boole; Veteran Car Club of Great Britain Library; Coventry City Archives; Annice Collett and Marie Tieche, National Motor Museum Library; Peter Critchley; Denise Critchley Salmonson; Mrs Mary Critchley Salmonson; Mrs M.M. Doré; Jack Fairman; David Fletcher, Tank Museum, Bovington Camp; Ray Frost; Ray Funnell, Royal Air Force Museum, Hendon; Les Geary; Ann Harris, Jaguar Daimler Archives; Walter Hayes CBE; David Holland; F.G. Hunt; Rupert Instone; Ivan Mahy, Autoworld, Brussels; Mercedes-Benz Archives; Kim Miller, Antique Automobile Club of America Library; Tim Moore; Simms Papers, University of London/Veteran Car Club; Sue Pearson, Jaguar Cars; Mrs Rosie Ramsay; Peter Richley; Colonel E.A. Rose; H.P. Small; James Smillie; Jonathan Stein, *Automobile Quarterly*; Desmond Stratton; Joan Williamson, Royal Automobile Club Library

Photographs courtesy of: *Automobile Quarterly* [AQ]; Museum of British Road Transport [MBRT]; David Burgess-Wise Collection [DBW]; Les Geary [LG]; Jaguar Daimler Heritage Trust [JDHT]; Mercedes-Benz Archives [M-BA]; National Motor Museum [NMM]; Desmond Stratton; [DS]

BOOKS

At the Wheel Ashore and Afloat by Montague Grahame-White (1935).

Autocar-Biography of Owen John (1927).

British Aviation – the Pioneer Years 1903–14 by Harald Penrose (1967).

British Car Factories from 1896 by Paul Collins & Michael Stratton (1993).

British Sports Cars in America 1946–1981 by Jonathan A. Stein (1994).

Chronicle of the 20th Century (1988).

Daimler 1896–1946 by St John Nixon (1946).

Geschichte des Deutschen Verbrennungsmotorenbaues von 1860 bis 1918 by F. Sass (1962).

Histoire de l'Automobile Belge by Jacques & Yvette Kupélian (nd).

History of British Aviation by R. Dallas Brett (nd).

Jaguar by Lord Montagu of Beaulieu (1990).

Jaguar by Andrew Whyte (1990).

Jaguar XJ40 by Andrew Whyte (1987).

Jaguar – Competition Cars to 1953 by Andrew Whyte (1982).

John, Lord Montagu of Beaulieu by Lady Troubridge & Archibald Marshall (1930).

John Montagu of Beaulieu by Paul Tritton (1985).

Lanchester Motor Cars by Anthony Bird & Francis Hutton-Stott (1965).

Memories of Men and Motor Cars by S.C.H. Davis (1965).

299

Motoring by A.E. Berriman (1914).

Motors & Motor Driving by Alfred Harmsworth (1902).

Motor Car Index 1918–29 (1929).

Munitions of War (BSA Group publication, nd).

Norah – the Autobiography of Lady Docker (1969).

Pierce-Arrow by Marc Ralston (1980).

Romance Among Cars by St John Nixon (1937).

Royal Daimlers by Brian Smith (1976).

Royal Rolls-Royce Motor Cars by Andrew Pastouna (1991).

Royalty on the Road by Lord Montagu of Beaulieu (1980).

Standard Catalog of American Cars 1805–1942 (1989).

The Glorious Tanks (William Foster & Co Ltd, nd).

The Humber Story 1868–1932 by A.B. Demaus & J.C. Tarring (1989).

The Hyphen in Rolls-Royce by Wilton J. Oldham (1967).

The Leyland Papers by Graham Turner (1971).

The Life of King George V by W.J. Makin (1936).

The Making of a Motor Car by Douglas Leechman (1908).

The Motor Car – Its Nature, Use and Management by Sir Henry Thompson (1902).

The Motor Car Industry in Coventry since the 1890s by David Thoms & Tom Donnelly (1985).

The Motor Car Red Book (1914).

The Motor Year-Book & Automobilist's Annual (1906).

The Motoring Montagus by Lord Montagu of Beaulieu (1959).

The South-bound Car by Owen Llewellyn (1907).

The World on Wheels by H.O. Duncan (1926).

The World Guide to Automobiles by Baldwin, Georgano, Sedgwick & Laban (1987).

W.O. by W.O. Bentley (1958).

What I Know by C.W. Stamper (1912).

MAGAZINES

Automobile Quarterly.

Automotive Industries.

Automotor Journal.

Car Illustrated.

Classic & Sportscar.

Classic Cars.

Country Life.

Cycle & Automobile Trade Journal.

Daimler Bulletin.

Horseless Age.

Horseless Carriage Gazette.

International Motor Review.

Motor-Car Journal.

Motor Commerce.

Motor Sport.

Motor Trader.

Omnia.

On Two Wheels.

Royal Automobile Club Journal & Motor Union Gazette.

The Aeroplane.

The Autocar.

The Driving Member.

The Motor.

Veteran & Vintage.

INDEX